iSpy

CultureAmerica

Karal Ann Marling
Erika Doss

SERIES EDITORS

iSpy

SURVEILLANCE AND

POWER IN THE

INTERACTIVE ERA

Mark Andrejevic

 University Press of Kansas

© 2007 by the University Press of Kansas

Published by the University Press of Kansas (Lawrence, Kansas 66045), which was
organized by the Kansas Board of Regents and is operated and funded by Emporia State
University, Fort Hays State University, Kansas State University, Pittsburg State University,
the University of Kansas, and Wichita State University

Library of Congress Cataloging-in-Publication Data

Andrejevic, Mark, 1964–
    iSpy : surveillance and power in the interactive era / Mark Andrejevic.
        p.   cm. — (CultureAmerica)
    Includes bibliographical references and index.
    ISBN 978-0-7006-1528-5 (cloth : alk. paper)
    1. Information society. 2. Interactive multimedia—Social aspects. I. Title.
    HM851.A65 2007
    303.48′33—dc222   007016410

British Library Cataloguing-in-Publication Data is available.

Printed in the United States of America
10 9 8 7 6 5 4 3 2 1

The paper used in this publication is recycled and contains 50 percent postconsumer
waste. It is acid free and meets the minimum requirements of the American National
Standard for Permanence of Paper for Printed Library Materials Z39.48-1984.

CONTENTS

ACKNOWLEDGMENTS

For the past several years, I have been fortunate enough to dwell, for the most part, in a world where interaction refers mainly to fruitful exchanges of ideas, informed debate, and productive challenges and correctives to underexamined thought. It is perhaps the contrast between the pleasures of this world and the pathologies of one in which interactivity serves as little more than a ruse of social control that prompted me to make the arguments I attempt to develop in the following pages. In this regard, I am deeply indebted to those who have provided me with a taste of the possibilities of meaningful interaction and thus of the potential for a world other than the surveillance state being assembled and celebrated, as I write, by the technicians, policy makers, publicists, pundits, academic apologists, and other assorted ideologists of what James Der Derian has dubbed the Military-Industrial-Media-Entertainment Network.

In particular, I am grateful to those who have provided me with a sense of academic community at the University of Iowa, including colleagues, graduate students, and several seasons of undergraduates in my seminars on new media technologies. I am indebted to the university not just for the atmosphere of inquiry it fosters but for the invaluable forms of material support with which it has provided me, including an Old Gold Summer Research Grant and an Obermann Faculty Research Semester Fellowship. With reference to the latter, I am grateful to Jay Semel, Jennifer New, and Karla Tonella for providing me with a quiet place to write, congenial coffee breaks, and access to TiVo.

In the Department of Communication Studies, I have benefited profoundly from the wisdom and wit of John Durham Peters, who graciously took the time to provide me with feedback on the manuscript and is always willing to talk theory—in the hall, on the run, or on the Ultimate field. His insights are as deft and true as his upwind forehand. Thanks to Kembrew McLeod and his partner, Lynne Nugent, for rescuing me from my office with welcome regularity when I was working on the manuscript—and for their humor, sanity, and laid-back friendship, which helped make Iowa feel like home. In the Department of Communication Studies and beyond, I have benefited greatly from the insights, observations, good humor, and intellectual generosity of David Depew, Tim Havens, and Rita Zajac as well from impromptu, after-hours, and conference conversations with Louis-Georges Schwartz, Loren Glass, Fred Turner, Frank Durham, Vicky Mayer, Sue Collins, Nick Couldry, Lynn Clark, Jan Fernback, David Silver, Greg Elmer, Andy Opel, Travis Ripley, Kristina Riegert, Katharine Sarikakis, Dean Colby, Sam McCormick, Joy Hayes, and Slavko Andrejevic. I am grateful to my colleagues in media studies at the University of Iowa for creating such a stimulating intellectual environment and to Kristine Fitch for helping to foster it—and for her ongoing support and encouragement.

I have benefited greatly from the talent and hard work of my graduate student research assistants at the University of Iowa, including Minkyu Sung, Jin Kim, Cate Monahan, and Huike Wen.

James Hay has served as intellectual mentor, good friend and sometime collaborator during the writing of this book, and I am profoundly grateful to him for welcoming me into a loose-knit group of thinkers whose ideas, insights, and writings have had an ongoing influence on my own: Toby Miller, Jack Bratich, Jeremy Packer, Craig Robertson, Kelly Gates, Laurie Ouellette, Anna McCarthy, and Bilge Yesil.

I remain deeply indebted to Janice Peck for her ongoing mentorship, as well as the model she has set as a rigorous and original scholar, a careful and passionate thinker, and a good-humored, caring friend. I am also deeply grateful for the ongoing support of Andrew Calabrese, who continues a long-standing pattern of intellectual, personal, and professional generosity toward me and my work.

I would also like to thank Nick Muntean and the rest of the crew at *Flow*, who have provided me with a forum to preview some of the arguments that appear in the following pages. I am profoundly grateful to the Centre for Critical and Cultural Studies at the University of Queensland and to Centre's Director Graeme Turner and Manager Andrea Mitchell for invaluable support during the preparation of the book manuscript. I am also deeply indebted to the academic community provided by the Centre and my colleagues at the University of Queensland. I am grateful, as always, to Helen Andrejevic for sharing her interest in the world—and a world of ideas—and to Zala Volcic for her support, patience, and persistence.

Finally, this book owes its existence to the talented, supportive, and professional folks at the University Press of Kansas, whose insight and feedback has been invaluable. I am grateful to Nancy Jackson, Ranjit Arab, Michael Briggs, Kalyani Fernando, Larisa Martin, Susan K. Schott, and everyone else whose collective labor made the book possible.

Meaningful interactions all—I feel fortunate to have had them, and they receive the credit for anything that is of interest in the following pages.

1

Introduction

Cyberspace is not a fairy realm of magical transformations. It's a realm of transformations all right, but since humans beings aren't magical fairies you can pretty much scratch the magic and the fairy part.

—Bruce Sterling

Enter the Digital Enclosure

In the spring of 2006, search engine giant Google announced its plans to bring the holy grail of next-generation Internet access to the United States' first city of technology: the entire city of San Francisco would be equipped with free wireless Internet access. The company wasn't doing this out of the kindness of its heart or to rid itself of an embarrassingly large budget surplus; it had a business model. In return for free wireless access, Google announced its plans to use the information it gathered about users' locations within the city to bombard them with time- and location-specific ads, or what it calls "contextual advertising." As one press account put it, "users linking up with Wi-Fi transmitters placed around cities can be located to within a couple of blocks, allowing [Google] to serve tightly focused ads on its web pages from small businesses in the immediate area."[1] If, in other words, you happened to be working on your laptop in a city park during lunchtime, you might find an ad on your computer screen for a lunch discount at the sandwich shop across the street. Given the fact that Google can also keep track of the search requests entered into its search engines and the e-mail messages sent over its popular Gmail service, it's not hard to imagine just how "contextual" the advertising it doles out might eventually become. Say you happen to be searching for information about a particular author while working in a neighborhood café. Perhaps you might find an ad for discounts on that author's work in the bookstore around the corner. Writing a friend about a trip you're planning to take to Las Vegas the following weekend? Maybe the ad will be for poker how-to manuals instead.

Google's plans for San Francisco represent the physical version of what I describe in this book as a *digital enclosure*—the creation of an interactive realm wherein every action and transaction generates information about itself.[2] Although the term implies a physical space, the same characteristics can apply to virtual spaces. The Internet, for example, provides the paradigmatic example of a virtual digital enclosure—one in which every virtual "move" has the potential to leave a digital trace or record of itself. When we surf the Internet, for example, Internet browsers can gather information about the paths we take—the sites we've visited and the clickstreams that take us from one site to the next. When we purchase items online, we leave detailed records of our transactions. Even our search requests are logged and preserved in the database memories of search engines. Google's plans for downtown San Francisco are, in other words, merely the implementation of this Internet model in physical space: an attempt to make the city "interactive" by enveloping it within the electromagnetic embrace of Wi-Fi.

I use the term *enclosure* not just to invoke the notion of a space—virtual or otherwise—that is rendered interactive, but also to highlight the *process* of enclosure, whereby places and activities become encompassed by the monitoring embrace of an interactive (virtual) space. Accompanying this movement is a not-so-subtle shift in social relations: entry into the digital enclosure carries with it, in most cases, the condition of surveillance. We can go into a bookstore and make a cash purchase without generating information about the transaction. But when we go online, we generate increasingly detailed forms of transactional information that become secondary information commodities: information that may eventually be sold to third parties or used by marketers for targeted advertising campaigns. When we turn on our wireless connection in the San Francisco of the future, we will find ourselves in a digital enclosure for which the terms of entry include submission to always-on, location-based monitoring.

The use of the term *digital enclosure* is also meant to evoke the land enclosure movement associated with the transition from feudalism to capitalism, the process whereby over time communal land was subjected to private control, allowing private landowners to set the conditions for its use. Over time, the enclosure movement leads to the formation of distinct classes: those who own the means of production and those who must sell their labor for access to these means, whether arable lands or factories. A similar division of groups can be discerned in the emerging digital enclosure between those who control privatized interactive spaces (virtual or otherwise), and those who submit to particular forms of monitoring in order to gain access to goods, services, and conveniences. If you want the benefits of mobile telephony, not only do you enter into a financial arrangement with a service provider, you also, perhaps unwittingly, surrender to the forms of surveillance associated with cell phone use. As we shall see, this means not only providing information about who you call and when, but about your movements throughout the course of the day, the types of music you like (based on the ring tones you download), and a range of practices that corresponds to the increasing functionality of mobile phones.

Enclosure might be considered a "movement" to the extent that the reach of the interactive embrace continues to expand. At present, many traditional forms of transactions can still take place offline: we don't *have* to buy our books online. But when the local bookstore closes down because it can't keep up with Amazon.com, that may change. For many services, however, we do find ourselves reliant on monitored transactions: digital video recorders, for example, come with submission to monitoring as a built-in condition of use. Cable companies may not yet be using the data they get from their set-top boxes, but they could. Internet access requires going through a service provider that can collect and store information about patterns of Internet use and online activity. Buying music online is a monitored transaction in a way that a cash purchase in a record store need not be. There is a pattern here: the use of interactive technologies—new media devices—lends itself to the generation of cybernetic information: feedback about the transactions themselves. This feedback becomes the property of private companies that can store, aggregate, sort, and, in many cases, sell the information to others in the form of a database or a cybernetic commodity.[3]

As we equip ourselves with interactive devices and become increasingly reliant on them for everything from talking to one another to listening to music and buying plane tickets, we find ourselves caught up in privately controlled networks whose owners set the terms for entry, communication, and transaction. Using a cell phone or credit card these days is deceptively simple: communicating and purchasing are streamlined and simplified, but we have very little access to the forms of information collection and circulation that are taking place behind the scenes and screens. Companies are able to track our movements, transactions, and communications without our permission or, in many cases, knowledge. An unprecedented level of convenience is enabled by a network of complex and costly information technology whose increasing functionality is inversely proportional to the typical user's knowledge about how the system works. Those who live in a wired world know, for example, that shopping has become virtually "friction-free": they can window shop, compare prices, and order products without leaving the privacy of their homes. But they likely have only the vaguest idea about what happens to the information they provide about themselves in the process—their addresses, product preferences, credit card numbers, clothing sizes, and so on. Cell phone users know that they can remain in constant contact with friends and family, but they might be surprised to know that in some locations, for example, their cell phones are being used to track traffic patterns, or that the pings sent out by their phones, even when they're not using them, allow their paths to be traced throughout the course of the day. Interactivity is not necessarily a two-way street; more often than not, it amounts to the offer of convenience in exchange for willing or unwitting submission to increasingly detailed forms of information gathering. This book is about some of the ways in which this information is being used—or might be used in the future—and why as citizens and consumers we might want to think carefully about the relationship between the interactive revolution and the power of commercial and state institutions over our daily lives.

Interactivity

Perhaps, when the multimedia histories are assembled, the turn of the current century will be portrayed as the dawn of the iCentury—a period in which the prefix signifying the promise of the interactive revolution became ubiquitous. The hip, tricky little "i" that appears in front of an increasing variety of popular products (many manufactured by Apple) and concepts (including, during the 2004 election campaign, iPolitics) is freighted with a timely double meaning, both solipsistic customization and the democratic promise of the ability to talk back—to "interact." And what could be friendlier and more progressive than devices that allow us to interact, not just with one another, but with marketers, celebrities, media outlets, and politicians? Isn't interactivity, like communication, an unadulterated good, something that can help eliminate misunderstandings, overcome differences, and even empower the masses? Isn't it, in fact, the antidote to the depredations of mass society, a technological enhancement of democratic participation, the ability not just to see and hear, but to be seen and heard?

To hear some of the more upbeat members of the digerati put it, the so-called interactive revolution arrived just in time to address the increasingly apparent fact that mass society wasn't turning out to be as democratic as we might have hoped. This celebration of interactivity remains both premature and largely unexamined. The term itself, although scattered enthusiastically and indiscriminately throughout popular and academic descriptions of new media (to the point that it has entered the spell-checker lexicon) is an ill-defined and slippery one that has been used to include everything from staying in constant contact with friends, family, and relatives to voting for our favorite "American Idol." The term's ubiquity is rivaled by its referential flexibility: as one group of researchers noted, "Even the 'experts' are not yet certain exactly what the concept means."[4] Or, as another researcher succinctly put it, "The academic [and, I might add, popular] usage of 'interactivity' is marginally inconsistent at best."[5]

Somewhere in the mix, the positive associations of interactivity as a form of two-way, symmetrical, and relatively transparent communication (in the sense of knowing where the information we send is going) have been assimilated to forms of interaction that amount to little more than strategies for monitoring and surveillance. But this is not a book about the so-called end of privacy, not least because the information economy is one in which personal information is being privatized on an unprecedented scale. Those who express their concern over the impending death of privacy as well as those who, like Sun Micosystems's former CEO Scott McNeally, tell us to "get over it," have the story only partly right.[6] It's true that citizens and consumers are losing control over information about themselves, that increasingly their movements and purchases, the details of their daily lives, are being recorded, gathered, and sorted. In this respect, it's also true that the public can no longer nurture one of the characteristic expectations of mass society: that of being able to pass relatively unnoticed in a crowd, of being able, for the most part, to fly below the radar of surveillance, whether in the form of state surveillance, commercial monitoring, or even neighborhood gossip. Most crowds these days flow past scores of closed-circuit surveillance cameras as they move through the city—cameras that will likely one day soon develop the capacity to recognize individual faces and link them to personal information.

The shift away from a culture of relative anonymity is pervasive—at least wherever interactive technologies are present. Not long ago, for example, loading software on a computer was an unmonitored act—a fact with consequences for software privacy (and piracy). These days, thanks to the spread of the Internet, the programs we load on our computers check in with their parent companies to let them know that they've been legally installed. As we use our frequent shopper cards, our credit cards, and our subway fare cards, and as we surf the Internet, we generate increasingly high-resolution pieces of an emerging data portrait, one that grows more detailed and comprehensive with each new interactive application.

Privacy itself is not only far from dead, it also forms the very basis for the value of detailed information about consumers and citizens. Companies make billions of dollars by gathering detailed information about consumers and claiming it as their private property. In so doing, they prevent members of the public from accessing information that has been gathered about them by invoking their own right to privacy. A cousin of mine who works at one of the nation's largest database companies refused, on privacy grounds, to send me a copy of the information the company had about me. But when she sent a copy of the information about her—including only the public record information and not the additional proprietary information (gathered from the commercial sector and law enforcement)—it was more than 20 pages long and included not only a list of all the places she'd lived, but the names of all of her former roommates and all of the cars she'd owned. This was the lowest-resolution data image available, and yet it contained much more information than most of us would have realized is routinely gathered and stored about us.

We as individuals may feel that we increasingly have less and less freedom from scrutiny by those who would like to know the smallest details of the rhythms of our daily lives. The flip side, however, is the return of privacy with a vengeance: we find it next to impossible to learn what is being done with all of the information about us, thanks to the shield of privacy claimed by commercial organizations and that of secrecy and national security invoked by the state. The result might be described as an asymmetrical loss of privacy: individuals are becoming increasingly transparent to both public and private monitoring agencies, even as the actions of these agencies remain stubbornly opaque in the face of technologies that make collecting, sharing, and analyzing large amounts of information easier than ever before.

Most of us have some vague understanding that marketers are gathering information about us when we use our credit or discount cards, register our preferences online, surf the Web, or use our mobile phone, but we have very little knowledge about what information is being gathered, who has access to it, and how it is being used. How many of us know, for example, that there are database companies that keep "lists of people who take Prozac for depression, believe in the Bible, gamble online, or buy sex toys," or that the "verification services" company ChoicePoint has more than 15 billion records about 220 million Americans?[7] We know in general terms that we're being monitored, but we are far from having a sense of how extensive, detailed, and sophisticated the monitoring system has become.

Increasingly, state surveillance, at least in the United States, follows the same model: as more information is gathered, less accountability is afforded to the general public. The post-9/11 Patriot Act is a telling example of this tendency. Although it has rightly received a fair amount of publicity for the forms of privacy protection that it sacrifices in the name of national security, it has received rather less publicity for what might be among its most significant provisions: the fact that it exempts monitoring activities under its aegis from the Federal Freedom of Information Act. The result is not just more intensive and extensive surveillance (which arguably has some value to national security) but decreased accountability on the part of the spy agencies—agencies that have become famous for past abuses of their surveillance power. The same logic is at work in President Bush's public insistence on his right to increase surveillance activities while at the same time bypassing the legal obligation to obtain search warrants—an obligation meant to ensure some degree of accountability. The goal is not merely increased surveillance, but increased surveillance with diminished oversight and accountability—

or, to put it another way, increasing asymmetry in the monitoring process: those who are increasingly subject to surveillance are prevented from learning about the details of the surveillance process itself. The watchmen don't want to be watched.

This asymmetry is pervasive in forms of commercial and state monitoring facilitated by new communication technologies and techniques. It is rapidly becoming a hallmark of the type of "interactivity" citizens and consumers encounter on a regular basis. Perhaps not surprisingly given their prevalence, such forms of asymmetry have made their way into the interpersonal use of "interactive" devices, which allow individuals to engage in forms of monitoring and surveillance that mimic commercial and state surveillance. Just as we are becoming increasingly accustomed to top-down forms of monitoring, so we are learning that new technologies mean friends, families, and peers have an unprecedented ability to surreptitiously monitor and record information about one another by, for example, tracking phone calls (via cell phone call histories) and computer use (by checking recently viewed searches, documents, and Web sites) or performing criminal background checks and public records searches. These broad-ranging forms of habituation to interactivity-as-monitoring reinforce one another.

All of which is not to argue that interactivity is either inherently pernicious (or, on the other hand, automatically empowering). Although this book explores various dimensions and proposed definitions of interactivity, it avoids defining interactivity in the abstract. Rather, it sets out to consider the contradictions and tensions that permeate the contemporary deployment of both the promise of interactivity (as a form of power sharing) and its practice (which often amounts to monitoring and surveillance). It takes interactivity as its guiding object of critique and analysis because of the central role played by this concept and capacity in the deployment of new information and communication technologies that have had a powerfully transformative effect on the media environment, the information economy, and, thus, on contemporary social relations.

At heart, this is a book that approaches some of the central issues surrounding the development and deployment of new media through the lens of one of their characteristic attributes. It is an attempt to debunk the false promise of the digital revolution and in so doing to rehabilitate rather than write off the democratic potential of interactive media. The standard strategy of ideology is to address a real perceived need with a false solution—often one that exacerbates the very need it promised to fulfill, thereby ensuring the unflagging demand that legitimates the ideology itself. Thus, for example, the market offers the image of control over nature as a means of selling powerful automobiles. Think of all the SUV ads that feature rugged vehicles ripping their way through tough terrain, climbing mountains, and slicing their way through snow drifts and streams. The ads cater to a desire to feel in control over nature even as they pitch a product that contributes to the threat posed by environmental degradation. The defining contradiction of every ideological strategy is that it acknowledges the reality of the need it fulfills while promising that it has already been addressed. By the same token, any attempt to debunk ideology runs the danger of dismissing the actuality of the need it addresses. As critic Fredric Jameson suggests, ideology cannot be dismissed as wholly false: it reveals its element of truth in the acknowledgment of the reality of a need or a contradiction to be addressed.[8] If we are to consider the promise of interactivity as ideological in this specific sense, we might start out by considering the need that it addresses. Or to put it somewhat differently, one approach to the notion of interactivity is to consider its implicit or explicit promise: why is it such a useful buzzword for marketing new communication technology? Rather than dismissing the marketing of interactivity as public relations froth, how might we extract the solid core of its appeal by working backward, as it were, from the proposed solution to the perceived need?

Instead of starting with a list of general answers, it is perhaps more useful to consider some specific examples chosen not so much for their sweeping social impact as for being suggestive—and typical of the promotional promise of interactivity. In the summer of the first year of the new millennium, for example, TV viewers were treated to an advertisement that featured a TV executive being tossed through the plate-glass window of his skyscraper office. The message of this tongue-in-cheek image of the impending interactive revolution was that interactive technology heralded a revolutionary shift in control over TV consumption from producers to viewers. As one account put it, glossing over the fact that the ostensible revolution had no impact on content whatsoever, "TiVo, a digital set-top unit that functions like a hyperintelligent VCR, allows viewers to create their own TV schedules."[9] By the time the advertisement aired, the rhetoric of the digital revolution had become easily recognizable: thanks to new, interactive, media technologies, consumers, viewers, and citizens were about to become radically empowered. Such rhetoric folded the images of *political* revolution—the violent dethroning of power figures in the TiVo ad, for example—into a promotional appeal for the latest generation of high-tech *consumer* goods.

Perhaps the archetypical image of this advertising campaign was the 1984 Apple computer ad featuring the revolutionary overthrow of Orwellian authoritarianism—thanks to the emergence of personal computing, Apple style. Not only would the revolution be televised and digitized, but it could be purchased . . . and the culture critics were buying. In its celebratory article about TiVo, the *New York Times* heralded the technology as "the beginning of the end of another socialistic force in American life: the mass market."[10] Against the background of the impending interactive revolution, the article's author argued, "the entire history of commercial television suddenly appears to have been a Stalinist plot erected, as it has been, on force from above rather than choice from below."[11] At the very least, such an observation amounts to dramatic historical revisionism for a publication like the *New York Times*. Apparently, by the turn of the millennium, thanks perhaps to the fall of communism in Europe, it seemed OK to admit that the mass culture critics had been right all along: there was a disconcerting similarity between the top-down control of capitalist mass media monopolies on the one hand and top-down state-controlled media on the other.

Perhaps it shouldn't have come as a big surprise that a mainstream media heavyweight like the *New York Times* would readily embrace a promise that had, after all, become commonplace in the hype surrounding new media technologies. But it was a bit surprising to discover that, at least in this instance, the mainstream media and the hip media critics who publish the magazine *Adbusters* were on the same page. According to *Adbusters,* TiVo is a subversive technology that "struck true fear into the hearts of the transnational bosses" (including, presumably, the networks who were investing in TiVo at the time) because it "sticks it to every broadcast advertiser."[12] The result, they noted, was "something revolutionary. Something almost purely democratic. Something essentially non-commercial, driven not by price but by value. At long last, the people—could it be true?—would have control of what they wanted to hear and see."

What helps make both reactions somewhat surprising is that the business model of TiVo's founders was, as the *New York Times* article noted, not to overthrow the corporate media, but to provide it with the most detailed information possible about viewers: to become information middlemen, providing customized content to viewers and detailed information about viewing habits to consumers. Far from fomenting revolution, TiVo promised to become the twenty-first-century realization of the Orwellian telescreen that watches viewers while they watch TV. Perhaps the most graphic instance of TiVo's surveillance capabilities came shortly after the notorious "wardrobe malfunction" during the 2004 Super Bowl, when one of the half-time performers, Janet Jackson, momentarily bared her breast. According to an enthusiastic press release put out by TiVo the following day, this brief moment was the most replayed in TiVo's admittedly brief history. The "freedom" allowed by TiVo—the ability to watch shows whenever one likes—came with a dramatically heightened level of viewer monitoring: the ability not just to determine which households are watching what shows, but the minutiae of how they are watching and when, including how often they rewind, fast forward, pause, and so on. TiVo promised a quantum leap in the ability of producers to monitor viewers.

The model, up until the advent of TiVo, has been to treat audiences as homogeneous masses in which the behavior of a small sample could be reasonably assumed to reflect the viewing patterns of society as a whole (without any way of checking for certain). With the development of interactive digital recording technology—which is also being incorporated into cable TV systems, thereby threatening to eliminate TiVo's coveted monopoly of the middleman role—the model shifts from one based on generalization and probability sampling to one based on the detailed monitoring of individual viewing habits. TiVo technology brings the mass medium of television into the customized, interactive network era. Just as Web sites like Amazon. com can remember the identity of individual visitors and sort through their past actions and purchases in order to target individual consumers with customized appeals for new products and services, TiVo—and other interactive video services—allow producers to keep track of the viewing habits of individual households. When television and Internet technologies merge, the amount of information gathered about consumers will likely grow exponentially, broadening from TV viewing to include, potentially, Web surfing and online shopping, digital radio listening, and downloading statistics.

The fact that digital VCR technologies allow viewers to program their viewing preferences adds a new dimension of predictability to ratings measurements: producers will know in advance the shows that specific households plan to view. Down the road, when the digital customization technology that futurists like Bill Gates have long envisioned becomes practical, advance knowledge of viewing habits will allow programmers to tailor advertisements to viewers. If, for example, a particular household has set its TiVo to record Monday Night Football every week during the football season, producers could conceivably use background information about the household to deliver customized advertising. The apparent drawback for producers is that digital VCRs make it possible for viewers to skip ads, a troublesome detail that they are addressing with product placement and the return of sponsored programming. Shows like *The Apprentice,* for example, rely heavily on sponsors who integrate their products into the content of the show. Thus, one of the likely consequences of digitization—a consequence that it both enables and necessitates (at least from the standpoint of advertisers)—is the continued blurring of the line between content and advertising.

It's worth pointing out that this process of de-differentiation goes far beyond straightforward forms of product placement, like the Reese's Pieces candy in *E.T. The Extra Terrestrial,* or the Coke logo on Simon Cowell's cup. Already the content of much television programming serves primarily as promotional material for other media commodities, either directly or in the form of packaging and promoting celebrities and hybrid entertainers like Jennifer Lopez. This convergence trend is, as media scholars and critics have pointed out, already well under way in the era of media conglomeration and cross-platform synergy. Reality shows like *Newlyweds* or *Making the Band* help promote the musical careers of their stars, while entertainment "news" shows and celebrity exposés promote the careers, movies, albums, and TV shows of featured celebrities. Watching *Entertainment Tonight* is like watching a long advertisement for movies, TV shows, and albums interspersed with shorter ads for personal care products and cars. If the advent of interactive TV heralds the end of advertising as we know it—vignettes distinct from the program content—it simultaneously anticipates the transformation of all content into advertising.

Critical theorists have for some time asserted that watching advertising might be considered a form of audience labor—value-generating work that is compensated for by access to "free" program content.[13] In other words, the informal media contract entered into by producers and viewers is that the latter agree to expose themselves to some amount of advertising in exchange for access to entertainment, news, and sports coverage. According to the unwritten rules of this contract, if no one were ever to watch any ads, presumably advertisers would take their business elsewhere, and funding for TV programming would dry up. The labor metaphor has its limits, but it is a suggestive way to approach some of the ongoing struggles that emerge around TV viewing, including attempts by viewers to shirk their viewing "responsibilities" by channel surfing or ad zapping, and counterattempts by producers to develop increasingly sophisticated techniques for monitoring viewers and thwarting their avoidance strategies—by, for example, synchronizing advertising slots and relying more heavily on ads that can't be zapped, such as product placement, sponsorship, and, more recently, advertising placed in the "crawl" space at the bottom of the screen.

TiVo, viewed from this perspective, is a technology that promises to greatly advance "workplace" monitoring, and, in combination with digital customization, to ensure that viewers work as efficiently as possible, which would mean that they are exposed only to those promotional messages that are relevant to them. Enhancing efficiency in this regard would mean cutting down on wasted advertising viewing, such as exposing retirees to acne cream ads or men to commercials for feminine hygiene products. The customization process, however, adds another, perhaps more literal, level of labor to the process. Targeted advertising relies on the collection of detailed information about consumer preferences, values, and behavior—information that, before the development of interactive technology, could be costly and time-consuming to obtain. Customization, in other words, increases the demand for demographic information to a new level: it creates new markets for the fruits of increasingly intensive and extensive forms of consumer surveillance.

To return to the example of TiVo, we can discern two different but interrelated forms of consumer labor and their relationship to one another: first, the work of watching described by media economists—the attempt to ensure that viewers are exposed to those ads that are most likely to be relevant to the needs, desires, and anxieties of individual viewers; and second, the work of *being watched*—the ability of the interactive technology to gather information about individual viewing habits. This second form of "labor" generates an actual product to be bought and sold in the form of what Vincent Mosco has described as cybernetic commodities: information *about* transactions and viewing habits.[14] When I buy a book at Amazon.com, I've purchased a commodity; if Amazon.com sells information about what books I've purchased and viewed to a data-mining company, it is selling what Mosco calls a cybernetic commodity.

The burgeoning personal information industry, which includes companies like Equifax, Choicepoint, Acxiom, and Lexis/Nexis, has grown up in part around the trade in such commodities, generated by individuals as they go through the routines of their daily lives. The value of such commodities lies in their ability to rationalize the marketing process—not just to ensure that ads are sent to the "right" viewers, but to determine strategies for marketing more efficiently to particular sets of viewers by capitalizing on detailed information about their personal lives: have they recently started buying diet products and larger-size clothing? Perhaps ads that target insecurities over weight issues might be inserted in the TV shows these viewers have scheduled for downloading. And that's just a mild version of the potential for invasive and manipulative forms of advertising facilitated by the combination of detailed data gathering and personalized marketing. The example of the woman who started receiving Safeway coupons for diapers and baby food nine months after she purchased a home pregnancy test at the store is only a crude foretaste of the marketing world to come—one in which advertisers may well have ready access not just to our purchases, but our movements throughout the course of the day, our medical and relationship histories, and perhaps even the changing state of our physiological responses.[15] Entrepreneurs are already working on interactive devices that store and respond to changes in level of anxiety, pulse, and body temperature. The attempt to use everything from eye-tracking devices to EKG scanning in order to hone interactive sales strategies is already well under way. Combine the marketing mind-set with the fervid and value-free imagination of entrepreneurial technocapital, and what might seem creepy to the rest of us becomes the next killer application: Web sites that rearrange themselves in response to our viewing behavior, interactive ads fired off to our cell phones in response to changes in our pulse rates and pupil dilation triggered by an advertisement;

samples for diet products sent to our homes when our pants size changes; or, perhaps somewhat more disturbingly, ads targeted to an emerging pattern of anxiety or insecurity (interactive ads for Viagra after visiting a Web site on impotency, for example). The question that we need to ask ourselves as we embark on the impending era of technologically facilitated "relationship" marketing is not what marketers want to know about us, but whether there is any information they *don't* want to know about our lives. The answer, one suspects, is a resounding "no."

The lesson of the TiVo advertisement, and the reason for dwelling on the example of digital video recording technology, is that it neatly encapsulates the marketing of surveillance as a form of revolutionary participation. What the TiVo campaign heralds is an era in which we are told that the consumer is being enthroned even as he or she is being put to work as never before. Thanks to the capability of interactive networked technology, consumers are being enlisted and equipped to assist in the process of their own manipulation. The defining irony of the interactive economy is that the labor of detailed information gathering and comprehensive monitoring is being offloaded onto consumers in the name of their own empowerment. To borrow from a formulation by critical theorist Slavoj Žižek, we are invited to actively participate in staging the scene of our own passive submission—and to view such participation as a form of power sharing.[16] As is evident from the recurring mobilization of the language of democracy, the promise of interactivity has implications that extend beyond the economic realm to that of the political—a theme that will be taken up in Chapters 6 and 7. Suffice it to note that the model of willing submission to comprehensive monitoring as a form of participation ought to be clearly recognizable to anyone who has been following the role of citizen "participation" in the Bush administration's war on terror and the Department of Homeland Security's "readiness" campaign. Willing submission to government surveillance and control is framed not just as civic duty, but as the public's participation in an interactive war.

iPromise: Interactivity's Offerings

In this book, I take as a given that there is no single correct definition of *interactivity* that can be used as a measuring stick to assess any given use of the term. Rather, through a consideration of particular applications, this book attempts to read the promise of interactivity against itself. To avoid begging the question, then, it discerns in the use of the term by promoters of the information economy the promise of interactivity as a form of power sharing: a democratic challenge to the economic, political, cultural, and social hierarchies of mass society. Interactive artist Celia Pearce, in her handbook on interactivity, captures the celebratory, revolutionary spirit of this promise when she argues that, precisely because of emerging forms of interactivity, "The digital age introduces a new form of international socialism, a new kind of democracy that Marx never even imagined."[17] The very premise of interactivity, she claims, "is one of intellectual, creative and social empowerment. It is anti-industrial."[18]

The celebratory "post–mass society" and postindustrial tone of these claims for interactivity extends to the media technologies that enable it, including networked computing. For example, Howard Rheingold, the populizer of the idea that computer networks can help revitalize a sense of community in an increasingly dispersed and atomized society, argues, "The political significance of computer mediated communication lies in its capacity to challenge the existing political hierarchy's monopoly on powerful communications media, and perhaps thus revitalize citizen-based democracy."[19] New media guru and futurist Derrick de Kerckhove goes even further, arguing that technological developments succeed where political struggle has failed: "In a networked society, the real powershift is from the producer to the consumer, and there is a redistribution of controls and power. On the Web, Karl Marx's dream has been realized: the tools and the means of production are in the hands of the workers."[20]

Read backward, all of these promises suggest that the current state of society is not altogether democratic, but rather is characterized by the concentration of power in a group of social, political, and economic elites. Further, as in the case of the *New York Times*'s reception of TiVo described above, the implicit message is that the forms of centralized, one-way, and top-down media characteristic of industrial capitalism facilitate an undemocratic concentration of power. In what is likely to be welcome news to the monopolists, this latest critique of concentrated power proposes a technological fix. There's no need for revolution if the technology itself is revolutionary: the market will heal itself, and citizens will become empowered by embracing new media technologies. Apparently unbeknownst to themselves, the very elites who are developing and popularizing the technology are crafting the tools of their own destruction. As Pearce puts it, "the Newt Gingriches of the world, who have inadvertently popularized the thing that will be their undoing should be very, very afraid,"[21] presumably because "no matter which way you look at it, interactivity is inherently subversive."[22] That such pronouncements reflect the euphoric techno-utopianism of the 1990s does not mean they have run their course. Indeed, the ongoing attempt to equate new media technologies with the promise of empowerment, individuation, and creative control remains alive and well even in the postbubble tech economy, as will become evident from several of the examples discussed in later sections of the book. The important ideological role that this equation plays in legitimating the ongoing rationalization of economic and political control suggests it's not going away any time soon.

Moreover, the unreflective, celebratory equation of interactivity with empowerment neatly sidesteps the more tangled and troublesome questions of revolutionary politics. An undemocratic affinity between monopoly capitalism and totalitarian culture can only be admitted—or even hinted at—once a technological fix has already been proffered. In its absence, such a critique would amount to a call for political action—a literal or metaphorical call to arms. A typically American faith in the redemptive power of technology, however, allows properly political issues to be transposed into the register of the technocracy. Media scholar James Carey describes the distinctively American faith in the ability of technological developments to properly resolve political issues as one aspect of "the rhetoric of the electrical sublime," which "massages in us all the belief that somehow advances in technology would solve the problems of the present and usher in a new century of peace, prosperity, and ecological harmony."[23] Technological politics, in this respect, functions in an era of generalized skepticism toward the political realm, as a form of *anti*-politics. We can avoid the messy work of collective deliberation and attendant struggles over power through an invocation of what Armand Mattelart called "the ideology of redemption through networks."[24]

There are two aspects of straightforward technological determinism embedded in the portrayal of interactive technology as inherently subversive and revolutionary. The first, typified by Pearce's comments, locates a political imperative in the technology itself insofar as it incorporates interactive capabilities. According to this account, interactivity is not a neutral capability that can be enlisted either for totalitarian control or democratic empowerment; it is, rather inextricably tied to the latter. The import of such a claim is to exempt particular uses of the technology from critical scrutiny: if they are interactive, they must be empowering. The second, related, claim asserts the inevitable development and implementation of networked communication technologies. The combination of these two claims exhibits the theme of fate that runs deep in the ongoing discussion of cyberspace: the assertion that, like it or not, the digital revolution is inevitable. As Negroponte puts it, "Like a force of nature, the digital age cannot be denied or stopped."[25] The breathless certainty of such claims is underwritten by the assumption that the digital revolution is a force for good.

By contrast, the man credited with coining the term that provided the prefix for the digital revolution—cybernetics—was less sanguine about the prospects for interactive technology. Norbert Wiener, the MIT mathematician whose neologism, derived from the word for "steersman," haunts the discourse on new media in the truncated form of the familiar "cyber-" prefix, observed that the technology we now call interactive facilitates increasingly sophisticated forms of centralized control. Throughout his writing on cybernetics, Wiener emphasized the link to questions of power and control, emphasizing them in his definition of the term itself: "We have decided to call the entire field of control and communication theory, whether in the machine or the animal, by the name cybernetics."[26] Rather than trumpeting the subversive potential of cybernetic technology, Wiener, writing shortly after the end of World War II, expressed guarded pessimism toward the scientific developments he helped pioneer and theorize: "there are those who hope that the good of a better understanding of man and society which is offered by this new field of work may anticipate and outweigh the incidental contribution we are making to the concentration of power (which is always concentrated, by its very conditions of existence, in the hands of the most unscrupulous). I write in 1947, and I am compelled to say that it is a very slight hope."[27]

If, as Spiro Kiousis's overview of the academic literature on interactivity and new media suggests, "any discussion of interactivity inevitably draws from its roots in Cybernetic theory, as outlined by Wiener," the latter's work—and his reservations—might be a good place to start in contextualizing and critiquing the promise of interactivity.[28] Obviously, the notion of interactivity in a general sense long predates Wiener's theories of cybernetics. The reason his work resonates through the literature on new media is not just the popularization of "cyber-" as a prefix for all things digitally networked, but also the resonance of his study of feedback with the rise of interactive media technologies. His theories focus on technology, whether organic or inorganic (and this persistent link in his work tends to assimilate the two), that relies on detailed data collection in an ongoing process of adjustment to shifting conditions.

In short, Wiener's theories bear directly on contemporary examples of interactive technology: Web sites that alter their appearance in response to viewer behavior, interactive billboards that customize their advertising appeals, TV shows that change their outcome based on viewer voting, smart homes that change climate conditions on the basis of the comfort level of residents, electronic "newspapers" that sort content in response to reader preferences. The persistent use of the prefix "cyber-" in the popular and academic reception of new media serves as an inadvertent but telling clue regarding the element of control that characterizes the deployment of interactivity in "cyberspace"—which, taking a cue from Wiener's work, we might rethink as "directed space" or "steered space." To put it in terms that will be developed in more detail in the following chapters, we might approach cyberspace as "governed" space, building on the etymological connection highlighted by Wiener: "we wish to recognize that the first significant paper on feed-back mechanisms is an article on governors, which was published by Clerk Maxwell in 1868 and that governor is derived from a Latin corruption of *kubernetes* [the Greek word for steersman]."[29]

If the genealogy of new media interactivity can be traced back to cybernetic theories of feedback-enhanced command and control, the latter took root in military research. Specifically, the task that occupied the attention of Wiener and his colleagues during their World War II research and an example that reappears throughout his work on cybernetics is the coupling of radar and servomechanisms in the development of guided antiaircraft artillery. Far from being anti-industrial, cybernetic theory envisioned the autonomization of industrial technology. Wiener envisions the possibility of automated factories equipped with devices that combine the mechanical "muscle" of the first industrial revolution with the "brains" (and senses) of the communication-based one. In predicting the eventual development of an "assembly line without human agents," he noted, "It has long been clear to me that the modern ultra-rapid computing machine was in principle an ideal central nervous system to an apparatus for automatic control."[30] Crucial to such control is the development of an interactive capability—the ability not just to communicate a signal or message, but to incorporate the process of an ongoing adjustment to shifting conditions of reception into the communication process.

Tellingly, Wiener highlighted the possibility that a cybernetic model might be deployed not just as a technique of mechanical control, but also as one of social control. Indeed, he considered strategies of scientific management (discussed in Chapter 3) as an early form of programming that presaged computer programming and the automated workplace. The use of cybernetic systems, he warned, might result in a society in which entrenched economic and political powers consolidated their control by modifying messages based on audience feedback. He describes a not-unfamiliar scenario, with undisguised bitterness directed toward his own contribution to military technology (in 1946, Wiener announced, "I do not expect to publish any future work of mine which may do damage in the hands of irresponsible militarists"):

A certain precise mixture of religion, pornography, and pseudo-science will sell an illustrated newspaper. A certain blend of wheedling, bribery, and intimidation will induce a young scientist to work on guided missiles or the atomic bomb. To determine these, we have our machinery of fan-ratings, straw votes, opinion samplings and other psychological investigations with the common man as their object. . . . Luckily for us, these merchants of lies, these exploiters of gullibility have not yet arrived at such a pitch of perfection as to have things all their own way.[31]

Note the guarded pessimism of the "not yet." The flip side of the revolutionary promise of interactive media, in other words, may well be the attempt to attain this level of perfection: to craft the perfect pitch.

One objection to such a line of argument may be that cybercelebrants like Celia Pearce and Nicholas Negroponte aren't talking about the same kind of interactivity that Wiener considers in his discussion of cybernetics. What they're interested in is the forms of person-to-person communication and collaboration facilitated by interactive technologies. Celebratory accounts of interactivity tend to blur this distinction, in part because they focus on the information gathering and sorting power of the technology itself (Nicholas Negroponte and Bill Gates love to talk about "smart" environments—that respond to the individuals moving through them), and in part because the distinction itself isn't as clear-cut as it might seem.

For the moment, most forms of interactive information gathering don't rely on autonomous machinery. As in the case of the antiaircraft gun, humans are in charge of managing the information gathering, setting the priorities, and overseeing the equipment. When we provide information about our shopping habits by, for example, letting Amazon.com know what books we're reading, this is not only a form of communication with a machine. It is also information that is used, albeit automatically, to consolidate marketing strategies devised by researchers and programmers. From Wiener's perspective, it is the use of feedback by decision makers to more effectively target advertising messages. This is precisely what the cybercelebrants call power sharing: the assertion that consumers now have the ability to talk back to producers and thus to have a say in production decisions—as if this information-gathering process allows them to take control of the production process itself. Are those who equate power sharing with a willing submission to surveillance to be numbered among the gullible, or among the accomplices of Wiener's "exploiters of gullibility"? The equation of feedback with power sharing is not a novel artifact of the new media era; it is the extension of the ideology of marketplace democracy into the digital age: the perfection of the promise of demand signaling as the essence of democracy. Later chapters will offer a critique of this equation in more detail. The following chapters offer an overview of the ways in which this equation functions in the economic, cultural, social, and political realms.

2

Three Dimensions of iCulture

And does not . . . the same hold for today's progressive computerization of our everyday lives in the course of which the subject is also more and more "mediatised," imperceptibly stripped of his power, under the false guise of its increase?

—Slavoj Žižek

iCommerce

In the summer of 2005, two of the biggest advertisers in the United States, Nike and Proctor and Gamble, unveiled interactive marketing campaigns that exemplified the equation of monitoring and empowerment. Nike's campaign was perhaps the more dramatic of the two: for the month of May, it created a twenty-three-story-high interactive billboard in New York City's Times Square. Passersby could call a toll-free number advertised on the billboard, allowing them to take control of part of the display to custom design an athletic shoe by picking the colors and watching the image on the billboard respond to their choices. When finished, they would receive a text message on their cell phone telling them where they could purchase the shoe, along with an image of their custom design, complete with their chosen lettering and a label noting that the shoe had been designed at Times Square. Passersby could watch the giant shoe change colors in real time in response to the commands of whoever had managed to phone in and take control of the billboard. This interactive campaign was part of the company's relaunch of its

NIKE iD Web site, which allows consumers to personalize their purchases from the privacy of home or office.

The marketing world greeted the Nike promotion with predictable technohype, describing the interactive billboard with headlines including, "Nike Empowers Mobile Users with Design Capabilities."[1] The NIKE iD Web site offered what, in the aftermath of TV shows like *The Apprentice* and *Rebel Billionaire*—shows that offered jobs in high-profile companies to selected audience members—might be described as the reality TV–inflected promise to enter, if only momentarily and symbolically, the hallowed halls of a corporate icon: "NIKE iD is your chance to be a NIKE designer" (note the telltale lowercase "i").[2] The site addressed consumers as apprentice producers, seizing the drawing board from those who have too long monopolized it: "You begin with a blank item—or an inspiration—and express your individuality by adding color and a personal iD."[3]

Because the Nike campaign efficiently exploited several facets of the promise of interactivity that will be taken up in later chapters, it's worth parsing the elements of the campaign in a bit more detail. First is the promise of individuation: thanks to the power of networked interactivity, mass marketing can surpass its own homogeneity. Interactivity promotes what the pundit Josh Micah Marshall has referred to, in political terms, as the "grand moral inversion." The corporate giant, an erstwhile foe of individuality, is miraculously revealed to be, on the contrary, one of its greatest facilitators, thanks to the alchemy of interactivity.[4] Drawing on the long-standing U.S. tradition of equating self-expression with freedom, the promise goes on to connect personal expression through customized commodities with shifting power relations. As the president of an interactive marketing company that worked on the NIKE iD campaign put it, "The Web gives the consumer empowerment and control. . . . Consumers own the brands, not the companies. The Internet allows the brand to adjust or adapt to fit the individual, not the other way around."[5]

In case the enthusiastically misleading rhetoric hasn't made it completely clear, the power shift is purportedly in the direction of democratization, even though any consumer who tried to use the brand for his or her own purposes would learn immediately that Nike is still very much the legal owner of the brand. Nevertheless, as one newspaper commentary put it, "Some see a political dimension to all of this, in that it points to a new market-based democratic egalitarianism."[6] Customization via interactivity represents, on this account, evidence of "a democratic desire": "Every person wants to say this is more them, and they're not part of mass culture."[7]

A third aspect of the promise of interactivity is the invocation of nostalgia for a lost sense of community, and the forms of participation, customization, and authenticity retroactively associated with pre–mass society. As Nike chairman and CEO Phil Knight put it, "NIKEiD brings us back to our roots when we designed and sold shoes one by one out of the trunk of my Plymouth. . . . We have now come full circle."[8] Thanks to its ability to reconnect consumers and producers, interactive technology moves us forward while recapturing what was best about a lost past.

The theme that runs throughout these aspects of the promise of interactivity is that of overcoming the forms of differentiation and abstraction associated with mass society, and in particular the separation between consumption and production. Haunting the promise is a romanticized vision of pre–mass society in which consumers had greater control over their consumption, in part because of their personal connection with shopkeepers and craftspeople and in part because they made many of the goods they consumed themselves. By the same token, they presumably had a more direct connection to their own labor conducted in a tradition-governed, craft-based setting rather than in an anonymous workspace populated by human cogs. Interactivity promises to overcome both forms of alienation in a single stroke: consumers will feel more connected to the products they buy because they receive "individualized" treatment. Moreover, they recapture a lost sense of direct connection to the product world because they are invited to participate in the production process itself. As in more traditional settings, they are consumer and producer at the same time, two reunited halves of a whole that had been sundered by the advent of industrial mass society. The key to this reunion is two-way communication facilitated by interactive media. As a spokesman for the advertising company TBWA/Chiat/Day put it, "Traditional media remains a little boxed in. . . . It's still a monologue. It's one message to a mass audience."[9] By contrast, "The interactive nature of the Web . . . opens marketers to limitless opportunities for personalization and dialogue."[10]

There are, of course, limits to the dialogue, as one activist-minded customer demonstrated in a much-publicized exchange with Nike's marketing department over his attempt to order a custom shoe with the personalized tag, "sweatshop." Noting that the NIKE iD Web site equated customization with "freedom to choose and freedom to express who you are," Jonah Peretti asked for the custom label because he wanted to, as he put it, "remember the toil and labor of the children who made my shoes."[11] Shared control over the production process, needless to say, doesn't extend to using the product as a means of protesting the working conditions of the people who *really* make the shoes. Nike turned down the request, at first contending that it contained inappropriate slang and finally conceding that even if the word *sweatshop* wasn't slang, it just wasn't something the company wanted to print on its shoes. Peretti's prank provided a nutshell critique of the limits of interactivity, albeit within the confines of what amounts to a practical joke with a point. It gave the lie to the political promise of democratization via consumption. The revelation of the limit to Nike's version of self-expression (that consumers can pick their color scheme and custom label, as long as it doesn't offend Nike's sensibilities—or, worse yet, engage in social critique) foregrounds the real role of the interactive site as a means of building brand loyalty while at the same time enticing consumers to participate in what marketers call the process of "co-creating unique value."[12] Customized shoes are not only more expensive, they also invite consumers to participate in the work of being watched. As one news account put it, "Profitable or not, the sneaker sites have one very practical application: They open up a wealth of market research possibilities. Thousands of shoppers logging their preferences on the minutiae of laces, tongues and soles amounts to a free focus group."[13]

The business literature has described the information gathered through interactive marketing as a technique for saving money "by offloading some of the duties of consumer interactions onto consumers themselves."[14] Market research "duties" once assigned to producers are being reconfigured as the responsibility of consumers. This use of interactivity as a technique for creating free focus groups is apparent across a variety of products, ranging from online shopping to reality TV. The producers of the *American Idol/Pop Star* franchise are probably kicking themselves for not having thought of it sooner. Now they can make money from the market-testing process instead of paying for it. Interactive marketing is, as one retail consultant put it, "a great way to insert the consumer into the process of product development."[15] It is truly a cybernetic process in the sense described by Wiener, one in which the manufacturing process is modified by consumer feedback. Interactive customization creates two products. In the case of Nike, it creates not just an athletic shoe, but also detailed information about consumer preferences. To the extent that this information can be traced back to individual consumers through their cell phone numbers, their credit card numbers, or online forms, the information can be personalized and aggregated.

Proctor and Gamble's attempt to equate participation in a nationwide focus group with democratic empowerment was a bit more direct: in what some might describe as an apt parody of what politics has become, it invited the public to vote for a new flavor of Crest toothpaste. The company set up a Web site for its election, specifying that participants had to be of voting age (presumably because of a prize giveaway associated with the "election") and introducing the three "candidates": "lemon ice," "sweet berry punch," and "tropica exotica." The somewhat disturbingly named "Whitening Expressions Vote" page of the Web site featured background photographs of a celebratory crowd with their fists raised in the air, power-to-the-people style. As the press coverage of the ad campaign noted, the "democratization" of marketing is more than an attempt to market-test products and build interest and loyalty; it's also a way to cut through the clutter of traditional advertising campaigns with the promise of participation. Like the Nike campaign, the Crest election included interactive, video game–like features, inviting would-be voters to create a campaign button online and to join an e-mail list that provided updates and interactive polls. Just as video games are becoming more and more like advertisements—integrating product placement in the form of background ads, celebrity characters, and theme music—interactive advertising is becoming more like a video game. Thanks to the interactive capability of networked digital media, advertising, entertainment, and retail merge: such is the logic of commercially driven convergence.

Perhaps one of the better publicized examples of this trend is the virtual digital enclosure of Second Life, an online digital world which users navigate in the form of virtual avatars consuming virtual goods as they go. Even though the products are virtual, the money paid for them is real—reportedly upward of $200 million a year.[16] Second Life serves as a kind of prototype for a digital enclosure in which every act of consumption, creativity, and customization is redoubled in the form of data about itself. It is not just composed of information; it constantly also generates new data about the actions of the digital doubles that populate it. As Reuben Steiger, the head of a company that seeks out commercial opportunities in Second Life, put it, the virtual world can serve as a research lab where marketers can observe consumer behavior and test products in their virtual—therefore less expensive—forms. For example, denizens of Second Life can purchase a virtual Toyota Scion for real money ($1.50) and customize it: "You're interacting with the brand in a fairly intimate way, you can customize it to your hearts content, change the color, the rims, in ways that fit your fancy, that's very interesting to companies."[17] The promise of interactivity serves as an invitation to submit to the monitoring gaze of market researchers and pay for the privilege.

There's nothing particularly new about using the promise of democracy to sell—or selling the market as an economic version of "democracy" (albeit one in which the somewhat less than egalitarian principle of "one dollar, one vote" prevails). What is distinct about the marketing of interactivity is its explicit critique of the market for not being democratic enough, and its resort to customization as an alibi for increasingly comprehensive forms of consumer monitoring. The mass market relies on feedback in the form of aggregate demand, and therefore exerts control at the group level. The interactive market relies on personalized feedback and thus seeks to exert control at the individual level. The former retains the anonymity of the mass, whereas the latter seeks to eliminate anonymity.

The consequences of such a loss will be taken up in more detail in later chapters, but for the moment, suffice it to say that the comparison to pre-mass forms of personalization is deceptive. Interactivity promises not a return to the relative lack of anonymity of village life, but rather to a state of affairs in which producers have more information about consumers than ever before, and consumers have less knowledge about and control over how this information is being used. Rather than the cozy image of the town cobbler with a custom-made template for every resident's foot, imagine an electronic village in which an omniscient and invisible shop owner keeps track of every detail of villagers' lives, storing them in a database to which they have no access, and using it not just to meet their needs, but also to prey on their anxieties and insecurities and to manipulate their hopes and dreams. This data-mining technocobbler knows what they are doing, but they, in turn, have little if any knowledge of the extent of the information he is collecting, how accurate it is, and what he is doing with it. Then imagine that they are told that providing personal information for the shoemaker's proprietary database—contributing to his increasingly invasive marketing schemes—is, paradoxically, a way of empowering themselves, and you get a more accurate picture of the grand moral inversion that characterizes the marketing of interactivity. It is a picture that is papered over by a barrage of ersatz forms of personal recognition. The hometown merchant who has a personal relationship with his or her customers is replaced by the cell phone text message that at first seems to be from a friend, but turns out to be spam, by the cheery voice of the targeted telemarketing campaign or the letter with the fake handwritten address that turns out to be yet another customized solicitation. Phony personalization abounds in the interactive era as a shoddy cover for the fundamental asymmetry of commercial surveillance.

To the extent that politics is embracing similar data-driven campaigning models, the same inversion insinuates itself into the political process, once again in the name of public empowerment—a strategy that will be taken up in more detail in Chapter 7. It's not that consumers aren't really participating. They are. But their participation is all too often limited to achieving the aims of marketers—aims not necessarily their own, despite the hype. Moreover, participation is not always the same thing as power sharing; sweatshop workers certainly participate in the production process, but that doesn't mean that the sweatshop can stand as a model for democracy.

iCulture

Mass culture, like the mass market that produces it, has long been criticized for being top down, homogeneous, and nonparticipatory. Indeed, one of the hallmarks of such culture is the way it replaces more participatory and interactive forms of popular culture: the parlor piano is displaced by the phonograph, the local band by the radio, the vaudeville troupe by the motion picture and the sketch comedy. The much-maligned result is the mass-produced cultural landscape of megabands and multiplexes, as abstracted and distant from local, participatory culture as the strip mall is from the mom-and-pop store, and as Starbucks, with its seasonal CD mixes, is from the local coffeehouse with its open-mike night. Against the background of the entertainment-industrial complex comprising the lumbering conglomerates that monopolize the mass media, the promise of interactivity is to bring active, participatory forms of cultural creativity back to the people—if they want it.

The promise of interactivity is that viewers can be cultural producers as well as consumers—that, furthermore, their participatory consumption can be creative and fulfilling. Thanks to the Internet and a host of increasingly cheap and easy-to-use do-it-yourself computer programs, access to publishing, recording, and even netcasting, is becoming increasingly widespread. If the commercial mobilization of the promise of interactivity is that consumption can be creative, its cultural corollary is that creativity is being made more accessible to a new generation of "prosumers"—or, in the parlance of media studies, "active" audiences.

The notion of the (inter-)"active" viewer, reader, and listener is central to many digital works and has been used to underwrite the claim that computer art radically "democratizes" the aesthetic experience. In his discussion of digital culture, Richard Lanham argues, for example, that the interactive character of the digital aesthetic counters the oppressive, antidemocratic nature of the artistic canon: "The traditional idea of an artistic canon brings with it, by the very 'immortality' it strives for, both a passive beholder and a passive reality waiting out there to be perceived."[18] Digital art, by contrast, promotes viewing as an active, transformative process, according to Lanham: "All of this yields a body of work active not passive, a canon not frozen in perfection, but volatile with contending human motive. Is this not the aesthetic of the personal computer?"[19]

Artists have experimented with interactivity as a form of collaboration, inviting readers to double as creators in, for example, the writing of an interactive poem, the creation of a collection of personal stories, and even the composition of a coffee table book devoted to anonymously submitted personal secrets. Margot Lovejoy's "Turns," an online work displayed at the Whitney Museum of American Art, is composed of the contributions of viewers who write essays about important moments in their lives. These essays can, in turn, be sifted through and sorted by viewers, who are invited to add to the project. An online work called "The World's First Collaborative Sentence" invited viewers to add their own thoughts, images, and links to a work that has become the world's longest run-on sentence. Within its first two years of operation, the site had logged more than 200,000 posts, in part, according to its Web page, because "it gives the world a space in which to speak its collective and its individual mind."[20]

An ongoing art Weblog called PostSecret features regularly updated images of homemade postcards devoted to previously undisclosed secrets sent in by anonymous members of the public. Contributions range from the humorous and quirky ("When I'm mad at my husband, I put boogers in his soup") to the poignant ("I call my ex at work when I know that she's not there, so I can listen to her voicemail greeting") and tragic ("I'm pretty sure that my confession to my dad that I had been abusing his prescription drugs had something to do with his suicide three days later").[21] The homemade cards are often imaginative and cleverly designed. Clearly the contributors put work into preparing them, conscious of their contribution to a collaborative and creative project. Suggestively, their willingness to contribute intimate details of their lives under the cover of anonymity evokes the information-gathering strategy of online marketers who collect detailed personal information by invoking both the promise of self-expression and the cover of anonymity: "we're gathering detailed information about you, but we won't link it to you" is the standard disclaimer (disingenuous not least because this decision could be revised later). The creator of PostSecret, Frank Warren, is the only one publicly identified with the project (he also admits to having sent in some of his own secrets), and he plans to publish a book of the secrets that have, for all practical purposes, become his property. Just to make sure, his site includes the following disclaimer: "By submitting information to PostSecret, you grant PostSecret a perpetual, royalty-free license to use, reproduce, modify, publish, distribute, and otherwise exercise all copyright and publicity rights with respect to that information at its sole discretion, including . . . incorporating it in other works in any media now known or later developed including without limitation published books." As of this writing, Warren says he has collected more than two thousand postcards and continues to receive new ones that he uses to update his Weblog at regular intervals.

The promise of participation, in short, has proven itself to be a particularly productive one—a fact that, despite some institutional inertia, has not been lost on marketers. Consider the creation of music mash-ups—homemade remixes that literalize and exploit the promise of an active audience. Thanks in large part to digitization, music fans are no longer limited to being passive audiences that merely listen to the music created by their favorite artists. Instead, they can make their own remixes—and even create original compositions by mashing, or combining, tracks from several artists. The resulting mash-ups have been at the center of the ongoing struggle over intellectual property rights exacerbated by digital file sharing: do such works represent "fair use" sampling, do they constitute new and original works, or are they purely derivative, requiring permission from and payments to the original artists? At the center of the debate in 2005 was a work called "The Grey Album" by DJ Dangermouse, who remixed Jay-Z's black album with a collage of samples taken from the Beatles' White Album. When EMI, which owns the rights to the Beatles tracks, issued a cease-and-desist order, the reaction was an online protest called "Grey Day" during which scores of Web sites changed their background color to gray; many of them offered free downloads of the album. The result, predictably, was a barrage of cease-and-desist orders and lots of free publicity for the album. The incident helped rally support for a challenge to the existing regime of copyright protection, which critics claimed to be anachronistic in the digital era because it discouraged cultural creativity. The ability of audiences to participate in the production of the culture they consume came to be portrayed, in keeping with the marketing of interactivity, as subversive, progressive, even, as the London *Guardian* put it, part of a "media revolution."[22]

As communication scholar James Beniger notes, the word *revolution*, which is borrowed from astronomy, originally meant the restoration of a previous form of government, and it's not yet clear which type of revolution is heralded by interactive media: a subversive challenge to centralized control, or the reestablishment of the media monopoly in a more participatory guise. Consider another example from the world of mash-ups: shortly after the Grey Day protests, the automobile manufacturer Audi partnered with David Bowie to promote the Audi TT Coupe with a "make your own mash-up" contest. Members of the public were invited to download samples from Bowie's latest album along with editing software to create and submit soundtracks for use in Audi's "progressions" advertising campaign. In keeping with the "embrace the new" theme of the commercials, which included a voice-over saying, "Where would we be if we always did things the way they were done before," Audi and Bowie inverted the standard industry approach to mash-ups: if people are going to download the music and create something new anyway, why not put them to work? Thanks to digital technology, members of the public could help market Audi (and Bowie) to themselves.

Working on a soundtrack mash-up meant not only familiarizing themselves with the Audi campaign, but also spending lots of time with the tracks from Bowie's *Reality* album. It would be hard to find a better example of what the business world calls "relationship" marketing. For their efforts, participants were offered the chance of winning a car or a second prize of audio mixing software—relatively cheap wages for the soundtrack of an entire ad campaign. Just to have a chance at the prizes, participants had to hand over any and all rights to their work. As the contest literature put it in no uncertain terms, contestants had to relinquish "all present and future right, title and interest of every kind and nature whatsoever, including, without limitation, all copyrights, all music and music publishing rights, and all rights incidental, subsidiary, ancillary or allied thereto (including, without limitation, all derivative rights) in and to the Mash-Up(s) for exploitation throughout the universe, in perpetuity, by means of any and all media and devices whether now known or hereafter devised."[23]

The fact that interactivity fosters audience creativity and productivity raises the question as to who will benefit from and control the labor of an increasingly (inter-)active audience. It is by no means a given that interactivity is automatically empowering. As the Audi example suggests, it may serve rather as a means of exploiting audience labor. The fact that mass society has been so roundly and routinely critiqued for not being participatory enough has resulted in a knee-jerk valorization of participation itself. The offer of participation has become its own reward, which helps explain, at least in part, why people might be willing to pay more for customized products, why they might be willing to pay to share in some of the "duties" of production, and perhaps even why they might be willing to go on reality TV shows that chronicle the details of their daily lives in exchange for payment that often amounts to less than minimum wage.

As I was writing this chapter, a reporter called me about a story he was doing on an upcoming reality show about a local high school football team in suburban Pittsburgh. ESPN had recruited the school by offering to pay for locker room renovations, weight room equipment, and a few other amenities. In exchange, the high school planned to open its doors to the camera crews to film the lives of its students and turn them into prime-time entertainment. Viewed from one perspective, the show, *Bound for Glory—The Montour Spartans,* might have seemed like a nice way to build community spirit (overlooking the fact that it continued the time-revered, all-American, bone-headed tradition of reducing the educational aspect of school to sideshow status for the football team). Viewed from a slightly different perspective, the decision looks disconcertingly like support for the exploitation of child labor. Apparently the students' parents and the school board were so hungry for attention and a new scoreboard that they were willing to sell ESPN access to their children for a pittance—a fraction of the cost of a prime-time TV cast. The show was not a documentary in the nonprofit, educational sense of the word; *Bound for Glory* was prime-time entertainment programming for ESPN, which means that its bottom line function was to use the images of Montour high school kids—of their triumphs and defeats, their conflicts, their personal dramas—to hawk soft drinks and cars.

It is perhaps testimony to the promise of participation—of inclusion in the formerly top-down medium of television—that our schools and parents are willing to sell their children so cheaply to the adjuncts of the advertising industry. The entire genre of reality TV might be considered a means of exploiting the promise of the interactive "revolution": that audiences can participate either directly or indirectly in shaping and creating the media they consume. In keeping with the commercial version of interactivity, much of this participation comes in the form of self-disclosure: participants' willing submission to monitoring, whether by the cameras in the *Big Brother* house or the voting hotlines and Web sites that gather information about viewer preferences.

iMonitoring

One of the more successful viral e-mail messages in recent years featured an advertisement for a product called Forget-Me-Not Panties: undergarments that allowed the wearer's location and biometric information to be monitored remotely. The ad was targeted to men with concerns about the love lives of "their" women and featured the tongue-in-cheek tagline, "Protect Her Privates." The Web site for the Forget-Me-Not Panties included testimonials from a satisfied father who bought his postpubescent daughter several pairs: "They work wonderfully . . . we can watch her around the clock, and if we see her temperature rising too high, we intervene by calling her cellphone or just picking her up wherever she is."[24] The fact that many people who circulated the link to the Forget-Me-Not Panties site (and at least one press account) failed to realize the ad was a hoax served as testimony not so much to online gullibility as to the way in which the prank tapped into real developments in the do-it-yourself use of monitoring technology. The general trend invoked by the panties prank is that of the technologically facilitated practice of mutual monitoring: the enhanced ability of people to track, monitor, and background-check one another via the Internet, cell phones, and other networked communication technologies.

At the most trivial level, consider the changes in telephony that have become commonplace in the cell phone world. When I was growing up, the phone was an inscrutable and insistent household object: when it rang, there was an element of mystery and suspense regarding who might be on the other end—suspense that could verge on the disagreeable if you happened to be avoiding someone's call (while trying to stay in touch with everyone else). If you missed the call, you might be left wondering who had been trying to call—what opportunities, invitations, or emergencies you had missed. In the cell phone world, this layer of uncertainty is all but eliminated. It is becoming impossible to call without leaving a trace, and screening calls has become commonplace. The once-familiar movie scene of failed communication in which someone calling to express a last-minute change of heart hangs up upon hearing a voice on the other end, leaving only a message of uncertainty, has become an anachronism. Now every call, even a hang-up, leaves an identifiable trace. The missed encounter has been replaced by constant contact.

In the cell phone era, instead of bemoaning the fact that the mute receiver can't talk, we have found ways of getting it to divulge its secrets: to tell us who tried to call and when, and to call him or her back with the push of a button. If, in the old days, the police had to go to the phone company to track call records, we now carry this information in compact devices in our purses and pockets. And increasingly, we find ourselves becoming habituated not just to the fact that we trail clouds of data as we go, but also to the fact that we can trace the trails of others. As the research presented in Chapter 6 suggests, it has become increasingly commonplace for people to conduct simple online background checks about one another, whether to check up on friends, learn about a new colleague, or profile a prospective date. Privacy scholar Jeffrey Rosen recounts the story of a friend who "after being set up on a blind date, ran an Internet search and discovered that her prospective partner had been described in an article for an on-line magazine as one of the ten worst dates of all time; the article included intimate details about his sexual equipment and performance that she was unable to banish from her mind during their first—and only—date."[25]

Activities that once would have bordered on stalking have become routine—a fact with implications not just for the ways in which we represent ourselves to one another, but also for shifting expectations regarding privacy and surveillance. Consider the admittedly trivial example of a former student who joined a popular campus Web site called Facebook, which allows students to post short profiles online and to link to friends—and friends of friends. Shortly after joining, at the invitation of one of her friends, she discovered that her boyfriend, unbeknownst to her, had his own Facebook page, on which he had listed his relationship status as single—a not insignificant fact considering that the site is devoted, at least in part, to online flirtation and dating.

The fact that "Google" has become a verb as well as a proper noun suggests the extent to which we are increasingly availing ourselves of the ability to translate interactivity into peer-to-peer monitoring. Now that, as the new media truism puts it, the Internet "allows everyone to become a producer of media content," we find ourselves generating information about ourselves that is increasingly available to our friends, acquaintances, and omnivorously curious Web surfers. [26] The poet Katha Pollitt recounted in the *New Yorker* magazine how she "stalked" her former lover online, putting together the pieces of past infidelities using only the tidbits of information gleaned from Google, HotBot, and AltaVista: "There on my screen glowed the programs of academic gatherings he had attended going back for a decade: the same female names appeared over and over entwined with his in panel announcements. Why hadn't it struck me as odd that his 'best friend,' a professor of English literature, was the respondent for papers he gave at conferences on art history and philosophy? . . . I had been so out of it!"[27] Shortly after the article appeared, readers went to the Internet to determine the identity of the faithless lover. Although Pollitt hadn't identified him by name, she had left enough clues scattered throughout to allow amateur Web sleuths to figure out his identity.

Sherry Turkle has observed that the computer helps bring postmodern theory "down to earth" by highlighting the role of performance in our everyday presentation of self. [28] Thanks to online chat rooms and role-playing games, computer users can experiment with different personas, perhaps acting out sides of their personality they aren't able to explore in day-to-day interactions with friends, family, and coworkers:

In the daily practice of many computer users, windows [on the computer desktop] have become a powerful metaphor for thinking about the self as a multiple, distributed system. The self is no longer playing different roles in different settings at different times. . . . The life practice of windows is that of a decentered self that exists in many worlds and plays many roles at the same time. . . . When people can play at having different genders and different lives, it isn't surprising that for some this play has become as real as what we conventionally think of as their lives. [29]

The flip side of this ability to get in touch with all sides of ourselves is a savvy recognition of the staging of the self—one that might help explain the use of interactive technologies for mutual monitoring. Consider, for example, the deployment of keystroke monitoring software (developed for businesses to keep track of what employees are doing on their computers) by parents to find out what their children are doing online, or by husbands and wives to discover how their significant others are whiling away their time in chat rooms: are they engaging in innocent discussions of shared interest, flirting online—or something more?

If the computer has made it possible for us to multiply our personal connections, to participate in what Howard Rheingold helped popularize as "online community," it has also highlighted the fact that many of the people with whom we interact remain strangers in very real ways. People who meet one another on Web-based dating sites, for example, may, thanks to the cover of online anonymity, misrepresent information about themselves—whether they are married, their age, their profession. One result is that the success of such sites has been accompanied by the proliferation of online background checking services that offer independent verification of such things as marital status and criminal history. CheckMyMate.com, for example warns online daters that they "will surely come across the same assortment of mischiefs [sic], criminals, and sexual deviants found in the real world."[30] The remedy can be found in its databases: "CheckMyMate.com was specifically designed to protect the dating community from sexual predators and devious individuals. With just a first and a last name, CheckMyMate.com can investigate almost anyone."[31]

Sites like CheckMyMate.com have an interest in playing up the risky side of online social interaction, but, as I discuss in Chapter 6, there are plenty of free online sites that allow curious Web surfers to collect information about friends, family members, and one another. In addition to googling one another, for example, many of the students I surveyed when conducting research for Chapter 6 reported visiting the state court system's online record site to see what information they could glean about people they knew. The spirit was one more of curious exploration than focused investigation, and yet there is an undertone of suspicion: a recognition that people don't always divulge telling details about themselves—that there is always more to find, and that, thanks to the powerful information-gathering tools increasingly available at home, work, and school, we have a variety of new ways to unearth additional information about them.

There is a progression apparent here, from a celebratory sense of the potential of new media (as a means of expanding social networks and experimenting with personal identity) to a savvy wariness toward forms of deception they facilitate, and finally to a sense of personal risk, exploited by commercial monitoring sites. As one of several testimonials for a background-check Web site puts it, "Thanks Net Detective. You saved my life. If I hadn't found out about my girlfriend's credit problems, I might have made the biggest mistake of my life."[32] The mobilization of risk will be a recurring theme in the following chapters, in large part because of the deployment of new media technologies as a strategy for offloading a variety of duties—social, economic, and political—onto the populace in the postwelfare era. The deployment of the specter of risk, as I will argue in more detail in Chapter 3, can operate as a management strategy for channeling the forms of "empowerment" enabled by new technologies according to priorities set by marketers, media corporations, and, in some cases, government authorities.

Thanks in part to the technological developments associated with the information society, citizens provided with the tools for accessing information are increasingly assigned the responsibility for tasks hitherto relegated to the state. It is no accident that the ideology of the information age described by Thomas Streeter and Paulina Barsook is one of anarchic market-based libertarianism.[33] If the technology is portrayed as empowering and democratizing (a portrayal subjected to critical scrutiny in subsequent chapters), then the need for welfare state measures that address social inequality or social welfare is largely obviated: the people have the tools they need—so much so that the outcome can be portrayed as entirely their responsibility, factually and (therefore) ethically. The government cannot assist you at this micromanagerial level, but the technology can: it can help you screen potential employees, lovers, nannies, colleagues—for a price. If the big-box wholesaler Sam's Club retails background-check software previously available only to private investigators, what excuse do members of the public have for *not* managing their own security?

Democratization of access to the means of monitoring coincides—in both the marketing industry and the prevailing political climate—with portrayals of ubiquitous and generalized risk. In a networked society, we find social and professional networks expanding even as we concede the contrived aspect of self-presentation. In other words, we're interacting with more people than even before, thanks to electronically mediated forms of communication, and we're more aware that they may not be who they say they are. Taken alongside a portrayal of the multiplying risks associated with the information society (for example, identity theft, Internet scams, sexual predators), this combination provides a potent recipe for a culture of detection and mutual monitoring. It shouldn't be particularly surprising that detection has become one of the watchwords of popular culture—not merely in the proliferating variants of shows like *CSI*, but also in the formats that offer to take us behind the scenes of the making of the video or movie, of the lifestyles of the latest pop culture heroes, or of the public image of a famous band or celebrity. The obverse of a culture of savvy debunkery—one that takes the performance of subjectivity as a given—is a culture of perpetual detection: a series of ongoing attempts to see behind the public performance, or at the very least to prove that one isn't taken in by it. We are nobody's fools, a society ostensibly immune to deceptive appearances, but captivated by the prospect of perpetually showcasing our own canny immunity from the fate of the duped.

A second monitoring trend that the Forget-Me-Not Panties hoax taps into is that of biometrics as a detection strategy: a means of isolating some empirical remainder—a trace of physical evidence that can't be staged. Early on, reality TV shows, in an effort to provide access to a *real* reality—one not simply staged for the cameras by the aspiring actors who populated the genre—incorporated scenes of biometric monitoring: lie detectors, skin galvanometers, and heart rate monitors (used on shows like *The Chair* and *The Chamber*). Similarly, police and marketers are both exploring the uses of biometrics as technologies for targeting criminals and consumers. The day when airport screeners will be able to keep track of who is showing signs of extreme nervousness as they attempt to check in (increased heart rate, sweating, and so on) and when advertisers will keep track of viewers' physiological responses to ad campaigns are not far off. Both systems are already being tested. Moreover, the notion that we will increasingly wear our technology on our bodies—integrated into our clothes—is one that both fashion designers and computer chip developers take as a given. As our interactive gadgets move closer to our skin, they are increasingly able to gather and record biometric information passively. Devices in development include clothing that monitors the vital signs of people with health concerns and even so-called smart underwear that adjusts indoor climate settings on the basis of changes in the wearer's body temperature.

The type of location-based monitoring envisioned by the Forget-Me-Not Panties scam is already anticipated by portable GPS tracking devices in use for patients with Alzheimer's disease and by radiofrequency ID chips implanted in pets and, more recently, in Mexico's attorney general (as a kidnapping precaution). Cell phones are already equipped with GPS devices that enable users to allow selected individuals, such as parents or significant others, to track the location of their users. A service called Teen Arrive Alive uses cell phone networks to generate an archive of information about the daily movements of teenage children so their parents can not only find out where they are at any given moment (as long as they have their cell phone with them), but also where they were—and even how fast they were driving.[34] Parents can also install a device called a *carchip* in their children's cars to record the details of their driving habits. Similar devices are used by long-haul trucking companies to monitor their drivers.

The constellation of real practices and technologies invoked by the Forget-Me-Not Panties advertisements cluster around the use of interactivity for risk management via peer-to-peer surveillance. That is to say, individuals are being invited to use the interactive technology in the same way that state and commercial entities do: as a strategy for asymmetrical, nontransparent data gathering. Consumers and citizens are invited to adopt a similar set of imperatives to those of the authorities: reducing uncertainty, increasing efficiency, and maintaining control at a distance. Thanks to the deployment of interactive monitoring devices in cell phones and cars, the power of law enforcement is extended and amplified through the actions of parents and other monitoring individuals. Whereas parents who lent or bought their children cars once had to rely on the police to enforce the laws—finding out only after the fact whether their children had been speeding or driving recklessly—interactive devices allow parents to watch more closely than the police ever could. To the extent that parents enforce adherence to the law, the technologies extend and multiply the power of policing by channeling it through the family network (a development whose political implications are explored in more detail in the following section). The flip side of interactivity as interconnectivity is that of interactivity as distributed monitoring: the democratization of the model of perpetual, perfectible surveillance embraced by government intelligence agencies and marketing services: an always-on strategy for keeping track of one another.

It is possible, of course, to argue that mutual monitoring has always been an important ingredient of community, and its online version merely confirms the notion that the Internet is rehabilitating the lost connectivity of more traditional societies. With community and connectivity come mutual monitoring. There is, however, an important difference—one highlighted by several of the examples described in this section. Whereas peer-to-peer monitoring in traditional communities is symmetrical and relatively transparent, the same cannot be said, in many cases, of networked, distributed monitoring. Background-check software, googling, and even sites like Facebook can be used without the knowledge of those about whom information is being gathered. Such monitoring can be one way and nontransparent. In the case of information about ourselves that we deliberately put online, the comparison might be made to public activities performed before a crowd: we may not know exactly who is watching, but we have no expectation of privacy.

The Internet audience isn't quite the same as a crowd. It is anonymous, but it is also largely invisible—facts that may well affect our perception of anonymity and our willingness to disclose information about ourselves that we might not be willing to divulge before a crowd. Moreover, information that is disclosed in one context online can easily migrate into other contexts—and to different audiences, because the audience itself is not localized either spatially or temporally. Consider the example, featured in a *Boston Globe* story about Google, of a man who wrote articles for an offline journal about his experience in prison (for burglary), not realizing that when those articles went online, they would pop up when his name was googled by prospective employers, dates, and so on.[35]

In traditional communities, information gathered via peer networks has a tendency to degrade over time and relies on interaction with others for both its collection and its retrieval. Someone must be asked, which means the person gathering information must be willing to make the search itself known. Online, searching can be done relatively anonymously—or through third-party intermediaries, whose monitoring activities remain nontransparent. Google, for example, has reportedly recorded every search request ever entered into its search engine (along with the address of the computer from which the query originated), but this remains proprietary information, accessible to neither the searcher nor the target of the search. At the same time, individuals are able to create their own databases—to gather and store information about one another for personal use, as in the case of the father who can access information about his son's whereabouts thanks to a GPS device in the car, or online daters who create spreadsheets and databases to keep track of their various contacts.[36]

The world of James Bond–style surveillance gimmickry for everyday use envisioned by the creators of the Forget-Me-Not Panties hoax is not as futuristic as it might seem. Those who imagine that the public at large will balk at such intrusive technologies would do well to consider just how readily we've accustomed ourselves to forms of information gathering that would have seemed like stalking only a decade or so ago. If the invitation proffered by such technology is to avail ourselves of the monitoring capacity of new high-tech devices for do-it-yourself monitoring, it is simultaneously an invitation to lower our threshold of concern regarding commercial and state surveillance.

After all, we will no longer be merely passive objects of surveillance in the interactive era. We will also be active participants in the process—ostensibly for our own good. To what extent does importing the model of interactivity as surveillance into the realm of interpersonal interaction help domesticate and normalize the model of "interactivity" as one-way, nontransparent information gathering—a far cry from "interactivity" as a form of democratizing empowerment?

iPolitics

Shortly after the September 11 attacks, Internet entrepreneur Jay Walker (the founder of the successful travel Web site Priceline.com) proposed an interactive system for protecting U.S. borders and other "soft targets" from attack. The system, called USHomeGuard, would enlist members of the public to monitor Web cameras equipped with heat sensors and microphones focused on vulnerable, unguarded facilities such as power plants and public reservoirs. If the cameras detected movement or a heat signature that indicated the presence of unauthorized individuals, they would trigger images to be sent by the Internet to human monitors, who could verify whether there was any cause for alarm and alert the authorities. Thanks to the networked technology, the human monitors could work inexpensively at home, creating what Walker's Web site describes as "a citizen corps" that would function as "a new kind of National Guard composed of ordinary citizens who serve their country working from home over any Internet connection."[37] USHomeGuard would serve as a kind of interactive reality show that allowed viewers to participate in the defense of the nation by creating a high-tech national neighborhood watch program.

Walker offered to sell the plan, which he reportedly spent $1 million to develop, to the government for $1. So far there has been no definitive public response, although Walker says government officials have told him they are looking into it.[38] The model is a familiar one to any Internet entrepreneur: use the interactive technology to offload labor onto the populace. In the case of USHomeGuard, Walker proposes paying spotters slightly more than minimum wage—about $10 an hour—for agreeing to monitor their computers for a fixed amount of time.[39] It's not hard to imagine supplementing paid monitors with a corps of volunteers—perhaps from among the ranks of the homebound, the retired, or even office workers with a USHomeGuard alert window on their desktop computers.

Already Web sites like Earthcam.com allow Web surfers access to Webcams around the world, documenting everything from sunsets in Mallorca to pedestrians in New York's Times Square. As in the case of the online background-check sites described in the previous section, USHomeGuard promises to take a seemingly undirected monitoring capacity—the ability to go online and visit various Webcam sites around the nation and the world—and refocus it through the lens of risk. If surfing Webcams can serve as a kind of aimless entertainment or online tourism, the practice can also be endowed with a renewed sense of purpose by being channeled toward the goal of protecting the homeland. Uncoordinated voyeurism can be redirected and reconfigured as a patriotic contribution to nation—and as a means of assisting the police and military.

As of this writing, USHomeGuard remains on the drawing board, but the logic of offloading some of the duties of national defense onto the populace has emerged as a guiding theme of the Department of Homeland Security's readiness campaign and related statewide campaigns. The state of New Jersey's Department of Homeland Security features a series of advertisements urging vigilance and participation in law enforcement activities. Citizens are advised to keep a watchful eye out for supposedly suspicious activities, including people wearing bulky clothes in hot weather, or unattended bags ("just an unattended bag . . . or a bomb?"), and to report them via cell phone. The always-on communication culture of the information age can serve, in this respect, as an extension and amplification of homeland defense through the mechanism of peer-to-peer monitoring.

This logic was taken even further in Australia shortly after the London terrorist bombing in the summer of 2005, when a former intelligence officer advised the public to turn their cell phone cameras into security tools: "Let's look at that technology being used by the public. . . . If you can take a photograph of the person who's wearing the backpack or carrying the briefcase that's fitted the criteria, the photo could be invaluable should anything occur."[40] If everyone is a potential suspect, surveillance must become ubiquitous and comprehensive, and thus distributed. There is no way for the police to watch everyone; machines or volunteers (or both) will have to help fill in the gaps.

Even if we agree, as seems only reasonable and sane, on the need to protect the populace and the national infrastructure from ambush, we might also find some cause for concern in the attempt to turn every citizen into both spy and suspect. At issue is not just the alleged need to pit all against all in a manner that undermines a sense of the social and threatens to replace community with a variant of hypersuspicious survivalist individualism, but also the more subtle logic of interactive participation, which invites unexamined identification with the priorities of those in power. One of the themes that I attempt to develop over the course of the next several chapters is that the promise of participation falls short of democratization in those contexts where it functions merely as a form of auxiliary guidance toward goals that are not necessarily those of audiences, consumers, and citizens. I describe this kind of interactivity as cybernetic participation, invoking the terms outlined above: citizens provide useful feedback in helping those who maintain control over the surveillance technology and the databases to pursue predetermined ends. Cybernetic participation enlists the labor of those who submit to monitored forms of interaction, but it stops short at the point of allowing shared control over shaping goals and designating desired ends.

Thus, for example, a politician who seeks support for a particular policy objective—say, for example, opposing a national health care system—can rely on public opinion polling to discover how best to market that objective: to manage the populace by means of its stated fears and concerns. Similarly, an advertiser can draw on market research to determine how best to package, promote, and sell a particular product. But the public feedback has little impact on the underlying imperative to sell as much as possible, for as large as profit as possible. These latter goals remain given and inaccessible to interactive feedback; they are the destination toward which marketers steer with assistance from public feedback. This feedback may help alter the course—but not the final destination. That the information received from the public is used to reach this destination is offered up as evidence of a harmony of interest between, for example, marketer and consumer, or politician and constituent. The fact of participation is equated with shared control over both means and ends, even though the latter were never on the table and remained inaccessible to the "participatory" decision-making process.

It is conceivable that the feedback process might induce a politician, for example, to adjust the policy objectives themselves—such is the premise, at least in part, of representative democracy. But asymmetrical monitoring allows for a managerial rather than a democratic relationship to constituents. It diminishes public accountability insofar as it allows for the fine-tuning of public relations as selective self-exposure. That is to say, to the extent that public officials and political candidates have access to more powerful and comprehensive monitoring techniques than does a public that relies for information on media conglomerates beholden to politicians (for their continued growth), information technology may well favor top-down forms of information management that more closely resemble marketing campaigns than democratic deliberation and accountability. Information technology does not benefit all equally. Those who control the means of interactivity (and the data it generates) are under no particular obligation to exercise this control democratically, and the evidence that they have no choice but to do so remains thin at best. Within the context of social, political, and economic inequality, the deployment of new technologies tends to consolidate and exacerbate asymmetry rather than redress it.

In the case of Homeland Security, the invitation to participate in defending the nation against terrorism doubles as an invitation to identify with the administration's policies and with its definition of the problem: terrorism is an inexplicable force of nature, born of irrational hatred and not amenable to shifts in foreign or domestic policy. Because there is no causal explanation for terrorism, according to this ideology, root causes cannot be addressed, and any attempt at understanding can be dismissed as appeasement. The focus thus shifts away from understanding or defining the problem to taking the formulation provided by authorities as a given—a shift that is reinforced by rituals of participatory readiness. If, as the philosopher Louis Althusser suggested, those beliefs we take to emanate from the innermost depths of our unique subjective consciousness can be understood as a function of our repeated daily rituals, participatory preparedness provides a set of practices that help embody a particular understanding of the threat of terror—an understanding that aligns itself with the terms set by the Bush administration.[41] Moreover, the portrayal of "readiness" as a form of interactive participation encourages a sense of identification with those who set the terms of interaction. Our definition of the situation must be the same as theirs since after all, we are active participants: we embarked on this collaborative process together. Interactivity, figured in these terms, invites participants to embrace the very goals that are exempted from deliberation as their own.

Positing a distinction between these goals and the possibility of different ones arrived at through a truly deliberative process—one in which participation applies to both means and ends—amounts to an attempt to secure that vexed space from which the realty of manipulation can be discerned. It entails the notion that there is a difference between a *deliberative* process whereby goals are collectively defined and a *manipulative* process whereby one group is induced to embrace the goals of another as its own, without deliberation, compromise, or revision.

The legal scholar Cass Sunstein offers a similar distinction in his attempt to differentiate between what he describes as consumer sovereignty and political sovereignty. The former takes preferences and priorities as given, and it draws on market research to manipulate them. Political sovereignty, by contrast, doesn't take priorities as given but views the process of decision making as a deliberative one in which individuals learn about one another and also about themselves. Through the process of deliberation, their understandings of the world evolve and come to embrace a sphere of interest broader than the narrowly defined tastes and preferences associated with the atomistic individualism of consumer sovereignty.

In contrast to consumer sovereignty, political sovereignty requires deliberation over policy preferences and the ability to publicly explain and defend particular choices—to give an account for political decisions (and it relies, therefore, on a process of political accountability on the part of elected representatives). Consumer preferences are commonly understood to be questions of taste—neither amenable to, nor in need of, public justification. Such is a core component of the popular understanding of private freedom: no one can tell me what type of food I ought to like or what kind of clothes I like to wear. I don't need to justify my decisions in these spheres because, presumably, they do not have any significant impact on others: they are purely private, individual decisions. Within the political sphere, however, decisions have impact beyond the purely individual, which means that aggregating personal preferences misses the point: individual decision makers need to take into account the potential impact on others. Therefore, as Sunstein puts it, political sovereignty "does not take individual tastes as fixed or given. It prizes democratic self-government, understood as a requirement of 'government by discussion,' accompanied by reason-giving in the public domain."[42]

The distinction proposed by Sunstein is not as clear-cut as it first appears. We live in a world in which, thanks in part to the expanding role of the market in all spheres of social life, decisions that have social and political impacts extending beyond the purely personal are increasingly portrayed as private consumer decisions (the individual choice of a consumer to drive, for example, a vehicle with low gas mileage and highly polluting emissions). On closer scrutiny, the model of consumer sovereignty falls apart. Marketers may portray themselves as slaves to consumer preferences, but when talking among themselves and their clients, they don't take these preferences as given. Consider, for example, one tagline for the BMG music corporation in an advertising trade publication: "If You Have Them by Their Ears, Their Hearts and Minds Will Follow." Marketers recognize that our ostensibly private tastes and preferences come neither from the inner recesses of a hermetically sealed consciousness nor from some uniquely determined genetic predisposition. They are largely the result of a sensibility shaped by the desires and anxieties, the fears, hopes, and dreams that derive their substance and shape from our interactions with one another—both direct and mediated.

Consumer sovereignty, in framing tastes as individual and given, partakes in a fundamental misrecognition of our relationships to one another: an inversion whereby that which is constructed through relations with others is assumed to emerge from the depths of isolated individual consciousnesses. This misrecognition is, from a commercial perspective, useful insofar as it backgrounds the role of advertising and marketing in shaping, inflecting, and channeling consumer tastes. The fiction that preferences are given underwrites the equation of feedback with participation: the promise that monitoring is a strategy not for control, but for unearthing the predetermined contours of consumer desire.

The model of consumer sovereignty is inadequate to political decision making because it backgrounds both the forces that shape individual preferences and the consequences of individual decisions made on the basis of ostensibly given sets of preferences. Where did I get the idea that driving an SUV is an expression of my independence and rugged individualism? Is this somehow a natural predisposition that reflects a core truth of my being? Did the marketers who portrayed this vehicle as a symbol of freedom and patriotism—of self-fulfillment and adventure—merely unearth a desire that was always already uniquely my own? Was it merely a convenient coincidence (for the automobile corporations) that so many people seem to share my deeply personal and individual desire at the same moment in time? By the same token, why might I believe that the impact my personal choice to purchase a highly polluting vehicle has on the environment is no one's business but my own? These are the types of questions that fall by the wayside when individual tastes are taken to be private and sacrosanct.

The wager of deliberative politics, by contrast, is that because my preferences are to a large degree shaped through my interactions with others, openly discussing their presuppositions and consequences might convince me to alter and adjust them. If the model of consumer sovereignty, understood from the perspective of marketers, is to draw on customer feedback in order to advance an imperative that remains beyond the reach of deliberation (profit maximization at the expense of all other concerns), the model of citizen sovereignty would be to make even that imperative amenable to deliberation and modification. The former remains a model of feedback-facilitated, top-down control, the latter one of power sharing. This distinction starts to suggest why the use of interactive technologies to pursue a consumer driven model of politics ends up compromising rather than advancing progress toward the democratic promise of participation.

Crucial to the consumer model of politics—voting as shopping—is the disaggregation of the public into niche audiences of individuals who can be targeted on the basis of individual preferences so as to ensure that they perceive their choices as individual ones—like choosing what to wear or eat—rather than collective ones. Relegating politics to the realm of private choice reduces both the resources and the impetus for deliberation. One commentator has suggested that a significant reason for voter alienation toward politics is that it doesn't yet live up to the model of consumer customization to which they have grown accustomed: "They have confused the norms and expectations that govern the political arena with those that govern the marketplace. Fundamentally, what they dislike about politics is that it isn't more like shopping. . . . We have become so accustomed to this sort of highly individualized service that some people, particularly the young, are tempted to wonder why their politicians can't be more like their favourite brands."[43]

The model of politics envisioned by those who would reduce it to interactive marketing is one that is becoming increasingly, disturbingly familiar: the use of voter feedback to craft the packaging of particular policies, rather than the choice of policies themselves. The failure of George W. Bush's plan to reform Social Security suggests that we have not yet reached the point at which policy makers can sell virtually any policy they like. Nevertheless, this is the direction in which cybernetics politics is pushing: increasing control over the message rather than enhanced democratic accountability. Such an outcome is not inevitable. Salvaging the democratic promise of interactivity is likely a lost cause if we continue to equate cybernetic control with power sharing. If, as democratic theorist Carole Pateman puts it, "we learn to participate by participating," the type of participation in which we engage is crucially important. [44] The danger of the emerging model of interactivity as cybernetic feedback is that it teaches a form of participation that amounts to actively staging the scene of our own submission: helping marketers—both political and commercial—increase their leverage over us. By contrast, the unrealized promise of interactivity contains a challenge to the forms of asymmetrical, top-down control that its deployment too often facilitates.

This last observation perhaps deserves a bit more explanation. When I have had the opportunity to present arguments critical of the deployment of interactivity as surveillance to academic and general audiences, I am frequently accused of being too negative. American culture is deeply imbued with the utopian optimism of the technological sublime, and we cherish fond hopes—all too frequently disappointed—that new communication technologies will resolve political conflicts, educate the masses, and deliver on the democratic promise. I have no interest in dismantling such hopes. On the contrary, my contention is that they can be realized only when we no longer depend on technology to sidestep political conflicts, when we engage in a political struggle over the deployment of the technology. The technological capacity of interactivity will not, on its own (*pace* Gilder, Pearce, and a litany of others), dismantle social, political, and economic hierarchies. It will not on its own foster a version of democracy based on collective control over the shaping of political goals. Only the deliberately political use of new media technologies can have such results—and only a political struggle for control over the means of interactivity and the databases can enable such usage.

The distance between commercial and activist forms of interactive participation was driven home to me by a relatively trivial but perhaps representative anecdote about Facebook. In fall 2006, a Facebook member who called himself Brody Ruckus issued a challenge to the online community, which was, at the time, mostly composed of college students: if 100,000 people joined an online group he had formed on his Facebook site, his girlfriend would consent to fulfilling his sexual fantasy of participating in a threesome with him and another woman. Within a week, Ruckus's group reportedly topped 100,000. The incident received a barrage of media publicity, and it was eventually revealed that the incident was a hoax designed as a promotional tool for the Ruckus Network, an online music service targeting college students. Shortly after hearing about the incident, I decided to see whether Facebook could be used to attract users to a group with a noncommercial, nonerotic purpose: political protest.

The decision was shaped by the conjunction of several incidents: the publicity received by Brody Ruckus, my recent encounter with an online essay by media scholar Henry Jenkins, and proposed legislation, supported by the president, that would legalize torture, detention without trial, and the warrantless wiretapping of American citizens. Jenkins, writing about online fan sites devoted to popular TV shows, suggested that audience interaction has a tendency to morph into political activism: "the response to reality TV teaches modes of engaging critically with television that may slide into activism around the Iraq war."[45] If that's the case, why not see whether the Facebook could be used to start a group opposed to the Republican administration's attempt to dispense with the writ of habeas corpus and to legalize its policies of torture and secret detention. So I formed a Facebook group announcing a public protest against the proposed legislation, outlined the reasons for doing so, and sent invitations to six of my Facebook contacts, all of whom had dozens of their own online contacts. A week later, the same amount of time it had taken Brody Ruckus to collect 100,000 members, my own group still had six. I'm not saying it's not possible to use social networking sites for political purposes; political consultant Joe Trippi did so quite effectively, at least for a while, for the ill-fated Howard Dean campaign in 2004.[46] But the move from marketing to social activism is neither simple nor automatic. Rather, it comes about through engaged social struggle rather than sanguine reliance on the character of the technology.

I find myself writing about interactive information and communication technologies during an historical period characterized by dramatic increases in economic inequality compounded by the concentration of political power in an increasingly intrusive and secretive White House. I would feel much more comfortable about the celebratory predictions of public empowerment via new media if these predictions took place in a very different historical context—one in which the galloping concentration of economic, political, and informational capital in the hands of the few was being slowed and reversed. I don't want to dismiss the potential of new media technologies, nor do I wish to downplay some of the very real ways in which they are being enlisted to both disclose and oppose the tendency toward the increasing concentration of power in the network society. Media theorists have made much of the use of the Internet by political groups, including the Zapatistas in Mexico and the antiglobalization movement in the United States and abroad, to challenge entrenched forms of political power.[47] Political bloggers have done a good job of circulating information overlooked by the mainstream commercial media and of holding media organizations themselves accountable for misleading and incomplete coverage.[48] Perhaps one of the reasons behind the generalized skepticism toward politics and politicians is the heightened level of scrutiny to which the political process has been subjected. Thanks to the Internet, it is easier than at any time in this nation's history for citizens to inform themselves about issues of public importance and to publish their own views and arguments. Their ability to reach a broad audience is another matter.

At the same time, much of this democratic potential remains just that—potential. The fact that citizens can inform or express themselves doesn't mean that they will, and the reasons why they don't are not reducible solely to individual preference. They have to do with the perceived impact of participation and with a shared sense of what political participation might mean. This book argues that the deployment of the promise of interactivity in commercial and political contexts underwrites participation in top-down forms of management and control rather than in democratic self-governance. Such an argument, to the extent that it depends on and elucidates concrete uses of new media technologies rather than their abstract potential, might help explain why the rise of the network society has paralleled the rise of social inequality and the concentration of economic and political power in the United States. The economist Paul Krugman has documented the end of a period of relatively increasing economic equality in the postwar era, noting the return to what he has described as a new Gilded Age: "Since the 1970's . . . income gaps have been rapidly widening . . . by most measures we are, in fact, back to the days of *The Great Gatsby*. After 30 years in which the income shares of the top 10 percent of taxpayers, the top 1 percent and so on were far below their levels in the 1920's, all are very nearly back where they were."[49] Suggestively, it was the Gilded Age that pioneered the forms of information-based management that come into their own in the network era. It is to this early history of the information revolution to which we now turn.

iManagement, the Early Years

The American phenomenon . . . is also the biggest collective effort to date to create, with unprecedented speed, and with a consciousness of purpose unmatched in human history, a new type of worker and a new type of man.

—Antonio Gramsci

Understood in its broadest sense, interactivity in one form or another has always been with us. Understood specifically as a type of cybernetic information gathering—a feedback control mechanism—it can be traced at least as far back as the rise of so-called scientific management in the late nineteenth century. The father—at least in spirit—of those complex algorithms that keep track of everything we watch on TiVo in order to suggest other shows we might also like—is Frederick Taylor, the scientific management pioneer, a man famous for standing over workers with a stopwatch and timing their every move. In a way, when we're buying books on Amazon.com, surfing the Web, or connecting to commercial wireless networks, Frederick Taylor's is the spirit of surveillance in the machine, watching over us, keeping track of our every move, noting it down, and finding ways to use that information to encourage us to consume as much as possible. If, as marketing pioneer Percival White wrote in 1927, the marketing process can be thought of as an extended factory for "the creation of demand, the merchandising of goods, [and] the delivery of articles purchased," this "social factory" might be made more efficient through the application of monitoring and management techniques that reached beyond the walls of the workplace and into spaces of consumption, recreation, and domesticity.[1] White was one of several marketing pioneers who explicitly invoked the spirit of Taylorism, even going so far as to write a primer on the principles of "scientific marketing management."[2] Much of what passes for interactivity in the digital economy might better be understood as techniques for facilitating the scientific management of consumption, understood as a reliance on detailed forms of continuous data collection to help allocate resources more effectively not just in the realm of production, but also in those of marketing and advertising. As Frank Webster and Kevin Robins put it in their study of the history of information technology, "The contemporary ideologies of the information society have their tap-roots in that philosophy of productivism and progress propounded by Frederick Winslow Taylor and the ideologues of Scientific Management. Everything begins with Taylor."[3]

Well, perhaps not everything. Taylor himself began with a mania for the application of science and engineering to the efficient management of human labor—a mania of the times, insofar as it fit neatly with the emergence of a distinctly American approach to the scientific study of human society in the late nineteenth century. If European sociology, born in the wake of revolutionary political transformation, took the overarching social order as its object of study, American sociology, born in the wake of the Industrial Revolution, fostered a tendency to focus on the problems of adjustment to the existing social order, according to historian Leon Bramson. He describes the former (European) version as a sociology of change and the latter as a sociology of conservation—one concerned with structural conflict, the other with "assimilating vast numbers of 'deviants'" to the norms of American society.[4] Social science similarly came to relegate questions about social justice and social structure to the deep background, directing its attention toward the engineering of improvements to the social order of industrial capitalism. Frederick Taylor merely adopted this approach at the microlevel of the firm, exploring ways in which techniques of observation, measurement, and experiment adapted from the natural sciences might be used to understand—and then manage—the workplace environment. In this regard, Taylor might be understood not as the grand initiator of scientific monitoring, but as an innovative adaptor: someone who transposed the methodology of empirical science and narrowed its scope to fit the imperatives of industrial mass production.

To say that information-based efficiency management started with Taylor is to suggest that the version of interactivity as monitoring with which this book is concerned can trace its genealogy through a progression that runs from the rise of social science to the development of scientific management and eventually to the "science" of marketing, from its inception to its most recent database-driven applications. This is not to say that every element of the so-called interactive revolution can be reduced to strategies for the surveillance-based rationalization of consumption. Even applications specifically designed for marketing purposes, such as experiments in consumer-generated media (which invite viewers to make their own versions of commercials and to share them with one another), can be turned to other ends, including criticism of the product or the sponsor, or even of the very marketing strategies being used. However, the goal of this book is not to recapitulate the predictions made about the empowering promise or potential of mediated interactivity, nor is it to explore the cases repeatedly adduced as evidence of this potential (how much more can be written about the Zapatista's use of the Internet?), but to zoom in on the deployment of the promise of interactivity that harkens back to techniques for the management of production and consumption in the early twentieth century. Put in slightly different terms, the goal is to explore the development of monitoring-based forms of management as they migrate, over the course of the late nineteenth and early twentieth centuries, from the realm of production to that of consumption; from information gathering in the workplace to data gathering in drug stores, supermarkets, and online; and, finally, from the surveillance-based management of the workplace to the contemporary commercial monitoring of so many aspects of daily life—a form of monitoring facilitated by the deployment of interactive media technology.

There is, in other words, a family resemblance between Taylor's passion for collecting detailed information about workers in order to customize and manage their working day and schemes such as Yahoo's customized advertising system, which "uses complex models to analyze records of what each of its 500 million users do on its site: what they search for, what pages they read, what ads they click on" in order to provide them with "advertisements that speak directly to their interests and the events in their lives."[5]

Tracing the relationship between surveillance-based management and interactive marketing is one way to highlight what might be described as a dialectical connection between production and consumption—a connection noted by members of the Taylor society in the early 1920s when they announced the formation of a sales section of their group with the rhetorical question, "Was there any real difference . . . between producing goods and producing orders?"—or consumers, for that matter.[6] Their interest in the connection between scientific management and marketing was reciprocated by marketing pioneers, educators, and administrators in the newly formed graduate schools in business, which emerged at the turn of the century and rapidly specialized in the Taylor-inspired science of managing production and distribution. Subsequent sections will consider this connection in more detail.

Far from representing a radically new economic model, the total information awareness economy promises to realize the dream of information-based management conceived at the dawn of industrialized mass production. The advent of interactive technology represents not the end of mass consumer society but its customized culmination: the prospect of its perfection in the form of markets that extract from each worker *and* every consumer the maximum productivity and profit. Whereas Taylor relied on the collection of detailed information about workers to customize workplace tasks and payment schemes, marketers rely on detailed forms of surveillance in order to customize advertising appeals, products, and pricing schemes that extract the maximum value from consumers. Taylor's influence, as we shall see, was ubiquitous in the formation of the marketing industry and the rise of the managerial side of business education and training. However, the drive toward customization, differentiation, and specialization characteristic of his system remained limited by the costs of information gathering and of the technological infrastructure for customization.

These limits, however, melted away in the face of networked, interactive communication devices and programmable manufacturing equipment. The interactive era made the comprehensive forms of data collection envisioned by Taylor both feasible and relatively inexpensive. Thanks to the development of interactive workplace and leisure technologies, as well as to the plummeting cost of data storage and manipulation, forms of monitoring that once required a costly battery of managers have become automated, programmable, and increasingly comprehensive. Far from countering the forms of managerial control associated with industrial mass society, these changes allow for its increased penetration into the fabric of daily life. Along with it come the attributes of scientific management developed a century earlier: disaggregation, individuation, the formation of increasingly detailed databases, and a focus on individual acts of production and consumption that take place against a largely obscured background of unequal control over the means of surveillance.

As historian Samuel Haber notes, one of the virtues of the scientific approach for political and economic elites is that, in the name of a misleading commitment to neutrality, it tends to take given arrangements of power and control as a given. Thus, "Taylor fashioned his methods after the exact sciences—experiment, measurement, generalization—in the hope of discovering laws of management which, like laws of nature, would be impartial and above class prejudice. Of course Taylor's science obscured his bias rather than eliminated it."[7] This formulation is perhaps a bit too personal: surely Taylor repeatedly exhibited the bias of his class toward the day laborers, whom he compared to draft animals. However, his commitment to a system that obscured the power relations within which it unfolded remains the central concern of a critical examination of the relationship between scientific management and the deployment of interactivity as consumer monitoring. Forms of interactivity that take place within a broader context of social and economic inequality exacerbate rather than redress these inequalities. There are those who will cite instances including the blogging "revolution," the use of the Internet by antiglobalization activists, or the rise of open-source forms of information and software production as counterexamples.[8] As of this writing, however, the evidence on the ground weighs more heavily in favor of the claim that the digital "revolution" coincides with an increasingly stratified society rather than an increasingly democratic one. This is a fact that needs to be addressed by everyone who would seek to mobilize the promise of the continually deferred democratic potential of interactivity to undo the very power relations it helps consolidate.

Historical Context: The Rise of Social Science

The turn-of-the-century drive for efficiency can be understood as the prehistory of Bill Gates's version of "friction-free" capitalism, the silicon rationalization of processes of production and consumption via the flow of information.[9] If, by the late 1800s, the process of industrialization had re-sulted in dramatically enhanced productivity along with the industrial by-products of urban squalor and exploitation, one proposed solution was *more* industrialization, not less. Such was the oft-stated credo of scientific management pioneer Frederick Taylor: in making workers more efficient, he claimed to be pursuing their own interests as well as those of their employ-ers. He argued that a more productive populace meant more and cheaper products for everyone—and thus increased prosperity and resulted in a higher standard of living. Crucially, increased productivity meant that work-ers could be freed up to engage in the forms of consumption required by a recently industrialized capitalist economy. As the sociologist Robert Gold-man put it, "To maintain capitalist expansion, it was imperative that new markets be created to provide outlets for both the investment of surplus cap-ital and the increasing abundance of goods. It was also necessary to provide a focus for workers' leisure compatible with the dictates of the workplace."[10]

In this regard, scientific management, consumerism, and the Progressive movement complemented one another. For our purposes, the decisive char-acter of turn-of-the century progressivism is the rise of an observation-based scientific approach to the management of social relations and activities. The late nineteenth century is a fascinating period insofar as it represents the intersection between these social science–inflected forms of social manage-ment and the creation of consumer society. It was a time when the United States adjusted itself socially, culturally, and even academically to the dra-matic transformations resulting from the development of technologies and techniques for industrial mass production—not just in the realm of produc-tion, but also in the processes of urbanization and industrialization.

For historian Thomas Haskell, the significance of "the early 19th century transportation revolution is that it carried the discipline of the market and the other consequences of interdependence into the lives of people who pre-viously had been protected by a moat of time and space. The whole pattern of human relationships in society was torn apart and made over again by the multitudinous influences thrust into men's lives by canal, steamboat, and railroad."[11] Just as the technology became more complex, demanding the cultivation of specialization and expertise, so too did social and economic relations become more interdependent and less transparent. The result was the professionalization of scientific expertise in technology alongside the development of social science, understood as the scientific study of increasingly interdependent social relations and their intricate interplay of causality and influence.

It is thus not surprising that the late nineteenth century saw the emergence of some of the most influential social theorists of modernity, including Ferdinand Tönnies, Max Weber, and Emile Durkheim (as well as Sigmund Freud, if we cast the net more widely). It was a time, to put things slightly differently, in which society itself emerged as a problem—an object of study and observation—at least in part because of the sweeping and disembedding effects of interdependence. As Haskell put it, more traditional, local communities were "drained of causal potency and devalued by interdependence."[12] That is to say, the relative transparency (if not predictability) of the variables affecting social life in more self-sufficient, autonomous communities gave way to the opacity of causes that exerted their influence "at a distance." Whereas, for example, market prices may have once depended to a large extent on local demand and conditions of production, the advent of the railroad and then telegraphy had the effect, as communication historian James Carey has noted, of increasing the reach and interdependence of markets.[13] Local prices became increasingly dependent on influences that remained largely invisible to purchasers: shortages or surpluses in distant regions.

Haskell describes this process as "the recession of causality," resulting from a "shortage" of independent (or causal) variables, understood as "things, events, or people to which genuine causal potency could be attributed and which could serve, therefore, as anchors for explanation and pressure points for purposeful action."[14] The rise of social science, which eventually extended its reach into the study of public opinion (understood as an increasingly "opaque" influence on both political and economic life), comes about in large part as a means of addressing the recession of causality, which "provided a market for expert advice in human affairs by discrediting traditional systems of belief."[15] It did so by attempting to transpose social theory into the realm of science, which had proven so successful in the development of manufacturing technology and the attendant exploitation of natural resources. The result, as Haskell notes, was that even as local, recognizable relations of causality receded into less legible forms of interdependence, helping to undermine traditional forms of authority, a space was opened up for an intermediate realm of expertise: that between transparent local knowledge and mystical communion with the gods. This space provided the sense of distance necessary for what communication theorist John Peters describes as the "Olympian" perspective of social scientists, who take a giant step back from the entanglements of locality and tradition in order to consider the emergent big picture.[16]

The modern notion of society and social science emerged hand in hand, the former as the explanatory problem addressed by the latter: "For men struggling to comprehend the changing texture of human affairs in the 19th century, 'society' was that increasingly important realm of causation located in an intermediate position between two more familiar realms of causal attribution: it stood 'behind' personal milieu, now increasingly drained of causal potency, but 'in front of' (less remote than) Nature and God, hitherto almost the only plausible loci of remote causal influence."[17] But with this shift in perspective comes a shift in method. The difficulty of discerning and tracing relations of causality within increasingly complex relations of interdependence gives way to an almost Gordian solution: seeking instead to discern patterns, and in particular statistical patterns derived through measurement and observation. The difficulty of puzzling through complex issues of causality could be displaced by a focus on pattern and correlation.

Think of the marketing expert who knows, for example, that a consumer who attended an East Coast liberal arts college is more likely to purchase a particular brand of razor, or the political consultant who knows that someone who drives a Mercury is more likely to vote Republican. The question of why is displaced by the apparent predictive power of correlation. Perhaps there is some useful information to be gleaned from figuring out why Mercury drivers vote Republican, but it is cheaper and easier to stick with an "Olympian" perspective that steps back far enough to isolate a bit of order in the midst of the apparent chaos. It is during the mid-nineteenth century— once again, the era of industrialization with which we are concerned—that, as statistics historian Ian Hacking notes, the practice of measurement becomes fully established, leading to what he describes as the precipitation of "an avalanche of numbers."[18]

The new social science relied on abstraction as a strategy for addressing the recession of causality. Quantification made it possible to disembed facts from their infinitely varied contexts and to array them side by side for the purposes of discerning patterns, norms, and deviations. As the currency of social science, numbers allowed for the portability, exchange, and comparison of information. Thus, as Haskell notes, "Positive science meant numerical science."[19] The neutrality of quantification carried over into the ethos of the social scientist for whom, as John Peters puts it, the moral force of scientific thinking "lies in the claim to see life cold, without reference to the mortal-size units in which experience is normally parceled out."[20] As Peters suggests, there is an element of stoic self-purification in such a stance: a form of self-overcoming and self-abnegation that accompanies the attempt to abstract away from mortal-size units. At its best, such a stance fosters a sense of humility and perspective—one that, as such stances do, can spill over into a form of self-congratulation: "Their shoptalk favors macho images of distance and detachment," as Peters notes—imagery whose afterimage appears both in Taylor's treatment of the workplace and in the contemporary business world, which privileges a certain cold-heartedness and clear-headedness, as well as a facility with and respect for the numbers arrayed along the bottom line.[21]

This ostensibly stoic stance may have made a virtue out of necessity. The adoption of a stance of scientific neutrality has the eminently practical effect of disembedding the expert from the nonquantifiable vagaries, superstitions, and prejudices of traditional life in order to confront the recession of causality. To make this observation, however, is to beg the question: whence the need to claim some understanding of interdependence? Why not just accept the unpredictability of interdependence as a new independent variable—the modern version of the unpredictability of the gods—and leave it at that? Perhaps some part of the answer lies in a modern sense of reflexivity: a concession to the role human activity plays in shaping this fate. Another part may also lie in the dismantling of traditional society and the forms of understanding and faith that sustained it.

According to sociologist James Beniger, however, the main impetus behind attempts to understand complex relations of interdependence is the need for control over the burgeoning forms of production resulting from the industrial revolution. If society can be viewed as requiring "the continuous processing of physical throughputs, from their input to the concrete social system to their final consumption and output as waste," it requires systems of feedback, coordination, and control to regulate and organize these processes.[22] The greater the interdependence, volume, and speed of these processes, the greater the need for information to coordinate and control their operations, and thus for the development of technologies and practices for managing information about the processes themselves. Before the rise of industrialization and interdependence, the need for specialized information managers and technologies was relatively minimal: "So long as the energy used to process and move material throughputs did not much exceed that of human labor, individual workers in the system could provide the information processing required for its control."[23] That is to say, information processing and production were relatively de-differentiated: the people who performed the tasks were the people who assembled and processed the information about them. When it came to distributed activities that predated industrialization, such as international or interregional trade, processing took place at what Beniger describes as a human pace. With speeds "enhanced only slightly by draft animals and wind and water power . . . individual workers in the system could provide the information processing required for its control."[24]

A crisis of control is precipitated, according to Beniger, at the moment when the speed of what he calls processing (the forms of production and distribution that sustain a particular society) outstrips its human pace and is amplified by the replacement of muscle power with first steam and then electrical power. The industrial revolution, with its escalating demands for information processing, storage, and communication, draws on and accelerates the information revolution. The latter might also be understood as the point at which industrialization becomes reflexive: when the machinery of production is turned to the task of managing the production process, or, to put it slightly differently, when the technology is turned to the production of information (about) itself. A telling example is the adaptation of punch-card technology developed for the Jacquard loom to the task of gathering, storing, and processing U.S. census data in 1890. A technology developed to speed the production of textiles would eventually be turned to measuring, among other things, changes in textile production.

This reflexive use of processing technology is revolutionary in the double sense invoked by Beniger: in the original (astronomically inspired) sense of the restoration of a previous regime and in its modern sense of a dramatic transformation (but not in its political sense of a fundamental shift in power relations). If the printing press—an information technology—was one of the first examples of technologically facilitated mass production, the use of the machinery of mass production for information processing on a grand scale completes the circle.

As Beniger points out, the span of a single (but rather long) lifetime starting in the 1830s would have witnessed perhaps one of the most rapid communication technology growth spurts in history, from the telegraph and camera, to the telephone, movies, radio, and TV (its invention, if not its installation as a mass medium).[25] Surely such technologies contributed greatly, in a variety of ways, to cultural and artistic expression. They were also crucial to managing and facilitating the processes of production, distribution, and consumption associated with the dramatic increase in manufactured goods during the same period. The telegraph, by allowing information to travel faster than material goods, facilitated control over their transport and distribution. Eight years after Samuel Morse's famous demonstration of the ability of the telegraph to relay messages from Baltimore to Washington, D.C., the number of miles of telegraph line in operation outstripped that of railroad lines by 10,000 (23,000 miles versus 13,000).[26] The nervous system of information control had surpassed in size and complexity the mechanical system that it helped control. At the same time, the development of telegraphic communication made possible the standardization of news content and advertising at the regional and national levels—a crucial task for the creation of a mass consumer society and one that was later taken up by radio and TV. In other words, the communication technology that helped make production more efficient also played a central role in the creation of mass consumer society.

The story of the role played by assorted mass media in promoting goods and services—and thereby facilitating (as well as profiting from) the creation of consumer society—is perhaps a familiar one. The story I want to develop in a bit more detail is, I think, slightly less so: the role played by the media industries in helping to foster the forms of surveillance-based management that carried over into the interactive era. As in the case of industrial production, the commercial media industries relied on increasingly comprehensive forms of surveillance-based rationalization in order to produce mass audiences for sale to advertisers. The parallel between the realms of consumption and production is a recurring theme in this chapter, and the following section returns to a more detailed consideration of workplace management to suggest some of the ways in which it anticipated the migration of monitoring techniques into the realms of consumption and mass marketing.

Frederick Taylor's attempt to develop a science of workplace management replicated the impulse of social science at the level of the firm. If the economy had become more interdependent, so too had the production process itself. Burgeoning forms of industrial production in the late nineteenth century relied not just on remote markets for products and supplies, but on the management and coordination of increasingly large groups of workers engaged in increasingly specialized tasks. Thus a material analogue of societal interdependence was the increasing opacity and specialization of manufactured products themselves to both consumers and producers. Because in the preindustrial era many products in daily use could be made at home or by local artisans, these items had a certain "openness" or availability to their users, who could see how they worked, manufacture them themselves, and repair them when they were broken. Industrialization, interdependence, and specialization, by contrast, contributed to the emergence of manufactured goods that became less transparent to their users, dependent as they were on a network of production processes in distant locations and on specialized technologies of production and forms of knowledge. As the production process came to rely on increasingly complex machinery and the coordination of specialized tasks, it too took on the character of increasing interdependence described by Haskell.

If, for social scientists, the problem of understanding society became central, for Taylor, the focus was on first understanding and then managing the process of collective production. Media theorists Kevin Robins and Frank Webster take the argument one step further: Taylor's strategy for information-based management served as the mediator between social science as a quest for knowledge and the deployment of some of its techniques by Progressive-era forms of social engineering. By turning techniques borrowed from the observational, natural sciences to the task of increasing efficiency and productivity, Taylor paved the way for the management of the workplace and the social factory.[27]

The Taylor System

Frederick Taylor did more than follow workers around with a stopwatch and notepad, monitoring and recording their every action in his quest for "the one right way"—the most efficient manner of performing a particular task. In his famous description of his management method—outlined in his informal lectures to the acolytes and recruits who made the pilgrimage to his suburban Pennsylvania home as well as in his treatise on scientific management—Taylor anticipates the type of research that has since become associated with marketers and demographers. Before selecting the workers that might prove most amenable to training—those whom Taylor was to continue to refer to as "first-class men"—he noted, "A careful study was made of each of these men. We looked up their history as far back as practicable and thorough inquires were made as to the character, habits, and ambitions of each of them."[28]

Taylor didn't just want to know whether they were able-bodied and energetic, whether they were hard workers who might also prove open to direction. He also wanted to know their life histories, their background, their hopes and dreams. By his account, all of this information could be of use in persuading them to work harder for a fractional increase in their pay (in the case of the ironworker whom he gave the pseudonym "Schmidt," Taylor noted that in return for quadrupling his output, the worker received a wage increase of about 60 percent).

Even though Taylor sometimes referred to hard workers as "first-class men," his writings make it clear that his motivation technique had less to do with his respect or empathy for the workers than with his drive for efficiency and profitability. His description, for example, of the process whereby he increased Schmidt's daily output is characterized by a patronizing and bullying attitude toward a worker he describes as "a man of the type of the ox . . . so stupid that he was unfitted to do most kinds of laboring work."[29] Playing on his understanding of Schmidt's ambitions and personality traits ("he had a reputation of . . . placing a very high value on a dollar"), Taylor depicts himself alternately threatening and cajoling the immigrant worker into following his every order in exchange for a promised increase of about 70 cents a day (more than half of Schmidt's daily pay at the time).[30]

Tellingly, Taylor's power over Schmidt resided not solely in control over the worker's livelihood (Taylor routinely fired those workers who refused to participate in his piecework experiments), but also in the knowledge he had gained about the worker through background research. The received version of scientific management tends to focus on a particular image of information gathering: that of the manager with a stopwatch or spreadsheet, dividing tasks into their most basic components and figuring out how to allocate them most efficiently and cost-effectively—that is to say cheaply—among workers. Taylor was not the first to pursue the economic logic of the division of labor. Pioneering political economist Adam Smith and proto-computer scientist Charles Babbage both dwelt in some detail on the economics of pin manufacturing, and in particular the efficiency gains to be had through the division of labor. Babbage famously anticipated the lowering of skill levels associated with the division of labor by noting the savings associated with separating out basic tasks and assigning them to lower-paid workers.[31]

This fine-tuning of the division of labor is an information intensive process. It requires not only a comprehensive overview and detailed analysis of the production process (perhaps not overly complex when it comes to making pins), but also information about the fit between the demands of specific tasks and the capabilities of individual laborers. But the Taylor system goes beyond the division of labor. His surveillance-based approach, at least in its paradigmatic example, relied on leverage gained through the accumulation of demographic information. The form of monitoring and information gathering he outlined anticipates the demographic research that has since come to be associated with the advertising and marketing industries. Taylor didn't just coerce Schimdt by relying on the threat of unemployment; he tried to sell him on the process of scientific management: to make him embrace and internalize the forms of workplace discipline developed by managers.

Taylor's repeated refrain in defending his system during a congressional hearing into its impact on workers was that the system was in the mutual interests of both management and labor—that it brought to the fore a fundamental harmony between the two and overcame an outdated sense of conflict. Managers were gathering information about workers for their own good, according to Taylor. This is a refrain that carries over into the marketing realm, where, once again, asymmetrical monitoring is presented as a means for achieving an underlying harmony of interests between, in this case, marketer and consumer. In this respect, Taylor had started to bridge the gap between the rationalization of work and that of consumption, between discipline and public relations, the use of information as a form of workplace coercion and its deployment as a strategy for consumer manipulation.

Whereas Smith and Babbage were men ahead of their times, anticipating the coming era of rationalization, Taylor was a man of his own time: someone whose attempt to bring science to bear on the management of humans—for their own good—epitomized the spirit of progressivism and its postromantic fascination with perfecting daily life through reason and science, tempered with attitudes of noblesse oblige, technological utopianism, and an abiding faith in "good" capitalism. If machines could help make society more productive and efficient, perhaps society itself could be made to run more like a machine. The industrial revolution suggested, to those caught up in its enthusiasm, the possibility of industrializing society itself: running it efficiently, by the clock, with a minimum of waste and a maximum of productivity.

There was nothing particularly new about the notion that surveillance might increase efficiency. As sociologist Anthony Giddens suggests, one of the main reasons for aggregating workers into shared workspaces during the industrial era was the need to supervise wage laborers.[32] Another was the increasingly capital-intensive nature of industrial production: its reliance on collective production processes incorporating the use of expensive equipment (such as steam-powered looms, belt-driven machinery, and eventually computer-controlled forms of electrical equipment). As surveillance historian Christian Parenti notes, the link between efficiency and surveillance goes back to colonial America and the founding figures of the United States: "George Washington kept a diary that he labeled 'where & how my time is spent.' Slave production was central in his musings, 'Their work ought to be well examined.'"[33] Record keeping allowed him to monitor his slaves for slacking, and he noted his displeasure when slaves fell below his expectations for their weekly productivity.[34] What is distinctive about Taylor's contribution is his ambition, in keeping with the times, to make a science of the role that observation plays in rendering the workplace more efficient. The underlying premise of this approach was of a piece with the dawn of the information era: the notion that detailed observation, record keeping, and analysis might yield the same benefits in the management of humans that the sciences and engineering had yielded in working with inanimate materials.

It is worth pointing out that not all information-gathering practices are necessarily managerial or supervisory. The accumulation of statistical information, including data about unemployment, pay rates, and other aspects of working life, can also be turned to politically progressive purposes. Monitoring technologies similarly can be turned to progressive ends, as was revealed, for example, by the release of protesters arrested during the 2004 Republican National Convention in New York City, thanks to video revealing that police claims that the protesters engaged in violent action and resisted arrest were false. Inventor Steve Mann has coined the term *sousveillance* to describe forms of monitoring that hold state and commercial authorities accountable, a process he describes as "watchful vigilance from underneath."[35] The focus of this book on forms of monitoring and data gathering that facilitate managerial control and economic rationalization is by no means meant to suggest that all forms of information gathering are exploitative and retrograde. Rather, the goal is to identify and critique those that are, to consider why, and to draw attention to the role that they play in the deployment of the participatory promise of interactive media.

Managing the Workspace

Historian Robert Kanigel locates the founding moment, in spirit, of the Taylor system in an 1886 address to the American Society of Mechanical Engineers, in which the association's acting president observed that the management of humans and their work processes was just as important to the production process as the engineering of their machines: "The management of works has become a matter of such great and far-reaching importance as perhaps to justify its classification also as one of the modern arts."[36] Despite calling it an art, Towne insisted it was a job for engineers—those familiar with the cold logic of numbers. The ethos of the scientific manager paralleled that of the social scientist: someone who studied human activities in order to gain a scientific understanding of them, and if one of the early goals of progressive social science was to reform the indigent and thereby improve society, the goal of workplace management was to reform the worker and thereby increase productivity.[37] In both cases—that of laborers and that of the destitute—those subjected to discipline in the name of progress belonged to groups for whom the offer to submit was hard to refuse.

In an era of interdependence, workplace management required a semi-Olympian view, which is why it was not to be undertaken by the workers themselves. Approaching the management process objectively meant treating workers as objects—of knowledge, manipulation, discipline, and managerial direction. Such treatment demanded a third-person position; the workers couldn't be expected to be at one and the same time managers and the objects being managed. Such a position is, as James Beniger suggests, necessitated by the sheer increase in volume of information to be processed: "The reason why people can be governed more readily qua things is that the amount of information about them that needs to be processed is thereby greatly reduced and hence the degree of control—for any constant capacity to process information—is greatly enhanced."[38]

The process of rationalization—a term that Beniger borrows from the writings of sociologist Max Weber to describe technocratic management in the name of efficiency—highlights the connection between the stoic neutrality of the social scientist and the dehumanizing character of bureaucracy. The humanity of workers, viewed from afar, can be abstracted away from. As Weber puts it in his discussion of managerial bureaucracy, "Its specific nature, which is welcomed by capitalism, develops the more perfectly the more the bureaucracy is 'dehumanized,' the more completely it succeeds in eliminating from official business love, hatred, and all purely personal, irrational, and emotional elements which escape calculation."[39]

Switching back to the realm of consumption, this posture is caricatured, as Erik Larson suggests in his history of marketing, by the scientism of contemporary market research: "The marketers talked not about flesh-and-blood people, but about BAR scales, market penetration, cluster analysis, conjoint analysis, convergent and divergent analysis . . . and noninvasive respondent-driven interviews."[40] The flip side of this ostensible neutrality, he noted, is a singularly hostile and aggressive approach toward consumers to be captured, manipulated, and controlled: "Companies did not merely target us; they targeted 'against' us. 'Conquest rate' was the rate at which one brand was able to steal customers from another."[41] Such language highlights the roots of cybernetic management, or feedback-based forms of control, in military research.

In both cases, the information generated by the target is used to reach it more effectively and efficiently.

As Beniger's analysis suggests, the corollary of the loss of traditional, community-based economic relations associated with industrialization is that managerial relations are depersonalized. Just as exchange becomes depersonalized, so too do forms of worker management and exploitation. Cruelty is transposed from the register of personal animosity to that of an impersonal bureaucracy that underwrites exclusion from, for example, forms of credit, mobility, education, or employment. The figure of the vicious tyrant is replaced by that of the indifferent bureaucrat—or rather, by the ostensibly democratic appeal to a depersonalized set of bureaucratically administered rules.

Frederick Taylor, in defending his management system before the U.S. Industrial Relations Commission in 1914, described the impersonal character of scientific management as a form of workplace democracy, noting that it wasn't the manger who made the decisions but "a code of laws." He highlighted his own submission and that of other managers to the rule of these laws: "There is nothing in the world more powerful than a code of laws. . . . The whole United States is run by a code of laws. . . . The code of laws is above all people."[42] Surely there is something admirably democratic about the notion that no person stands above the law; however, the laws that Taylor references—his "scientifically" derived laws of workplace behavior—are not the result of deliberation, legislation, and collective choice, but purportedly the hard and fast laws of nature derived from his own observations about the workplace. It is perhaps not surprising that these supposed "laws," particularly regarding the inadvisability of rewarding workers too handsomely, incorporate the prejudices of his class and managerial status.

The neutrality of the system promises a democracy of indifference: all are treated equally as objects and exploitation is not to be taken personally (even if success often is). This scientific neutrality is characteristic of Frederick Taylor's ostensibly democratic approach to workshop management. As Taylor wrote in his correspondence, his system "prevents arbitrary and tyrannical action on the part of foremen and superintendents quite as much as it prevents soldiering [slacking] or loafing or inefficiency on the part of workmen. . . . Thus you see we have under scientific management a greater democracy than has ever before existed in industry."[43]

There is also an oddly egalitarian feel to Taylor's willingness to devote his concentrated attention to the niceties of the most menial of tasks, as in his detailed consideration of different techniques for shoveling during his congressional testimony. In her glowing portrait of Taylor for the *Saturday Review of Literature,* muckraking journalist Ida Tarbell praised his system for its salutary impact on labor and for "boldly announcing that there is no task so humble that is not worthy of scientific study."[44] Taylor emphasized his own ostensible egalitarianism, frequently invoking the fact that he had, unlike many other members of the class of factory owners and administrators, done an apprenticeship stint as a shop-floor worker.

As his biographer Robert Kanigel suggests, Taylor invoked his shop-floor credentials as a means of preempting charges of elitism and exploitation. His paternalistic attitude toward workers was at its strongest when he engaged in debates over the benefits that workers should receive in return for their increased productivity. In his response to Upton Sinclair's public critique of his system, for example, Taylor, perhaps reflexively, adopted the cover of ostensibly scientific research to argue that he had the workers' best interests in mind when he limited their pay increases: "when . . . they receive much more than a 60 per cent increase in wages, many of them will work irregularly and tend to become more or less shiftless, extravagant and dissipated . . . for their own interest it does not do for most men to get rich too fast."[45] The category of "most men" presumably excluded those business owners and managers to whom he advocated the financial benefits of his system.

Taylor's tendency to push the logic of scientific management as far as possible highlighted its limitations: its inability, most tellingly, to determine scientifically what the optimal pay for an "honest day's work" might be. The logic of his system suggested that such a day's work would be attained when the worker exerted the maximum amount of effort possible without resulting in diminishing returns over the long term. By extension, such logic might be enlisted to suggest that the worker should be paid the maximum sustainable amount possible—a suggestion that Taylor never made, preferring to base his payments on percentage increments over existing pay scales, whose existence he took, rather unscientifically, for granted as the amount workers in a particular industry could reasonably expect to make. Moreover, he based these increments on his study of the minimum amount it would take to get workers to adhere to the system.[46] His repeated assertion that workers employed under his system wouldn't need recourse to collective bargaining systematically overlooked the role of power struggles between management and labor in setting prevailing wage rates.

In other words, his assumption of an underlying harmony between the interests of management and labor served as justification for a system of de-collectivization. Labor organization was unnecessary under Taylorism, he argued, because the system improved working conditions by allocating tasks and compensation "scientifically." Whether deliberately or not, the Taylor system relied on detailed monitoring, differentiation of tasks, and customization of payment as a means of disaggregating the workforce, mobilizing a narrowly defined conception of self-interest as a means of dispensing with the collective bargaining process. This process of disaggregation, paradoxically, remains a theme of mass culture and resurfaces with a vengeance in the realm of surveillance-based mass customization.

Several of the principles of the Taylor system have endured and have even come into their own in the digital era, including the systematized process of disaggregation and the formation of proprietary databases to aggregate and sort information gathered by increasingly detailed and comprehensive forms of monitoring. In Taylor's own time, the technology for recording, storing, and making use of data couldn't keep pace with his ambitions for amassing it. The cost of comprehensive data collection and management is presumably one of the reasons why he claimed during the course of his congressional testimony that, despite the popularity—indeed, the notoriety—of his system, he was aware of no company that had adopted it "in its entirety."[47] The level of monitoring and data sorting he required was just too expensive to be cost-effective, given the available technology.

In this respect, perhaps Taylor really was ahead of his time—if not conceptually, at least in terms of his demand for data. Whereas timing a worker in Taylor's day required paying a relatively expensive management trainee, now, in many cases, the worker's equipment itself can do double duty, keeping track of performance even as it facilitates it. Keystroke monitoring programs, for example, deter employees from using computers for non-work-related activities while they simultaneously provide a detailed record of worker productivity. Bar code scanners in supermarkets serve not only to record prices, making the checkout worker's job faster and easier; they can also keep track of the checker's scan rate to monitor productivity, as can portable, networked,

GPS-equipped devices for delivery workers and truckers. Forms of information gathering and storage that were once prohibitively costly are becoming trivially inexpensive. The same is true of the technology for aggregating and analyzing the data that is collected. Such devices allow the extension of the monitoring gaze to reach beyond the workplace, a process considered in more detail in the following section.

Monitoring at a Distance

The continued development of industrial techniques and technologies of production in the early twentieth century highlighted yet another crucial element of interdependence: the reliance of the rapidly growing economy on increasing levels of consumption. As technology critic Darin Barney puts it, "while the Industrial Revolution enabled the production of vast quantities of an increasing variety of goods, the question remained as to how their consumption could be incited on an equivalent scale."[48] The managerial "problem" shifted from one of production to one of consumption, or, as Arch W. Shaw, a central figure in the history of marketing management and business education, put it, "the problem of distribution."[49] If, as Shaw argued, this "problem" posed the challenge of arousing "the desired maximum demand at a minimum expense," the reach of effective business management would have to extend beyond the factory walls to embrace the realm of consumption.[50] The effective manager must become "a pioneer on the frontier of human desires and needs."[51]

A disciple of Taylor's management system, albeit one who thought it was too narrowly focused on plant management, Shaw would go on to play an important role in the formation of the curriculum in some of the nation's leading business schools early in the twentieth century. He struck up an enduring friendship with Edwin Gay, the founding dean of Harvard's Graduate School of Business Administration (where Shaw also taught and served on the administrative board shortly after the school was founded in 1908), and he contributed to developing business education programs at both Northwestern University and the University of Chicago.[52] Under Shaw's influence, Gay brought Frederick Taylor in for regular lectures at Harvard, where the focus was shifting from an emphasis on plant-based forms of management toward a focus on the "problem of distribution." Shaw's focus on distribution represented the next wave of management, which not only overflowed the bounds of the factory walls, but also absorbed the social-scientific ideals of professionalization and empirical observation. Historian Alfred Chandler noted that by 1914, the required course in American commerce at Harvard's business school had become a marketing class that "comprehended the whole process of physical distribution, demand activation, merchandising, pricing."[53] No longer was the problem of manufacturing to be considered in isolation from conditions of demand and distribution. No more would the scientific study of business management be limited to gathering information about conditions of production. Consumers were to be considered just as important an object of study as workers, for without the former, the increasing efficiency of the latter would go to waste. As advertising historian Roland Marchand put it, "An economy organized for efficient production through economies of scale, rationalization in the working place, functional specialization, and a rapid and integrated flow of materials and communications also needed a high 'velocity of flow' in the purchase of goods by consumers."[54]

Thus it was during the first half of the century that marketing evolved into an industry designed not just to get the word out about particular products, but also to induce demand by portraying shopping itself as a fulfilling and even entertaining process: not just a means to an end but a lifestyle in itself. As the psychologist author of the 1911 book *Influencing Men in Business* notes, "The man with the proper imagination is able to conceive of any commodity in such a way that it becomes an object to him and to those to whom he imparts his picture, and hence creates desire rather than a mere feeling of ought."[55] It was perhaps this appeal to nonmaterial desires that led Calvin Coolidge to declare that "advertising ministers to the spiritual side of trade."[56] The development of twentieth-century advertising might be distinguished by both its emphasis on lifestyle and its reliance on detailed research coupled with the incorporation of developments in the fields of individual and social psychology. It represents, in the realm of consumption, the application and extension of principles developed in rudimentary form by Frederick Taylor's exposition of his principles of scientific management. In this respect, as one commentator notes, the "ideas of Frederick W. Taylor constituted an all-encompassing world view."[57]

What might it mean to describe Taylorism as a worldview? Among other things, it would mean acknowledging that even if the workplace is subject to forms of direct control quite different from those associated with the market-place, there is a still complementary relationship between the two that allows strategies associated with one to be transposed into the management of the other. As Frank Webster and Kevin Robins argue, it would mean seeing the surveillance-based rationalization of both as characteristic of an information-based economy that got under way not at the end of the twentieth century, but from its very beginning, with the emergence of social Taylorism. Webster and Robins argue, "in so far as they represent endeavors to better manage affairs of the corporation beyond the workplace, then the development of market research, mail order, credit agencies, annual product models, public relations, advertising and so forth can be interpreted as an extension of Taylorism from the factory throughout society."[58] If watching workers helped make them more efficient, monitoring consumers became an integral component of managing the "problem" of distribution. The trick was to find a way of expanding the reach of commercial monitoring beyond the workshop to reach the places where the consumers were: spaces of leisure, shopping, and domesticity.

Monitoring Audiences

If one of the hallmarks of modernity is the increasing differentiation between sites of production and consumption, we shouldn't be deceived into ignoring their close relations of complementarity and interdependence. Even Karl Marx, who is misleadingly famous for his seemingly single-minded focus on the production process, noted, "consumption also mediates production, in that it alone creates for the products the subject for whom they are products. The product only obtains its 'last finish' in consumption. A railway on which no trains run . . . is not used up, not consumed, is a railway only . . . [potentially], and not in reality."[59] An industrial revolution without a consumption revolution would remain an example of dramatically unfulfilled potential.

Managing consumers, however, poses some rather distinct difficulties when compared with managing the workforce. One of the most important differences, alluded to earlier, is that marketers don't have recourse to the threat of termination of employment (at least not directly). Another has to do with the issue of scale: managing a workplace requires controlling a sometimes large, but clearly delimited, space. Issuing directives and promulgating guidelines to employees in a defined workspace is the province of workplace managers. How might a comparable method be developed for managing a dispersed mass to make them prolific and "productive," not just as workers but also as consumers?

With the advent of industrial mass society, the recession of causality referred both to an increasingly intricate economy and to the management of an increasingly interdependent society. Cultural historian Stuart Ewen argues in his account of the rise of public relations that as the influences buffeting public life became more interdependent and less transparent, so too did the notion of what constituted the public and what comprised public opinion. When economic and political interdependence increased in a country whose local identities were becoming caught up in and reliant on national economic and political developments, there emerged a corresponding notion of a public shaped (or produced) by influences both opaque and remote, geographically and psychologically. As Ewen put it, citing the influential work of the French sociologist Gabriel Tarde, "the modern public was, Tarde asserted, an essentially, 'spiritual collectivity, a dispersion of individuals who are physically separated and whose cohesion is entirely mental."[60] This was the "imagined" public of a mass society and an emerging mass media, a public that, notwithstanding its virtual character, was crucial to processes of democratic self-governance at the national level—as well as to that of that of mass consumption. Resolving the problem of distribution meant studying the various interdependent influences on the formation of consumer desire and demand. Robert Bartels, a prolific historian of the marketing industry, notes, in terms that tend to equate economic imperatives with a natural process of evolution, "Interest in advertising increased around 1900 as a natural consequence of two circumstances—the need for promotional stimulus as buyers' markets began to replace sellers markets and the application of new psychological findings to the motivation of consumers in this evolving marketing situation."[61]

In the era of mass production, the marketers' opaque object of desire, the mass consumer, receded into a frustratingly anonymous distance. If, in premodern society, producers benefited from a direct relationship with consumers that enabled them to gauge their needs and desires directly and personally, in the era of mass production, these consumers became part of an imagined consumption community—a "spiritual collectivity" whose needs and desires needed to be both studied and, crucially, managed. The notion of a spiritual collectivity was the obverse of the all too physically palpable urban "crowd" associated with urbanization and industrialization in the nineteenth century. If the latter posed the threat of immediate and perhaps unpredictable action, the former held forth the prospect that, prior to acting, it might be amenable to the influence of more abstract forms of persuasion, including rational argumentation and, later on, psychological influence. It might be a reasoning and judging public—one for whom the mass media could serve as instruments of education and the transmission of both expert opinion and the information and evidence that supported it. As centralized institutions, the media could serve as a vehicle for channeling the expert knowledge generated by those whose training and research allowed them to address what I have been describing, following Haskell, as the "recession of causality."

In addition to providing entertainment and diversion, the progressive hope for the mass media was that they might help compensate for the recession of causality by telling stories that explained the complexities of interdependence in terms readily understandable to the public. But the public itself was implicated in this process, insofar as its collective decisions influenced public policy, which meant that as an imagined collectivity of dispersed individuals influenced by a variety of nontransparent factors, the public needed to be explained to itself. Hence the emergence of public opinion research as an extension of social science: the public was one more opaque object of modernity, one whose composition and shifting opinions were also subject to the "recession of causality." It was an object that needed to be understood— by itself for the purposes of democratic self-governance, and by the political and economic elites for the purposes of influencing public opinion.

With the development of the advertising and public relations industries, the split between a conception of a "public" engaged in reasoned deliberation and a crowd or mass subject to irrational impulses becomes obscured. Incorporating the lessons of psychoanalysis and a paternalistic attitude toward audiences, public relations pioneer Ivy Lee summed up the attitude of what Stuart Ewen calls the "consciousness industries" with the observation, "People are guided more by sentiment than by mind."[62] The public's sentiments thus became an increasingly important object of study for those who sought to influence it—industries whose practitioners would have to become as Ewen, paraphrasing public relations pioneer Edward Bernays, put it, "tireless student[s] of the sociological terrain: of public propensities, opinions, and behavior."[63] Detailed forms of monitoring and observation, in other words, were no longer solely the province of scientific study or workplace management. They had become crucial to the management of a mass audience.

Knowing what influenced consumers was not enough, on its own, to solve the problem of distribution, just as gathering information about the iron-worker Schmidt's desires and ambitions was insufficient to make him a more efficient worker. What was needed was a way of getting messages to a mass audience on a mass scale, large enough to encompass markets at the regional and national level. It is no coincidence that the first national mass medium in the United States—the mass-circulation magazine—emerged alongside the development of industrialized mass production in the nineteenth century, not least because its success was reliant on the same technologies that made the mass production and distribution of other manufactured goods possible. The magazine, like the industrial factory, relied on the railroad and the steam engine for its production and distribution. Equally important, the commercial success of national magazines depended on the emergence of advertisers who sought to reach beyond local and regional markets to national ones. The ability to assemble a national audience allowed the dispersed public's "entirely mental" cohesion to be organized, at least in part, through its relation to the mass media.

It's a very short step from the progressive hope that the mass media, properly managed, could help create an informed and enlightened public to the belief that "mindfully employed, the press could shape and control public discourse."[64] If, to reproduce a tenuous distinction, media content might be enlisted to help organize public opinion, by extension, the advertising alongside it could be turned to the management of desire. The result is perhaps the defining contradiction embedded in the oxymoronic concept of commercial news: the split public is to be treated, on the one hand, as a rational, deliberative body in need of information to participate in democratic self-governance, and, on the other hand, as a mass to be molded to serve the ends of advertisers.

The mass media provided the most obvious way of reaching a dispersed audience and attempting to manage its shared opinions and attitudes through the promulgation of instructions for living and images of a desirable lifestyle in a newly industrialized and urbanized consumer society. This form of management, of course, was the most direct one available, barring the possibility of counting and timing people and ordering them what to buy, when, and where, Taylor style. In contrast to the management of action and attitude in the workplace, the management of consumption had to rely heavily on the attitudinal side of the equation. The attempt to shape behavior indirectly has led advertising to be described by one historian as "the only institution we have for instilling new needs, for training people to act as consumers, for altering men's values and thus for hastening their adjustment to potential abundance."[65] The value-shaping ministrations of the industry were perhaps facilitated by the fact that industrialization had helped erode more traditional lifestyles and their attendant value systems, providing an opening for the introduction of the values of modern consumerism on a mass-mediated scale. As Robert Goldman argues, the standard sociological account points to the "the decline of craft hierarchy and occupational community and the resultant breakdown of status mechanisms within the working-class community. In the wake of the disappearance of these mechanisms, the 'life plans' of workers . . . had to be reoriented around the pursuit of status through money and the commodity display."[66] The goal of the marketing and advertising industry was to provide the symbolic resources for this new orientation.

Defenders of the advertising industry tend to claim, paradoxically, that it doesn't work very well, a strategy for protecting the industry by what might be described as the Edsel argument: advertising can't be a very effective form of mass management because most new products fail to succeed economically, often despite aggressive advertising campaigns. This argument is a red herring to the extent that it pretends to answer the broader question about the cumulative effect of advertising and marketing in conjunction with changing modes of social and economic life by posing a purely administrative question regarding the success of an individual campaign, considered in isolation, for a specific product. For our purposes, the key question has to do not with whether an expensive advertising campaign can sell a particular model of car, but with the role played by the growth of the entire marketing industry alongside very real increases in productivity in a rapidly transforming socioeconomic landscape. Even the more skeptical accounts of advertising, such as that elaborated by media sociologist Michael Schudson, concede,

"Advertising not only promotes specific products but also fosters a consumer way of life. . . . there are many other factors that also promote consumerism, but this does not mean advertising's contribution can be overlooked."[67]

As emerging businesses, the marketing and advertising industries drew on the management techniques of their era, including the monitoring-based approaches of scientific management. The lesson of the rise of social science's "instrumental association" with social management—an association that had been "brewing since the late 19th century"—was that effective forms of control and guidance relied on knowledge derived from close observation and detailed research.[68] This is the shared understanding that provides a vein of continuity between scientific management, marketing, and corporate and political public relations. The affinity between the last three has been well documented, but it is their connection to the first—workplace management—that tends to be downplayed by the tendency to separate the analysis of consumption from that of production. The notion of "social Taylorism" reconnects these spheres and identifies the affinities between them: "As Ford's assembly line utilized 'expensive single-purpose machinery' to produce automobiles inexpensively and at a rate that dwarfed traditional methods, the costly machinery of advertising . . . set out to produce consumers, likewise inexpensively and at a rate that dwarfed traditional methods."[69] A further link between the spheres of production and consumption is highlighted by the fact that increased worker productivity was a precondition for the production of consumer goods and for the formation of what might be described (through analogy to the term *workforce*) as a "consumerforce" with the time and resources to afford a consumption-oriented lifestyle: "Under Taylorism and various other forms of scientific management, workers were encouraged to work as rapidly as possible in order to make more money so that they could 'buy pleasure in their leisure time.'"[70]

If the Progressive movement represented a response not just to the recession of causality, but also to the rise of industrial capitalism and the concentration of vast wealth in the hands of a few, the strategies of efficiency and social management it embraced were easily adapted to the purposes of economic and political elites, as were the techniques of social science, which, as one historian put it, "appealed less in their ability to create an informed public than in their promise to help establish social control."[71] It is beyond the scope of this chapter to trace a history of the rise of national advertising and the national mass media in the period of the late nineteenth and early twentieth centuries—a crucial period for the rationalization of consumer culture. However, it is worth noting that all too often, these histories and their related fields are treated as distinct. Students study advertising and marketing in business school, whereas the media industries are studied separately in journalism or communication programs. Journalism, entertainment, and advertising, because they purportedly treat different forms of content, are similarly approached as distinct forms of professional practice. Viewed from the perspective of career training and specialization, the fields of journalism, marketing, and advertisement remain distinct forms of social practice. Viewed, however, as business concerns, they are thoroughly intertwined. Media critic Robert McChesney notes, "Those media that depend upon advertising for the lion's share of their income . . . are, in effect, part of the advertising industry."[72]

The implication of this fact, for our purposes, is to consider the role that the mass media play in the feedback loop whereby marketing messages are targeted to consumers. It is to argue that, in important respects, the commercial mass media, decried by the promoters of the new media "revolution" for being too one-way and top-down, have been interactive from their inception—or, to put it slightly differently, the version of interactivity on offer by commercial media in the digital era represents not a decisive break with previous forms of mass media, but an extension and intensification of the forms of monitoring that their development helped pioneer. We encounter again the slippery nature of the term *interactive*. Scholarly accounts of early newspapers argue that, for example, their production was truly participatory in the sense that the boundary between readers and writers—the consumers and producers of the public conversation—remained blurred.[73] All this changed with the increasing commodification of information and the emergence of commercial mass media. As they became more commercial, increasingly professionalized, and less participatory (in the sense of allowing readers to share in the production process), mass media simultaneously engaged in more systematic forms of consumer monitoring and information gathering, largely driven by their dependence on advertising. As readers came to have less direct input into content, they made a greater indirect contribution in the form of the data they provided about themselves to pollsters, the ratings industry, and market researchers.

Focusing on Audiences

Although the origin of market research proper can, as James Beniger points out, be traced back to the gathering of sales data in the early 1900s (an extension of information-based management processes to the realms of marketing and distribution), at least one ad agency started to research its customers and markets as early as 1879. Beniger notes, "Although such market information seems obviously useful to us today, manufacturers and distributors had little need for it before crisis in the control of consumption made it necessary and the rise of mass media and mass advertising enabled it to be exploited."[74] This is not an attempt to reduce the role of the media to their economic function or to discount the various ways in which mass mediated news coverage and entertainment have helped serve democratic and progressive ends in the United States. It is, rather, to emphasize the necessity, within a commercial context, of a connection that tends to be portrayed as incidental—as if news, entertainment (including the production of a celebrity culture that is used to sell culture and to model consumer lifestyles), and advertising were separate, autonomous entities.

If the national media helped to serve as the informational nervous system of a nation that was rapidly becoming economically and politically integrated, they also served as a rudimentary form of virtual enclosure within which consumers could be both monitored and provided with the implicit and explicit blueprints for a consumerist lifestyle. In this regard, the media industries allowed corporate America to continue to extend techniques for the management of consumption into the texture of everyday life. The economic engine that made the growth of this symbolic nervous system possible was fueled by the profits generated by industrialization and the attendant rise of consumerism, which was in turn the result of monitoring-based approaches to the management of production and consumption.

Selling advertising entailed measuring the elusive product that was being purchased: the attention of readers, listeners, and viewers. These became additional examples of opaque commodities that needed to be measured and managed by an emerging category of experts equipped with techniques and technologies for audience monitoring. It is not exaggerating to say that surveillance of the populace became the economic lifeblood of the commercial mass media. On the one hand, the model of journalism championed by those who hoped it might provide useful information to the citizenry depended not just on reporting, but also on a judicious study of the populace to determine what information might be important or useful for the purposes of democratic self-governance. On the other hand, marketing to the public required detailed monitoring of its practices and preferences. Given the amount of time, energy, and resources that went into the latter, it is clear which of these functions took precedence. Even now, in the era of perpetual opinion polling, techniques for discerning which stories might be most useful to citizens remain at best rudimentary and for the most part all but nonexistent—except insofar as they are conflated with marketing research. That the commercial side of the mass media became one of the driving forces for the managerial monitoring of the populace is evidenced by the role played by the advertising industry in pioneering practices and techniques for demographic monitoring—techniques that eventually carry over into the realm of political marketing described in Chapter 7. Reliance on advertising led newspapers and magazines to generate information first about the number of readers and eventually about their demographic and even "psychographic" (attitudinal) characteristics. As advertisers started to find ways to double-check dubious circulation figures promulgated by publishers, the latter banded together to subsidize the formation of the Audit Bureau of Circulation in 1914 to provide standardized, independently verified circulation numbers.[75]

If, from the consumer's perspective, the commercial mass media served as what Cass Sunstein calls "general interest intermediaries," gathering together news, information, and entertainment to be shared simultaneously by dispersed audiences, from the publishers' and advertisers' perspectives, the same media helped manufacture audiences that could be measured, monitored, and targeted. By 1914, the same year the Audit Bureau of Circulation was formed, the publisher of *Ladies Home Journal* and the *Saturday Evening Post* completed lengthy research studies of markets for the products advertised in his publications (including department stores, automobiles, and farm implements), and the advertising agency J. Walter Thompson commissioned a comprehensive study of "consumer populations surrounding all major cities."[76]

The goals of audience research conducted by advertisers and publishers overlap. Both gather detailed information about what media theorists have described as the audience commodity—publishers because they are marketing this commodity to potential buyers, advertisers because they want to know what they're buying and how to make the most effective use of their purchase.[77] Market research is devoted, on the publisher's side, to attempting to assemble and deliver the most desirable audience commodity, and on the advertiser's side to learning how best to manage and influence this audience once it has been assembled by a media outlet.

As media theorists Kevin Robins and Frank Webster have pointed out, the formation of the industries of consumer management in the early twentieth century—marketing, advertising, and the mass media they supported—was characterized by the development of a form of cybernetic interactivity, an increasing reliance on feedback-based forms of social control. The portrayal of the mass media by promoters of the "interactive revolution" tends to downplay or overlook this fact, perhaps in part to highlight the contrast between interactive media and their mass media precursors. Relegating to the background the forms of interactivity that characterized the mass media industries from their inception makes it easier to portray interactivity—even in its cybernetic form—as inherently democratizing and subversive of centralized forms of command and control.

By contrast, recognizing the central role that feedback played in the development of the mass media and their auxiliary industries highlights the continuity between the old media and the new, as well as between ostensibly novel forms of interactivity and the strategies of cybernetic management they extend and perfect. Such an approach also allows for a refinement of the critique that is being leveled by the champions of the new media against the old, by the promoters of interactivity against the monolithic, imperious, centralized, and top-down media that comprise the so-called Stalinist character of mass society invoked by the *New York Times*. If indeed it turns out that the simple opposition between new media and old, between mass and interactive media, is a false one, if it turns out that the deployment of information-gathering forms of interactivity remain constant from one media era to the next, then it is to a critique of these forms of interactivity themselves that we must turn. The following chapters explore some of the ways in which new media interactivity extends the same feedback-based management techniques that inspired the critique of the commercial mass media. It is only against this background that a reformulation of the promise of interactivity can take shape—one that considers not just the potential of the technology, but also the concrete circumstance of its contemporary deployment.

The Rise of the Ratings Industry

Before moving on to a consideration of interactive media proper in the following chapters, this concluding section expands the discussion of monitoring systems pioneered by the commercial mass media in order to address the "recession" of the audience brought about by broadcasting, the nation's first electronic mass commercial medium. The problem faced by early broadcasters was that the very technology that brought messages to the masses with unprecedented ease also rendered the audience harder to monitor: "Since no visible connection was required between broadcaster and receiver, who could tell who was receiving the message?"[78]

The development of radio merely continued and highlighted a trend associated with the rise of mass-produced media products. If community newspapers served identifiable local groups, some of whom participated in the production process, then large urban newspapers and national magazines catered to an increasingly anonymous readership, remote from both editors and writers and from one another. In the publishing industry, there remained, however, some form of discernible link insofar as readers had to acquire in one way or another a physical copy of the publication, which made rudimentary forms of monitoring possible by counting the number of copies sold, when, and where. The advent of broadcasting removed even this physical link: content and advertising were sent out to whoever might be listening or watching, and the receivers didn't talk back (at least initially). It became the task of the sampling-based ratings industry to make audiences visible again, this time on a mass scale, to broadcasters and advertisers.

Suggestively, one of the early signs of the reappearance of the audience for the new medium of radio came in the form of traces from a much older medium. Advertisers reportedly realized the advertising potential of broadcasting when an over-the-air promotion for the cosmetics company Mineralava drew hundreds of mail-in responses to an offer for free signed photos of the actress Marion Davies.[79] Given the right incentives and the interactive capability of the mail service, the largely invisible audience was willing to make an appearance: "lacking any other yardstick, the number of fan letters for stars was an important clue to the unparalleled audience response that radio generated. NBC received 1 million letters in 1929, 2 million in 1930."[80] The use of auxiliary communication technologies—including writing—was to become a staple of the ratings industry, which incorporated viewing journals, telephone surveys, and automated recording devices into its measurement system. The goal was to take a one-way medium delivering content to a remote audience and find a way to get as much information back about who was paying attention.

Although twentieth-century broadcasting has been portrayed as a synoptic form of media delivery—the many watching the few—the economic model was, from its inception, panoptic: the few watching the many. George Orwell's notorious telescreen—the TV that watches you while you watch—was not a fictional authoritarian deviation from the capitalist model of commercial TV, but its logical extension. The economic advantage of the broadcasting model was its reach and economy of scale, but the initial condition for reaching a large remote audience was its decreasing visibility to content producers. The ratings industry emerges alongside broadcasting in an attempt to restore this visibility on a scale large enough to keep pace with the rapidly growing broadcast audience.

Perhaps not surprisingly, the pioneers of the broadcast ratings system in the 1920s and 1930s got their start in the emerging field of market research. The first attempt to gain a glimpse of the audience was provided by Harvard professor and pioneer market research consultant Daniel Starch, who collected more than 17,000 personal interviews with families in cities and rural counties east of the Rockies to determine how many owned radios.[81] This was, obviously, before the era of scientific random sampling—and it anticipates the goal of total coverage resuscitated by the development of interactive technologies that dramatically reduce the costs of audience monitoring. Starch's research fell short of developing a ratings study proper, as industry historian Hugh Belville notes, because it "did nothing to measure listening patterns insofar as stations and programs were concerned . . . it had minimal impact on the advertising world."[82]

Starch had proven the audience existed, but he hadn't provided any useful information about its habits and behavior. It was market research entrepreneur Archibald Crossley who provided the first detailed accounts of audience listening habits, thanks to his deployment of a more interactive, individualized, communication technology, the telephone, which allowed marketers to penetrate viewer households without actually taking to the streets. Crossley, who is credited with coining the term *ratings,* started his career as a market researcher before founding his own firm, which conducted telephone surveys of radio listeners for the Davis Baking Company and Eastman Kodak, eventually assembling a 1929 report entitled "The Advertiser Looks at Radio." What was really being looked at, however, was the audience.[83] The report, which was based on some 31,000 telephone interviews (again, before the era of scientific sampling), led to the formation of the advertiser-supported Cooperative Analysis of Broadcasting surveys, which inaugurated both the media industry's fascination with (and increasing reliance on) ratings as well as the long history of innovations designed to help render viewers as visible as possible to advertisers.

Crossley's innovation was to collect information about the use of a one-way medium—broadcast radio—with the assistance of the two-way medium of the telephone. As he put it in "The Advertiser Looks at Radio," "We conducted a little test and discovered that at the time, most radio-set owners had telephones. This meant we could reach a lot of people cheaply in a short period of time over a wide area."[84] Because it allowed for a form of electronic entry into spaces of leisure and domesticity, and because it was a two-way medium, the telephone extended the monitoring reach of advertisers and marketers, making it easier to gather information about viewers.

Crossley proved to be particularly innovative and adept at devising strategies for collecting information about consumers and viewers, as evidenced not just by his pioneering work in ratings research, but also by the recognition he received, in the form of a Harvard Business School prize, for his use of household garbage to collect information about purchasing patterns. Crossley's insight was to recognize that the waste stream, augmented by the development of branding and packaging as strategies for managing consumption, could double as a form of information: a by-product of consumption that could provide data for the marketing industry. So he signed up households to allow his company to pick up their household waste in specially tagged bags and bring it back it to a sorting facility, where it was sifted and cataloged. If this sounds like dirty work, it demonstrated the lengths to which marketers were willing to go to render consumers visible. It also perhaps highlights the relative ease with which marketers can now gather increasingly detailed information about consumer habits thanks to interactive, digital technologies. Cataloging trash is costly and time-consuming compared with contemporary automated forms of consumer monitoring facilitated by credit cards, loyalty cards, bar code scanners, online shopping sites, and so on. In the world of digital capitalism, it's much easier to induce consumers to submit to detailed forms of information gathering, in part because the work of generating information about purchasing habits can be offloaded onto consumers themselves, a process considered in greater detail in the following chapters.

One of the drawbacks of the telephone as a feedback mechanism, highlighted by media scholar Eileen Meehan, is that it relied on the explicit consent of viewers. It was an "active" rather than a passive form of information gathering.[85] The fact that it biased the sample of households toward those affluent enough to afford both telephones and radios was probably not a significant concern to advertisers, because these households represented the affluent, influential, and early-adopting audience they hoped to reach. A more significant problem lay in the methodology: the Crossley surveys originally relied on the respondent's recall of radio-listening activities over the past twenty-four hours. As Meehan points out, this method encouraged inaccuracy: "Should householders find onerous the task of detailing twenty-four hours' worth of listening for a perfect stranger on the telephone, they could politely escape the situation by suddenly remembering that they hadn't listened yesterday."[86] The recall method was eventually replaced by the so-called telephone coincidental (developed by C. E. Hooper), which was conducted at different times throughout the course of the day and relied on asking respondents whether they were listening to the radio, and if so, what were they listening to at the time of the call. If it wasn't quite Taylor calling with a stopwatch in hand, it started to come close.

It was up to another marketing pioneer, Arthur C. Nielsen Sr., to develop a more passive technology for gathering continuous data about audience listening patterns. He did so in large part by making first radios and then TVs interactive, in the narrow sense that they came to be equipped, in selected homes, with devices that recorded audience behavior in real time. These Audimeters monitored where the radio dial was set during particular times of the day when the radio was on. Similar devices for TVs were eventually augmented with devices called People Meters that allowed individual viewers within households to punch in when viewing, so that the ratings devices could capture not only what station the TV was tuned to at a particular time, but who in the household was watching.

With the advent of the Audimeter and then the People Meter, audience monitoring took a step in the direction of more continuous, passive forms of feedback, anticipating the TiVo era, in which the very act of viewing simultaneously becomes a form of feedback. Such devices might be considered precursors of the extension of commercial monitoring beyond the confines of the workplace and the marketplace into the household. Indeed, the long historical association in the United States between the electronic mass media and commercial forms of audience monitoring may be one explanation for lower expectations of privacy protection than in European countries, where radio and TV were developed according to a public service model, funded by the government and therefore not reliant on commercial monitoring. If, in the United States, the media model was from its inception an interactive one predicated on increasingly detailed forms of audience monitoring, this was not true of the public service model of broadcasting.

Perhaps the clearest indication of the importance of audience feedback to the media industries is the ongoing series of attempts to gather as detailed and accurate information about viewers as possible. The holy grail of audience measurement is to be able to determine which viewers have been exposed to which ads and how that exposure correlates with consumption behavior. Audimeters represent only a distant approximation of this goal: they indicated when the radio was on and which station it was tuned to, but not whether anyone in the household was in the room when a commercial aired. People Meters are supposed to indicate who is in the room, but they are hampered in their effectiveness by the fact that they are an "active" technology: they require compliance on the part of respondents, who may not feel like punching in when they enter a room, or punching out when they leave. Even when they are in the room, viewers may not be paying attention when a particular advertisement airs. A famous 1965 study of television viewing revealed not only that TVs played to an empty room 19 percent of the time, but that even when viewers were in the room, they spent 21 percent of their time "so involved in something else that they couldn't see the screen" (a fact that even People Meters couldn't register).[87]

The history of the attempts to address the shortcomings of audience-monitoring technology highlights the cybernetic character of commercial mass media: their reliance on forms of interactivity narrowly construed as submission to detailed information gathering. Failed technologies—such as the 1965 attempt to develop a ratings truck "capable of capturing the tuning of televisions while passing on the street"—are as instructive as those that were eventually adopted, insofar as they reveal the surveillance imperative of the marketing industry.[88]

If we recall that cybernetics as an automated system of command and control traces its roots back to guided missile targeting during World War II, it is telling fact that in 1981 Nielsen hired as director of engineering a former designer of "surveillance and targeting systems for submarines and bombers."[89] The audience-monitoring schemes devised during his tenure included an infrared sensor that would scan the room for "hot bodies"—to determine whether there were viewers in the room when the set was on—and a "wall-mounted sonar set that scanned living rooms in exactly the same way a ship scans New York Harbor."[90] Both systems had the drawback of counting large dogs as audience members, and the infrared device could be fooled by hot water pipes in the walls. The sonar device also counted ceiling fans as audience members.[91]

Nevertheless, the overlap between surveillance technology and the cybernetic mass media continues to this day, with passive People Meter prototypes incorporating facial recognition technology and tiny monitoring devices called radio frequency ID chips (discussed in more detail in Chapter 4). Made famous after the September 11 attacks amid the stampede of surveillance innovations devoted to countering terrorism (as well as crime), facial recognition technology is supposed to allow cameras to recognize particular faces on the basis of information that has been programmed into them. Nielsen, drawing on this technology, is experimenting with devices that would be able not just to record the fact that someone is in the room watching TV, but also to identify that person and even detect whether he or she is facing the screen when a particular advertisement is aired.[92]

Thanks to recent developments in information technology, the audience-monitoring process is going through many of the same changes as content delivery: it is becoming increasingly customized, pervasive, multiplatform, and convergent. Symptomatic of this change was an announcement in 2005 by the radio ratings company Arbitron of plans to team up with Nielsen Media Research to develop a multimedia Portable People Meter (PPM), a device designed to provide a comprehensive portrait of individual media consumption. The PPM is the ratings industry response to the rise of ubiquitous media—the fact that we are exposed to commercial media (and the ads they contain) virtually everywhere we go. As Arbitron CEO Steve Morris put it, "Media is following you not just when you consciously turn on your satellite radio in your car, or when you consciously flip open your cellphone and get some cable channel delivered to it. . . . It's also coming at you when you walk through Grand Central Station. It's on the floor and on the walls. . . . Advertising is becoming incredibly ubiquitous, so you need measurement that is equally ubiquitous."[93]

The PPM works by detecting embedded audio frequencies, whether in radio songs and commercials or TV shows, which means the wearer has to be close enough to hear the broadcast. Headphone attachments would allow the device to monitor iPod and other portable forms of media consumption. Ratings researchers are also considering ways of integrating PPMs with GPS devices and radiofrequency ID (RFID) chips. Down the road, the idea is to develop a convergent multimedia ad-exposure detector that would be able to capture information about the music users listen to, the TV they watch, the billboards they are exposed to, and even the magazine and newspaper ads they are near enough to see (thanks to RFID chips embedded in articles and ads). The result would be as comprehensive a portrait of individual advertising exposure as possible—one that included not just a list of which ads were seen, but where, for how long, and at what time of day.

In the near future, the goal is to create a fully monitored media enclosure by matching up this information with consumption behavior, as measured by consumers who scan their purchases at home. When products are equipped with RFID chips, the PPM could double as a consumer meter, gathering information about purchasing behavior and advertising exposure. Nielsen calls this merging of viewer and consumer data *fusion*—a futuristic, vaguely utopian moniker for a goal conceived in the early twentieth century: the perfection of the scientific management of consumption. An all-knowing PPM is the automated equivalent of a personal scientific manager for consumers: a way to stand over them with a stopwatch (and a battery of other data-recording devices), measuring their every move and figuring out how it correlates with more effective marketing—that is to say, an increase in the speed and volume of consumption.

This is not to say that the emerging regime of total media monitoring is without its stumbling blocks. Nielsen backed out of the Arbitron deal but has since announced its own consumer total information awareness campaign, dubbed "Anytime Anywhere Media Measurement" (or A2/M2). The problem with equipping viewers with passive, always-on monitoring devices, according to Stan Seagren, executive vice president for strategic research at A. C. Nielsen, is finding a way to ensure that selected viewers carry this device with them at all times. The company is exploring ways of incorporating the device into an item of clothing or jewelry to make it less obtrusive and easier to carry. The cybernetic imagination of market researchers at play in the fields of new media even envisions the possibility of a device small enough to be implanted under the skin like an RFID chip, although, as Seagren points out, "our cooperation rates would go down substantially if we started asking people for implants." The array of technologies that facilitates the monitoring of the audience sounds like a summary of high-tech surveillance over the past half-century—not just in the realm of marketing, but in policing, detection, and warfare. As Seagren put it, "We're always looking for different things—especially in the security market."[94]

As in the case of scientific management before it, achieving the goal of comprehensive monitoring, whether of workers or consumers, requires time, effort, and technology. From a management perspective, twentieth-century limits on the ability to gather and store detailed information about consumers and workers may well be all but eliminated by the development of pervasive, inexpensive forms of monitoring and data storage. Convincing members of the public to submit to this type of monitoring, or rendering surveillance so passive and invisible that they may not recognize it, remains the challenge of the twenty-first century. Social Taylorism, like Taylorism, is information intensive, not just because it relies on ongoing feedback and thus a continuing relationship with workers and consumers, but also because it is based on specialization and customization, whether in the form of Taylor's variable piece rate system (which paid workers at different rates according to how efficiently they worked) or in the form of customized pricing and target marketing. As in the case of the workplace, the scientific management of consumption relies on constant contact: always-on relationship monitoring. Thus, consumer relationships, like labor relations, have become increasingly contractual (think, for example, of music subscription services or cell phone contracts), allowing for continual monitoring. Increasingly, these forms of consumer surveillance depend on the development of interactive spaces that permit a mobile population to be caught up in the flexible monitoring embrace of the digital enclosure described in the Introduction and taken up in more detail in the next chapter.

iCommerce
Interactivity Goes Mobile

At the dawn of the new millennium, the U.S. National Academy of Engineering praised the dramatic increase in the mobility of the nation's population as one of the greatest achievements of the twentieth century: "In 1900 the average American traveled about 1,200 miles in a lifetime, mostly on foot, and mostly within his or her own village or town. By the end of the century, the typical American adult would travel some 12,000 miles by automobile alone, in just one year."[1] If the figures seem somewhat suspect, the general trend is unquestionable: Americans are a lot more mobile than they used to be. The dramatic increase in mobility reflects a feat of engineering—of highway building and automobile making, of designing and constructing the infrastructure for suburban sprawl and shopping malls—but it also represents a crucial spatial component of the dramatic increase in levels of consumption and production associated with twentieth-century consumer society and related forms of industrialized mass production. What the French theorist Henri Lefebvre described as the "productive consumption" of space associated with increased mobility helped to stimulate a productive spiral: suburbanization and its associated technologies of mobile and static privatization increased demand through spatial dispersion.[2] Each household came to serve as the repository for a private set of appliances that displaced or replaced forms of collective consumption: the automobile displaced the trolley and train, the phonograph and radio the concert hall, and the TV set the downtown movie theater. Thus began the trend toward personalization and individuation that eventually yielded the Walkman, the iPod, and the cell phone. If this process initially relied on a retreat into private spaces for media consumption, it eventually burst back into shared public spaces by going mobile. Thus, one might trace the progression from the collective space of the movie theater to the private TV room of the suburban home, to, finally, the semiprivate spaces of cell phone–saturated malls and airport lounges.

The replacement of collective forms of consumption by individualized ones helped to absorb the surfeit of goods produced by an increasingly rationalized and efficient industrial sector. More recently, the consumption of space itself—the continued trend toward mobility—helps reinforce demand for mobile communication devices such as portable computers, PDAs, and Blackberries. The consumption ideal is no longer simply that of, for example, the single-TV household, or even that of the multiple-TV household, but that of the TV-equipped SUV with an iPod bracket on the dashboard. The fact that many portable devices are being equipped with the capability for wireless networking renders mobility doubly productive: it generates the demand for an increasing array of portable devices, and it enables information gathering about the "space-time paths" of users—information that can be used for both commercial and law enforcement purposes.

Within a monitored space, mobility allows not just for detailed forms of information gathering, but, as this chapter argues, for increasingly fine-grained forms of social sorting, customization, and surveillance. The trend continues that associated with 1950s suburbanization, which offered an escape from urban congestion as surely as it served as a form of sorting, exclusion, and differentiation. The interstate highway system mobilized the myth of the freedom of the road while simultaneously channeling movement through specified areas and around others. As the French philosopher Gilles Deleuze put it, "people can drive infinitely and 'freely' without being confined yet while still being perfectly controlled."[3]

Perhaps one of the reasons that mobility carries with it—at least in the American mythos—such a sense of freedom is the recognition that enclosed spaces and stasis are associated with the strategies of control and rationalization implemented during industrialization. The specialization of labor was associated with its spatialization—a connection that, as sociologist Anthony Giddens suggests, carried over into the dimension of time as well as space. The result was the emergence of "two opposed modes of time-consciousness, 'working time' and 'one's own' or 'free time'—and their associated spaces."[4] The suburban home removed itself as far as possible from the work space, highlighting its role as the counterbalance to wage labor: a domestic refuge from the factory or office (but not, of course, from the unremunerated labor of the housewife and mother). Leaving the factory walls behind meant leaving behind the monitoring gaze of managers and supervisors. Such "free spaces" remained subject to other forms of monitoring—by the state and by peers and nosy neighbors. But up until relatively recently (and barring some exceptional cases, including the enclosures created by the internment camps of World War II), the monitoring technologies to which these "free" spaces were subject remained less comprehensive and often more rudimentary than those associated with the workplace.

As the previous chapter suggested, the difficulty of monitoring increasingly mobile consumers and the expectation of relative freedom from constant oversight beyond the workplace walls posed a challenge for those who would broaden the reach of their monitoring gaze. This chapter explores some of the ways in which mobile interactivity—the proliferation of networked wireless communication devices—addresses these challenges and facilitates the expanded reach of surveillance-based rationalization. The focus of the following sections is thus on the spatial dimension of information gathering—the creation of a widening "digital enclosure" within which a variety of interactive devices that provide convenience and customization to users double as technologies for gathering information about them. In the marketing world and the popular press, the promise of information-based customization within this virtual enclosure has been dubbed "m-commerce" and is associated with what we encountered in the first chapter as "u-life"—a world of ubiquitous computing. The goal of this ubiquity is to endow physical spaces with the interactive character of the Internet, allowing consumers to retrieve useful information (such as directions or movie listings) while simultaneously narrowcasting information about their movements and preferences to those who own and operate the means of interaction.

It's the Phone, Stupid

The first interactive communication technology used by the marketing industry—the telephone, which provided ratings researchers with access to the inner reaches of domestic space—is emerging as the so-called lifestyle tool of mobile interactivity.[5] Because of its popularity as a portable communication device, the cell phone has become the locus of futuristic fantasies of friction-free capitalism. In the m-commerce world envisioned by corporate futurists, cell phones will do much more than take pictures and download ring tones (not to mention allowing people to talk to one another). They will also serve as interactive digital credit cards and mobile Internet access points. As the marketing director for one major cell phone company put it, "The first thing people are going to drop is their keys and then their wallet. . . . You will eventually be able to fulfill all their functions using your phone as your personal service device."[6]

As an m-commerce tool—or what another enthusiastic corporate spokesman called a "digital lifestyle hub"—the cell phone will become a bare-bones, wireless PC, streamlined to facilitate mobile consumption.[7] It will allow remote banking, Internet access, and, with the added security of a PIN number, the ability to make both remote and on-site purchases. As one press account put it, "Imagine being able to use your cellphone to pay for a taxi fare or to top up a parking meter remotely from your office cubicle."[8] Enthusiastic technofuturists predict that cell phones will be used "to manage everything from paying bills to the temperature of your home."[9] A mania for efficiency and hyperinteractivity—or hyperconsumerism—runs through these press and public relations narratives about the future of the cell phone. Time not spent shopping, banking, investing, reading the news, playing games, or tweaking the thermostat via the network is time wasted. Thanks to the wonder of mobile interactivity, we can multitask wherever we happen to be: on the train, in the park, at the café, riding the elevator, on the john.

The developments in wireless technology that render mobile telephony suitable for always-on connectivity include the personalization of the technology, its networked character, and its traceable mobility. The private phone used by the ratings pioneers in the early twentieth century to gather consumer information was not personalized; it reached into a private household where it might be shared by several individuals. The "addressability" of the cell phone, by contrast, is more precise insofar as it associates one number with a particular individual, wherever he or she may happen to be. Just as the family car and TV set were, in the pantheon of American affluence, replaced with individual TV sets and cars, so too has communication technology become further individualized: to each his own phone (and with it, eventually, his own TV, radio, camera, and portable computer).

Unlike cars and TVs (at least for the moment), telephones allow for personalization and for entry into an interactive network—a virtual enclosure that allows individuals to stay in constant contact with one another and with commercial and state entities interested in tracking their whereabouts. The trackability of cell phones received a big boost thanks to the legal requirement in the United States that they be equipped with GPS technology to allow their location to be pinpointed in case of emergency. This requirement, promulgated in the name of security, promises to facilitate the rationalization of consumption by allowing marketers to reach individual consumers when they are on the street "poised to make spending decisions," as one m-commerce pioneer puts it.[10] The world envisioned by the promoters of m-commerce is one in which "'location-based services' will alert you that a friend happens to be nearby, that a store you are passing is holding a sale, or that you have made a wrong turn on your way to a new restaurant."[11]

Within the electromagnetic enclosure formed by mobile phone networks, individual users trail data throughout the course of their day: "Wireless contributes a critical piece of information to the business model. When a wireless device is on, businesses can know where the user is (within 300 feet, in fact, using GPS technology), so businesses can offer location-aware services"[12] There are some undeniable conveniences associated with such services: the ability, for example, to get personalized directions in real time—perhaps even in the form of voice instructions (as in the case of automotive GPS systems), or the ability to instantly track friends and relatives in case of emergencies. Soon the person listening to his or her cell phone on a street corner might be getting directions to the nearest sushi bar, or perhaps listening to reviews of a movie playing in a nearby cinema.

Increasingly, we are likely to find ourselves using the telephone not to communicate with people but with automated services and databases. These automated services will also talk back to us—providing both on-demand information and, most likely, unsolicited, customized marketing appeals: electronic coupons for stores we happen to be passing by and real-time offers for personalized goods and services in the vicinity. Users will likely have the capacity to block these customized ads, as we now have the ability to block Internet tracking cookies. But as in the case of these cookies, exempting ourselves from monitoring will come with a cost: loss of access to information and convenient services. There is a price to be paid for convenience and customization—and we will likely end up paying it not just by sacrificing our privacy, but by engaging in the work of being watched: participating in the creation of demographic information to be traded by commercial entities for commercial gain and subcontracted forms of policing and surveillance.

Above all, these interactive services will be listening and watching, assembling databases of personal information that dwarf the current data sets accumulated by search engines like Google and retailers like Wal-Mart. Taken to its limit, networked monitoring promises to approximate the memory of Jorge Borges's Funes, who could remember "the shapes of the clouds in the south at dawn on the 30th of April of 1882, and he could compare them in his recollection with the marbled grain in the design of a leather-bound book which he had seen only once, and with the lines in the spray which an oar raised in the Rio Negro on the eve of the battle of the Quebracho."[13] Except, of course, that the focus of the databases will be somewhat more prosaic, recalling not only what each consumer purchased and when, but where—and relating this information to the behavior of everyone else at any given time and place.

Mapping Mobility

The portrayal of the Web as a customized medium that allows users to unfold their unique interests, needs, and desires within a virtual space by surfing the Internet transposed the promise of the open road into cyberspace (Microsoft's "Where do you want to go today?" slogan is exemplary). Thanks to the Internet, one could "travel" freely through cyberspace from the privacy of one's home. But this was a static promise: although it increased virtual mobility, it restricted physical mobility by tethering Web surfers to stationary access points. The stereotypical image of the Web surfer, presumably highly mobile in virtual space, is one of physical stasis: users are parked in front of a glowing screen, with only restlessly flitting fingers doing the walking. Virtual mobility potentially undermined the demand-enhancing function of physical mobility, as highlighted, for example, by the fact that Bill Gates once predicted computers might help lessen pollution by cutting back on physical travel (primarily commuting).[14] Increased virtual mobility, on this account, would correspond to decreased physical mobility. The more we traveled virtually, the less we would actually have to move. Perhaps broadband could empty out the L.A. freeway and allow us to painlessly break our oil addiction.

The brute economic fact is that to the extent that it dampens consumption, stasis is not particularly desirable for producers. Wireless commerce offers to counter this dampening effect: consumers can go mobile while they surf the Web and generate information about themselves. Virtual and physical mobility can complement and redouble one another. When the elastic boundaries of cyberspace extend beyond the confines of the home or office to contain the movements of the mobile consumer, this mobility becomes the real-world analogue of Web surfing. The promise of wireless networked technology, from the standpoint of m-commerce, is thus to inscribe the productive spiral of spatial dispersion into the interactive economy. Consumers' motions through space aren't just productive in the sense of generating demand for resources (such as cars and gas); they also open up new informational dimensions that can be used to further facilitate consumption, as in the case, for example, of the "direct to your cell phone" promotional offer.

The interactive overlay of physical space is neatly described by venture capitalist David Bennahum in an article about Vindigo, a U.S.-based interactive city guide for portable devices such as cell phones and Palm Pilots. At the time, Vindigo's headquarters featured a computerized map that tracked the movements of consumers in New York City on the basis of information gathered from portable devices translated into visual form:

Most maps of Manhattan show a straightforward grid of streets. On this one, coagulating splotches of red portrayed an additional network. The speckles were densest along vertical axes, where one would expect the avenues to be. They thinned out in perpendicular strands, following what would normally be the side streets. . . . The clustering of dots around any given point corresponded to the location of restaurants or bars in the Vindigo database that people had inquired about. The thicker the clump, the more interest people had shown in that particular place.[15]

The map was not functioning in real time because Vindigo was not fully wireless at the time. Users downloaded the program from the Internet to their Palm Pilots and received regular upgrades by connecting their devices with a networked computer. Each download was interactive insofar as it provided new information regarding such things as movie schedules and gallery shows, while simultaneously sending information on user requests back to Vindigo. The future of Vindigo-style applications is the retrieval of information on a real-time basis so as to transform the map described above into a fluid tracing of the flow of consumers through the city.

Already some municipalities, including the city of Baltimore, are using cell phone data as a traffic management tool, monitoring the movement of cell phones to keep track of traffic flow and congestion. This type of monitoring relies on the fact that cell phones, even without GPS technology, are not purely passive devices; they search for nearby cells and connect with them, switching from tower to tower as they move. The result is that cell phone companies can retrieve data from each phone that indicates which tower it is connected to at any given moment. As long as the phone is turned on, it serves as a passport into a monitored electromagnetic enclosure. State and company officials, sensitive to privacy concerns, have stressed that the traffic monitoring program doesn't gather information about particular individuals, only aggregated, anonymous data. This self-limitation is the result of the current whims of corporate policy, and not due to any inherent limits of the technology. The very existence of the traffic monitoring program suggests that the ability to gather detailed information about the movements of particular users already exists. As one privacy advocate noted, "We are basically developing the surveillance infrastructure that has the capability to track people individually—even if that system is not being used to do that yet."[16]

The reluctance of state authorities and private corporations to admit to individual tracking is likely to dissipate at the very moment when commercially viable applications are developed to take advantage of the technology. If the recent erosion of privacy protection is any indication, individualized monitoring will be portrayed as the latest in customized convenience: "Wouldn't you like your car to tell you how to avoid traffic jams on your way to work or the beach?" Don't be surprised if it throws in a few ads—or customized electronic coupons—for nearby shops along the way. The promise of convenience will, in the spirit of a rejuvenated Taylorism, be supplemented with an appeal to the benefits of rationalization: "'The potential is incredible,' said Phil Tarnoff, director of the Center for Advanced Transportation Technology at the University of Maryland, who said the monitoring technology could possibly help reduce congestion in some areas by 50 percent."[17] To

those steeped in the workings of the Internet—which functions as the prototype of a "smart" network, in which information is routed according to the
most efficient path—the sight of a dumb network like the interstate highway
system, in which individual travelers have little or no knowledge about the
state of the network beyond their particular location, looks frighteningly in-
efficient—a problem to be solved through the addition of a little interactive
monitoring.

Such surveillance isn't limited to highway travel. The existing technology
makes it possible to differentiate between modes of transportation and to
keep track of the movements of anyone equipped with a phone: "The . . .
system, which can receive several hundred thousand signals at once, uses
complex computer algorithms to tell whether a signal is coming from a car,
a bicycle or someone sitting still."[18] Customized traffic control is perhaps a
gateway application for personal monitoring—one that will help lower the
threshold of resistance and raise the wage of convenience offered in exchange
for comprehensive monitoring. Applications already in the works include
personalized directions, the ability to track friends or family members' locations, and even the use of cell phone monitoring for health care: "Mobiles
could automatically send signals from sensor devices monitoring a person's
health status to care providers—an instant network that triggered alerts and
interventions when needed."[19]

M-commerce is not yet fully upon us, but it is nevertheless a central
component of the speculative future of electronic commerce—a sector that
seems to have survived the dot-com meltdown. Preliminary forms of m-
commerce—the ability to pay for goods and services with a cell phone—
have become commonplace in Scandinavia and Asia, while Europe and the
United States have yet to sort out the wireless standards that will allow m-
commerce to become a widespread phenomenon.[20] So far the uptake has
been largely lukewarm. There is a certain novelty to paying for a vending
machine candy bar by dialing a cell phone number, but in the end, it's probably still just as easy to carry around some change. However, emerging forms
of cell phone commerce—including the purchase of ring tones, games, and
screen savers—anticipate a time when music, video, and customized news
and information services will be readily available via cell phone. Lehman
Brothers has predicted that Europeans will spend more than $1.7 trillion by
2010 on cell phone–facilitated m-commerce.[21]

The marketing strategy is to offer geographic customization as a form of convenience: an attempt to cater to individual desires, including that for the individualized recognition associated with mass customization. Spatial customization can thereby serve as an incitement to the consumption of space as a form of productive self-expression: we are where we go. In contrast to the modern assumption that the essence of an individual's identity is expressed in the intimate realm of the home, in the wired world of m-commerce, subjective expression is projected outward through the consumption of space. [22]

The appropriation of individual space-time paths as a useful demographic category and thus a valuable information commodity casts a somewhat more instrumental light on French literary critic Michel De Certeau's description of the process whereby pedestrians create a unique spatial calligraphy of their own as they roam a city's streets: "they are walkers . . . whose bodies follows the thicks and thins of an urban 'text' they write without being able to read it."[23] The fact that these traces are produced unintentionally and idiosyncratically while at the same time capturing the rhythm of daily life provides them, according to De Certeau, with a poetic character that falls below "the threshold at which visibility begins."[24] The countergesture of electromagnetic monitoring within the digital enclosure is to lower this threshold, perhaps until it disappears, resulting in total visibility. The fantasy implicitly invoked by companies like Vindigo—a fantasy that may soon become a reality—is to embrace the celestial point of view that so tempted Icarus in De Certeau's account: "His elevation transfigures him into a voyeur. It puts him at a distance. It transforms the bewitching world by which one was 'possessed' into a text that lies before one's eyes. It allows one to read it, to be a solar Eye, looking down like a god."[25]

Digital technology helps bring this celestial viewpoint down to earth—where it can, predictably, be turned to the ends of commerce. The m-commerce fantasy entails the creation of a virtual enclosure in which the details of every digitally enabled transaction can be gathered, collected, and analyzed. One marketer summarized the cosmic ambitions of marketers in a description of a process that tags objects (including clothes) so that they can be tracked by radio sensors: "Ultimately, we'll be tagging every item in the universe."[26] The process of naming everything in the universe turns out to be a prelude to enfolding it into a monitored totality subject to the manipulations and ministrations of marketers. It's hard not to see the recurrence of a post-Enlightenment technological hubris in these ambitions: the desire to realize (in the sense of "making real") an omniscient gaze for the purposes of convenience and profit. As the engineers at Intel put it, their intention is to build "planetary scale systems." In keeping with the animation of smart objects and clothes, much of the activity of data transfer and processing will, on this account, become automated, exempting users from having to actively monitor the streams of data that surround them and through which they send ripples: "We will continue to interact with a few of our computers, but the vast majority will be embedded deep within our physical environment where they will capture and may act on data without human intervention."[27]

If, in an ostensibly postmetaphysical era, enlightened science has helped undermine the notion of an invisible other who keeps track of our actions, one of the resulting compensatory gestures is to literally recreate this other in the form of networked monitoring. More than a decade ago, the attempt to gather so much information would have seemed pointless and absurdly costly and time-consuming—scientific management run amok, hemorrhaging reams of data along the way. Even if all this information could be gathered, who on earth would be able to sort though it and make sense of it? Enter the promise of the algorithm: to sort and analyze data automatically. In the breathless rhetoric of relationship marketing, the combination of database and algorithm is portrayed as the recuperation of an enhanced version of personalized service: "Technology has brought us back to an old-fashioned way of doing business by making it possible to remember relationships with individual customers—sometimes millions of them—one at a time."[28]

Such formulations are disingenuous, to say the least: it is a machine that does the "remembering"—not just of individual customers, but of recurring patterns of consumption that generate marketing strategies based on predictions of consumer behavior. The goal is not just to remember individual shoppers, but to consider how they might be enticed or manipulated to buy more. It's one thing to remember a customer's preferences in order to serve them up "the usual," and quite another to use information about the fact that their clothing size might have changed recently to market them diet pills, or to use the fact that they recently subscribed to an online dating service to try to sell them a book on relationships. In the United States, the uber-retailer Wal-Mart has already collected a database of transactions, purchases, and consumer activity that is the largest corporate database in the world—reportedly larger than the indexable contents of the World Wide Web.

The benefits of accumulating such information remain, for the moment, mostly speculative because algorithms don't always get it right—as suggested, for example, by the experience of TiVo subscribers who find bizarrely off-target recommendations downloaded to their machines, or of anyone who has received a misguided "personalized" advertising appeal. We may also have had the uncanny experience of a customized ad getting it right—an experience that may well get creepier in the future, when, for example, after visiting a doctor (or a Web site) for a particular complaint, we find ads for remedies popping up on our favorite Web sites. Such ads will provide further evidence of the automated monitoring network: it has registered our complaints, our reading and shopping habits; what else does it know? The answer may turn out to be: lots more than we'd like.

In response to examples of misguided customization, the wager of m-commerce is that the most effective remedy would be not less monitoring, but more—more comprehensive, more extensive, and more precise. Information about the space-time paths of consumers remains one of the more recent additions to the growing quiver of demographic tools for targeting consumers—but it is one that guides futuristic marketing fantasies: "It's the dream out there about GPS," according to one marketer. "It's the soccer mom, picking up her kids, and she gets into the car and she gets a discount ad targeting her for McDonald's, just as the kids are finishing up practice."[29]

Rendered legible, the traces of personal mobility—of our wanderings through city streets and of our circulation through the arteries and capillaries of suburbia—become hieroglyphs of consumer desire that, read correctly, provide instructions for unlocking pocketbooks by catching consumers at their most vulnerable and impressionable moments. Transposed by digital data gathering into the register of m-commerce, what De Certeau describes as "the chorus of idle footsteps" that inscribe unique, personal, evanescent traces across the landscape sounds to marketers more like the clamor of cash registers.

The Digital Enclosure Continued

The name of MIT's ubiquitous computing initiative, Project Oxygen, invokes the goal of making interactive computing as omnipresent and invisible as air. The digital future it envisions is one in which the electromagnetic enclosure, rather than fencing us in or tying us down, will be the medium through which we move. The open, flexible character of the digital enclosure differentiates it from earlier enclosures whose boundaries helped enforce the differentiation of "free" time and space from other spaces and times. The very notion of an enclosure implies notions of walls and limits—means of marking off one space from another. The digital enclosure, however, is a virtual one, whose limit is not necessarily spatial (because in its ideal form it would enclose the entire planet) so much as technological. Entrance into the digital enclosure, as the following section suggests, is not a matter of crossing physical boundaries but of equipping oneself with the appropriate technology: devices that allow users to communicate with the network, to gather information from it, and to supply information to it. Entering the enclosure is about embracing interactive technology.

One reason for the use of the term *enclosure* is to invoke a more classical theoretical instance of enclosure: Marx's description of the land enclosure movement that forced the rearrangement of labor relations by separating workers from the land. The result was a wage-labor model of production that allowed for the extraction of surplus value from workers rather than the appropriation of surplus product (in the form, for example, of a portion of each year's harvest). By the same token, one might consider the advent of ubiquitous computing as an attempt to compel or entice entrance into a monitored space that helps rearrange relations of consumption and production. The fact that the threat of force isn't directly invoked, at least for the moment, shouldn't discount the possibility that real forms of exclusion may well be visited on those who resist entry. Indeed, it is likely that sometime soon, labor contracts will require workers to enter the enclosure as a condition of their work supervision. This requirement is already the case, for example, in the trucking industry, which relies on the rationalization of transportation via GPS technology that keeps track of the location of individual trucks.

In the case of consumption, the profitability of demographic commodities relies not just on the ability of companies to claim proprietary rights to them, but also on the ability to store and manipulate vast quantities of data. Information that has little value in isolation gains value to the extent that it becomes part of an extensive database. Thus, the ability of consumers to choose whether or not they enter into the digital enclosure increasingly comes to resemble the forced choice of the wage-labor agreement. Consumers are free not to interact, but they find themselves compelled to engage in interactive exchanges (and to go online) by what Lester describes as "the tyranny of convenience."[30] To the extent that goods and services become available only over an interactive network, the consumer is faced with a forced choice that complements that of the worker: either submit to monitoring, or go without. Taken to the limit, one might imagine an economy completely reliant on, for example, an electronic bank card. Purchasing any good or service would then require entry into a monitored relationship.

The digital enclosure promises to dispense with physical boundaries: rather than restricting movement, it feeds on it, exploiting the productive potential of mobility. French philosopher Gilles Deleuze described some of the attributes of this emerging flexible enclosure in his description of the rise of "societies of control." Whereas industrialized societies characterized by routinized forms of homogenous mass production and consumption were associated with the rigid "molds" of the factory enclosure and the prescripted, repetitive routines of mass production, societies of control are characterized by the more flexible paradigm of modulation: a flexible, "self-deforming cast that will continuously change from one moment to the next . . . a sieve whose mesh will transmute from point to point"[31]—in short, a flexible network.

For workers, the emergence of a flexible enclosure means that the monitoring gaze of managers can extend beyond the factory or office walls—even to the extent of facilitating long-distance labor. At the bottom end of the economic scale, this implies the ability of capital to seek out low-wage workers around the world and to draw on the labor of low-paid immigrants (many of whom, despite predictions of postindustrialism and the demise of disciplinary society, continue to work in old-fashioned sweatshops). At the high end, it refers to always-on-call professionals who carry their work with them as they travel the globe and who move from company to company with an increasing degree of frequency: "Work anywhere anytime is the new paradigm. . . . It amounts to a massive disaggregation of work, spinning outside the walls and confines of the traditional office."[32]

In this respect, the promise of the digital enclosure may well mark a rearrangement of the boundaries of what French theorist Michel Foucault described as the rise of the great enclosed institutions of the modern era:

hospitals, prisons, factories, and schools. In each case, a widening digital enclosure is allowing for the spatial dispersion of institutional control—the dissolution of the walls of the enclosure. Prison officials are increasingly relying on digital tethers for nonviolent offenders; the work space has expanded beyond the office and factory walls, schools are embracing distance learning, and even the medical profession is considering the benefits of digital outpatient monitoring as a lower-cost alternative to hospitalization: "We could offer a wireless monitoring system—which could be as simple as a bathroom scale that registers weight gain due to water retention—that would alert a nurse to check on the patient. . . . If you keep one patient out of hospital at least once a year, you are providing better care for the patient and saving the health system up to $9,000."[33]

At the same time, the eroding significance of physical boundaries facilitates the de-differentiation of labor and leisure. It means not only that work can take place remotely, but also that activities formerly undertaken beyond the reach of the monitoring gaze can become (doubly) productive. A world in which we can log in to work from the neighborhood café or from the airport is simultaneously a world in which our weekend drive can generate marketable commodities: demographic information about the rhythms of our daily lives.

Two levels of digital de-differentiation characterize predictions about the wired workforce: first, the spatiotemporal de-differentiation between places of work, leisure, and domesticity; and second, the de-differentiation between acts of production and consumption. Digitally facilitated interactivity within the enclosure brings out the productive character of consumption: the fact that each transaction generates information about itself that can be bought and sold as a commodity. The productivity of consumers can be registered along with the activity of viewers once considered to be passive. It turns out that the media scholars who championed the notion of an "active audience" were right all along. Viewing can be, quite literally, a productive act—but perhaps not quite in the way they intended. Or to put it slightly differently, the structure of the emerging digital enclosure seems poised to capitalize on the productive labor of audiences and viewers: to enfold their efforts into the marketing and rationalization process. The labor of fans who make Web sites for their favorite TV shows or who entertain one another with critical online commentary can, as the next chapter suggests, be just as useful from a marketing perspective as is willing submission to detailed forms of consumer monitoring.

With respect to the fate of labor in the digital enclosure, media critics Kevin Robins and Frank Webster have argued that networks provide the "technological means to break the times of working, consumption, and recreation into 'pellets' of any duration, which may then be arranged in complex, individualized configurations and shifted to any part of the day or night"[34]—or, we might add, any place of the day or night: hotel room, airport, home, café. However, as the second aspect of de-differentiation described above suggests, such pellets of consumption and recreation are also internally de-differentiated: an act of consumption doubles as an act of production to the extent that it generates feedback commodities. Thanks to de-differentiation, "'free' time becomes increasingly subordinated to the 'labor' of consumption."[35]

Gilles Deleuze's version of modulation is defined by this kind of interactivity: the network's "sieve" adjusts itself to conform to the details of its interstices: the workers and consumers who are redoubled by the digital records of their actions. Deleuze refers to the emergence of the informational doppelganger of the consumer-worker in the form of the "dividual"—a subject split between its physical manifestation and the digital profile that emerges from its interaction with data-gathering devices. Similarly, theorist Mark Poster uses the notion of the "second self" to refer to the data image of consumers stored in data banks, and new media theorist Philip Agre calls it a "digital shadow."[36] The density of this shadow, or what might be described as the resolution of this second self, depends on the information-gathering capacity of the digital enclosure and on the interactive capabilities of the individuals moving within it.

An individual's activities may be only partially embraced by the digital enclosure, depending on the limitations of the interactive capability of both the space and the individual moving through it. Thus, for example, cash transactions may fall partially below the radar of the network. When, as some futurists predict, cash is replaced entirely by electronic transfer of funds via cell phone or some other device, all economic transaction may fall within the purview of the enclosure. In this respect, we might describe a digital enclosure movement whereby activities previously invisible to the network are gradually (or rapidly) engulfed by it.

One ready example is the fate of sound recording. Back in the days of vinyl, once a recording was purchased and released from the monitored enclosure of the record store, it had moved, for all practical purposes, beyond the range of commercial or state monitoring. The owner could play it as many times as desired, lend it to friends, give it away, sell it, or destroy it, all without the manufacturer being any the wiser. In the era of digital music—which seemed initially to usher in an era of lack of control over recorded music—it is becoming easier for corporations to continue to monitor music usage even after a song is purchased. The success of iTunes and other online music stores represents the beginnings of the digital enclosure of sound recording. As anyone who has bought music online has discovered, no longer does the fact of purchase mean that one has complete control over the recording. Digital rights management tools restrict the number of times a file can be copied or moved, and in some cases, the number of times it can be played. Down the road, when most audio devices are interactive, music files will carry identifying information that will allow the network to determine whether their use has been authorized by the seller. So-called musical piracy—unauthorized duplication and file sharing—will not disappear, but it will require a greater degree of technological sophistication on the part of pirates, as well as an increasing tolerance for the real threat of legal action. When your iPod cell phone keeps track of every song on its hard drive, it may someday be able to let the network know whether or not a particular music file has been legitimately purchased. Indeed, it will likely make it difficult, barring illegal hacking, to play illegally obtained music files—and the risks of trying to get away with file sharing will, for most of the general public, outweigh the benefits.

The heady Napster era of free and uncontrolled downloading was reliant, paradoxically, on a relative lack of interactivity and the resulting anonymity afforded users. As consumer devices become increasingly networked and interactive, it will be harder to retain that level of anonymity. Reportedly, some digital recordings of movies have embedded code that notifies copyright holders when an unauthorized copy has been played—and pinpoints the offending computer. Anyone who has purchased computer software recently knows that copyright holders rely on the Internet to require registration and prevent unauthorized usage. If you don't register online and type in the proper code, the software shuts down after a set period of time. Such systems require that a computer be networked (as anyone who has tried to call in to register software offline has discovered): they compel entry into the digital enclosure that provides them with a degree of control. Similarly, as a friend who recently traveled to Australia with a DVD he had legally purchased featuring a high-definition version of a movie in Microsoft's proprietary format discovered, interactivity can be restrictive. When he tried to watch the movie, which he had purchased in the United States, in Australia, he was required to go online to get a license from Microsoft. When he attempted to do so, he was notified that because the DVD had been purchased in a different region, Microsoft would not supply the license. Barring some hacking, there was no way to watch the high-definition version of the movie he had purchased perfectly legally.

The clear trend is toward increasing reliance on the network and the foreclosure of unmonitored, noninteractive transactions. Access to goods and services will be increasingly tied to interactive monitoring as a condition of purchase, either implicit or explicit, as the digital enclosure expands—all of which means that consumers will be required to be always-on interactors. As the requirements of maintaining interactive relationships with producers outstrip our ability to keep track of them, the technology will take over for us, shouldering the burden of the myriad forms of data transmission required by the version of "relationship" marketing and consumption fostered within the digital enclosure. As users decide to switch from relying on public pay phones to cell phones, for example, they enter into an interactive relationship that allows for the types of monitoring described in the previous section: cell phone companies will be able to keep track not just of who they're calling and when, but where they are and how they move throughout the course of the day. As users switch from paper copies of the daily newspaper to electronic, online versions, they relay detailed information that was previously impossible to gather: which stories they click on and download, which ads they click on, when they read the paper, how much time they devote to individual articles, and whether they click through to the jump. The result is a detailed portrait of individual and aggregate behavior: a wealth of data to crunch, sort, and exploit in an effort to more effectively manage the marketing of news and the placement of advertising.

Users tend not to recognize just how much information they are relaying to various parts of the enclosure as they read their online newspapers, surf the Web, pay with debit cards, or carry their cell phones with them wherever they go. Instead, the devices do the work for them, quietly translating their actions into bits of information that flow upstream along the same channels and pipes that carry data, images, music, and e-mail to consumers. One result is that the promise of interactivity is quietly but systematically undergoing a downgrade that will require a lot less activity on the part of the user—and a lot more on the dispersed smart objects that will come to populate their lives.

The reason for the transformation is twofold: the work it would take to intentionally generate the quantities of detailed digital data anticipated by promoters of new media would be prohibitive—and it would draw attention to the degree of privacy surrendered by users immersed in an increasingly inquisitive environment. The invitation to interact is consequently being replaced by the invitation to immerse ourselves in a digital enclosure that takes on the burden of heightened interactivity for us. The promise of what Intel researchers call "proactive computing" is one not of frenetic interactivity—endless "talking back" to the media that surround us—but of a heightened form of passive interaction: the gathering of detailed information in an increasingly unobtrusive manner. Indeed, the goal of much of what is described as "ubiquitous computing" is to render interactivity itself invisible. This goal is to be achieved in part by inviting users to delegate many of their interactions to increasingly smart portable devices. According to the promoters of proactive computing, we won't have to remember details of conversations, directions, or scheduling, or even our own consumer preferences, because various smart devices will keep track of them for us. As one corporate futurist put it, "Society in the next 10 to 15 years will involve people being surrounded by electronic gadgets with ambient intelligence."[37] Similarly, ubiquitous-computing pioneer Mark Weiser predicted, "Over the next twenty years computers will inhabit the most trivial things: clothes labels (to track washing), coffee cups . . . light switches . . . and pencils."[38] Although this third stage of computer development remains in its infancy, some of its first traces have already started to emerge: portable networked devices, cars, and cell phones that know where they are, radiofrequency ID (RFID) tags that allow shelves to keep track of the products stored on them, even restaurant drinking glasses that notify nearby waiters that they need refilling.

Use It and Wear It

From the perspective of these emergent forms of ambient intelligence, un-wired humans will come across as singularly unintelligent, nonconversant, and incomprehensible. Once the external world becomes wired—overlaid with an interactive interface—individuals moving through it will need to be equipped with devices that can interact with a smart world, even if they remain oblivious to the electronic conversations taking place around and about them. Making users visible to the network and vice versa requires the development of a flexible, portable, and unobtrusive interface. Rather than adding yet another portable device to the growing quiver—cell phone, beeper, Palm Pilot, laptop—one solution is to endow those items that we take with us almost everywhere we go with an interactive capability. Hence the advent of so-called smart clothes, which, according to one account, will eventually "provide personalized information about the surrounding environment, such as the names of people you meet or directions to your next meeting, and can replace most computer and consumer electronics. The key idea is that because the room or the clothing knows something about what is going on, it can react intelligently."[39]

One of the paradigm shifts of this brave new world of proactive computing is away from the user model of interaction and toward a wearer-based model, according to researchers working on MIT's wearable computing project (dubbed MIThril, in reference to the magic armor worn by Frodo in *The Lord of the Rings*): "One might *use* a hammer or PDA, but a person *wears* a watch or a shirt; the watch and shirt are always functioning and require a minimum of the wearer's attention."[40] Integrating computing into every aspect of daily life means finding ways of making it less intrusive, more portable, and, as one group of researchers note, more intimate: "Underlying such a vision is the notion that computers in their many forms will be pervasive and anticipatory. Arguably, to achieve this, computing appliances will have to become more intimate, more knowing about who we are and what we desire, more woven into the fabric of our daily lives, and possibly woven into the fabric of our (cyber)bodies."[41]

Smart clothes revive in digital form the promise of the nineteenth-century bourgeois interior as "a space providing the illusion of individuality while protecting its inhabitants form the shocks of modern life. The domestic interior sustained the private fictions of control and subjective agency."[42] The appeal of the ability to carry one's casing with oneself is evidenced by the burgeoning popularity of the SUV, which, with its telephones, television, and stereo, is increasingly coming to resemble a cockpit of bourgeois interiority. Smart suits shrink the interior even further, allowing it to follow us out the door of the car and into the street.

Smart clothes promise to serve as the mobile cockpit for digital flaneurs, storing detailed records of the user's movements, preferences, encounters, purchases, and even vital signs. In a futuristic vision with somewhat disturbing overtones, smart clothing, thanks in large part to its proximity, will not only feed off of the energy generated by the body, it will also transform this energy into information: "The fabric itself will be woven from conductive fibres capable of generating electrical power from body heat or movement. Buttons and zippers will contain information-gathering sensors. Imagine a wedding dress that records all of the sights and sounds of the day, including that heart arrhythmia at the moment you say, 'I do.'"[43]

As they press close to the skin, smart clothes promise to offer a new range of biometrics that will likely make their way into demographic databases. Just as we now leave a trail of cookies on the Internet as we move about, perhaps one day we will leave a comprehensive inventory of our vital signs as we encounter advertisements and interactive entertainment, providing cybernetic feedback for further customization. If this sounds intrusive now, it is worth recalling how readily we have accepted forms of monitoring that would have seemed absurdly invasive only a short time ago: the ability, for example, of cell phone companies to keep track of our movements throughout the day, or of online marketers to map our online behavior. As in the case of these other forms of monitoring, biometric tracking will be portrayed as a means of enhancing and facilitating personal convenience through customization: "Would you like to have us discover music custom-tailored to your individual tastes and preferences? If so, wear this feedback headset, and we'll be able to find music that's guaranteed to please—or your money back." Marketing researchers are already pioneering the field of so-called neuromarketing: the ability to gauge consumer response to advertisements on the basis of their physiological responses.[44]

In addition to facilitating the advent of what Bill Gates once described as a "fully documented life," smart clothes will, so their promoters say, keep us on time for appointments, gather information about people we meet, and process this information to provide us with salient details, topics of conversation, and shared interests. As one enthusiastic press account puts it, "Clothing of the future will be smart, so smart it will organise your day. It'll take you jogging, massage your ego and even fix your love life."[45] One scenario envisions clothes that, with the aid of strategically timed chemical releases, would help shape the wearer's mood to fit the situation: "Smart-smelling clothes will sexually arouse you, boost your confidence at an interview or business meeting, enhance your appetite, uplift your mood, freshen you at work, wake you up or send you to sleep."[46] Moreover, clothes will undertake the chores with which they have become associated: "You will not need to wash them because they will self-wash, self-condition and repair themselves," according to Jennifer Tillotson of London's Sensory Design Lab.[47] Our portable casings, in short, will take on a hyperactive life of their own: they will serve not just as passive recorders but as active participants: digital butlers, as Negroponte puts it.[48] Indeed, their very activity will serve as a form of insulation from the data overload associated with the information society by taking on the increasingly intrusive and ubiquitous duties of interaction. In this respect, smart clothes fulfill the age-old function of clothing by serving as a protective layer to shelter us from the invisible data storm in which we are immersed.

At the same time, the technologically enhanced second skin that will one day serve as a mobile interface represents one site of a struggle over power, information, and control. On the one hand is the prospect of a customized digital servant that looks after the user. On the other is that of clothes that do the bidding not just of their wearers, but of their manufacturers: proprietary labels that, for example, allow clothing companies to track products even after their purchase. The future portrayed by Steven Spielberg in *Minority Report,* in which billboards direct customized appeals to shoppers on the basis of their past purchases, is not as far off as it might seem, at least according to the fashion futurists. According to one report, entrepreneurs at MIT working on the RFID tag–based Auto-ID project pitch it as an individualized form of real-time demographic data gathering: "One scenario will alert shopkeepers to wealthy individuals entering their store, calculating their net worth based on the tags hidden in their clothing, and comparing their type against a demographic database. Bus shelters and other public spaces might be fitted with RFID tag readers connected to display devices, which will pitch products at consumers based on their tags."[49] Instead of a world in which our clothes help us through the day, we are presented with one in which confederacies of smart objects murmur information to one another on inaudible frequencies as they conspire to sell us products. As one upbeat news story puts it, "desks and doors, TVs and telephones, cars and trains, eyeglasses and shoes, and even the shirts on our backs are changing from static, inanimate objects into adaptive, reactive systems that can be more friendly, useful, and efficient."[50]

In the vocal world of smart objects, clothes, which have long served as a visible signifying system and as an interface between the private and the public, may be delegated the additional task of providing an interactive second skin that allows users to navigate the information-rich world of the digital enclosure. The interactive interface might then be considered to be composed of two layers: that of the digital enclosure through which we move, and that of the portable networked devices we wear as we move through it. The promise of this interface is to make the entire external world a container that recognizes us in order to supply us with information and, in turn, to gather information about us. It is this projection of an interior world—a customized digital living room, as it were—outward onto the external world that is taken up in the following section.

Interiorizing the External World

If interactivity in the 1990s entailed a retreat into the stasis of a technologically enhanced interior, the goal of ubiquitous computing is to transform the whole world into such an interior. Computer guru Mark Weiser describes the 1990s as the era of "second-wave" computing—networked, but static. It is the era of the PC potato, cultivated by the ability of personal computers to introject the outside world into the privacy of one's home, thanks to the creation of broad ranging computer networks. It was a convenient world for the hermetic, Bill Gates–style geek, perhaps even more at ease with machines than people. Gates's 1995 futurist manifesto, *The Road Ahead*, is filled with examples of ways in which computers can displace human interaction and allow us to retreat into our technologically enhanced shells. Consider, for example, a Gates-inflected version of the videophone—a device that promised, perhaps, to make mediated communication more like face-to-face interaction. The Gates twist is to suggest that we could have our own images digitally replaced by whomever we wanted to look like—and our voices digitally altered as well. The result, rather than heightening a sense of interpersonal interaction, is to dissimulate it.[51]

As we find ourselves able to conduct more and more of our daily activities online, the need for real face-to-face interaction may drop precipitously: our computers could do our shopping and other chores, and we could work, surf the Internet, and "socialize" without leaving the privacy of home. Microsoft's advertising campaigns have exploited the double meaning of its flagship operating system's name, which refers not just to the multiple windows that characterize its graphical user interface, but to the notion that in the era of networked computing, each of these windows has the potential to open up a virtual vista of the external world. The networked user can roam the world from the privacy of home.

Perhaps the archetypical example of this version of interiority is provided by the case of a young man from Texas, who in 1999 decided that he would demonstrate the benefits of the Internet by moving into an unfurnished suburban home, not leaving for a year, and acquiring everything he needed from the outside world over the Internet. The man, who legally changed his name to DotComGuy, bought his groceries and his furniture online, courted a woman he met in an online chat room, hired a cleaning service online, and received his information from the world via the Internet and cable television.[52] He could even work from home, insofar as his "job" was to serve as an online advertisement for the services he used. His Web site featured an automatic camera that beamed images of his enclosure, surrounded by messages from sponsors, to others watching from the privacy of their homes and offices. This combination of interiorization and self-display is mirrored, as the following section argues, in the exterior world by mobile networked consumers who carry their network connections with them, leaving traces and gathering information as they interact with the world around them.

For DotComGuy, the computer screen served, among other things, as a technologically augmented version of the nineteenth-century window mirror described by the philosopher Theodor Adorno in his discussion of the bourgeois interior. The window mirror was a kind of rearview mirror for the urban apartment whose function was to "project the endless rows of apartment buildings into the isolated bourgeois living room. . . . The window mirror testifies to objectlessness—it casts into the apartment only the semblance of things—and isolated privacy."[53] The hermetic yet fully networked suburban home of DotComGuy rehearses and expands on this process of interiorization.

The Web surfer freed by physical immobility to roam virtual worlds recalls the image of the "promenades in the parlor" envisioned by philosopher Soren Kierkegaard's early writings, in which the pseudonymous character Johannes Climacus, forbidden to go outside, takes imaginary walks in the sitting room with his father: "As they now went up and down the hall, the father pointed out everything they saw; they greeted others passing by, cars noisily crossed their way, drowning out the father's voice; the cakes in the bakery window were more inviting than ever."[54] This conjunction of interiority with its apparent opposite—promenade and self-display—anticipates the DotComGuy fantasy: the ability to roam the world from the privacy and security of home.

It is easy to discern in such language the undertones of escapism. In the nineteenth century, the bourgeois interior was figured as a site of refuge for the privileged from the increasingly anonymous and alienated world of urban industrial capitalism.[55] Critic Walter Benjamin describes the interior as a form of protective armor, suggesting its kinship with the shell, a covering customized to fit its inhabitant: "The original form of all dwelling is existence not in the house but in the shell. The shell bears the impression of its inhabitant."[56]

More than a protective housing, the bourgeois interior compensates for the homogenous and anonymous character of industrialized mass production. If the home is a site free from the monitoring gaze of the factory, it is also a site of individuation and self-expression. The interior was the space within which individuals could make an impression—in which they could discern the traces they made upon their surroundings—traces formerly embedded directly in the idiosyncrasies of handicraft production, perhaps in the paths one wore through the fields, and in the impression made by each individual on the close-knit communities that came before mass society. Benjamin uses the image of the plush-lined case as a metaphor for the way in which the bourgeois interior recaptured this sense of individuation by molding itself to fit its inhabitant. As Benjamin puts it, "the bourgeois has shown a tendency to compensate for the absence of any trace of private life in the big city. He tries to do this within the four walls of his apartment. It is as if he had made it a point of honor not to allow the traces of his everyday objects and accessories to get lost."[57] The logical extension of the proliferation of "cases, receptacles, and coverings" was the conception of "the domestic interior as a whole in terms of an environment in which the individual himself might be contained"—and leave an impression.[58] At the limit, the apartment becomes, as Benjamin describes it, "a sort of cockpit" that takes the form of its inhabitant.[59]

If the bourgeois interior served as a refuge of the privileged from the alienated world of commerce and the reified fate of public life, its digital enhancement promises to perfect this form of refuge. The promise invoked is an old one; it is the solution that is new: replace the plush comfort of the nineteenth century with the silicon flexibility of the digital era. If, in other words, the alienated world is "out there," the promise on offer is that of an escape into DotComGuy's world of around-the-clock interiority—with a twist. Instead of confining oneself to a "DotCompound," as he described it, the promise of the digital enclosure is to transform the entire external world into an interior on which each occupant makes an impression and leaves a trace. In keeping with this vision of interiority, mobile commerce envisions a digital enclosure equipped with smart objects it describes as "street furniture"—billboards that recognize us, kiosks that provide us with customized news announcements. The move from second- to third-wave computing envisions this process of enclosure: the transformation of the physical world into a customizable interior with the ability to recognize the wired users passing through its electromagnetic ether, respiring information.

Digital Arcades

The fantasy of enclosing and domesticating the external world is not a new one and probably traces its roots back to that first perfect Edenic enclosure. In the era of industrial capitalism, it harkens back to the Paris shopping arcades studied by Benjamin—overarching structures of glass and steel designed to enclose a sidewalk shopping mall and provide it with the homey, cluttered feeling of the nineteenth-century bourgeois interior. As one commentator notes, "The construction of the arcade involves a particular alteration—or rather, inversion—of space; the street, that which is exterior to the building, became interiorized, was part of the building itself."[60] The arcades enlist the appeal of the bourgeois interior as a commercial strategy for transforming the streets into sites for consumption and commodification. As in the case of their descendants—suburban shopping malls—the arcades privatized public space, turning the entire street into a shop.

A smart landscape, populated with receptors for portable digital devices, conserves the promise of interiority described by Benjamin: users will be able to make an impression on their environment. It also conserves the promise of subsuming all physical space to the imperatives of a virtual marketplace. Thanks to the digital enclosure, we can shop anywhere. In this respect, the digital enclosure surpasses the arcades in scope and ambition: thanks to its flexible boundaries, mountaintops and rivers, forests and automobiles can double as sites of consumption. We can download sports scores to our cell phones wherever we happen to be; we can shop online in any space caught in the embrace of the wireless Web.

Read together, the models of the digital bourgeois interior (inhabited by DotComGuy) and the digital arcade trace the double movement of the impulse of interiorization: the attempt to domesticate the external world in the privacy of one's home or office and to extend the reach of a customized interior to encompass an increasing range and variety of spaces. Smart clothes straddle this double movement: they bring the world to users and help users domesticate and customize the objects through which they move. Thanks to the flexible wearable interface, the interior shrinks to the size of a portable shell and expands to fill the interactive landscape with which the suit communicates. The smart suit becomes the interface for an arcade not of iron and glass, but of electromagnetic radiation through which the wired consumer moves. This enclosure is perhaps one of many afterimages of the arcade, one that emerges contemporaneously with the decline of its twentieth-century descendants: urban shopping malls with their faux boulevards, park benches, and indoor foliage. With the help of portable wireless devices, the digital enclosure promises to succeed where its predecessors failed, encompassing the entirety of the external world.

The Paris arcades were not merely bourgeois interiors for parlor promenades sheltered from the elements; they were also shopping malls that comprised, according to Benjamin, "the original temple of commodity capitalism."[61] As commentator Graeme Gilloch puts it, "The arcade was also the ultimate 'theater of purchases,' the space where everything was to be bought and where one could buy everything."[62] The same might be said of the digital enclosure, which, although affording neither the material structure of the arcades nor protection from the elements, nevertheless constitutes an analogous process of interiority: the facilitation of commerce that is based on subsuming the object world to the universal medium of information exchange: the bit.

The digital enclosure is a virtual enclosure that promises not just the universalization of the space of consumption—allowing one to consume anywhere—but also the ability to render this space increasingly productive through the ongoing generation of information about consumer behavior. Looking backward, it is difficult not to discern the afterimage of a giant shopping arcade in Bill Gates's description of a networked world in which every digital interaction can be monitored, sorted, and commodified. [63] Thanks to the wireless embrace of interactive technology, no spaces and no activities are exempt. The external world is subsumed within and encompassed by the network. Similarly, the vegetal inertia of DotComGuy, confined to his house and yard and supplied with digital sustenance thanks to his Internet umbilicus, is prefigured in a quote about the Paris arcades cited by Benjamin: "I hear they want to roof all the streets in Paris with glass. That will make for lovely hothouses: we will live in them like melons."[64]

The development of smart clothes and smart objects is, according to the account outlined above, an economic one designed to facilitate the rationalization of both consumption and production. The enclosure promises not just efficiency and customization, but also the perfection of market research. The former serves as the alibi for the latter. To take up Benjamin's description of bourgeois interiority, the promise that we can make an impression, that our environment will recognize us (sending us coupons, perhaps, for a store we like that happens to be nearby), is a double-edged promise. It offers to provide us with information suited to meet our location, the time of day, and our tastes. At the same time, thanks to the interactive character of the enclosure, it gathers detailed information about our movements, our tastes, and our consumption habits. All of this is portrayed as information gathered in the name of serving consumers better. Indeed, it is thanks to the fact that the world of ubiquitous computing envisioned by corporate futurists is a privatized one that it skirts the specter of Big Brother. This isn't the government watching, we are told (although the government is currently tapping into corporate databases for policing purposes—more on this in Chapters 6 and 7); it's just companies that want to be able to serve us better.

Thus, the private sector tends to dismiss protests over the loss of privacy as little more than lip service to an outdated conception of privacy: complaints unlikely to deter consumption in the face of the lure of customization and convenience. Sun Microsystems CEO Scott McNealy once famously admonished those who raised privacy concerns with the observation that "you have no privacy, get over it"—and the public seemed inclined to heed his advice.[65] Much to the frustration of privacy advocates, consumers continue to embrace privacy-atrophying technologies like digital video recorders, portable GPS-equipped devices, and the commercialized Internet, shedding data as they go. Privacy, according to the promoters of e-commerce, may be relegated to the dustbin of modernity, an atavistic longing that impedes the conveniences associated with the brave new world of interactivity. After all, if one of its purposes was to clear a space of refuge for personal development and self-expression, the paradoxical promise of perpetual monitoring is to facilitate this process. Thanks to the detailed information made available within the digital enclosure, our needs and desires can be slavishly catered to: the anonymity of the external world for which the bourgeois interior once provided a compensatory space of refuge and recognition will itself be eradicated, or so the story goes. The alienated character of industrial production will be overcome by the promise of interactivity, which promises not just to dispense with the homogenous character of mass production, but to shatter the barrier that separated consumers from the production process. They will be able to recognize in the goods they consume the product of their own "labor": the imprint of their interactive participation in the production process itself. Should such labor come to seem burdensome, it can, in turn, be automated.

The sting of the loss of privacy will be assuaged, in this scenario, by the fact that it will be impersonal. We won't have to know, precisely, what type of information is being collected, and we won't have to do the work of generating it. In the world of ubiquitous computing, smart objects will communicate among themselves. To use the benign example outlined by MIT Media Lab guru Nicholas Negroponte, our alarm clock will check in with the computer to determine the weather (or the traffic) and wake us in time to make it to work. Smart objects will assist producers as well as consumers. In the *Alice in Wonderland* world of our digital future described by the promoters of a world populated by intelligent inventory, products will communicate information about their progress through the supply chain, notify stores when shelves need restocking, and cry thief when they are stolen. Technology promises to reanimate the world—this time with the intentionality of humans rather than that of the spirit world. Instead of river sprites and wood nymphs, we will have appliance animism: devices that talk to one another, buildings that recognize us, and rooms that adjust the climate, music, and lighting to fit our preferences—or perhaps to shape our moods (based on biometric feedback). Technology's demystification of the external world promises to infuse it with human intentionality. The result promises nevertheless to remain uncanny: the literalization of an omniscient, networked other that monitors our actions and registers them in a unified database of databases.

The purported advantage for humans is that they will be able to delegate much of the grunt work of daily life to smart objects, including not just errands and busy work, but also the tasks of remembering directions, names, and perhaps faces. Researchers at MIT, for example, are working on smart glasses that will recognize people and places and provide subliminal cues to the user about how to respond: "The computer could be programmed, for example, to remind the wearer of topics to discuss when he bumps into someone with whom he has unfinished business. Or to remind a doctor of medical procedures at the operating table. Or flash a list of desired movies upon entering a video store."[66] What emerges is an image of a world in which objects take on an uncanny alacrity, increasingly usurping the active role from the humans they ostensibly serve. Within the digital enclosure, we will be able to embrace the hothouse inertia of melons in the global greenhouse.

By contrast, the digital devices we rely on will become not just interactive but hyperactive. If, as one newspaper headline put it, the new generation of ultralightweight wireless interactive ID tags will eventually make products "talk," a privileged topic of their discussion is likely to be detailed information about consumers.[67] RFID tags are being miniaturized to the point that they can be incorporated into clothing without being noticeable to consumers. RFID tags, touted as the wireless version of universal product codes, are more versatile and more specific than bar codes. Their versatility lies in their ability to be scanned by radiofrequency, which means that they don't have to be visibly exposed to be read. A tag in a wallet or on a shirt label could be read by a nearby scanner. Unlike bar codes, the RFID tag would specify not just the general type of item—a pair of jeans, for example—but the individual product.

As a form of identification, RFID technology promises to reindividualize mass-produced products so that each one, if not unique in appearance, becomes uniquely identifiable. The implications for monitoring and marketing are significant: the space-time path of an RFID-equipped item can be individually traced, and a particular purchase can be linked with a uniquely identifiable item rather than just a product class. In other words, marketers will know much more than the fact that someone bought a pair of Levi's boot-cut jeans; they will know precisely which pair of jeans was bought, when, and where. Conceivably the pair of jeans could be tracked even after purchase. As long as the RFID tag remains "live," it is readable by the scanners that will presumably be placed in stores and shopping malls. As one critical commentator notes, "As an extra added bonus, when shoppers take their Big Brother–branded purchases home (and wherever RFID 'readers' are located) their purchase will be tracked."[68] A slightly more upbeat article focuses on the possibilities for consumers: "Imagine tiny chips that emit radio waves embedded in clothing, food packaging or your wallet to broadcast information about what you have and what you may want."[69] In the digital future, technologically augmented humans may not recognize us, but the store itself will—along with the cash register and the products on the shelves that cry out to us. This recognition is portrayed by the promoters of e-commerce as a recuperation of the lost intimacy of traditional society: thanks to the new technology, we can enter a space in which everything—if not everyone—knows our name.

In the interactive world of smart clothes and the objects with which they commune, wired consumers will carry their demographic information on their sleeve, as it were, to be read by any scanner with the appropriate technology. The staggering quantities of data that the digital enclosure could potentially generate might be considered the mother lode of the data mine: abundant raw material for managing consumption and production in the information society. Wired consumers participate in the generation of this information just by going about their daily activities within the monitored space of the digital enclosure. The promise of individuation—of the ability to "make an impression"—serves as an incitement to productive self-disclosure, a technique for differentiating and specifying consumer attributes by multiplying the categories of available information and pursuing them with increasing tenacity and exactitude.

Pathologies of the Enclosure: Surveillance, Sorting, and Privacy

The extension of a digital enclosure offers to extend the embrace of interactivity and thereby to redouble the productivity of mobility. It is perhaps not surprising that the ongoing development of the wireless Internet coincides with a new benchmark of mobile privatization: as of September 2003, the United States reached the point at which the number of working cars in the country surpassed that of legal drivers. Far from abandoning the crowded roadways and retreating to the wired privacy of their networked homes, people equipped with cell phones, laptops, portable DVD players, and iPods, are going mobile at unprecedented levels.[70] If the appeal of the PC world was that of accessing the world from the privacy of home, that of pervasive interactivity—what its promoters call *ubicomp* (ubiquitous computing)—is of being at home wherever one happens to be.

Feeling at home in the digital enclosure is a luxury available to a particular group: those with the resources to view the enclosure as a friendly—rather than a claustrophobically oppressive—one. The consumption of space as a means of individuation is, in general, a form of consumption limited to affluent groups (as is the promise of individuation through the consumption of customized goods and services). As the British media scholar David Morley has observed, the mobility of affluent classes is "quite different from the mobility of the international refugee or the unemployed migrant as a social experience."[71] Such mobility stands in stark contrast to the immobility of groups unable to relocate from regions of poverty, famine, and warfare, or from the tightly monitored and controlled mobility of migrant workers.

The vast discrepancies in wealth that characterize the contemporary global economy are reflected in dramatically different levels of access to the means of mobility. The consumption of space by affluent groups becomes one more form of conspicuous consumption. The bourgeoisie have endowed themselves with what might be described, with a nod to French theorist Michel Foucault, as a "garrulous mobility," one that permeates the ads for cell phones, cruise lines, and sports utility vehicles. Just as there is what might be described as a bourgeois form of monitored mobility (advertised as a means of individuation and self-expression), there are also class mobilities associated with very different forms of surveillance. Economically disadvantaged groups are subjected to surveillance in the form of policing and exclusion, whereas wealthy groups are increasingly subject to productive forms of surveillance: they are monitored in order to be provided with individualized goods and services.

The law enforcement correlative to consumer monitoring, especially in the recently terrorism-conscious United States, is what sociologist Gary Marx has described as categorical suspicion. Monitoring is not limited to particular suspects but is extended to broad categories—indeed, at the limit to the entire populace: everyone is a potential suspect.[72] Of late, the spatial component of this type of monitoring has been developed as a technique to permit the automated recognition of criminal activity: computers are programmed to recognize, in their monitoring of a particular space, interaction patterns associated with criminal activity, and then to draw those interactions to the attention of human monitors.[73] Benjamin noted the crucial difference between those who find themselves at home in the street, and those who are forced to make the street their home. A similar distinction might be made in the digital enclosure between those for whom interactivity means the delivery of customized goods and services and those for whom it means subjection to inescapable forms of disciplinary monitoring and sorting: the difference between the Palm Pilot and the electronic tether. It may be fashionable to joke that the former is only a version of the latter, but to do so is to overlook very real differences in access to and control over economic, legal, and social resources. At the same time, it is worth pointing out that even elite groups will find themselves increasingly the targets of workplace and commercial monitoring in which function creep is inevitable: details revealed in one context will be available for other uses, including marketing and policing.

From a policing perspective, the digital enclosure offers new dimensions of data gathering and sorting. The intersection of spatiotemporal paths can be treated as hieroglyphic representations to sort and flag social interactions. The goal is to automate the monitoring process by endowing cameras with a form of intelligence: the ability to pick out patterns of action or behavior deemed suspicious. The automation of surveillance reduces the need for human monitoring and eliminates the uncertainty associated with generalized surveillance. If we don't have enough people to monitor the surveillance cameras, the work of watching can be delegated and automated. But this means equipping cameras with algorithms that define behaviors associated with "normal"—nonthreatening or noncriminal—behavior and imposing these norms on individuals. Failure to adhere to these norms may trigger sanctions and more intrusive forms of monitoring, such as police visits for follow-up investigations. Both commercial and police monitoring will build pattern-recognition databases designed to reduce uncertainty in targeting consumers and criminals alike. Technology promises to eliminate any slack in surveillance systems.

The commercial analogue is the elimination of the slack of consumer surplus: the ability of consumers to pay less than they might have been willing to pay for a particular product. The goal of mass customization based on interactively generated demographic information is to disaggregate the demand curve, or to put it another way, to get rid of standardized unitary pricing. Prices may well be customized along with products to meet the profile of the consumer, including the size of his or her bank account.

From an economic perspective, the Internet as we currently know it is overflowing with slack. In many respects, it operates according to an old-economy model: a relatively uniform price for access, regardless of how much you use it. Thus someone who spends eight hours a day online, sends scores of e-mail, and shares hundreds of files might pay the same monthly fee as someone who checks his or her e-mail for a half an hour a day and shops online every few weeks. Not for long, if those who control the pipes through which the information travels have their way. As one news account describes it, "Verizon, Comcast, Bell South and other communications giants are developing strategies that would track and store information on our every move in cyberspace in a vast data-collection and marketing system, the scope of which could rival the National Security Agency."[74] The goal is not just to gather detailed information about users for marketing purposes, but to use this information to customize both services and pricing. Instead of people paying one set rate regardless of their online activity, users might be charged on the basis of the number of e-mails they send, the number of files they download, and so on: "Industry planners are mulling new subscription plans that would further limit the online experience, establishing 'platinum,' 'gold,' and 'silver' levels of Internet access that would set limits on the number of downloads, media streams or even e-mail messages that could be sent or received."[75]

A smart network will be able to read files that traverse it, sorting and discriminating between forms of information, spiking illegal files, slowing down those files that are considered to be low priority (perhaps because they're going to lower-tier, low-paying clients), and expediting those sent by premium clients. In short, the network—previously open and nondiscriminatory—will be formally subsumed to the logic of the market. As the cost of monitoring and sorting information drops precipitously, thanks to the ease with which files can be tagged and read as they pass through the network, the level of monitoring and sorting will increase dramatically. Networks will keep detailed accounts of what type of information we access and send over the network, where and when the information is sent, and where and when it is retrieved. Imagine a mail service that gathered information about every packet sent (its type, its size, and its cost), recorded it, and created a database that included every package we've received—as well as when and where we opened it—and every postcard we've sent—along with when and where we sent it.

An obvious consequence is the restriction of the free flow of information online—and the sorting of users into groups with varying degrees of access to online information and services. If the Internet of the late 1990s was a relatively open architecture in which information could travel relatively freely, the digital enclosure envisioned by the cable and phone companies is a tightly closed one. It is entirely possible that the network structure envisioned by the developers of the digital enclosure will take a wide pendulum swing from an almost unimaginable degree of freedom to an equally extreme degree of control.

Information control means not only the ability to charge for varying types of service and information—to extract a payment for every microtransaction—but also the ability to sort and segregate information. A smart network, combined with a wireless digital enclosure populated by smart objects and the clothes with which they interact, will make possible hitherto unprecedented levels of what communication scholar Oscar Gandy has described as social sorting: discrimination in the distribution of information and access to goods and services.[76] The emerging digital enclosure continues to foster the growth of what Gandy describes as "a cadre of professionals whose very existence is based upon the ability to draw finer and finer distinctions between segments of the public."[77] Part of the job of this cadre will be to decide who has access to what kind of information—in the form of advertising and special offers—and what kind of services, including financial services such as loans. This type of "weblining," as Gandy calls it, enables discrimination practices that are more opaque and harder to target because the decisions are made according to complex algorithms that may disguise the role that, for example, race plays as a basis for discrimination.

Given the potential scope and depth of the digital enclosure, it is worth pointing out that there is no easily discernible limit to just how much information marketers might seek to collect. In a society in which every realm of life, from the most intimate to the most public, from the exceptional to the mundane, is colonized by consumerism, it is hard to rule out any aspect of the life as not being of interest to marketers. Just consider the range of products that cater to people's sex lives, from birth control technologies to STD medications and performance-enhancing drugs and devices. We are already inundated by the mass media with ads for all of these products. It is worth raising some concerns about how such marketing will take place within a digital enclosure.

Mass advertising (like mass politics) accords a degree of anonymity to the "general public" toward whom advertising appeals are directed. The promise of mass customization, by contrast, shatters this anonymity: messages can be addressed not just to particular groups or subcultures but to specific individuals. The implications for the marketing of certain types of products—from medical remedies to self-help books—are at best unsettling. It's one thing, for example, to encounter a general ad for products to treat impotence or a sexually transmitted disease, and quite another to encounter a personalized ad for the same products—perhaps one that integrates a variety of personal details culled from related databases: dating history, recent weight changes, divorce records—perhaps even medical information. Medical records are, of course, protected, but the fact that someone may have visited several sites (or a clinic) devoted to a particular disease, may have sought online advice, or visited a chat room or online support group are not.

For the most part, consumers seem to be making their peace with the rather dramatic increase in consumer monitoring in recent years, encompassing everything from clickstream monitoring by companies like Double-Click to Gmail's use of the contents of e-mail messages to target advertising. Indeed, the Gmail model might be considered a significant example of the direction in which the digital enclosure is headed. Bucking the trend of limiting the size of ostensibly free e-mail sites, Gmail's innovation was to invite users to store as much information as possible on Google's computers. Google's wager is that by inverting the model of free e-mail—expanding it rather than limiting it—it can realize a payoff that is based on its enclosure of personal information. The company's attempt to shift networked personal computing back to the server-client model of the early days of the Internet is predicated on the logic of digital enclosure. To the extent that Google becomes a storehouse for all of our personal correspondence, for archives of our online chats, perhaps even to the contents of our hard drives through its search tool, it can use this information to more efficiently and effectively customize marketing appeals for goods and services.

The Gmail project remains one of Google's most daring and innovative strategies: turning over relatively large chunks of storage space in the hopes that data-mining technology will eventually be able to sort through and make profitable use of the detailed demographic information that can be gleaned from the content with which users entrust it. Gmail lays out the details of this arrangement in its terms of service agreement: "As consideration for using the Service, you agree and understand that Google will display ads and other information adjacent to and related to the content of your email."[78] The company stresses that the search process is "completely automated"—as if this is enough to assure our privacy. The hope is that users will feel that their privacy is protected as long as the "eyes" going through their personal e-mail aren't human. It is, in some ways, a quaint and perhaps slightly disingenuous interpretation of what privacy means: that what really bothers us is the thought of a stranger's gaze falling on private letters and our concern over the illicit pleasure that someone else might gain from peeping into the private corners of our life. The assumption appears to be that as long as these details are registered by a mechanical gaze and stored not in any individual's memory but in a rapidly expanding database, users will feel comfortable and protected. In other words, what people know somehow counts, but what a machine knows doesn't, because, after all, machines don't have the power to really know anything.

In reality, as anyone who has applied for a bank loan or a credit card, who has attempted to renew a driver's license, or who has undergone a background check knows, what machines know counts for quite a bit in contemporary society. To the extent that, as Gandy argues, providers of goods and services use databases to sort consumers, Google is developing a tool for increasingly fine-grained forms of discrimination. The company's privacy agreement stipulates that personally identifiable information will remain protected—that is, that the link between personal data and personalized ad will remain an anonymous and automated one. If a user happens to mention a sexually transmitted disease in an e-mail message, for example, and then receives an ad for treatment in a subsequent message, the company that paid for the ad won't necessarily know the circumstances of why an ad was placed or who received it. The message seems to be, as long as the machines are doing the snooping and sorting, questions of privacy can be sidestepped. Human recognition is portrayed as the threshold condition for a loss of anonymity or privacy.

This is a misleading threshold, not just in light of the fact that humans who control the databases are likely to have ready access to their contents but also with respect to the role of function creep in the information age. Consider, for example, the errant spouse who learns that the device that allows rapid passage through highway toll stations can be used in divorce proceedings to track his or her whereabouts.[79] Information gathered benignly for one purpose can be readily retrieved for another. Even if it is only a machine that registers the information, it can migrate into more sentient hands, or can be used, automatically, for invasive and manipulative forms of marketing. Google, like other Web sites, reserves the right to change its privacy policies—the binding character of which remains in question—and once they've got a complete archive of personal correspondence and information, even if an account is canceled, the information is warehoused. Moreover, Google concedes that the information it stores can be disclosed to law enforcement authorities pursuant to subpoena. Information initially gathered for marketing purposes can do double duty as legal evidence. At a time when the president of the United States has made it clear that he and his legal advisors do not have any qualms about bypassing congressionally mandated legal protections against surveillance, there is little doubt that databases—including those amassed by Google—will come to be perceived as temptingly rich veins of information for legal data mining.

In closing, it is perhaps worth noting that as the digital enclosure develops, the forms of target marketing that once seemed relatively benign—a suggestion by Amazon.com regarding a new book, for example—might start to become a bit more disconcerting. As increasingly detailed databases merge and recombine, we may find ourselves facing much more sophisticated and personalized forms of customization—products and services targeted not only on the basis of past preferences, but on the basis of increasingly high-resolution data portraits that combine details about our personal lives with demographic, psychographic, and biometric information. Will those who currently adopt a sanguine attitude toward proliferating consumer surveillance finally find cause for concern when they learn that details of their love lives, combined with their Web surfing habits, the size of the clothes they buy, the terms they've entered in search engines, the places they've traveled, and their daily commuting habits are used in combination not just to inform them about products, but to manipulate them on the basis of anxieties and insecurities as well as hopes and fantasies?

Marketers are likely not going to be abrasive enough to say things like, "We notice that you are recently divorced, that your waist has increased 10 inches, that you've signed up for a dating site, and that you have been pricing Rogaine online. Face it—you need a makeover and hair replacement surgery." But one can perhaps imagine more subtle strategies based on targeting consumers during times of vulnerability and anxiety with calculated advertising appeals. At what point does the amount of information available to advertisers constitute a form of power over consumers, especially in a context wherein consumers have very little knowledge about what information marketers have and how they are using it? This might be considered an empirical question. Will consumers start to perceive marketing both as a form of intrusion and as unfair leverage when products are priced according to information about past purchasing patterns and individual wealth? What about when advertisers start to use biometric information to determine when consumers might be most inclined to respond to an advertising appeal?

The question of power is more than merely a question of attitudes and expectations; it is also an issue of asymmetrical access to information resources, databases, and processing power. Finally, it is an issue of control over the benefits that accrue to the use of information consumers generate about themselves. As in the case of the land enclosure movement, within the digital enclosure, those who control the resources—in this case, information-gathering technologies and databases—can lay claim to the value generated by those who enter "freely" into the enclosure. The use of scare quotes to qualify the notion of free entry is meant to indicate that when submission to monitoring becomes a condition of access not just to work, but to goods and services (from food to telephony), relations of unequal access to and control over resources structure the terms of entry. When, for example, all stores implement forms of electronic surveillance and payment, the "freedom" to avoid monitoring becomes, in practice, a largely theoretical one. Consumers will be free not to divulge information about themselves—as long as they don't buy anything. The proliferation of monitoring technologies will likely be accompanied by technologies that are designed to ensure anonymity and that are available to those with the knowledge and resources to obtain them. Opting out will come at a cost in terms of both convenience and cash, and monitoring technologies are likely to continue to outstrip anonymizing technologies.

In short, the forms of recognition and interactivity that take place within the digital enclosure are shaped by asymmetrical power relations. As this enclosure is currently envisioned, it will represent a privatized overlay upon public and private spaces alike: our cell phone companies, for example, will be able to track our locations whether we are at home, at work, or flying down the freeway at midnight. In its abstract form, a digital enclosure describes a space of universalized recognition and communication in which the places through which we move and the objects they contain recognize individuals and communicate with them (via portable devices). It is a space within which cars know their location and can rapidly access information about their surroundings, in which supermarket shelves know when they need to be stocked and when they are being approached by someone likely to buy a particular product. In more concrete terms, the enclosure is being built to serve particular ends: the facilitation of commerce and policing.

For the most part, the infrastructure of the digital enclosure is a privatized, commercial one fueled by large investments in third-generation wireless technology and ubiquitous computing. According to the chief of research at computer-chip manufacturer Intel, the company is devoting most of its $4 billion annual research and development budget to products that anticipate the advent of an era of ubiquitous and "proactive" computing.[80] In South Korea, a consortium of private developers in partnership with the tech company LG CNS plans to raise $25 billion to build New Songdo City—the first comprehensive urban digital enclosure in which wireless computing will be ubiquitous.[81] In the United States and Western Europe, mobile telephone companies are spending billions of dollars to develop third-generation wireless networks that will enable cell phones to serve as mobile Internet connections and data storage devices. As in the case of some of the most ambitious physical enclosures of the twentieth century, including the giant shopping malls, the digital enclosure will be a commercial one. The universal, convergent medium of the binary digit—the *bit*—underwrites that of the marketplace: a dematerialized digital currency that can flow faster than the real thing.

Within a commercial enclosure, interactivity is shaped by commercial imperatives and their resulting asymmetries: consumers will become increasingly transparent to marketers even as the algorithms used to sort, target, and exclude them become increasingly complex and opaque. The privatization of the network allows for the enclosure of personal information gathered not just in public and commercial spaces, but in the privacy of one's home. In this respect, the digitization of the enclosure doesn't merely de-differentiate the public from the private. In so doing, it favors commercial information gathering over the protection of personal privacy. It allows, in other words, for the privatization of public space to broaden its reach even as it reprivatizes personal information as commercial property. The result is not the end of privacy but rather its repurposing in commercial form. As we search the Internet from home, download information to our mobile phones, and so on, we generate information that becomes both the property of information intermediaries and the raw material of demographic databases for mining, sorting, and sale to third parties.

Thus, the model of commercial interactivity falls short of the promise of power sharing and hierarchy leveling. If, as marketers like to observe, customization technologies help recapture the lost element of personal knowledge associated with traditional, preindustrial society, they do so only partially. Retail outlets may be able to "recognize" their millions of consumers just as shopkeepers of yore did, greeting them by name and recalling their tastes and preferences, but the relationship will not be mutual. Consumers will find themselves interacting not with a well-known local shopkeeper but with a sprawling and opaque database, mediated, at times, by anonymous low-paid workers.

Famously, it is the corporate, mass-produced big-box chain of Wal-Mart that has compiled the largest consumer database in the world—the chain responsible not for the resuscitation of the local mom-and-pop store, but for its obliteration. Within the digital enclosure, the accumulation of detailed information about consumers requires the automation and autonomization of the monitoring process. The result is a fundamental asymmetry: the value of increasingly detailed, centralized information about consumers is predicated on the exclusive character of this information—the fact that not everyone knows it. The model of interactivity on offer is not one of power sharing, but of submission to productive forms of monitoring and surveillance. We are invited by the promise of interactivity to participate in marketing and—from a state perspective—policing ourselves.

iMedia

The Case of Interactive TV

Since focus groups aren't the real world, they're working damn hard to make the real world a focus group.

—Carrie McLaren

The new media trend story of the post-Napster era was, arguably, the widespread embrace by wired youth of social networking sites like Friendster, Facebook (for college students), and MySpace. These sites might be considered the Internet embodiment of Webcam diva Ana Voog's breathless anticipation of the day when "everyone has their own TV show." Thanks to digital cameras, MP3s, and the spread of Internet and computer literacy, the social networking promise seems to be that everyone can become a multimedia publisher. The result, so far, hasn't been the virtual reconstruction of the eighteenth-century coffeehouses hinted at by Web futurists like bloggers Andrew Sullivan ("blogs . . . seize the means of production") or Rebecca Blood: a world in which the Internet revives a participatory public by continuing public conversation "by other means."[1] The result might better be described as the democratization of publicity as self-promotion. The German philosopher Jürgen Habermas has documented the shifting role of the public sphere associated with what he describes as "refeudalization": the relegation of members of the public to the role of observers of the spectacle of power—a spectacle framed by the mass media in the form of pundits, celebrities, and political elites. In an era of refeudalization, the financial interests of mass media industries militate against holding political and economic elites publicly accountable. Instead, media organizations serve as publicity vehicles for the rich and powerful—one-way bullhorns amplifying the spin concocted by the few for the consumption of the many. As Habermas points out, the changing associations of the word *publicity* embody the shift from a society predicated on public scrutiny of government decisions to one in which publicity has become a synonym for public relations.

One result is that providing the public with access to the publication process (through, for example, the interactive capability of the Internet) has resulted in the generalized embrace of "publicity as public relations" as a model for the online presentation of self. Instead of a revitalized public sphere in the Habermasian sense, the interactive ethos privileging self-promotion and self-marketing: widespread access to the machinery of publicity and public relations. In the reality TV and Webcam "revolutions," self-presentation as a form of self-commodification coincides with self-expression through participation in customized marketing and advertising. Driving this point home, one researcher describes the way in which young people are using social networking sites as "egocasting, the thoroughly personalized and extremely narrow pursuit of one's personal taste . . . people who use networks like Facebook have a tendency to describe themselves like products."[2] It turns out that the so-called discussion groups that university students create at Facebook look "a lot like direct mailing lists"—and seem to do very little in the way of promoting or facilitating actual discussion. Some of these groups are "barely distinguishable from mailing lists compiled in *The Lifestyle Market Analyst,* a reference book that looks at potential audiences for advertisers."[3] Researcher Christine Rosen has noted the irony of the fact "that the technologies we embrace and praise for the degree of control they give us individually also give marketers and advertisers the most direct window into our psyche and buying habits they've ever had."[4] The social networkers' apparent identification of the marketing process as a form of self-expression recalls the impulse for recognition described in the previous chapter—an attempt to make one's impression on the cultural landscape, even if this means little more than receiving customized products and advertising.

Critic Walter Benjamin's description of the "empathy" for the commodity experienced by the nineteenth-century flaneur represents the prehistory of interactivity as a form of identification with the marketing process.[5] Just as the flaneur expresses this sense of identification not just through an "empathy with inorganic things," but also by identifying with the process of self-display itself, the online flaneur engages in the process of promoting his or her own image—even if that means "advertising" oneself online, as in the case, for example, of Internet dating and social networking sites. Undoubtedly some Silicon Valley startup has already proposed a business plan based on mining information from social networking sites, as sites like MySpace are already doing. Moreover, as a flurry of popular media coverage has noted, social networking technologies allow commercial and state authorities (employers and the police) to check individuals' backgrounds. Online self-expression, it turns out, provides a rich vein of information for data miners. Interactive self-disclosure is productive to the extent that the information it generates can be collected, aggregated, sorted, and retrieved for a range of managerial purposes that span the realm of commerce, politics, and even (as we shall see in the following chapter) homeland security.

The productive character of the promise of interactivity within a commercial context is taken up in this chapter, which previews the impending era of interactive media through an exploration of one precursor form: the fan-feedback Web site. The goal of the detailed case study offered in this chapter is not to provide a comprehensive overview so much as it is to offer some suggestive insights into the uses of convergence. The relatively narrow focus on one popular online fan site allows for a consideration of the ways in which interactivity can be enlisted by producers as a form of instant feedback—a free online focus group, as it were—as well as a marketing tool and an invitation for viewers to identify with the imperatives of producers. As the example of social networking sites suggests, such forms of identification aren't limited to online fan sites, and the intention of the chapter is to identify patterns that have more general applicability, in particular the exploitation of the promise of interactivity as a technique for encouraging viewers and consumers to participate in the process not just of marketing themselves (as in the case of online dating sites and social networking sites), but of marketing *to* themselves.

In this respect, my treatment of the online fan community discussed below might be considered the obverse of some of the more celebratory descriptions of fan activity in the cultural studies literature, in particular, for example, those influenced by the work of Henry Jenkins, who has described the members of fan communities as "readers who appropriate popular texts and reread them in a fashion that serves different interests, as spectators who transform the experience of watching television into a rich and complex participatory culture."[6] My intent is not to diminish either the complexity or pleasure that results from viewer participation in online sites like the one I consider in this chapter. Rather it is to explore the ways in which the work that gets done by participatory viewers within the digital enclosure serves the interests of producers. That is, my intent is to consider the ways in which the promise of interactivity doubles as a means of capitalizing on this work, much of which is significantly more creative and interesting than the raw material from which it is crafted.

As I write these chapters, I often stumble across marketing strategies that further develop the tendencies to which I'm attempting to draw attention. One case in point is the USA Network's social networking site, "ShowUsYour-Character.com," introduced in 2006. Designed as a cross-platform marketing tool, the site invites viewers to upload original, humorous, and eye-catching videos and photos as part of a competition to select online "characters" to be featured in USA-sponsored online Webcasts. A marketing executive for the network described the "grass-roots" competition as an "incubator for great new characters to live on air."[7]

Within the digital enclosure, producers avail themselves of the productivity of viewers, and the promise of interactivity is deployed as a means of encouraging and facilitating their efforts. Mediated interactivity, we are told by its promoters, is a way of recapturing a lost, more participatory past by moving ahead into an era in which viewers can talk back to the TV—and actually be heard. As training wheels for the coming era of interactivity, many television shows have created official Web sites, and some incorporate the comments of online fans, who are encouraged to e-mail comments and requests while they watch. Similarly, reality game shows invite viewers to vote for their favorite contestants via text messaging and offer online contests to build viewer loyalty between shows. Such developments deploy the umbrella promise of interactivity: that new media will challenge the passive forms of media consumption associated with mass society. Consider, for example, the description by the creator of the spy show *Alias* of online fan sites as an "integral part" of the production process: "If the Internet is your audience, TV is quite like a play. . . . Movies are a done deal—there's no give and take—but in a play, you listen to the applause, the missing laughs, the boos. It's the same with the Internet. If you ignore that sort of response, you probably shouldn't be working in TV right now."[8] In an era in which the mass audience is becoming increasingly visible thanks to a variety of sophisticated monitoring technologies, viewers are also increasingly encouraged to climb out of the couch to embrace a more active approach to their viewing experience. One result is an evolving culture of online fandom, which relies on the Internet to unite far-flung viewers in ongoing discussion and critique of an increasing number of television shows.

For producers, such fan sites can serve as an impromptu focus group, providing instant feedback to plot twists and the introduction of new characters even as it helps imbue the show with the kind of "stickiness" coveted by Web site owners through the creation of an online community of sorts as an added component of the show. As a *New York Times* article about online fan sites notes, "It is now standard Hollywood practice for executive producers (known in trade argot as 'show runners') to scurry into Web groups moments after an episode is shown on the East Coast. Sure, a good review in the print media is important, but the boards, by definition, are populated by a program's core audience—many thousands of viewers who care deeply about what direction their show takes."[9]

As in the case of the interactive economy more generally, viewer feedback promises to become increasingly integrated into the production process in a cybernetic cycle that offers to reduce uncertainty and, at least according to the marketing industry, increase customer satisfaction. Indeed, many of those who visit the online site Television Without Pity (TWoP), which includes forums devoted to some three dozen shows, are convinced that their feedback has had some sort of impact on writers or producers. The Web site is one of the more prominent, smart, and professional viewer-oriented sites, and it has received a fair amount of media coverage and industry recognition—enough to suggest to participants that producers might be listening. One respondent to my online survey of TWoP participants commented, "The decision makers can come and see what specifically the audience liked and disliked about the way they handled various things, and why . . . which, if they choose to pay attention, can help them to improve their work." Although the site, as its name suggests, encourages critical, "snarkastic" commentary, many of those who post do so in this spirit, adopting the viewpoint of assistants who can help producers and writers do their job better by providing detailed commentary not just on plot development, but also on technical aspects of the show, including continuity, wardrobe, and makeup. The recappers, who are hired by TWoP to craft lengthy, detailed, and humorous summaries of the shows, often focus on production details, including lighting and editing, thereby helping direct the attention to the formal aspects of the shows they describe.

The result is the merging of two forms of audience participation: the effort viewers put into making the show interesting to themselves, and the effort they devote to taking on the role of production assistants and attempting to provide feedback to writers and producers. Part of the entertainment value of a site like TWoP, in other words, relies on the implicit promise to erode the boundaries between the sites of passive consumption and those of sequestered power over media production—what Nick Couldry has called the "place of media power."[10] If interactive technologies help de-differentiate sites of consumption and production in the contemporary era, according to this promise, they also pose a challenge to the boundaries that reinforce the concentration of control in the hands of the few.

In keeping with the celebratory predictions of those who champion the democratizing potential of new media, respondents to an online survey I posted to TWoP overwhelmingly agreed with the assertion that online fan sites will make TV producers more accountable to viewers.[11] One respondent wrote, "I think producers/writers etc. would be well served to see what their 'constituents' want. TV should be more viewer-driven and I think TWoP is a foundation for a movement toward that."

The promise of accountability seems to cut both ways: if TWoP provides producers with direct and immediate access to the viewpoints of the audience, it also fosters identification on the part of audiences with the viewpoint of producers. Market and production imperatives like show promotion, mass audience appeal, and technical details are taken up in depth by TWoP participants who, in missives directed to producers, suggest ways to more effectively tailor a particular show to a specific set of viewers.

At the same time, TWoP posters, who pride themselves on their savviness, can be quite cynical about the prospect of shared control, or even the willingness of producers to pay attention to fan feedback. Several survey respondents noted that producers view Internet fans as mildly obsessed cranks representing the geek fringe of a show's audience. This perception was underscored by an infamous incident in TWoP lore: the fallout from a visit to the forums by producer Aaron Sorkin, creator of the popular show *The West Wing*. After a heated online exchange with critical fans, Sorkin scripted an episode that, according to a *New York Times* account, portrayed "hard-core Internet users as obese shut-ins who lounge around in muumuus and chain-smoke Parliaments."[12] The incident was taken as a sign that the producers were, at the very least, paying attention, and TWoPpers are perpetually on the lookout for other "shout outs" that refer directly or indirectly to TWoP. The recapper for a show on the WB Network called *Popular* noted, for example, that in a backhanded gesture of recognition for his praise of the show, the writers named a character after him: a junkie who was killed in a car accident. He also received e-mail from cast members who reportedly told him that the show's executive producer, in an effort to find something positive written about the show, printed out his recaps and distributed them to the cast and crew. As he put it, "That was weird because all of a sudden we weren't students sitting around snarking on shows anymore. We were a focus group whose comments were heard by the executive brass." Other shout outs included the use of one recapper's name by the writers for NBC's *Ed* and the appearance of the TWoP logo on a bag in an episode of *Once and Again*. However, the line between real and perceived impact is not always clear. Fans and recappers have a tendency to interpret changes in the show that seem to be direct responses to online criticism as having been prompted, at least in part, by their comments.

The embrace of interactive sites and the marketing power of online communities by producers do not go unacknowledged by posters, some of whom expressed concern that fan sites might be reduced to one more marketing strategy. As one poster put it, "the majority of producers/execs either fear the internet community or feel that if they try hard enough, they can manipulate it right back." However, direct manipulation by producers isn't necessary to make even an often critical site like TWoP an effective form of promotion. About a third of those who responded to my online survey indicated that they watched more television because of TWoP, and a large majority said that the site made television more entertaining to watch. Indeed, it is the collective effort of viewers to enlist the Internet to enhance the entertainment value of their television viewing that emerges as a recurring theme in the remarks of respondents. Interactivity allows the viewers to take on the work of finding ways to make a show more interesting.

The case study that forms the basis for this chapter's discussion of interactive media draws from the results of two online surveys posted to the TWoP Web site for one week. The first survey, which was largely quantitative, received more than 1,800 responses; the second, made up of open-ended questions, received more than 500 responses. The responses were uniformly thoughtful, articulate, interesting, and witty—in keeping with the general tenor of the site, which is tightly monitored and places a premium on smart, entertaining writing. The vast majority of the responses to the surveys were from women, a fact that is explained, at least in part, by the site's demographics and also perhaps by a self-selection bias on the part of respondents. Seventy percent of the respondents indicated they were in the 18-to-34 age range—the demographic group most prized by advertisers and marketers. The respondents, of course, were self-selected; they represented visitors to the Web site who clicked on a link to the survey, but the large number of responses provided a rich set of observations, as well as several clear trends, discussed below, that demonstrate the ways in which viewer participation, while providing perceived benefits to viewers, doubled as a form of free labor for producers.

Interactive Labor

The emerging interactive economy requires the creation of new, more active—or interactive—type of viewer. The evolution of the television remote control is suggestive of the type of transformations underway: early remotes that facilitated the growing passivity of the couch potato stressed simplicity and ease. The goal was to reduce the amount of effort, such as it was, associated with the viewing experience. Over time, the remote has evolved to encompass an increasing range of functions and the convergence of multiple devices, a process that has led to remote controls for recording and playback devices, sound systems, and cable boxes. These days, mastering a remote control can require a fair amount of time and effort poring over awkwardly worded instruction manuals. Some of the more advanced devices come equipped with their own miniature screens to be both watched and interacted with. Remote control has, in some respects, thereby transformed itself from a passive activity to an active one. By the same token, one of the central problems facing the promoters of interactive television is how to transform a passive pastime into an active one—one in which the relationship to the screen is more akin to that of the computer user: looking and listening, but also interacting.

A site like TWoP provides a neat transition to this era of interactive viewing. Many of the survey respondents noted that even if they weren't online while watching TV, they often took notes as they watched TV, writing down choice morsels of dialogue and observations to help them prepare for their posts. Moreover, some TWoP participants go beyond watching and commenting on the show; they conduct online research and even cultivate studio connections in order to be able to provide information on topics ranging from media coverage to upcoming cast changes and plot twists. The goal is not just to participate in the forums, but to do so in a way that adds value for other participants—to entertain them with both witty observations based on a close analysis of the show, and to inform them with tidbits gleaned from the Internet or industry connections. Participating on TWoP can be, for the devotees, a bit like creating a blog about an admired—or reviled—show: it requires time and effort. A quarter of the participants who responded to my online survey indicated that they spent between five and ten hours a week in the TWoP forums, and 13 percent said they spent more than ten hours a week on the site (much of which reportedly took place at work). Additionally, many TWoPpers devoted time not just to watching (and sometimes taking notes on) particular shows, but to gathering information about them from other sources. The TWoP forums provide a pool of research expertise available not just to fellow fans, but also to producers. The result has reportedly been, at least at times, a welcome corrective to writers who learn from avid fans that a recent or upcoming script includes a continuity flaw or plot inconsistency. This is precisely the type of effort that the theorist Tiziana Terranova has described as the "free labor" characteristic of the relationship between the online economy and what, following the Italian autonomists, she terms "the social factory."[13] She invokes this term to describe the process "whereby 'work processes have shifted from the factory to society, thereby setting in motion a truly complex machine.'"[14]

The notion of the social factory coincides with the creation of a new type of consumer-viewer: one prepared to devote time and energy to developing the skills necessary to participate in an increasingly interactive media economy. The list of such skills is growing longer and includes not only the ability to operate a computer and surf the Internet, but to master an array of devices including video remote control programmers, cell phones, Palm Pilots, and video games. This work is productive not just in the sense that it facilitates the consumption of an increasingly technologically sophisticated array of media products and services; it also becomes directly economically productive to the extent that it allows producers to offload work onto consumers. A privately controlled digital enclosure allows for the capture and repurposing of transactionally generated information and for the mobilization of the promise of interactivity to help generate information for marketers, content for producers, and added value for media products.

It is perhaps not insignificant that the work offloaded onto the consumer is referred to by marketers as a "duty" of interaction. The notion that consumers are increasingly required to take on a broad array of interactive responsibilities ties in neatly with the forms of "governing at a distance" elaborated by the Foucault-inspired literature on governmentality. The interactive consumer is the market analogue of the responsible citizen as construed by the proponents of the neoliberal postwelfare state. As social theorist Nikolas Rose puts it, neoliberal forms of governance envision the citizen as an "entrepreneur of him- or herself" who is "to conduct his or her life, and that of his or her family, as a kind of enterprise, seeking to enhance and capitalize on existence itself through calculated acts and investments."[15]

It doesn't seem far-fetched to extend this analysis into the realm of consumption, where the consumer is increasingly encouraged to make the investment of time and energy it takes to be an interactive consumer—increasingly responsible for one's own viewing and consumption practices and experiences. The promise is that the final product will be more satisfying the more effort one invests in preparing (oneself for) it. Thus, the promoters of mass customization encourage us to take on the "duties" of consumer interaction in order, presumably, to help them craft a product that addresses our specific needs and concerns, and for which, not incidentally, we might be willing to pay more, essentially buying back the added value we contributed. As the digital enclosure makes it easier to capture and capitalize on consumer labor, the consumer is urged to take on responsibility for an increasing array of interactive forms of participation. At the same time, this labor, productive as it might be for those in a position to exploit it, is portrayed as a means of overcoming the forms of alienation associated with both mass production and mass consumption. Consumers are invited to become part of the production process in order to recognize—and to gain satisfaction from this recognition of—the traces of their own contributions.

Not surprisingly, many of the contributors to the TWoP Web site suggested that the effort that they put into the shows they watch increases their own viewing pleasure. As one fan put it in a column about her passion for collecting behind-the-scenes and advance information about her favorite show, "At the most basic level, being plugged-in means becoming invested in the creation of the show, rather than simply a passive recipient."[16] To the extent that such sites—even those that are ostensibly critical—promote this sense of investment, they similarly enhance the viewing experience. One TWoP fan writes, "TWoP has definitely made me pay closer attention to the shows I watch (ie script, direction, set decoration, etc.). While at times I can be more critical of a show, for example more aware of continuity errors and obvious audience manipulation, it also makes me more appreciative of the work that goes into creating a show, and insanely, more loyal to a show." This post and several similar ones suggest that the more the boundary between the "offstage" site of production and that of consumption is eroded, the greater this sense of participation-based loyalty becomes.

Although TWoPpers pride themselves on belonging to a cynical, canny, and occasionally jaded subset of viewers, many nonetheless find themselves captivated by those moments when producers, actors, or writers participate in the forums or agree to be interviewed online for the site. One respondent described the experience of hearing from those involved in a favorite show as "unbelievably weird and simultaneously wonderful. Their feedback and insights made my love for the show grow exponentially! If actors and other persons affiliated with shows regularly showed up, I might end up watching much more TV, simply because of the stronger connection I would feel." This is marketing advice that producers seem to have taken to heart in their attempts to promote and capitalize on such loyalty by creating official Web sites, the savviest of which provide interactive interviews and the kind of behind-the-scenes information that gives fans the sense of at least partial entry into an inner circle of producers and writers.

Official sites, however, don't have the luxury of deliberately fostering the critical, sarcastic repartee that has become the staple of TWoP, which provides visitors not just with tightly monitored and witty forums, but also with lengthy, often sarcastic, and savagely funny recaps of selected shows. The combination of enthusiasm and criticism that infuses the site is in part a function of the fact that there are two, not entirely distinct, types of forums: those populated by serious fans, and those devoted to viewers who love to mock the shows being discussed. The "fan"-oriented forums at the time of the survey tended to coalesce around dramatic shows like *24, Buffy The Vampire Slayer,* and *Alias,* whereas shows like *Joe Millionaire* and *The Bachelor* served as the brunt of the more snarkastic forums, whose viewers are nonetheless avid viewers of the shows they pan. The boundary between the two types of forum is far from clear: fans of shows like *24* enjoy criticizing it, and snarkastic viewers become invested in the show that they follow online. In both cases, the goal is not uncritical fannishness, but rather for viewers to use the site as a springboard for entertaining one another. The show itself can in some cases become merely a precursor to the real entertainment: its online comeuppance in the form of the gleeful dissection that takes place after it airs.

I first noticed this phenomenon when I was spending a fair amount of time in the official chat rooms for the first U.S. version of the *Big Brother* reality game show. Despite much hype, the show was often mind-numbingly boring, as were the round-the-clock live Internet video feeds. The chat rooms became, for at least some viewers, the only way to make the show interesting. While watching the contestants attempt to entertain themselves in a drab, media-free ranch-house holding pen on a lot in Studio City, online viewers took upon themselves the task of amusing themselves by speculating on plot twists that might make the show more interesting, sharing information about the various contestants, and starting online debates. Viewers created their own Web pages devoted to the show, including the popular BigBrotherBlows.com. There was, in short, more to host Julie Chen's closing observation to fans that "your participation made this a truly interactive show" than she might have realized. Faced with a show that was routinely dull and contrived, online viewers did the creative work of making the show entertaining to themselves, often by coming up with innovative ways to poke fun at it.

Similarly, TWoP fans focused their attention on the lengthy recaps written by paid freelancers and on the ongoing discussions of fellow fan-critics in the forums. Within this context, the show is no longer the final product, but rather the raw material to which value is added by the labor—some paid, some free—of recappers and forum contributors. Not only did roughly one-third of the survey respondents indicate that they watched more TV because of TWoP, but a similar number indicated that there were shows that they would not have watched without the concurrent TWoP recaps. The most frequently mentioned of these shows were the reality formats *Joe Million-aire, Married by America, Are You Hot,* and *The Bachelor.* Respondents said that, taken on their own, such shows were too contrived and cheesy to merit watching, but that they provided wonderful raw material for the TWoP recaps and forums. As one respondent put it,

I watched parts of *Married by America* simply because Miss Alli [one of the favorite recappers] was recapping it and I wanted to see what she was so hysterically mocking. This week, during *For Love or Money,* I had to visit the site because I knew that people would be hilariously mocking the "robot" bachelor and I was not disappointed. So, yes, TWoP can get me to watch bad TV, at least for a short period.

Another viewer expressed similar enthusiasm for Miss Alli's sardonic prose: "I absolutely will watch a show just to be able to keep up—*The Amazing Race!* Miss Alli's recaps were just so damn SMART, I had to know what she was skewering." Others said that they tuned into a show after reading a particularly hilarious recap and continued to watch in order to enjoy future recaps. Interestingly, a few respondents said that they followed some shows entirely online, because the recaps were entertaining and thorough enough to stand on their own. Although not the norm, these "viewers" had found a way to consume TV-based entertainment without having to watch TV. Perhaps out of a desire to encourage the kind of participation that fosters loyalty to a show—even if it's a program that viewers love to hate—producers have said publicly that they find Web sites to be useful sources of feedback. The executive producer of *ER,* one of TWoP's staple shows, said, "I don't overreact to the boards, but I pay real attention to messages that are thoughtful. If you ignore your customer, you do so at your peril."[17]

As in the case of other forms of interactive commerce, the information provided by viewers doesn't just add value to the product, it doubles as audience research. Fan communities have been around for a long time, but the growth of online bulletin boards received a boost with the reality TV boom, perhaps in part because of the way in which such shows foster a sense of participation by proxy. Indeed, some formats incorporate fan participation online or by cell phone in order to exploit the promise of an ersatz democratization—a promise that is often repeated in the media coverage. As one article on reality TV explains, "The popularity of this format with youth also has a lot to do with their growing up in a democratized society, where the Internet, Webcams and other technologies give the average Joe the ability to personalize his entertainment."[18] The ready equation of commodity customization with democratization echoes the marketing rhetoric of the interactive revolution. In keeping with this theme, a *New York Times* article about the reception of the pan-African version of *Big Brother* suggested that it appealed to a longing for democracy: "'Big Brother' defenders are many. Though it may be subtle, one theme they point to is democracy. The contestants are nominated for eviction by their housemates and then voted off by viewers on the Internet or by cellphone text messaging. The will of the people decides how the show unfolds."[19]

If the implicit message of reality TV is one of increasingly shared control, it is not surprising that network executive Chris Ender says the power of the Web-based fan groups first caught his attention during the airing of the smash hit reality series, *Survivor:* "In the first season there was a groundswell of attention in there. . . . We started monitoring the message boards to actually help guide us in what would resonate in our marketing. It's just the best market research you can get."[20] TWoPpers may be working for free, but that doesn't mean they're not producing value. The work they do—that of making their preferences transparent, of allowing themselves to be watched as they do their own watching—is, as the previous chapters have suggested, an increasingly important component of the emerging interactive economy.

Productive Consumption

One of the ancillary effects of the promise of shared control mobilized by producers who publicize the impact of online fans is that of an implicit bridging of the production-consumption divide. If viewers are, to some limited extent, allowed to participate in the production process, then the notion that a new set of duties has devolved upon them becomes much more palatable. Furthermore, the promise of shared control, the invitation to participate in the production process, doubles as an invitation to internalize the imperatives of producers. There are entire threads on TWoP devoted, for example, to the marketing of a favored show. Posters frequently bemoan the ineffectiveness of promotional ads for the shows they follow and offer suggestions as to which characters and images ought to be included to increase audience appeal and viewership. Even in the face of a still relatively nonresponsive industry, the formal introduction of an interactive element helps foster a sense of identification with producers. Although there are instances where the feedback seems to have had an impact, for the most part, the impact of the boards is limited and indirect. For interactive viewers, the fun comes not so much from watching the implementation of their suggestions—because very few of these have any directly discernible impact—as from embracing interactivity that makes it possible to identify with the position of the producer.

If, as social theorist Nikolas Rose puts it, in the emerging form of neoliberal society, "One is always in continuous training, lifelong learning, perpetual assessment, continual incitement to buy, [and to] to improve oneself," then the imperative for consumers is to become not only more efficient, but more informed and even more critical viewers. To borrow some loaded terms from the political sphere, if the passive viewer is an artifact of the welfare "culture of dependency," then the active viewer is invoked as being of a piece with a postwelfare culture of individual responsibility and self-activation. If TV is low quality, unentertaining, or unintelligent, the post–welfare state interactive viewer can take on the duty of making it more interesting, entertaining, and intelligent. One survey respondent writes, "I would like my TV to be smarter, better written, more intellectually stimulating, and more emotionally engaging. With TWoP, at least my watching of TV can be those things."

In contrast to the image of television as a mind-numbing addiction that promotes a culture of passivity, that of TWoP-enhanced TV is one of active participation, self-improvement, and actualization, even creativity. Respondents thus repeatedly reiterated their assertion that TWoP allowed them to develop and hone their critical skills—the very skills that were ostensibly threatened and eroded by their dependency on the "plug-in drug." One survey respondent summed up this recurring refrain as follows: "My inner critic was always apparent, now it is in a better, more intelligent form." As another put it, TWoP has "certainly made me more snarky/critical of television. However, it's also made me more critical of my own writing in that it's highlighted some clichés and contrivances that we systematically use without thinking about them. All in all it's made me more creative."

The portrayal of interactivity as a means for revitalizing a self-actualizing form of participation parallels the marketing of the digital economy as one that counters the stultification and homogenization of mass society. Indeed, one of the recurring marketing strategies of the increasingly interactive, mass customized economy is the suggestion that, thanks to the addition of interactivity, signified by the telltale lowercase "i," forms of media that were once passive and mind-numbing are transformed into means of creative self-expression and empowerment. One survey respondent noted that a site like TWoP "changes TV from a brain-dead pastime to an art and a science." Or, similarly, "bad TV becomes good TV when combined with TWoP." The element of reflexivity, combined with a snarkastic savviness, inoculates the viewer against the depredations of the passive form of the medium.

The intriguing result is that, thanks to inclusion of the formal element of interactivity, the entire character of a particular show changes from that of a mass-produced product of the culture industry into a tool to hone and develop one's critical thinking and viewing skills. As another respondent put it, "Being able to see through the stereotypes and clichés bad shows propagate is a useful skill, much like being able to deconstruct and analyze advertising. At least if you are able to hone your critical thinking skill during a tasteless show, it's not a total waste." Another TWoPper invoked a famous indictment of the mass media for fostering a form of "narcotizing dysfunction."[21] The ostensibly stultifying effects of the mass media—those bemoaned in the critiques of mass society—can, on this account, be overcome by reflexive, critical humor: "Applying such a smart, dark sense of humor to the thing that pervades our lives takes away some of its hypnotic power. When you look at it critically it is something you are experiencing and participating in, rather than something that is narcotizing you."

Several respondents suggested that the development of critical viewing skills, combined with the feedback supplied by increasingly sophisticated viewers, might result in improved programming. However, even if such a result is not forthcoming, savvy reflexivity serves as a kind of coping mechanism—a strategy for salvaging the very same advertisements and programming that, when viewed uncritically or nonreflexively, are relegated to the category of the shallow manipulations of the culture industry. In other words, it's not the content itself but the attitude taken by the viewers that defines whether the medium is stimulating or invigorating. It is, in other words, the way in which viewers watch—or, more precisely, the way in which they are seen to watch (or see themselves watching)—that makes the difference. TWoPpers esteem savvy, critical posts highly, and those who are active contributors to the site say that while they like the idea that producers may be paying attention, they post mainly for the benefit of fellow posters and the moderator. The goal is not so much to influence the group of producers and production assistants referred to in posts as TPTB (The Powers That Be) as it is to entertain and impress the TWoP community with wit, insight, and, above all, snark.

"Thanks for Listening (Or Not)!"

Despite the stories of shout outs and other examples of the impact of the online community on producers and writers, the savvy attitude of TWoP-pers includes a marked skepticism toward the notion that they might actually be making a difference. One poster notes, "The producers are such prostitutes to advertisers and whatever other show may be popular that giving advice would be pointless. It is all about the Benjamins." Indeed, most of the respondents took pains to suggest that they didn't have any illusions about transforming or improving the culture industry. The recurring theme in the responses was that contributors post primarily for one another, and that if producers feel like paying attention, so much the better. Some respondents cautioned against the dangers of TWoPpers believing the media hype about the influence of the boards: "Although the artistic personnel of some shows probably read TWOP, I think the posters on the forums think they have more influence than they probably do. If they write posts for the series creators, they are deluded as to their influence." The more cynical posters recognize that there's a certain amount of public relations value to be gained by producers from suggesting that online fans have some kind of influence over the production process.

For those who see through the hype and have no illusions about the impact they're having on the industry, the appeal of critique is not just its entertainment value, but also the recognition that they receive online. Respondents repeatedly emphasized the satisfaction they gained from having their posts noticed and responded to in the online forums. A typical example was the observation by one regular poster that "when posting, my main goal is to make the other posters laugh, to be witty. If I get a 'word' out of the deal, my day's pretty much made." Another respondent, highlighting the work done by viewers in making the viewing experience more entertaining wrote, "My 'job' on TWoP is the class clown—almost all of my posts are humorous in nature and I love it when posters respond to them in their posts. I guess I enjoy the validation that I can indeed be funny."

A premium was placed on the ability to get some kind of shout out, not from the producers or writers, but from fellow viewers: "The pleasure kicks in when I've helped to expand someone's knowledge or world-view and when I'm quoted or declared funny. (I like making other people laugh)." The high expectations that posters have for the level of wit, sarcasm, and snark in some of the forums apparently has the unintended result of keeping some readers from posting, partly because they're worried that their own posts won't live up to the standard set by the regulars. As one avid TWoP fan put it in a parenthetical aside to an effusive description of the quality of the discussion on the boards, "I should note that I'm a lurker—too afraid to post!"

But for those who do post, the goal is not just to be heard, but to be seen in a particular way: as savvy viewers who aren't taken in by the transparent forms of manipulation practiced by producers. The ability of the viewers to make themselves seen—or, to draw on Walter Benjamin's terminology from the previous chapter, to leave a trace—is one of the characteristic attributes of the impending era of interactivity, and its implications are worth exploring in a bit more detail. The celebratory promise of the interactive era is that transparency will result in greater democratization in the political and economic spheres (although the latter is often conflated with the former). This promise is underwritten by the unexamined equation of participation with shared control: that any medium that increases interaction is necessarily politically progressive. If lack of participation is bad, then participation must be good.

However, the exploitation of participation as a form of audience labor—and even as a source of demographic information that can be appropriated and commodified—suggests that this equation needs to be approached with a bit more caution. The political theorist Jodi Dean argues that the interactivity fostered by new media promotes a form of publicity without publics: a drive to advertise one's own opinion that falls short of the political commitments of the public sphere.[22] For her, the characteristic mode of subjectivity associated with new media is that of universalized celebrity: "The subject is driven to make itself visible over and over again. It has to understand itself as a celebrity precisely because the excesses of cyberia make it uncertain as to its place in the symbolic order."[23] Dean is here following cultural theorist Slavoj Žižek's diagnosis of the pathologies associated with what he describes as the decline of the symbolic order in postmodernity, by which he means the debunking of the systems of meaning that facilitated collective action and deliberation.[24] The result is a generalized and demobilizing skepticism, a universal savviness that places a premium on detached cynicism, sarcasm, and, of course, snark.

Furthermore, as Dean suggests, this skepticism translates into the self-contradictory (and self-stimulating) logic of the attempt to make some kind of impression on a symbolic register whose very existence is in doubt. The savvy subject, wary of metanarratives, repeatedly attempts to assert this wariness as a sign that he or she is no dupe. The paradox lies in the attempt to register the fact of one's own nonduped status—a process, which, of course, implicitly smuggles back in the effectivity of a symbolic order (one that might "recognize" someone's "nonduped" status). The impasse of the desire to be seen as savvy results in the properly perverse logic of celebrity described by Dean, one in which the subject takes pleasure in the very failure of its attempt to make an impression on a debunked symbolic order. Savvy contemporary subjects know better than to imagine that interactivity would actually allow them to make an impression on The Powers That Be of the entertainment industry—one whose claims to represent the demands of consumers is little more than a ruse of the marketing process. Moreover, the narratives that underwrote both the democratic claims of the market (that consumers can "vote with their dollars") and those of contemporary democracy have been eroded to the point that both the market and politics come to be seen as autonomous forces, independent of the control of either consumers or voters. As one survey respondent wrote, "TV producers are kind of like politicians, I think, in that no matter what they do some people will complain, so they just do what they want and/or follow the advertising dollars." Or, as another post put it, "Producers of TV (and here I include the entire range from network execs through creators, writers, actors down to the grips) firmly and completely believe that they are the Gods who know 'how to tell the story' and that we the viewers are the idiots watching the shadows on the cave wall."

Translated into the terms of TWoP, the savvy, snarkastic response is not incidental to the prevailing skeptical attitude toward the promise that the boards will democratize the viewing process. Rather, the point for posters is to be seen by others as nondupes—to make it clear to one another that they have not been caught up in the illusory, breathless promise of a kind of immaculate revolution, painlessly effected by technological developments.

Surely there are participants at TWoP who imagine a world in which producers will pay more attention to viewers, and in which viewers may play an active and creative role in producing the culture they then turn around and consume. However, the characteristic attitude encouraged by the site and its posters is much more skeptical. Even if feedback is taken into account, the snarkastic subject suggests that the result would be one more form of market rationalization: the use of just-in-time focus groups to fine-tune a show, or the exploitation of online communities as a form of viral marketing: a way to spread buzz by word of mouth rather than relying solely on advertising promotions.

In a world in which the half-life of co-opting ostensibly subversive cultural forms seems to have shrunk almost to zero, in which the notion of revolution itself has become a marketing slogan, the savvy subject might well look askance at the promise of power sharing. Rather than buying into the promise that interactive technology will fundamentally alter the power relations between consumer and producer, the interactive viewer enlists the proffered technologies to, if nothing else, let others know that he or she hasn't been taken in by the ruse. The consequence is a sense of political inertness: only the dupes imagine that things could be otherwise: the nonduped may well crave social change, but they are not so naive as to be fooled by their desire into believing that it is actually possible.

Media critic Todd Gitlin neatly describes the politics of the savvy subject: "savviness flatters spectators that they really do understand; that people like them are in charge; that even if they stand outside the policy elites, they remain sovereign. . . . [S]avviness appeals to a spirit both managerial and voyeuristic. It transmutes the desire to participate into spectacle—one is already participating, in effect, by watching."[25] The promise of interactive television is to take this equation literally: in the digital future, watching really will be a form of participation precisely because we will be able to talk back to the tube. The savvy subject will be realized in the form of the active viewer. TWoP caters to a form of savviness described by Gitlin: its premium attitude is that of not being taken in by the machinations of the culture industry. If the viewers can't be insiders, at least they can make it clear that they are not being fooled by the insiders, and this is the closest that the interactive technologies can bring them to the inner sanctum.

Helping the Producers

As Gitlin notes, savviness encourages viewers to identify with insiders by defining the issues as they define them, which is an apt description of much of what goes on in the production-oriented strands of the TWoP boards. Posters who identify problems in continuity, in plot and character development, in makeup and lighting, and even in publicity and promotional material are using the interactive forum to imagine themselves in the position of the producer so as to understand the imperatives that shape the programming they consume. In this respect, they adopt a standard critical procedure: an attempt to demystify and explain the behind-the-scenes functioning of the media.

However, the goal of such knowledge for the savvy subject is not so much to reshape the media—to imagine how things might be done differently—as it is to take pleasure in identifying with the insiders. The next best thing to having power, on this account, is identifying with those who do, rather than naively imagining that power might be redistributed or realigned. In this respect, the snarkiest and most critical of the fan sites runs the danger of partaking in what Gitlin describes as "the postmodern fascination with surfaces and the machinery that cranks them out, a fascination indistinguishable from surrender—as if once we understand that all images are concocted we are enlightened."[26]

The stance of the savvy viewers is twofold: an insider's skepticism toward the notion that the *real* insiders are paying any attention to the boards, combined with a sense that understanding the insider's perspective sets the savvy viewer apart from the masses who comprise the majority of the audience.

Thus, one respondent described the pleasure of TWoP as follows: "It is hard to explain, but I feel like an 'insider' when I read TWoP. Like we are a community of those in the know, not a bunch of clueless losers." Another poster observed, "Reading and participating in the forums makes me feel that all hope for humanity is not lost. If there are so many people watching reality TV, at least not all of us are taking it seriously. . . . TWoP makes it easier for us to convince ourselves that we are smart, while watching DUMB television."

Such is the fate of the savvy viewer: to search for the redeeming value of the media not in the content—over which their newly enhanced, interactive participation has little influence—but precisely in understanding why their participation must be ineffective: in their insider knowledge of how the system works. Within this context, the lure of interactivity loses some of its luster. Rather than a progressive challenge to a nonparticipatory medium, it offers to divert the threat of activism into the productive activity of marketing and market research. Interactivity turns out to be rather more passive than advertised. The drive of savvy viewers to make themselves seen (as nondupes) overlaps with the invitation proffered by interactive media: for audiences to reveal themselves in increasing detail to producers.

The logic of a savvy site like TWoP, which allows viewers to take pleasure in critiquing the programming within which they are immersed, stages Žižek's description of a resigned savviness that derives "satisfaction from actively sustaining the scene of one's own passive submission."[27] The hope of nonduped subjects is that by actively embracing a reality that "could not be otherwise," they escape the fate of the naive victims who end up victims of circumstances beyond their control. Similarly, if the emerging interactive economy fails to provide an authentic vision of shared control, it nevertheless invites us to take a more active role in staging the scene of our passive submission.

Refeudalization and the Publicity Sphere

If, as Habermas has argued, the political public sphere can trace its origins to the literary public sphere, perhaps we can discern its decline in the televisual publicity sphere enacted by sites like TWoP.[28] Such sites exhibit many of the attributes of Habermas's version of the public sphere: open admission, discussion of topics of communal interest, and, at least on TWoP, a relatively scrupulous adherence to norms of noncoercive speech. TWoP moderators, for example, ban anyone who directly insults another poster, and they generally delete offensive, sexist, and other forms of inflammatory or insulting commentary. Many posters described the site as a variant of a public sphere that allows them to discuss topics intelligently with strangers and thereby to develop their own critical and analytical skills and to learn from one another. Moreover, the Internet is, at least in some respects, more open than the literary societies and secret societies described by Habermas. One poster suggested that, at least for women, the Internet remains *more* open than other venues of social interaction, "in which men still tend to dominate conversations, meetings, and classrooms, and women's opinions are often ignored or marginalized, even if they have something valuable to contribute. Online forums give us the chance to be heard, and the reader can choose to ignore it or pay attention—but the point is, WE GET THE CHANCE TO BE HEARD. It isn't any wonder that the majority of posters in most chatrooms are female?" Such sentiments echo cyberfeminist Sadie Plant's suggestion that the medium lends itself to a dismantling of gendered power relations in part because of the decentralized forms of communication it facilitates: "the roundabout, circuitous connections with which women have always been associated and the informal networking at which they have excelled now become protocols for everyone."[29,30]

Removed from traditionally male-dominated public spaces and accessible from home or work, bulletin boards like TWoP make it hard to differentiate posters on the basis of gender. Perhaps not insignificantly, the form of unpaid labor that goes into a site like TWoP bears a certain similarity to the unpaid labor of the homemaker. The ability of the new media to de-differentiate sites of production, domesticity, and leisure has been portrayed by the promoters of the new economy as a form of liberation from spatial constraints: telecommuters will be able to live wherever they want, skip the traffic, and work from home (or the beach, the corner coffee shop, or any other wired location). At the same time, as one social theorist has pointed out, the de-differentiation that takes place within the digital enclosure makes it possible for employers to offload the costs of the workplace onto workers, and it encourages the transformation of the home into a workplace in which domestic labor and paid labor take place simultaneously: "When performed at the same site where cooking, cleaning, and diaper-changing waits to be done, network-mediated telework enables women to exceed even Aristotle's designation of their utility: they can be, simultaneously, unpaid domestic managers as well as poorly paid . . . wage slaves."[31]

Furthermore, de-differentiation allows formerly nonproductive activities to generate valuable information commodities if they take place within the monitoring reach of the digital enclosure. The work of being watched doubles as yet another form of unpaid labor—one to which men as well as women are subjected. In this respect, it is tempting to read Plant's techno-utopianism in the opposite direction: if the traditional gender hierarchy is challenged online, the result is not necessarily an emancipatory privileging of decentralized networking, but the universalization of forms of exploitation historically associated with women's work. The free labor performed by fans might be considered a subset of the work of being watched, insofar as it doubles as a form of marketing and promotion for television shows, and a way of making such shows more entertaining, and thus desirable, to viewers.

Viewed in this light, the exploitation of free labor represents the obverse of fan participation as the potentially subversive form of "textual poaching" described by media critic Henry Jenkins.[32] Jenkins's formulation relies on and compounds a misleading appropriation (poaching?) of a production-oriented metaphor suggested by the French cultural theorist Michel De Certeau: "readers are travelers; they move across lands belonging to someone else, like nomads poaching their way across fields they did not write, despoiling the wealth of Egypt to enjoy it themselves."[33] The metaphor breaks down in the transition from fields to texts: the consumption of crops is exclusive (or, as economists put it, "rivalrous"), the productive consumption of texts is not (because information is a "nonrivalrous"). Far from "despoiling" the television texts through their practices, TWoPpers enrich them—not just for themselves, but also for those who benefit economically from the added value produced by the labor of viewers. The "poachers" are helping to work the field for its owners. Online viewers' responses confirm what producers have already figured out: that their participatory activity gets them to watch more TV more attentively and builds their loyalty to particular programs. In short, it helps deliver more eyes to producers—and not just any eyes: those that belong to a demographic group coveted by marketers.

That the Web site, according to many of the survey respondents, doubles as a form of online community in no way detracts from or undermines its potential productivity. On the contrary, as media theorist Jan Fernback notes, in the era of relationship marketing, community is an increasingly valuable marketing apparatus.[34] The advantage to marketers of online communities is that they help build allegiance to particular products, serving as forums for practices of self-disclosure that generate detailed information about consumers. As one company quoted by Fernback put it, the systematic development of product-related community sites represents "a trend toward the transformation of ad hoc e-communities into established forums that drive product innovation and contribute to profits."[35]

TWoP remains an independent site as of this writing—unaffiliated with any particular show—and posters continue to make the most of its largely critical approach to the TV shows it recaps. The site may have the potential to serve as an instant focus group, as one respondent put it, but perhaps even more importantly, it helps draw viewers to particular shows and allows them to accumulate social and information capital that increases their commitment to viewing. Several posters noted that they continued to watch shows that they once enjoyed but no longer really liked because they wanted to participate in the ongoing online dissection of the program, its characters, and writers. As a public sphere the site also retains certain pathologies of online community, including the passion for a friction-free form of community, what Kevin Robins has described as "the desire to be free from the challenge of difference and otherness" and a "a culture of retreat from the world."[36] The words of one respondent echo Robins: "The site also provides a sense of community, without the tangles of actually knowing the people."

TWoP also provides a form of publicity without, as Dean suggests, a public—or, put in slightly different terms, a public that has dispersed its activity into a savvy but domesticated interactivity. If the Web facilitates the self-promoting celebrity subject engaged in a repetitive cycle of self-disclosure associated with the drive to make itself seen, it stands diametrically opposed to the subversive potential of the literary public spheres described by Habermas. As Jodi Dean astutely observes, secrecy was a crucial component of the emergent public spheres described by Habermas, precisely because of their potentially subversive nature.[37] Publicity as a politically subversive strategy enacted not the drive toward self-exposure associated with the celebrity subject of Cyberia, but the exposure of the secret of power. The challenge was not directed toward those private secrets associated with the personal lives of public figures, but toward the principle of secrecy governing public affairs. The contemporary Habermasian diagnosis of "refeudalization" suggests a return to the principle of the secrecy of power accompanied by the pomp of public display: a historical shift away from a media model that fosters the continuation of political conversation by other means toward that of the society of the spectacle. Such a shift coincides with the return not of the subversive secrecy that challenged rulers' lack of accountability, but of the secrecy within which power itself was cloaked. In the United States, for example, the Bush administration combines its well-honed, Reaganesque publicity strategy with an increasingly secretive attitude toward public records.[38]

However, what the diagnosis of refeudalization misses—and what is highlighted by the form of savvy critique associated with sites like TWoP—is the way in which the emerging (interactive) constellation of voyeurism and self-disclosure facilitates identification with the "insiders" on the part of outsiders. If the impulse is to show what one knows, then what savvy viewers know is the manipulative, profit-oriented character of the mass media: the entire set of imperatives that generate the content they love to mock. Perhaps the most fascinating aspect of this identification with producers and insiders facilitated by interactive media is the way in which it fosters acceptance of the rules of the game. In an era of interactive reflexivity, the media turn back on themselves. The new media mock the old, while tellingly failing to deliver on the promised transformative shift in power relations. It is perhaps possible to discern in the savvy self-criticism of the media a certain resentment over a failed promise: that information would double as a form of power sharing—that once the secret of power was exposed, it could be shared. The perceived dissolution of the democratic promise of publicity, in an era in which information is increasingly available and in which power and wealth (and the media) are simultaneously becoming increasingly concentrated in the hands of the wealthy few feeds a savvy attitude toward the media itself. The critical impetus shifts away from political leaders—witness a Pew poll that indicated almost half of the population felt the media were becoming too critical—and toward the media themselves.[39] The result, however, is not a transformed media, but rather a reflexive redoubling that amounts to an active form of self-submission. As in the online world of TWoP, spectators take their pleasure in knowing—with the insiders—just why things are as bad as they are, and why they couldn't be any different.

6

iWar

Fitter, happier, more productive, comfortable, not drinking too much
Regular exercise at the gym, 3 days a week . . .
No longer empty and frantic like a cat tied to a stick

—Radiohead

Shortly after the 9/11 attacks, *Time* magazine observed that "every war has its signature medium," and it dubbed the government's declared war on terrorism the "first Internet war."[1] Because the war on terrorism is so diffuse, complex, and multitiered, according to *Time,* it "defies more linear mediums like print and television." Moreover, because the war on terrorism is an information intensive one—one in which the hallmark of so-called homeland defense is a well-informed and proactive public—it lends itself to the participatory model of information consumption associated with the Internet. The public no longer has to rely on the judgment of editors, and it doesn't have to wait until the end of the workday for the latest news. Rather, as *Time* notes, "The war on terrorism is the first war you can access from your desk."[2] The unspoken subtext is that ready access to extensive and updated information is more than a convenience. It has become a *duty* within the context of an ongoing battle in which civilians are part of the conflict. Tom Ridge's readiness campaign makes this duty clear: it is the role of the citizen not only to prepare one's home and one's family, but also to remain vigilant, alert, and aware. Ridge, when he unveiled a series of commercials for his readiness campaign, said, "The next attack could happen to any community at any time. The random, unpredictable nature of terrorism itself requires, hopefully, everyone to take our recommendations to be prepared regardless of where they live."[3]

The Department of Homeland Security's (DHS) readiness campaign pushes the participatory model one step further than *Time*: it's not just that citizens can now participate in the information gathering process, but that the war itself is interactive. In a disturbing twist to the interactive promise of the Internet, once-passive spectators are urged to become active participants. According to *New York Times* columnist Maureen Dowd, one of the original proposals for Ridge's readiness commercials—rejected by the focus groups—was to invite the viewer "to be a solider in your own home."[4]

It is hard not to see the parallels between the marketing of interactivity and the advertising campaign for readiness. In this century of de-differentiation, when we can work from the corner Starbuck's, the airport lounge, or the beach, when we can multitask thanks to the proliferation of networked devices, we are invited to participate in the war on terrorism from the privacy of our homes and from our offices, or wherever we might happen to be. At the same time, as the once ubiquitous terror-alert logos in the corners of our television sets and computers suggest (and it is possible to download an application that will keep one's desktop appraised of the current terror alert level), citizen-soldiers are presented as primary targets in the war; they are no longer just collateral damage. Hence the notorious duct tape recommendation: our homes must be retrofitted to deal with the possibility not of a nuclear catastrophe, but of an attack whose very randomness implicates everyone. As Ridge put it, in a finger-shaking anecdote: "In one newspaper last week, a man was quoted as saying, 'The chances of getting hit are too small.' I would say to him, 'Not small enough,' ladies and gentlemen, 'Not small enough.' I hope he reconsiders his statement and at least goes home and gets prepared."[5] As should we all, according to the government's latest marketing campaign.

The interactive character of the DHS campaign makes it amenable to the critique of interactivity developed in previous chapters. The transition from the previous chapter's case study of a TV-themed Web site to the current chapter's focus on the "global war on terror" is admittedly a dramatic one in scope and scale, but the intent is to note the shared logic in the deployment of the promise of interactivity (from a micro to macro scale—and across commercial and state applications). The thread of continuity that holds the two examples together is the use of interactivity as an information-gathering strategy and as an invitation to identify with the imperatives of those in positions of power, either cultural or political. If the Television Without Pity participants contribute to the production process by adding value to cultural commodities and adopting the perspective of TV producers, the citizen-warriors envisioned by the DHS's "readiness" campaign contribute to national security by amplifying and extending state surveillance and adopting administration imperatives uncritically. The interactive marketing of security offloads duties of homeland defense onto the populace, inviting it to define the threat in the terms adopted by the administration (or else to expose themselves to the vague dangers invoked by Tom Ridge's ominous admonition that the odds of becoming a victim are "not small enough"). The following sections explore the interactive side of the war on terror and examine its strategic use of monitoring and managerial strategies that par-allel (and exploit) commercial forms of interactivity enabled by the digital enclosure. It turns out that the information gathered by commercial entities can serve the double purpose of consumer *and* citizen profiling, and that the terrorist threat can be mobilized as a reason for submitting to comprehen-sive forms of surveillance in the name of national defense. When it comes to mobilizing public consent to interactive monitoring, convenience is the car-rot and risk is the stick.

Offloading Homeland Security

It is certainly possible to argue that there is nothing new about the strat-egy of enlisting the contributions of the civilian population in the name of homeland defense. After all, previous wars' efforts included attempts to mo-bilize the populace through enlistment, conservation, and war bond cam-paigns. The notorious cold war threat portrayed all Americans as potential victims and thereby helped to mobilize do-it-yourself defense strategies ex-emplified by backyard fallout shelters and the "be prepared" duck-and-cover campaign.

What is new in the framing of the war on terror is that its post–welfare state effort to offload duties of homeland defense onto the populace coincides with the triumph of the neoliberal ideology of the Bush administration. Conservative presidents in the postwar era have a history of running up budget deficits, but the Bush administration remains the first to attempt to run a multifront war while at the same time cutting taxes. Cold war readiness adopted a mass society welfare state model in which civilians remained the potential victims of technology beyond their reach. The injunction to prepare was, on the individual level, a defensive one, and, at the level of the welfare state, a kind of contribution at a distance: to support a formidable escalation and investment in the military-industrial complex.

The current version of homeland security promulgated by the U.S. government, is, by contrast, neither collective nor welfarist: citizens are urged to take on the responsibility of preparing for a variety of potential catastrophes and of participating in an ongoing homeland security surveillance program against terror. Rather than conserving, citizens are urged to consume and seek out investment opportunities that disconcertingly capitalize on the terrorist threat. The message is not so much one of unity and sacrifice in the name of collective defense as it is a form of encouragement to leverage opportunities in a society in which the populace is admonished not to rely solely on the state and its agents. The public is told to take on some of the responsibilities for its own defense while availing itself of the opportunities that arise in the post-9/11 economy. As the New Jersey Department of Homeland Security's Web site puts it, because terrorists "know federal, state, and local authorities cannot be everywhere," citizens need to take on the responsibility of defending the homeland, making their eyes and ears extensions of the monitoring capacity of the state. The war on terror is an interactive war in which the populace has a role to play not only by watching over one another, but also by watching over themselves, as we shall see in subsequent sections. As President Bush noted during his second inaugural address, "Self-government relies, in the end, on the governing of the self."[6]

Finally, the war on terror is portrayed not in terms of collective political action so much as in terms of individual market choice. As right-wing Senator Rick Santorum (R-Pa.) noted in a speech to the National Press Club, "This is a truly modern war—a war fought not just on the battlefield, but on the Internet, a war decided less by armies and warplanes than by individuals making individual choices."[7] This is not, in other words, a war that should foster a sense of dependence on the state. It is a war to be waged by individuals making the "right" choices. Collective action is displaced by individual choice, with terrorism just one more instance of the jungle of marketplace competition in which risk is rampant, to the detriment of some and the benefit of others. As in the case of the social safety net provided by Social Security and Medicare (targeted by neocons for replacement by personal investment accounts) and the associated war on poverty, so too with national security and the war on terror. In both cases, the neoconservative impulse is to decollectivize and depoliticize, to replace citizens' dependency on state agencies with their version of individual responsibility.

The active participants in homeland security envisioned by the DHS's readiness campaign must invest in themselves and their homes. They must acquire the necessary equipment and training to take on the duties offloaded on them by the state. Thus, the contemporary version of homeland security has spawned a host of relatively new forms of expertise and has coordinated them with more familiar ones: experts in "preparedness" and "readiness" tutor the prudent citizen in strategies for self-defense via self-care in accordance with more familiar teachings in realms ranging from personal investment to personal hygiene. Even as they are repeatedly reminded of the failings of government bureaucracies in securing the nation against terrorists, the savvy consumer and investor are invited to consume their way to safety through speculation in the "growth market" of homeland defense. Expertise in all spheres of social practice is redoubled against the background of perpetual threat. Taking care of one's finances or one's health becomes not solely a personal responsibility, but one with a direct link to homeland defense. Complementing the neoliberal privatization of national defense is the attempt to enfold the private sphere into the managerial embrace of homeland security—an attempt facilitated by the expanding reach of the digital enclosure.

One example of this intersection of personal consumption with the entrepreneurialization of homeland defense was provided by the cover of a nationally circulated stock-tip sheet with the screaming headline, "Making America Safe: A $215 billion a year business. Now a hot new bomb detection technology is making it safe to fly again . . . and could make you rich."[8] It is this combination of threat and opportunity that characterizes the neoliberal mobilization of the war on terror. Savvy investors can make money while helping finance homeland defense. To paraphrase a New Yorker cartoon, if the specter of terrorist attack is rife with unimaginable horrors, the preat-tack scenario presents plenty of opportunities for profit. It also presents the opportunity for the mother of all fear appeals, as exemplified by the blurb for a nuclear war survival skills manual advertised on the for-profit Web site AreYouPrepared.com: "You can prepare and survive. Nuclear terrorism is coming. Know what to expect and how to prepare. Vital life saving instruc-tions. A must for every home and serious survival library." Available for the miraculous bargain price of $29.95.[9]

The flip side of the truism of the *Fountainhead* version of heroic capital-ism, that high returns are earned by those willing to take big risks, is that the threat of risk and the promise of security can be profitably leveraged. The literal realization of such logic was, of course, the ill-fated terrorism fu-tures market, proposed by DARPA's short-lived Total Information Awareness Office. The so-called Policy Analysis Market (PAM) "envisioned a potential futures trading market in which speculators would wager on the Internet on the likelihood of a future terrorist attack or assassination attempt on a particular leader."[10] The logic of the terrorism futures market is that of con-sumer interactivity in the digital enclosure: that each act of consumption doubles as an act of information production—a market signal that has its own predictive value. Although Total Information Awareness Office director John Poindexter reportedly lost his job after the PAM debacle, his market-based approach lives on in the form of the private subcontracting of the war on terror and the ongoing attempts to enlist marketing databases for surveil-lance purposes.

Selling Securities

It is characteristic of the Bush regime's market-oriented-solution mental-ity that homeland security would be sold to the public by an advertising campaign, complete with focus groups, and, in one early proposal, celeb-rity spokespeople.[11] The citizen soldier becomes the military analogue of the participatory consumer. The result is the marketing of homeland security as the latest form of self-help: a militarized enterprise culture that offloads du-ties of homeland defense on to a citizenry trained in the "norms and values of the market including those of 'responsibility, initiative, competitiveness, risk-taking, and industrious effort.'"[12]

The Ready.gov Web site makes it clear that one of the responsibilities of the citizenry is to accept the state of heightened risk—to learn to live with it—and to "begin the process of learning about potential threats so we are better prepared to react." The time for a culture of dependency is over: those who plan, those who prepare and ready themselves, those who practice good hygiene (visitors to Ready.gov are advised to "use common sense, practice good hygiene and cleanliness to avoid spreading germs"), and those who take the initiative in preparing the young and the elderly will be able to exchange their fear for readiness. Ridge's tagline for one of the Ad Council's readiness spots sums up the false choice outlined on the Web site: "we can either be afraid or we can be ready."[13] The version of readiness on offer, however, entails not the abolition of fear but a stance of perpetual anxious diligence.

Mobilizing Risk

To call the war on terror an "interactive" Internet war is not merely to emphasize that is it arguably the first broad-ranging U.S. conflict in the full-fledged Internet era. It is meant not just to suggest that the notion of the citizen-solider in the enterprise culture of triumphant neoliberalism aligns itself with the dawn of the era of interactivity. It is also to emphasize the distributed character of this so-called war and the way in which making the threat virtual can help render warfare generalized and ubiquitous.[14] The goal of analyzing the interactive character of this "war" is to highlight how citizen participation is mobilized to foster public identification with and support for administration policies within the context of what sociologist Ulrich Beck has described as the reflexive character of the contemporary "risk society."[15]

The war on terror might be described as the political mobilization of a climate of generalized risk: the exhortation to be always on one's guard indefinitely postpones a critical examination of the terms in which risk is defined and the interests served by this definition. In this regard, one of the more disconcerting aspects of the national security response to the 9/11 terrorist attacks in the United States was to emphasize the ease with which everyday objects could be transformed into devastating weaponry. As author Martin Amis noted shortly after the attacks, "A score or so of Stanley knives produced two million tons of rubble."[16] One of the recurring themes of the government and media response to the attack, consequently, was to enumerate the variety of ways in which innovative terrorists might work their destructive alchemy with the raw materials of daily life: tainted water supplies, contaminated ventilation systems, poisoned produce. The administration's call for "infinite justice" framed itself as a response to a climate of infinitely varied and dispersed threat—an atmosphere of generalized risk in which the most familiar aspects of daily life took on the somber aspect of potential targets or tools of terror.

The threat was all the more disturbing—and perhaps mobilizing—precisely because it appeared in the guise of daily life and not in the form of overtly military technology. In the wake of 9/11, the specter of threat that animated national defense appeared not in its exceptional form—a sudden intrusion of the military other—but as the uncanny doppelganger of daily life. The novel element of the so-called war on terror was that the enemy's weaponry took the familiar form of passenger jets, cars, computer code, and even the daily mail: technologies of communication and transportation. If an unattended backpack can, when viewed through the lens of ubiquitous threat, double as a dirty bomb, we are invited to anxiously ask ourselves an infinite series of related questions: "Is the steam rising from the street just exhaust— or a toxic gas?" "Is that white powder talcum—or anthrax?" "Is that rust in the water—or a biological agent?" The corollary of generalized suspicion is a paranoid redoubling of the world. The need for verification technologies multiplies along with the responsibility of individuals for monitoring a climate of proliferating risk.

The Reflexive Threat

One commonplace of the post-9/11 media coverage was the portrayal of the attacks as the result of, as one magazine put it, "a pre-modern religious Weltanschauung."[17] This portrayal neatly aligned itself with the Bush administration's assertion that the United States had become a target not because of its policies or behavior, but because it stood for the freedoms associated with modernity. By contrast, Islamic terrorists were portrayed as the fanatic guardians of an archaic and oppressive way of life struggling violently against western hegemony and modernization. The portrait was one of uneven modernization: as the modern world spread, it encountered resistance in some of the more "backward" corners of the globe, where those whose traditional power was threatened reacted violently and irrationally. This portrayal allowed the Bush regime to dismiss the notion that there might be historical reasons for the hatred and mistrust fomented against the United States. The hatred was portrayed as irrational by definition.

Consequently, arguments that the United States might be able to reduce animosity toward itself by ensuring that its policies lived up to its stated values of liberty and justice were portrayed at best as naive attempts to reason with irrational groups, or at worst as self-hating complicity in the irrational hatred directed toward the freedoms of the West. Conservative commentator and former U.S. Secretary of Education William J. Bennett was one of the more vociferous mouthpieces of the conservative line: "We are not hated because we support Israel; we are hated because liberal democracy is incompatible with militant Islam. . . . America was not punished because we are bad, but because we are good."[18] In other words, if there is a connection to be made between U.S. foreign policy and terrorism, it is that the latter is a symptom of the former's virtue rather than its vices. Thus, as Bennett puts it, "These are not times that should try our minds": there is no need to make the situation more complex than it is: a righteous nation faces an irrational, premodern hatred.[19]

The portrayal of terrorism as an irrational and archaic hatred not only allows for the dismissal of any consideration of the role of U.S. policy in triggering or exacerbating animosity toward the West, it also overlooks the distinctly contemporary aspects of terrorist organizations, many of whose international members are western educated and multilingual, and who rely on the latest information and communication technologies to coordinate their activities. News accounts of police raids on terrorist targets are frequently accompanied by detailed description of the computer disks and cell phones seized. Indeed, it has been hard to miss the similarity between the media portrayal of Al Qaeda and that of the stereotypical postindustrial organization characteristic of the new "flexible economy": a decentralized, dehierarchized organization that relies on fluid and temporary connections—a distributed, postmodern organization. The terrorists circulate through international transit hubs alongside international business travelers, keeping in touch via cell phone and carrying computer data. If we are to believe the media portrayals, Al Qaeda operates even more on the model of a distributed network than the most flexible of global corporations. The cells serve as independent nodes whose destruction needn't impair the functioning of the rest of the network. Consequently, we are told, on one hand, that the counterterrorist goal is to get Osama bin Laden, but on the other that the activities of the terror network will continue unabated without him. The organization is more Gnutella than Napster: it can't be shut down by taking out the command center.

In attempting to make sense out of an apparently archaic postmodernism, the media coverage at times seemed to be working at cross purposes: portraying bin Laden as a singular archenemy whose capture would constitute victory in the war on terrorism while simultaneously undermining the notion that fundamentalist terror organizations can be conceived in the centralized, hierarchical terms more appropriate to nation-states. As the model of the distributed network suggests, an organization like Al Qaeda cannot be approached simply as a regressive or archaic remainder of premodernity. One alternative to the ahistorical perspective that situates terrorism in an autonomous realm of irrational and radical evil is the explicit recognition of the ways in which, as sociologist Ulrich Beck suggests, terrorism emerges as one of the reflexive consequences of political and economic globalization.[20]

Beck's original formulation of the risk society draws on environmental politics to consider the ways in which the universalization of scientific skepticism becomes a reflexive and self-undermining gesture whereby scientific reason turns back on itself.[21] One result is the public recognition that the technology used to dominate nature turns into an oppressive and dangerous second nature that generates its own risks, many of which, in contradiction to the self-image of technological rationality, emerge as unseen and, as Beck suggests, incalculable (the threat of global warming, for example).

In the wake of the 9/11 attacks, Beck has included the threat of international terrorism as one of the reflexive risks of globalization: "The novelty of the world risk society lies in the fact that we, with our civilizing decisions, cause global consequences that trigger problems and dangers that radically contradict the institutionalized language and promises of the authorities in catastrophic cases highlighted worldwide (like in Chernobyl and now in the terrorist attacks in New York and Washington)."[22] However, he doesn't make explicit the parallel to his environmental example: that globalization, like technological rationality, has followed a calculus of domination and control that contributes to the formation of the incalculable risks of biological and nuclear terror haunting the contemporary imagination. The development of science and technology and the emergence of the terrorist threat have become entwined at all levels—from the forms of social, political, and cultural domination associated with the extraction of raw materials to the chemical and biological discoveries that allow deadly toxins to be manufactured relatively simply and, finally, to the role of the global mass media in broadcasting and amplifying the terrorist threat. As Beck puts it, "the risks of terrorism exponentially multiply with technological advancement. With the technologies of the future—genetic engineering, nanotechnology, and robotics, we are opening a 'new Pandora's box.'"[23]

The logic of those who ignore the reflexive aspect of terrorism—the way in which it emerges, at least in part, as a by-product of the instrumental logic of what Beck describes as neoliberal globalization—is that of the scientist who refuses to acknowledge the reflexive character of environmental hazards. Both prescribe more of the cause as the only possible cure, a prescription that stimulates a self-proliferating spiral of domination and catastrophe.

The reflexive model is ultimately one of self-implication: our own actions participate in the generation of risks in ways that remain largely opaque. A reliance on cheap gasoline is so far removed from the suffering of a village in Nigeria or Ecuador and any one individual's responsibility so diluted that it becomes seemingly impossible to trace or register the connection. Put differently, the web of interrelations has become so complex that it becomes impossible to imagine how *not* to remain caught up in it; the avoidance of one form of consumption results in the necessity of another.

The distributed and diffuse complicity on the part of "developed" nations is paralleled by the concentration of risk in the emergent form of the tyrannical figure of the "premodern" terrorist. In the era of reflexive modernization, a country recognized as an unchallenged global hegemon can fall victim to a handful of men armed only with box cutters or a test tube full of genetically engineered bacteria. Against the background of the challenge to the monolithic structures of industrial society posed by the new "flexibility" of the network society emerges the challenge of flexible, customized, and distributed violence. If the industrial era ushered in an era of warfare waged on the scale of mass society, with its mass armies and weapons of mass destruction, Ulrich Beck suggests that in the era of reflexive modernity, "we are on the threshold of the individualization of war."[24] This emerging portrayal of the terrorist serves as the sinister obverse of the new entrepreneurialism. The militant extremist brewing chemical or biological cocktails in the attic is the violent counterpart of the geeks tinkering with computers in the garage. As former Senate majority leader Bill Frist wrote in his recently published self-help manual on family protection against bioterrorism, "In general, neither sophisticated knowledge nor significant resources are required to launch a bioterrorist attack, and the materials are relatively easy to acquire. It has been estimated that a substantial biological arsenal could be developed in a fifteen-foot-square room with just $10,000 of equipment."[25]

The threat of a rival superpower engaged in a battle of military-industrial titans is replaced by the specter of a simple, cheap, but devastating attack on national security by a lone terrorist hunkered down in a suburban garage. The shift is the political analogue of the claim that in the information economy even a titan like Microsoft has to be on the lookout for threats not just from rival industrial heavyweights, but from the next generation of garage hackers. Thanks to the rapid spread of information, the networked economy can amplify a threat dramatically, whether in the form of a new source code, a computer virus, or media-circulated warnings of the heightened risk of a terrorist attack. As the French theorist Paul Virilio suggests, highlighting the reflexive nature of the threat in the era of the information society, "terrorism is intimately connected with technologization."[26]

"Not Small Enough . . ."

The process of the individualization of war anticipated by Beck corresponds to the universalization of threat and the de-differentiation of spatiotemporal divisions associated with the network society. The infinite justice pursued by the publicists of the war on terrorism mobilizes a complementary dis-aggregation of defense to correspond with the decentralization of the terrorist threat. As former DHS director Tom Ridge put it in one of the Ad Council radio spots for his readiness campaign, "We need all Americans to be engaged . . . down to the point where we ask mothers and fathers to think about doing some simple things at home to protect themselves and protect their children."[27] As of this writing, the latest addition to the DHS's Ready.gov preparedness site was a "ready kids" Web page with a series of games to help train children to prepare for both terrorist attacks and natural disaster. When he announced the program at a Chicago elementary school, DHS Secretary Michael Chertoff emphasized that "preparedness is not just a government challenge. We all have to learn how to plan for the unexpected."[28]

The recurring message is an admonitory invocation of self-reliance as a compensatory response to the disconcerting revelation that the lumbering institutions of mass society—mass armies and their hyperexpensive equipment—aren't nimble enough to counter the flexible threat of terrorism. Some duties of defense must be offloaded onto the civilian population. As the risk is generalized, individual participation at every level is required. This participation takes two forms: the "interpassive" one, in which data about every transaction, every purchase, and every movement is aggregated within the government equivalent of the demographic database; and the interactive form, in which citizens are encouraged to take responsibility for their role in the war on terror even as they go about their daily lives at work, at home, and at school.

Interpassive and Interactive Participation

After 9/11, the prospect of a technological fix along the lines of old-style weapons defense became a target of ridicule. So-called Star Wars antimissile defense technology was designed for the era of a standoff between superpowers, not for the new era of individualized warfare. A satellite network provides little in the way of defense against suicide pilots armed with box cutters. However, the logic of the technological fix resurfaced in the register of the information age: what was needed was not a missile defense system, but a vastly enhanced information system, which took the form of a superpanopticon: a database of databases administered by the Total Information Awareness Office. To the extent that even the most routine transactions, ranging from credit card purchases to video rentals, library loans, and online searches, already generate a digital record, this information could be aggregated and cross-indexed with government records. As the *New York Times* put it, "Total Information Awareness could link for the first time such different electronic sources as video feeds from airport surveillance cameras, credit card transactions, airline reservations and telephone calling records. The data would be filtered through software that would constantly look for suspicious patterns of behavior."[29] The office's goal would be to piggyback on the extensive demographic research accumulated by the private sector. Thanks in part to commercial monitoring and in part to existing technology, an extensive surveillance system was already in place in the form of surveillance cameras (soon to be equipped with facial recognition technology) and computer databases. All that was needed was a program to unite all of these "little brothers" into an all-encompassing "Big Brother" database.

Despite its reliance on the interactive capability of new information and communication technologies, the prospect of "total information awareness" anticipated by Poindexter's DARPA program remains decidedly nonreflexive in its approach to terrorism. Indeed, it serves as a strategy for abstracting the terrorist threat from the techniques of control and the relays of power that amplify it. In general terms, it offers the prospect of greater control—and a more global reach of techniques for both monitoring and enforcement—as the solution for risks that have been generated at least in part by the global expansion of economic and political domination. It's hard to escape the sense of a vicious cycle at work in an approach based on the notion that the threat of terrorism, which emerges in part from the globalization process, can only be countered by accelerating this process. Conversely, as Beck puts it, "the not yet publicly noticed strange natural law has proven itself that to resist globalization—whether you like it or not—only accelerates its engine."[30]

Thus, the Bush regime, after embarking on a policy of conservative isolationism, finds itself responding to the threat of terrorism with a strategy for global hegemony—globalization with a U.S. face—that entails remaking the entire Middle East, starting with Iraq. This version of globalization, as repeated media reports suggest, runs the danger of exacerbating the problem it addresses: the U.S. invasion threatens to inflame antiwestern sentiments and accelerate the pace, scope, and reach of terrorist attacks. Well over a year after the U.S. invasion and President Bush's well-publicized declaration of the "end of major combat operations," NBC News reported that Islamic terrorism attacks since 11 September 2001 "are on the rise worldwide—dramatically."[31] It is the lack of reflexivity—the externalization of the threat (as something entirely unrelated either to western policy or to the military response)—that accelerates and reinforces the cycle.

The fantasy is that this reinforcement is somehow temporary and provisional rather than systemic—that it is the result of incomplete globalization, domination, and control. What keeps the cycle spinning is the infinitely deferred perfection of control—or of surveillance, as in the case of the now defunct (in name only) Total Information Awareness Office. The cycle stops at the unattainable point of total awareness, an endpoint that, for the theorist Paul Virilio, recalls Goebbels's observation that "he who knows everything is not afraid of anything."[32]

Active and (Inter-)Passive Participation

In an era of individualized warfare—the military corollary of mass customization and the triumph of the niche market—systems of command and control rely on the proliferation and intensification of information-gathering technology and strategies. Just as in an interactive economy, consumers "participate" by contributing increasingly detailed data about their purchasing habits, their preferences, and their lifestyles. During a time of individualized warfare, this information doubles as their contribution to the security apparatus. The more information they provide about themselves, the more effectively they participate in their own defense. The power of interactivity is redoubled: the digital shadow cast by interactive consumers provides not only demographic information for the rationalization of consumption, but potential-threat profiles for security agencies. This was the recognition that inspired Admiral Poindexter's attempt to piggyback the intelligence-gathering effort on commercial databases. Poindexter may be gone, but the Bush administration has managed to preserve the general intent of his program by subcontracting it to private database firms and seeking to obtain commercial database information for policing purposes.

Perhaps the most convincing evidence of the link between mass customization and the "interactive" war on terror was the rapid repurposing of marketing database companies for antiterrorist surveillance documented by *Washington Post* reporter Robert O'Harrow Jr. in his book *No Place to Hide*. O'Harrow recounts how the government has outsourced its data-mining operations to database companies including ChoicePoint and LexisNexis. The result, he notes, is one more end run around the 1974 Privacy Act, which was created in response to covert government surveillance operations. Outsourcing surveillance means that government agencies don't have to worry about restrictions that set limits to the ability of government agencies to create database dossiers about individuals.[33] Moreover, privatizing surveillance operations means that the government can sidestep the law's accountability provisions, which are designed to ensure the accuracy of information stored about particular individuals. As one report quoted by O'Harrow puts it, the subcontracting of surveillance databases allows companies like ChoicePoint, working in the government's name, to "amass huge databases that the government is legally prohibited from creating."[34]

To the extent that this information is gathered with a minimum of friction, perhaps even without the explicit awareness of users—through transactionally generated data or unobtrusive cameras with facial recognition technology (perhaps coupled, eventually, with the "gait recognition" and "biometric" capabilities anticipated by the Total Information Awareness Office)—it requires a minimum of extra effort on the part of data collectors. Much of the information used for surveillance purposes by database companies was generated for other purposes, such as marketing or government record keeping. Its repurposing for terrorist profiling is one of the many forms of function creep that take place within the digital enclosure: information gathered for one purpose can easily be reconfigured for other uses, thanks to the ease of copying, storing, searching, and transporting digital data. In this respect, consumer participation in the creation of government surveillance databases may be largely inadvertent. Just as the digital enclosure allows commercial entities to capture transactionally generated information for marketing purposes, it allows the state to capture the same information for surveillance purposes.

The information gathering process is made even easier by the current climate of self-disclosure facilitated by interactive technology. The popularity of online journal writing, blogging, and social networking has helped generate a treasure trove of information for data miners, whether for marketing or policing purposes. The Pentagon's National Security Agency has already funded research into "the mass harvesting of the information people post about themselves on social networks."[35] One news account suggests that data harvested from freely available online sites could be combined with information from other databases about "banking, retail, and property records, allowing the NSA to build extensive, all-embracing personal profiles of individuals." Posting information on MySpace, in other words, can double as a form of active participation in creating a government data dossier about oneself.

Comprehensive monitoring programs like that envisioned by the Total Information Awareness Office don't distinguish between suspects and the rest of the populace in the collection of information. Rather, the data-gathering process is a fishing expedition, designed to generate suspects by sifting through the data and identifying potentially high-risk individuals. Data gathered about the rest of the populace is essential to the process: it helps set a baseline pattern of behavior for investigators, one from which any evidence of deviance triggers suspicion and further investigation. Data like that provided from social networking sites might be described as the result of inadvertently active participation in the surveillance process: people providing more information about themselves thanks to the available technology, but without the expectation that the information might be used for policing purposes.

By contrast, the active component of participation in surveillance comes in the form of the call for practices of mutual monitoring that complement and enhance centralized monitoring. In his book on bioterrorism, for example, Bill Frist suggests that one of the most important forms of civilian participation in the battle against terrorism is to "become the eyes and ears of our law enforcement agencies": "You know your communities better than anyone else. You know when something looks out of place, whether it's a package left on the subway or someone acting in an unusual or suspicious manner in your neighborhood."[36] Shortly after the 9/11 attacks, the government started a call-in program called TIPS that so closely echoed the participatory character of the popular TV show, *America's Most Wanted,* that one White House secretary reportedly forwarded a TIPS call to the switchboard for the television show.[37]

The invitation to participate in lateral surveillance was literalized by a CIA postcard campaign that invited residents to participate in a species of "neighborhood watch program against terrorism." According to one newspaper account, thousands of postcards were sent to Virginia residents in the neighborhood near CIA headquarters, asking them to "report anything unusual or serious associated with your community and/or the Headquarters." In an apparent attempt to personalize and humanize the request, the cards were accompanied by a friendly explanation signed, enigmatically, only by "Marie."[38] Just as the CIA watches over the neighborhood, so too are neighbors invited to watch over the CIA—through participation in mutual monitoring.

The interactive medium of the Internet lends itself to the mobilization of distributed forms of participatory surveillance, as evidenced by the New Jersey city of East Orange's creation of an online Virtual Community Patrol. The police department announced its plans to provide selected residents with access to "a Web site that provides panoramic views of their block, allows them to type in general complaints, pinpoint a problem location, immediately send that information to police headquarters, and simultaneously activate hidden police surveillance cameras."[39] The police department described the initiative as a civilian-participation program that provides privileged access to the means of surveillance: "We plan on giving the community control of a very powerful technology."[40] In return, members of the public are asked to help extend the monitoring reach of the police force. They will add "intelligence" to an existing network of closed circuit surveillance cameras and an "acoustic gunshot sensor system," thereby helping to solve the staffing problem posed by the proliferation of monitoring technologies. Thanks to the promise of interactive participation in the policing process, the authorities can exploit the free labor of selected members of the community. The wager, of course, is that entrusting members of the populace with access to surveillance technology will encourage them to internalize the norms of state surveillance and policing: they will identify the problem the same way the police do, thanks, at least in part, to having been accorded the role of an agent of the state. Thus, the threat of pervasive and proliferating risks underwrites the invitation to participate in self-policing by providing for the capillary extension of surveillance into households and surrounding neighborhoods—a strategy that enlists the appeal of participation as a shared responsibility. As social theorist Mitchell Dean suggests, the invitation to participate in the process of risk management accompanies the mobilization of an increasing range and scope of risks by authorities who serve as "tutors in the multiple forms of risk."[41]

With the homeland security campaign, such forms of tutelage come full circle: the consumption of surveillance technologies and the cultivation of monitoring techniques by corporations and private citizens are reclaimed for national defense in an era of generalized threat. Online and off, a recent trend in surveillance has been the mass marketing of investigatory tools once restricted to the realm of law enforcement to consumers interested in backgrounding nannies, potential mates, or in-laws, and in monitoring the activities of children, spouses, and significant others.

A populace increasingly well versed in spy skills and habituated to a culture of surveillance is invited by the mobilization of a proliferating array of risks to put its training to work. The ostensibly democratic character of such participation—the implication that the monitoring process is no longer solely the province of professionals, but can be shared with those normally excluded from the command centers of the intelligence industry—is, in this instance, supplemented by the promotion of a shared sense of civic responsibility in an era of perpetual, decentralized warfare. As a public service announcement put out by the state of New Jersey's Domestic Security Preparedness Task Force put it, "Terrorism is a fact of life that's not going away."[42] Complacency, the PSA admonishes, plays into the hands of the terrorists and must be replaced by generalized vigilance: "Terrorists count on you not paying attention, you can prove them wrong, we can fight back using our eyes, our ears and just our plain old gut to report anything that looks suspicious."[43] The populist appeal is not just to civilian expertise in mutual monitoring, but to the trustworthy instincts of the good citizen. The PSA continues with a brief primer in threat detection for the masses and an invitation to visit the state's online do-it-yourself homeland security guide. As in the case of the federal Ready.gov site, the information is disconcertingly sparse and simplistic, and the recurring theme is one of universal suspicion and generalized fear.

Self-Monitoring

The participatory, interactive character of the war on terror extends beyond mutual monitoring to embrace a characteristic element of reflexive governance: self-surveillance. The need to prepare oneself and to train and inform oneself (and one's family) how best to practice the proper forms of participation in homeland defense comprises the core of the government's readiness campaign. The Ready.gov readiness pamphlet provides a list of tasks and procedures designed to foster a sense of preparedness. Recommendations range from tips on stocking emergency food supplies to the injunction to "be informed." They are supplemented with some simple summaries of threats (biological, chemical, nuclear, and radioactive) and pictograms suggesting possible responses ("If you have a thick shield between yourself and the radioactive materials more of the radiation will be absorbed and you will be exposed to less").[44]

The information comes across as simple, clear, sanitized, and frustratingly inadequate. The image of a man standing in the path of nuclear radiation with a timer pointing to him ("minimize time spent exposed") defaults to self-parody, the twenty-first-century version of "duck and cover." Fear is both countered and exacerbated by a litany of tasks and activities: in the face of a threat that deliberately thwarts planning, it is not so much the substance of the planning that is at stake, but the fact that one is perpetually planning, continually informing oneself, always calculating, evaluating, and watching. As an enterprise, security is an ongoing affair, a Sisyphean task without end. The familiar tune of "lifelong learning" is transposed into the key of homeland defense. The risk is so diffuse, the possible forms of attack so varied and, ultimately, so impossible to anticipate, that preparation can extend to include all aspects of life, from physical fitness to child rearing, piety, and, once again, good hygiene.

The terrorist threat invigorates the deployment of what social theorist Mitchell Dean describes as "the new prudentialism": "the multiple 'responsibilization' of individuals, families, households, and communities for their own risks."[45] The new prudentialism multiplies and extends the domains to be managed, monitored, and subjected to the productive discipline of personal security—a discipline that compels consumption of surveillance and security technologies, up-to-date information about risk, and market-based forms of insurance and security.

Similarly, *When Every Moment Counts*, the post-9/11 primer on biological threats by surgeon-legislator Bill Frist makes clear the connection between bioterror and biopower (the management of the life processes of the populace). In response to the prospect of generalized risk, Frist advocates the enhancement and rehabilitation of a new and improved normalcy that relies on the enhanced care of the self. To adequately cope with the stress of terrorism, Frist advocates regular exercise ("exercise can actually . . . give you a greater sense of control"), proper nutrition ("avoid too much caffeine, sugar, or alcohol"), a regular sleep cycle, and the embrace of a daily routine ("If you're feeling like your life is spinning out of control, the simple, productive daily routines . . . offer calming reassurance that life does go on").[46]

In short, participation in the war on terror—in which we are all participants, like it or not, in this account—is a method of inciting the productive deployment of self-care. It is not difficult to discern the links that can—and are—being made between the threat of individualized warfare and the promotion of neoliberal versions of individualism, self-discipline, and self-reliance. One apparent goal is the reform of "institutional and individual conduct so that both come to embody the values and orientations of the market, expressed in notions of enterprise and the consumer."[47] Frist's list serves as an elaboration and amplification of National Security Adviser Condoleezza Rice's post-9/11 call for productive patriotism: "It's every American's duty to get back to doing the things that make us American. . . . Going to work and going to shop and taking your kids to school."[48]

Read through the bleak and fractured lens of the terrorist threat, all "normal" activities are redoubled as combat duties, and perpetual threat is in turn normalized. Consumption-based activities double as civic duty, just as the citizen's duty is to engage in the consumption of security and the forms of self-training and self-education ostensibly necessitated by a perpetual and ubiquitous threat. This is "pure war" in the sense invoked by French theorist Paul Virilio but transposed into the register of decentralized risk: "war is no longer in its execution, but in its preparation. The perpetuation of war is what I call Pure War, war which isn't acted out in repetition, but in infinite preparation."[49] It is the combination of the market-based responsibilization of the populace with the atmosphere of militarization and threat that characterizes the homeland security campaign. Risk is not merely associated with the diffuse and multiplying threats of modernity, from economic to environmental uncertainty, but with a specific (albeit diffuse) threat.

It has hard not to catch the note of opprobrium in the appeal to duty and the stark admonitions of the Homeland Security ads: what part of the blame is allocated to those who fail to heed the call for preparedness? Perhaps, as in one theorist's formulation, the victims may find themselves defined as those "in need of counseling and help" in part because "they have failed to manage their own risks as individuals, as households and as neighborhoods."[50] Such is the substance of former DHS director Tom Ridge's warning to the man who thought that the odds against his being a target were too small. The implicit accusation is doubly unsettling: not only is everyone a target of a threat that is by nature unpredictable and constantly shifting, but the victims may face the accusation of not having suitably prepared themselves.

Future Map

The suppression of the reflexive character of terrorist risk by the Bush administration underwrites a reaction that is the exact opposite of that anticipated by sociologist Ulrich Beck: "After the terrorist attack even the [United] States recognized the power and possibilities of transnational cooperation. . . . All of a sudden the opposite of neoliberalism, the importance of the state, becomes once again omnipresent. . . . The times of 'everyone to the best of their abilities and will' are certainly over."[51] It's hard to overstate, in the wake of events including the attack on Iraq, just how wrong Beck's predictions were (at least in the short run). Rather, what has emerged in the wake of the individualization of warfare and the spread of a generalized terrorist risk is, at least in the policies of the Bush administration and the formulation of its readiness program, the individualization of defense. Underwriting this response is the nonreflexive externalization of the terrorist threat as evidenced by the readiness campaign's equation of terrorism and natural disaster: "Families in Florida prepare themselves for the hurricane season; families in California prepare themselves for earthquakes. Every family in American should prepare itself for a terrorist attack."[52] Terrorism is portrayed as a form of second nature: an additional uncontrollable force in the world, just as independent of national policy as a tsunami or earthquake.

In the face of generalized risk, the proposed response, which draws on the rhetoric of participatory self-empowerment suitable to the era of networked interactivity, is the displacement of the monolithic public welfare model of governance by the multiple and flexible agencies of risk management and self-empowerment. Bill Frist, while adopting the mantle of Senate leadership, simultaneously used the climate of pervasive threat—and the implicit inadequacy of welfare-society defense programs—to publicize his self-help primer on bioterror. It is a humorous but perhaps telling detail that the much-ridiculed advisory issued by the DHS urging citizens to prepare for the threat of impending terrorist attacks with duct tape (among other items) ended up boosting sales for a staunch Bush supporter. Several news accounts noted that the founder of the company that manufactures almost half of all the duct tape sold in the United States gave $100,000 to the Republican National Committee and other GOP committees during the 2000 campaign. The company's CEO, John Kahl, reported that after the homeland security advisory, "'we're seeing a doubling and tripling of our sales, particularly in certain metro markets and around the coasts and borders.'"[53] In the wake of the duct tape announcement, the company saw sales increase 40 percent over the same time the previous year.

Duct tape was just the tip of the iceberg: the DHS's admonition to all citizens to "be prepared" doubled as taxpayer-supported advertising for a burgeoning industry in do-it-yourself defense technology, marketed by companies with names like "Safer America," "Safety Square," and "Security Planet"—entrepreneurs in the latest, and most urgent, self-help industry. It is in keeping with the enterprise culture promoted by the homeland security campaign that it would lend itself not just to individual responsibilization, but to the promotion of markets in risk-management technologies. In what seems almost a parody of the offloading process, the privatization of homeland security fostered emergent retail markets in technologies once reserved for the professionals: lie detectors, handheld explosives detectors, security wands, and even walk-through metal detectors.

Successful entrepreneurs—along with the patriotic shoppers hailed by national security advisor Condoleezza Rice—were invited to construe their private economic activity as public service. In the neoliberal risk-enterprise culture, as one theorist notes, "No longer is there a conflict between the self-interest of the economic subject and the patriotic duty of the citizen."[54] The Safer America Web site, for example, which offers many of the products described above, as well as the "Executive Chute"—a parachute for those who work in skyscrapers—notes that in the wake of 9/11, the company's founder "came to the realization that he had two options: sit and listen to the confusing news and heightened security alerts, or do something productive. He also understood that the feelings of fear and anxiety that so many are feeling are rooted in the feeling of helplessness. . . . [He] realized that the key in answering this problem is providing people tools, resources and solutions that negate the feeling of helplessness."[55] In a climate of generalized and reflexive risk, in which even prosperity produces threat, as the Bush administration repeatedly asserts, anxiety is especially productive, and risk can be leveraged for profit.

Despite the entrepreneurial rhetoric, it's not only the do-it-yourself security startups that benefit. Private contractors like Halliburton, Titan Industries, and other suppliers of security equipment and personnel (most of whose training was subsidized by taxpayers via the military), have, as press accounts during the first year of the Iraq war suggest, benefited greatly from the prosecution and privatization of the war on terror. Richard Perle, former chair of the Defense Policy Group and one of the influential administration advisors in the war on terrorism, was named as managing partner in a business venture registered shortly after 9/11 devoted to investing "in companies dealing in technology, goods, and services that are of value to homeland security and defense."[56]

One result is that centralized forms of social control and risk management associated with the welfare state are replaced by niche markets for security. Bill Frist's business endeavors highlight the logic of this strategy in its various manifestations. In addition to capitalizing on the demand for terrorism protection, Frist, whose family fortune comes from a for-profit hospital chain, is a leading congressional advocate for the privatization of Medicare. What is taking place, in the face of a generalized and omnipresent risk—to which terrorism can assimilate itself, and which it comes to symbolize—is the marketization and ultimately the privatization of risk management. However, this shift is best understood not as a form of deregulation but of reregulation, whereby society comes to be governed not through the direct mechanisms of the welfare state, but "through the government of the mechanisms, techniques, and agencies of government themselves."[57] Such government relies on the participation of the citizenry in their self-government and therefore on the public sector version of interactivity-as-participation described in previous chapters: active collusion in the process of one's own manipulation and management.

Significantly, once government has been fragmented into a collection of markets including health care, insurance, unemployment, and security, the management of the social is transposed into the calculation, monitoring, and manipulation of markets. Public opinion management defaults to market management, as in the reliance of neoconservative commentators on stock market performance as a guide to the prosecution of the Iraq war. In the wake of 9/11, the occasional humorous parody of the way in which the Bush administration has linked a variety of seemingly unrelated programs to the prosecution of the war—programs ranging from environmental deregulation to cutting corporate taxes and reforming Medicare—miss the way in which these programs and the war itself remain integrally connected by a strategy in which "the individualization of risk is linked to new forms of liberal government."[58] The market model, as this chapter's discussion of neoliberalism is meant to suggest, substitutes public identification with market imperatives for collective deliberation: it shatters the collective character of public deliberation into discrete and individualized market choices. In so doing, it further incorporates a set of economic and political imperatives that accord with the state's definition of the war on terror as well as with its economic priorities. To put this in slightly different terms, although any form of democratic governance might be described as a strategy for offloading duties of the state onto the populace, the market model privileges a disaggregated model of decision making over other possible alternatives, while simultaneously structuring the terms of participation according to the imperatives of state authorities.

The model of participation on offer in the interactive war on terror, in other words, contributes to the experience of the recession of causality described in previous chapters. There is a logic to the pattern of individual decisions (insofar as they are structured by state and market imperatives), but it remains opaque to the participants. The standard liberal-pluralist interpretation of the market suggests that this opacity is symmetrical or evenly distributed: no one has any greater impact over the outcome than anyone else, such that there is an ungovernable logic to the process whose pattern can only be discerned in retrospect.

A critical approach influenced by the Foucault-inflected literature on governance, by contrast, suggests that the privatization of public deliberation through market mechanisms might be described as a form of governing at a distance. This is to say that control is exerted on the public by means of the very guidelines for participation that define terrorism as an external threat unrelated to government policy and that serve to maximize the economic productivity and political docility of the populace. Preparing oneself means taking on the duties of being a good consumer and an efficient producer, a self-disciplined and self-monitoring contributor to the very economy whose systematic and at times violent expansion contributes to the proliferation of reflexive risks in both the political and environmental spheres.

The instructions for preparation in the face of a terrorist threat described in Senate majority leader Bill Frist's primer on preparedness, for example, recall the forms of socialization to which Henry Ford's workers were subjected at the turn of the century: training in forms of economic self-management, personal hygiene, and lifestyle designed to increase the efficiency and reliability of the labor force. The critical point is that relegating politics to the marketplace has political implications of its own: it coordinates and channels individual decisions while avoiding the forms of self-conscious coordination and deliberation associated with collective action. Neoliberal forms of interactivity allow for the shaping of collective action without an associated public—merely an aggregation of private, atomized decision makers. The version of interactivity on offer is far from democratic, a theme that is taken up in more detail in the following chapter on interactive politics in the digital enclosure.

7

iPolitics

The threat today is not passivity but pseudo-activity, the urge "to be active" to "participate" to mask the Nothingness of what goes on.
—Slavoj Žižek, *The Parallax View*

In the spring of 2006, as the nation's political parties trained their sights on the upcoming midterm elections and, farther down the road, on the next presidential election, the chosen weapon of at least one candidate was the database. An advisor for former first lady Hilary Clinton announced plans to create a $10 million company that would amass as much detailed information about prospective voters as possible. As one news account suggested, the data-mining push, heavily funded by financier and outspoken Bush administration critic George Soros, would help close the database gap between Democrats and Republicans. Although Democrats have historically had an edge over Republicans when it comes to grassroots, get-out-the-vote campaigning, the GOP's successful adoption of target marketing technology reportedly made a significant difference in the 2002 midterm elections: "For the first time in recent memory, Republicans ran better get-out-the-vote programs than Democrats. . . . Democrats have become increasingly fearful that the GOP is capitalizing on high-speed computers and the growing volume of data available from government files and consumer marketing firms—as well as the party's own surveys—to better target potential supporters."[1]

Suggestively, the Democrats proved highly effective at using the Internet to raise campaign funds—thanks at least in part to their legacy of grassroots campaigning, which was facilitated and amplified by the social networking capacity of the Internet and, famously, by the Meetup.org Web site in particular. What the Republicans did more effectively, thanks in part to database tools and the strategies devised by consultant Karl Rove, was to target campaign spending. If Democrats were better at harnessing the power of social networking, the Republicans did a better job of marketing.

Political campaigning, to put it in slightly different terms, has entered the database world, a realm of asymmetrical data gathering, data mining, and target marketing. As one pair of researchers describes it, "the panoptic aspect of such political surveillance . . . reflects the extent to which the political and the commercial are inherently intertwined and inseparable under current articulations of American democracy."[2] This connection perhaps explains why the business-oriented Republican Party was more effective in its database-driven marketing campaign. The flip side of the championing of privatization by post–welfare state neoliberalism is the ongoing adoption of private-sector strategies for political purposes. In the era of electronic mass media, this is far from a novel strategy; political consultants have long made careers out of finding ways to use electronic media to market their candidates. The point is not merely to observe that politics has become a form of marketing—this happened quite some time ago—but rather to consider the impact on the political process of emerging interactive marketing strategies facilitated by monitoring techniques and technologies. This chapter first outlines some of the trends in political marketing and then develops a theoretical framework for a critique of mass customized politics. Finally it draws on this framework to critique the impact of data-driven forms of separation, sorting, and surveillance on democratic politics, arguing that not all participation is democratic in character.

The Political Promise of New Media

The mobilization of the promise of interactivity comes into its own in the realm of politics—the realm from which the popular reception of new media as tendentially democratic is drawn. The sentiments of new media theorist and game designer Celia Pearce neatly complement those of ubiquitous political consultant and cybercelebrant Joe Trippi. Both, for example, invoke the promise of technologically facilitated democratic revolution. As Pearce notes, "The digital age introduces a new form of international socialism, a new kind of democracy that Marx never even imagined."[3] The political and economic elites that have developed and promoted the technology have, she suggests, spun the Web into rope for their own hanging: "The Newt Gingriches of the world, who have inadvertently popularized the thing that will be their undoing should be very, very afraid. Because when it comes right down to it, an online underclass is much more powerful than an armed underclass."[4] Joe Trippi evinces a similar revolutionary fervor: "Every institution that doesn't understand that the technology is finally here to allow people to reject what they're being given and *demand what they want* had better start paying attention. The revolution comes for you next."[5]

The story of the political deployment of the Internet is, according to Trippi, a story of the revitalization of democracy: "Most of all it's the story of people standing up and making themselves heard. It's the story of how to engage those Americans in a real dialogue, how to reach them where they live, how to stop *selling* to them and start *listening* to them."[6] This opposition is, as I have been arguing throughout the course of this book, not just a false one, but a usefully misleading one. It suggests that technologies that facilitate "listening" necessarily empower those invited to disclose information about themselves. However, the emerging model of data-driven relationship marketing undermines the opposition described by Trippi: the sellers are able to sell more effectively precisely because they are able to listen more efficiently. In the end, the marketing-based model enlisted by the Republican Party triumphed, whereas the high-profile challenge by the Dean campaign, managed by Trippi, famously went down in flames, fanned by the viral spread over the Internet of the candidate's famous screech speech.

The facts not withstanding, the general promise of empowerment outlined in Chapter 1 has been explicitly taken up by scholars studying the role of media in politics and, according to one account, "a number of theorists have argued that such technologies may help contain or provide the public sphere necessary for true participatory democracy."[7] Cybercelebrants are engaged, perhaps unwittingly, in parroting the litany of claims that have greeted each new electronic medium in the twentieth century, from the telegraph to cable TV. It is worth rehearsing some of these claims to provide a bit of historical context for the current enthusiasm bubbling up around the democratic potential of new media.

What emerges from a survey of the celebratory responses to new media technologies during the twentieth century might be described as a form of repetition compulsion: a stubborn ahistorical reiteration of the mantra that any device that facilitates the transmission of information is inherently democratizing, not least in the sense that it enhances mutual respect and understanding—resources for collective action and reasoned deliberation. In their early history of the telegraph, for example, Charles Briggs and Augustus Maverick wrote that the device "binds together by a vital cord all the nations of the earth. It is impossible that old prejudices and hostilities should longer exist, while such an instrument has been created for an exchange of thought between all the nations of the earth."[8] An early fan of radio directly applied this line of thought to the new medium: "How fine is the texture of the web that radio is even now spinning! It is achieving the task of making us feel together, think together, live together."[9] Speaking of the medium that would, toward the end of the twentieth century, become dominated by figures including Rush Limbaugh and Howard Stern, another commentator observed, "Radio might even produce a new kind of politician, a man without the ordinary tricks of delivery, but possessed of a quiet, logical persuasiveness."[10] As for TV, authors Barry Schwartz and J. G. Watkins predicted cable TV, the medium that provides us with *Fear Factor, Blind Date,* and professional wrestling, would not only "create great access to information; it will also greatly assist self-identity, democratic processes, educational environments and community cohesion."[11] Media scholar Vincent Mosco has devoted an entire chapter of his book, *The Digital Sublime,* to the utopian predictions surrounding electronic media, and he draws on the work of another noted scholar, James Carey, to sum up his findings: "As Carey . . . notes, starting with the telegraph we observe a renewed triumphalism asserting that every improvement in communication would end isolation, link people every-where, realizing in practice the 'Universal Brotherhood of Universal Man.'"[12]

Just a little familiarity with history adds some grains of salt to our reception of claims, such as those of futurist William Wriston's, that "the force of microelectronics will blow apart all monopolies, hierarchies, pyramids, and power grids of established industrial society," or author George Gilder's assertion that the personal computer will become "a powerful force for democracy, individuality, community, and high culture."[13] New media technologies have done a much better job of assimilating themselves to the interests of established political and economic hierarchies than blowing them to bits. Even as cybercelebrants hype the revolutionary power of blogs and social networking, media moguls like Rupert Murdoch enlist the rhetoric of revolution as a marketing strategy. Shortly after buying the social networking site MySpace for half a billion dollars, Murdoch observed, "Technology is shifting power away from the editors, the publishers, the establishment, the media elite. Now it's the people who are taking control. . . . We're looking at the ultimate opportunity. . . . The internet is media's golden age."[14]

Given the historical context, it is perhaps testimony to a persistent case of technological amnesia that media theorists still feel confident making claims like, "Far from the telescreen dystopias, new media technology hails a rebirth of democratic life."[15] New media guru Howard Rheingold is more circumspect, noting that whether the Internet comes to serve as an online agora or a virtual panopticon will depend on who controls it and for what purposes. Still, his outlook remains on the whole more optimistic than pessimistic, and he insists, "The political significance of computer mediated communication lies in its capacity to challenge the existing political hierarchy's monopoly on powerful communications media, and perhaps thus revitalize citizen-based democracy."[16]

Considered in the abstract, enhanced interactivity, information access, and the ability to build community over long distances certainly sound like positive, if not necessarily revolutionary, additions to the media landscape. The argument of this book is, however, that an abstract consideration of such technologies is both incoherent and misleading: incoherent because it makes claims diametrically opposed to the evidence supplied by concrete applications; misleading because it implies that actual applications are determined by the technical capabilities themselves—that, for example, the Internet, by its very nature, ought to be inherently threatening to centralized, hierarchical power relations.

The real question that needs to be addressed is how new media technologies are being turned to political ends not in theory, but in practice. And this practice increasingly takes place within a context characterized by the accumulation of control over information facilitated by the digital enclosure. Thus, any consideration of political uses of new media needs to explore not just the capabilities theoretically available to individual users, but the actual application of these capabilities in the age of "digital capitalism."[17] It is one thing to say with Joe Trippi that the Internet could be the "most democratizing innovation we've ever seen," and quite another to consider the ways in which it is being used as one of the most powerful technologies for centralized information gathering, sorting, and management that we've ever seen.[18] The following sections consider the ways in which the Internet has been enlisted by politicians and their consultants as a tool for management and marketing—a model borrowed from and based on target and relationship marketing. An important consequence of the political adoption of this model is, as one group of researchers notes, "an opening up of *the market for political information*."[19]

Political consultants—never far behind the marketers—have realized for some time that market-research algorithms can yield information useful not just for selling products, but for recruiting voters. The problem was finding cheap and efficient ways to gather and sort the information. One political consultant, for example, recalled how research revealed several decades ago "that Mercury owners were far more likely to vote Republican than owners of any other kind of automobile—data that was so constant across the country . . . that it couldn't possibly have been the product of chance. 'We never had the money or the technology to make anything of it. . . . But of course, they do now.'"[20]

Generating the type of information useful to political parties requires accumulating as much information as possible about voters in order to sift through it and discern reliable patterns of voting behavior that might be exploited by political operatives. Just as background details like education level, place of residence, and reading habits help predict what type of products a consumer is likely to buy, they can serve as reliable indicators of which hot-button political issues voters care about—at least, that's what political consultants are telling parties and candidates. As the former head of the Republican National Committee put it, "We can tailor our message to people who care about taxes, who care about health care, who care about jobs, who care about regulation—we can target that way."[21]

The clues and cues that guide targeted political marketing campaigns are not always obvious, but they can be extracted by sifting through large databases for unexpected or unanticipated correlations. One Republican consultant commented, "The microtargeter would tell me, 'You know, if you own a Ford Explorer and you garden and like the outdoors and you're over 50, there might be a high likelihood that you care about tort reform.' . . . I don't know how they do this, and I was skeptical, but it works."[22] The result is a change in the mode of address adopted by political campaigners—instead of tailoring a general message designed to maximize common appeal and minimize offense, the goal is to target individuals and groups based on key motivating issues—to provide not a generalized, blurry portrait of the candidate, but a customized, high-resolution perspectival portrait that can be modified to meet the interests and concerns of specific audiences.

During President George W. Bush's second term, the prevailing political wisdom was that Republicans under the leadership of former direct-mail consultant Karl Rove had the database edge—and were using it very much in keeping with standard marketing strategies that were based as much on emotional as on rational appeals. During the 2002 elections, one report stated, "Consultants working for the Republican National Committee developed strategies to design messages targeting individual voters' 'anger points' in the belief that grievance is one of the strongest motivations to get people to turn out on Election Day."[23]

Detailed databases allowed for some significant changes in campaign strategy. Whereas the prevailing political wisdom had been to avoid districts heavily populated by opposition party voters, target marketing allowed for tactical poaching: "The advantage of data-based targeting is that political field operatives can home in on precisely the voters they wish to reach—the antiabortion parishioners of a traditionally Democratic African American church congregation, for instance."[24]

The result, in short, is the attempt to manage masses of voters, Taylor style, by disaggregating them. This niche-marketing approach requires the same asymmetry of information in the political as in the commercial realms: the accumulation of detailed information about consumers combined, ideally, with a corresponding lack of information about alternatives (or undesirable aspects of the product being pushed) on the part of consumers. Conservative field operatives picking off the abortion foes in a traditionally African American church congregation want to make sure to avoid touching on the other campaign planks that might alienate these voters and make them hesitate to become one-issue voters.

As in marketing, so in politics: compiling detailed information about voters in a cost-effective manner largely depends on their entry into the digital enclosure. In theory, political operatives could develop detailed databases about voters by going door to door, conducting in-depth interviews about everything from political preferences to shopping habits, and compiling public and private records, but the cost would be prohibitive—not least because voters would likely find the process disturbingly invasive. By contrast, the privatized digital enclosure provides access to extensive databases of information gathered for other purposes. Like marketers, political data miners can avail themselves of the migration and accumulation of information in marketing databases. Moreover, they can harness emerging interactive technologies to the ends of political research.

Consider, for example, the case of Knowledge Networks, an instant polling company founded by two Stanford political scientists who realized, as had market researchers before them, the information-gathering capability of interactive communication technology. Knowledge Networks turned the TiVo model of interactive content delivery into an instant political polling mechanism by spending millions of dollars to equip more than 40,000 homes of selected viewers with Web TVs. The viewers received the interactive TV device—their portal into the digital enclosure—free of cost in exchange for agreeing to spend ten minutes a week answering pollsters' questions over the Internet.[25]

In order to raise the more than $40 million needed to purchase, install, and link the 40,000-plus Web TVs that form the virtual infrastructure of Knowledge Networks' digital enclosure, the professors had to make it dual purpose: a system for both market and political research. Political polling is, perhaps not surprisingly, a few steps behind commerce when it comes to the development of relationship marketing—a process that Knowledge Networks pushes toward its logical extreme: always-on information gathering. In addition to the weekly polls, the Web TVs gather detailed information about viewing habits and Web surfing behavior that can be used to create profiles of the respondents. The device that is used to gather instant responses to, for example, the performance of candidates during a political debate also collects a constant stream of information about viewers even when they aren't directly engaged in the polling process. The invitation to participate in the process of instant online polling, in other words, doubles as a perhaps less obvious inducement to enter into a relationship characterized by always-on monitoring.

The use of interactive TVs as a polling tool is continuous with a long-standing tradition of the deployment of communication technologies that provide access to the private sphere as a means of simultaneously extracting information from it. As we saw in Chapter 3, the early polling and ratings industry embraced the telephone as a technology for catching people at home and gathering information about them in discrete bursts: the radio show that they happened to be listening to at the time of the call, which products they had recently purchased, and, eventually whom they planned to vote for.

Recent debates surrounding government surveillance in the United States have demonstrated that the telephone remains an important monitoring technology—one that promises, thanks to the development of cell phone networks, to become increasingly individualized and continuous. In addition to the telephone, specially equipped radio and television sets can become monitoring technologies, thanks to the invention and development of Audimeters and then People Meters. Digital TV and the Internet represent both the continuation of this trend and a quantum leap forward in information gathering technology thanks to their built-in interactive capability. Whereas telephone surveys, Audimeters, and related devices require the audience's active consent and participation, interactive networked technologies come with a built-in, passive information-gathering capacity that promises broader coverage and decreased audience awareness of monitoring practices.

Nielsen households, for example, have a constant reminder that information about their viewing habits is being gathered: the requirement to fill out viewing diaries, or to punch in when they are watching TV. TiVo viewers, by contrast, receive no such reminder. As in the case of the Internet, the monitoring that takes place is largely passive in the sense that it is generated as a by-product of using the technology itself. The result is what might be described as a passive form of interactivity—what the philosopher Slavoj Žižek has described (in a different context) as "interpassivity."[26] The machine does the interacting for us. Viewers are active in the sense that they are always providing information about themselves—but not critically active in the sense of being aware that monitoring is taking place and how the information is being used.

In the political context, the smooth functioning of niche campaigning depends on this precritical or passive form of participation. The effectiveness of niche campaigning depends, at least in part, on voters not realizing that they are being provided with a customized appeal, one that may look very different from those received by voting groups with different political views from their own. As researchers who have studied this new breed of political research tools have noted, even when participants are informed about the information-gathering capability of their Web TVs (which the researchers liken to spyware that covertly gathers information about online activity), over time, this awareness tends to fade into the background: "Spyware is sometimes installed with the generally underinformed agreement of the user, who often later forgets about its presence."[27]

In addition to the information collected through dedicated devices like those installed by Knowledge Networks, political researchers, like marketers, are able to make use of information that people disclose both offline, in the form of public records and proprietary databases, and in the form of the "free" information that millions of Internet users post online. Thus, for example, the popular press has highlighted the ways in which personal information posted online to social networking sites like MySpace and Facebook has been used for research purposes and background checking by police and potential employers. A student who posted a photo of himself drinking beer in his dorm room to his Facebook site, for example, found himself accused of violating university policy, an accusation supported by evidence he had supplied himself.[28]

Thanks to the ease with which digital files can be transported, large amounts of data gathered, for example, by the state for driver registration or property tax records can be imported wholesale into commercial databases and used for target marketing purposes (depending on local laws, some of which charge hefty fees for information gathering, restricting it to well-heeled corporations; or they place other restrictions on the availability of some public records). The information that we enter into magazine subscription forms finds its way into direct-mail databases, and the information we enter into online forms can rapidly be assimilated into marketing algorithms. Perhaps one of the defining characteristics of the digital enclosure is that within it, information constantly flows and migrates. This does not mean, however, that it can't be controlled. Yes, firewalls and databases can be breached, but for the most part, the flow of information is not as anarchic as the high-profile press coverage of file-sharing networks might suggest.[29] Large amounts of information can be gathered, stored, and transmitted cheaply and efficiently along well-controlled channels. One of the goals of market research within the context of the digital enclosure is to tame the anarchy of available information: to gather data about Web-surfing behavior, MP3 listening patterns, and self-disclosure sites like MySpace and impose order on it by aggregating it, sorting it, and extracting usable patterns. To capture this kind of information, political marketing research firms, such as marketers, rely on automated information gathering: "Their spider programs crawl through the Web, automatically collecting website content, such as a person's email or physical address, or an organization's press releases."[30]

One of the reasons for the increasing value of information captured within the embrace of the digital enclosure is that it does treble- and quadruple-duty: for marketing, policing, campaigning—and, as I will argue in the following chapter, for interpersonal or peer monitoring. However, the shift in information-gathering capacity facilitated by the enclosure is both quantitative and qualitative. By embracing sites of domesticity, leisure, and labor and permitting always-on connectivity, the enclosure provides information not just in discrete packets—a survey here, a focus group there—but a continuous flow of data. Consider, for example, the latest version of Apple's iTunes, which can relay a continuous flow of information back to "headquarters" about what music you're listening to while you're listening to it. Similarly, the Web TV devices installed by the researchers at Knowledge Networks do more than capture the information from spot polls (although they do this also); the devices capture a continuous flow of information about viewing habits, Web surfing, and so-called clickstreams (information about which hypertext links viewers click on). What emerges is a detailed, personalized image of consumer behavior: the twenty-first-century version of the forms of personalized monitoring pioneered in the workplace by Frederick Taylor and his associates. The cost problem has been solved, thanks to automated forms of information gathering and sorting. Politicians and marketers alike can incorporate detailed and automated forms of listening—or feedback monitoring—into their attempts to sell consumers on products and voters on candidates.

Some Consequences

Democracy, understood as a political system in which rulers are held accountable to the citizenry, relies on the interplay between two mechanisms of publicity: one that allows for public scrutiny of government decisions, policies, and actions; and one that makes public opinion manifest to policy makers. Critics of mass society have made much of the so-called refeudalization of the public sphere, understood as the default of government mechanisms of publicity to public relations, in conjunction with the relegation of the role of citizens to that of passive observers saturated by the mediated spectacle of power. In its most popular form, this critique manifests itself in the denigration of infotainment—the triumph of news that entertains without providing citizens with the information they need to hold their rulers accountable. Spectacular entertainment keeps the masses occupied and politically isolated, while real politics takes place behind their backs. According to critical theorist Jürgen Habermas in his discussion of the fate of public debate and deliberation in mass society, the result is "a *staged and manipulative* publicity displayed by organizations over the heads of a mediatized public."[31]

The tendency Habermas critiques is exemplified by the usurpation of public debate by talking heads, spin doctors, and political spokespeople on cable news. Debate has defaulted from participatory public endeavor to spectator sport for the masses. Instead of cultivating public participation in the process of democratic deliberation, such shows display viewpoints as a range of "givens" among which viewers are left to choose. Habermas laments, "Publicity loses its critical function in favor of a staged display; even arguments are transmuted into symbols to which again one can not respond by arguing but only by identifying with them."[32]

A related result is the decline of a countervailing force of publicity—that which comes in the form of public opinion, or the public expression of the will and judgment of the populace to which political rulers are to be held accountable. Just as the public needs to be informed about the actions of its leaders, so too do the leaders need to be informed about both the public's reaction to policy decisions and its policy priorities. As Habermas, among others, has argued, when media-managed spectacles replace deliberation, the formation of public opinion is itself impaired. Without accurate knowledge about government actions and policies, the formation of public opinion takes place in a vacuum—or, little better, amid the predetermined viewpoints and policy options promulgated by political and media elites. Furthermore, without mechanisms to facilitate engaged political debate (rather than mere spectatorship), public opinion remains underdeveloped and incoherent, and therefore increasingly subject to manipulation.

Political theorist Benjamin Ginsberg has argued that public opinion polling—a "science" that emerged out of the late nineteenth-developments discussed in Chapter 3—changes the terms for the expression of public opinion. This latter might be described as *citizen publicity:* the right of citizens to have their opinions heard by their rulers. Specifically, public opinion polling shifts the expression of public opinion away from its manifestation in the form of action (such as public demonstrations and protests) and toward the measurement of attitude. The shift is a crucial one because it allows for the management of public opinion before it is expressed in action. The measurement of attitude, combined with the expansion and proliferation of mass-mediated forms of communication in the early twentieth century, anticipates the goal of the scientific management of public opinion. The development of the marketing and public relations industries coalesces around this goal of feedback-based opinion management. These industries do not spring full grown from the heads of public relations and marketing pioneers like Ivy Lee and Alfred P. Sloan. Rather, as Chapter 3 suggests, they harken back to nineteenth-century ideals of information-based management—and in particular to the notion that observation and measurement provide the information necessary to "rationalize," or make more efficient and effective, a variety of human endeavors.

Thus, the crucial element of the structural transformation of what might be described as "citizen publicity," understood as the public expression of public opinion, is the shift from publicity as public action to publicity as the preemptive measurement of attitude. That is to say, what takes place in the early twentieth century is not the silencing of the masses, but the probing, observation, and measurement of the citizenry. Citizen publicity is re-doubled: it occurs not just in the form of the actions taken by the citizenry in response to or anticipation of government action, but also in the monitored expression of opinions about what the public is likely to do and why. As in the case of the scientific management of production, the gathering of this information by public relations practitioners (whether public or private, corporate or political) is prompted by the attempt to more effectively manage the populace: to influence action not by directly, physically impinging on it, but by helping to shape attitudes before they result in action.

The advent of the digital enclosure and its deployment for political purposes (in the form of increasingly detailed databases and continuous monitoring, as in the case of Knowledge Networks) doesn't challenge the logic of previous forms of marketing and campaigning so much as it promises to perfect them. If strategies for public opinion management rely on the gathering of detailed information about attitudes, behavior, and their interrelationships as well as on information asymmetry (marketers know the details of consumer behavior, but consumers don't know the details about how this information is being used to target or manipulate them), the digital enclosure facilitates market-based campaigning techniques on both counts.

In other words, the obverse of the world described by political consultant Joe Trippi—one in which "the Internet is the most democratizing innovation we've ever seen"—is one in which interactive technology can be used to perfect strategies for target marketing and the centralized management of public opinion by political elites.[33] It is the world imagined by a privacy consultant with government experience: "The nightmare scenario is that the databases create puppet masters."[34] In this nightmare vision, the one whose monitoring apparatus is currently being assembled by political consultants and database experts in anticipation of upcoming elections, "every voter will get a tailored message based on detailed information about the voter. The candidate would know what schools the voter went to, any public records that showed they supported some cause, any court case they've been involved in. There might even be several different messages sent by a candidate to the same home—one for the wife, one for the husband and one for the 23-year-old kid."[35] Far from public empowerment and democratic rebellion, such a scenario envisions what one commentator describes as "a nearly perfect perversion of the political process": "The candidate knows everything about the voter, but the media and the public know nothing about what the candidate really believes."[36]

At stake in these alternative versions of the future—one of empowerment, the other of centralized control—is the very meaning of the term *democratic participation*. By participation, do we simply mean the ability to provide increasingly detailed information about ourselves? If so, then the offer of participation can double as an alibi for the perfection of marketing strategies—both political and commercial. If, however, by participation we mean a conscious, considered, informed, and meaningful contribution to the governing process, it is important not to distinguish this at every turn from a version of participation that equates submission to detailed monitoring with participation.

Defining Participation

What is the difference between meaningful participation and consumer or citizen feedback? What, in other words, might one mean by a notion of "meaningful participation"? One way to think about the difference between these two versions of participation is by revisiting the distinction between feedback and shared control in Chapter 1's discussion of cybernetics. A heat-seeking missile may be cybernetic insofar as it adjusts to signals from its target, but to call it "interactive" or "participatory" would be to suggest a misleading commonality of interests between projectile and target. As the target shifts and changes direction, it inadvertently relays information about its new trajectory back to the guided missile. The relation between target and missile—or targeted and targeter—might, in this respect, be described as an interactive one. It is this version of interactivity that is invoked by marketers who, perhaps not coincidentally, make use of the vocabulary of "aiming" and "targeting" to describe their advertising campaigns and strategies.

This is not to overlook an obvious and important difference between target marketing and missile attack: in the case of the former, the impact on the target isn't fatal (at least in most cases, cigarettes excluded)—but it may well run counter to the self-expressed interests of the targeted. Despite what they may say, marketers have a bottom-line goal that remains inaccessible to the needs and desires of consumers, even if information about those needs and desires is crucial to attaining this goal. We can thus differentiate between two layers of feedback in its broadest sense: the first allows for the adjustment of strategies to achieve a given end (boosting record sales, destroying a rocket); the second influences the goal-setting decisions themselves (whether profits are more important than, say, diversity of music or quality). The market-based model of interactivity promises shared control at the second level, but it delivers only on the first.

Democratic politics, by contrast, promise public participation all the way up, as it were, to the goal-setting process itself. Indeed, this level of participation might be considered one element of the definition of meaningful participation, elaborated in more depth in Chapter 9. A second element—one emphasized by constitutional scholar Cass Sunstein—is the creation of optimal conditions for public deliberation about shared goals. As Sunstein suggests, the adoption of marketing and advertising techniques by political campaigns ignores an important difference between consumer decisions and political decisions: the former relate to individual preferences and only indirectly influence society as a whole, whereas the latter are explicitly about collective decisions that (directly) influence society as a whole.[37] My decision to buy a particular laundry detergent does not have broader social consequences in quite the same way as does my vote for a new school tax proposal or a congressional candidate. Moreover, as Sunstein argues, political participation envisions a decision-making process that "does not take individual tastes as fixed or given. It prizes democratic self-government, understood as a requirement of 'government by discussion,' accompanied by reason-giving in the public domain."[38]

The database-informed customized campaign model of political marketing transposes the perfection of what Sunstein might describe as a consumerist model onto the political process. Far from contributing to democratic participation and deliberation, the version of interactivity envisioned by the database consultants and target marketers offers to perfect a cybernetic form of public relations: the customization of marketing appeals that are based on detailed profiles of individual voters. The consequences of this model of interactivity are threefold: the further disaggregation of the citizenry, the facilitation of sorting and exclusion when it comes to information access, and the further normalization of surveillance as a legitimate political tool. In the following pages, I explore each of these consequences in a bit more detail.

Customization and Disaggregation

The French social critic and activist Guy Debord described consumer capitalism as a society characterized by the triumph of the spectacle—one in which consumers and viewers were "linked only by a one-way relationship to the very center that maintains their isolation from one another."[39] The mediated spectacle, as Debord notes, "unites what is separate, but it unites it only in its *separateness*."[40] Consider, for example, a description of Manhattan's Upper West Side on the evening of September 11, 2001, by one New Yorker who, looking out the window of his ninth-floor apartment at nightfall, noticed something unusual about the view. Usually the buildings visible across the way presented a patchwork of lit and unlit windows. On that evening, however, almost every window was lit, in part by the bluish glow of a TV screen.[41] With the city for all practical purposes closed down, everyone had returned to the privacy of their apartments to watch the news coverage, each to view the same horrific images repeated over and over on their separate screens. They were united by their relation to the images that each received separately in the privacy of their honeycombed apartments. This is perhaps an extreme example occurring in response to an exceptional situation, but the process of separation and unification it illustrates arguably characterizes everyday consumer and political conditions. Our media-saturated society provides us with (at least for the moment) shared images, information, and culture, which we experience, for the most part in conditions of relative isolation, from the privacy of home via the television or, more recently, the Internet.

From the perspective of democratic participation, the process of separation identified by Debord undermines the conditions for debate and deliberation. It disavows and suppresses the collective character of democratic politics, reinforcing a consumerist model in which citizens are treated not as part of a deliberative body, but as isolated shoppers in the marketplace of ideas. As critical theorist John Brenkman observes, the tendency of consumer society is to "destroy the space"—of deliberation and collective action in which critical public opinion can be formed.[42] Countervailing publicity—the citizenry making known its wishes to public officials and representatives—is reduced to the privatized polling of spectators.

The promise of interactive media is predicated in part on a critique of this process: thanks to the Internet, the public no longer need depend on centralized, top-down, mass media; nor are citizens all sharing the same images. Moreover, the interactive capability of the network allows media consumers to become media producers. New media guru Howard Rheingold, for example, envisions a world in which citizens equipped with souped-up versions of cell phone video cameras could engage in distributed peer-to-peer journalism: "Imagine the power of the Rodney King video multiplied by the power of Napster. . . . Would it be possible to turn the table on the surveillance society and counter the media monopolies?"[43]

The promise, in short, is to rearrange the relationship between spectators so they are no longer linked only by a "one-way relationship to the very center." Instead, they could be linked in a myriad ways to dispersed centers, participating in the shared production of a proliferating series of spectacles. Instead of tuning into the network news, viewers could surf the Internet for all kinds of publicly generated "news" about the world covering a range of interests and perspectives. If you're tired of watching Americans interview other Americans about the war in Iraq, you might be able to tune in to video narratives about life in Baghdad that were shot, edited, and posted to the Internet by Iraqi residents—or defense contractors, for that matter. *Wired* magazine has dubbed the prospect of distributed information production a form of "crowdsourcing"—turning over the duties of production to the populace, which, thanks to the development of interactive technology, can "solve problems [and] even do corporate R & D" in addition to providing "content" in the form of more images for shared consumption.[44]

Two questions need to be addressed regarding the promise of distributed media production—the crowdsourcing of the spectacle. The first has to do with whether a distributed spectacle overcomes the atomism that undermines conditions for collective deliberation. The second has to do with the impact of customized information on the populace. If the citizenry, relegated to the role of spectators, has surrendered the task of critical deliberation and accepted the model of politics as one more form of individualized consumption, could the promise of participation revitalize interest and participation in the deliberative process? Does peer-to-peer journalism undo the default of publicity to public relations, and does it furnish improved conditions for public deliberation? The hope of distributed reporting is that it might provide citizen-journalists with a more complete and accurate understanding of the world around them and the political issues affecting their lives.

One possible danger, anticipated by legal theorist Cass Sunstein, is the loss of shared resources for collective deliberation. People need an overlapping knowledge base of some kind to be able to engage in meaningful political discussion. In a world of information glut, it becomes possible, Sunstein argues, for people to become so specialized in their information consumption that they lack the resources to engage in debate on topics of general interest in a democratic society.[45] Thanks to the proliferation of information resources online and on television, it is conceivable, for example, to devote one's news consumption entirely to NASCAR racing, fantasy baseball, or online gaming. Nevertheless, the danger that more information could lead to less shared knowledge doesn't provide a convincing argument against the importance of providing the populace with a variety of perspectives and information. It was even easier to have nonoverlapping knowledge sets before the proliferation of always-on, customized news and information outlets, because lack of information is equally a hindrance to collective deliberation.

The real danger posed by the proliferation of information resources lies in the tendency to reinforce a savvy postmodern skepticism that threatens to default to an incoherent relativism. Sunstein worries that, for example, political polarization might result from conservatives only getting their news from Fox, the *Washington Times,* Rush Limbaugh, and conservative Web sites, and liberals limiting themselves to *Democracy Now* and *The Nation,* with the result that neither group would face challenges to its political predispositions. The real threat to deliberation lies a bit deeper: in the mind-set that allows individuals to feel comfortable deliberately seeking out only a select group of news sources with predictable slants. The standard explanation of this phenomenon—sometimes called "selective exposure"—is that people, loathe to having their opinions unsettled or challenged, seek out information sources that confirm their values, attitudes, and prejudices. But this explanation doesn't do justice to the deeper pathology of the savvy postmodern attitude, which provides a specific justification for choosing those outlets that fail to challenge one's worldview: because all portrayals are biased in one way or another, there is nothing to prevent viewers from selecting those that present the views with which they identify and screening out the rest.

Political commentator Josh Marshall describes this popularized version of postmodernism as one characterized by the belief that "ideology isn't just the prism through which we see world, or a pervasive tilt in the way a person understands a given set of facts. Ideology is really all there is."[46] This savvy reductionism equates the recognition that all viewpoints are biased with the assertion that bias is all there is. That this formulation is incoherent in its absolute dismissal of absolutes does not detract from its popularity among not just the tragically hip, but also, as philosopher Bruno Latour suggests, an increasingly savvy and skeptical populace.[47]

The result is what might be described as a preemptive defense against the charge (recklessly popularized by critical theory) of being a dupe. It is a fate that can ostensibly be avoided by asserting in advance the claim that all truth claims and statements of fact are simply ruses of power. Latour, referring to the proliferation of conspiracy theories after the 9/11 attacks, asks, "Remember the good old days when revisionism arrived very late, after the facts had been thoroughly established, decades after bodies of evidence had accumulated? Now we have the benefit of what can be called *instant revisionism*. The smoke of the event has not yet finished settling before dozens of conspiracy theories begin revising the official account, adding even more ruins to the ruins, adding even more smoke to the smoke."[48] The savvy preemptive deconstruction of facts and truths—which are always invoked in scare quotes—levels the playing field on which conspiracy theories and investigative journalism find themselves rubbing shoulders, on which *The Da Vinci Code* finds itself pitted against the Catholic Church, and fictional novels about global warming vie with scientific evidence for the attention of the president of the United States. It is, to the say the least, a slightly vertiginous world—one in which the task of sorting through opposing arguments has been complicated by the increasing difficulty of establishing the basis for distinguishing between conspiracy theory and conspiracy.

One potential downside, then, to the Internet as the great information leveler where do-it-yourself news sites and blogs rub shoulders with the BBC and the *New York Times*, is the tendency for the proliferation of information to reinforce a popular if incoherent postmodern relativism. Absent this mind-set, the proliferation of news and information sources could serve as a crucial resource for public deliberation, allowing citizens access to more varied perspectives and arguments and to a more complete picture of the debate and the available evidence. I want to be careful to note that the proliferation of information is not necessarily the cause of a mind-set that "makes it easy to ignore the facts or brush them aside because 'the facts' aren't really facts, at least not as most people understand them. If they come from people who don't agree with you, they're just the other side's argument dressed up in a mantle of facticity."[49] But once this mind-set about facts prevails, the Internet makes it that much easier to "go out and find a new set of [facts]."[50]

Sorting and Exclusion

The prospect of customization and target marketing envisioned by the promoters of database campaigning doesn't necessarily counter the logic of the spectacle. Rather, it promises to perfect the process of separation: in the privacy of their homes and cars, on their personal laptops, Palm Pilots, and iPods, readers, viewers, and listeners will continue to receive mass-produced information and entertainment, but it too will be personalized and individualized. The spectacle will mask its mass-produced character through feedback-based customization. John Brenkman anticipates this trend in his analysis of a society of the spectacle in which audiences "are atomized as they receive *back* a message that has been produced from their own signifying practices as groups. The mass communication effaces its own genesis by displacing the subject from his or her position as a participant in a collective expression to the serial position of an isolated receiver of a pre-packaged message."[51] The one revision of this formulation we might add in the era of mass customization and digital enclosure is that, increasingly, signifying practices themselves will be individualized: data will be gathered from audiences not as masses or groups, but as individual viewers and listeners.

The process of customization not only allows for targeted political appeals as described in previous sections, but it also facilitates discrimination in the provision of public information. As communication scholar Oscar Gandy has argued, the development of database politics allows forms of social sorting practiced by the marketing industry to be imported into the realm of political campaigning. Just as some groups—often those in the lower socioeconomic income brackets—can be excluded from targeted marketing appeals and discriminated against in the provision of special offers for goods and services, customized political marketing may foster more disturbing forms of social exclusion: an exacerbation of the gap between the information haves and have-nots. As Gandy notes, "People who are deemed unlikely to vote are unlikely to be identified as the target for the 'Get Out the Vote Campaign' next time. . . . Excluding people from the flow of information because they have been deemed unlikely to vote means that those who are most in need of information are least likely to receive it."[52] Or, as another group of researchers have noted, "the same dataveillance technologies that allow the market to distinguish between consumers of different commercial value will inherently allow powerful players in the governmental field to distinguish between voters of different political value, and treat them disproportionately."[53] This unequal treatment may well privilege the views of established political majorities at the expense of the interests and concerns of those who are already largely excluded from the political process. Rather than promoting inclusiveness and diversity, target marketing traces a vicious circle of exclusion: those who have been less active politically are less likely to be solicited by political campaigns, and "as a result, their ability to articulate their concerns remains underdeveloped."[54]

Customization, then, means not only that citizens will receive customized campaign appeals that are based on their politics, background, and preferences, but that they may receive different levels of information—and some may be excluded entirely. This information discrimination is not a departure from past practice but the extension and culmination of its logic. As political coverage by the TV networks—the nation's main source of news—continues to decline, political campaigns have become increasingly reliant on paid advertising and targeted get-out-the-vote campaigns, which, in the interest of efficiency and cost-effectiveness, need to allocate time and resources where they have the greatest likelihood of benefiting individual candidates, rather than the populace as a whole.[55] Targeted forms of information discrimination contribute to the individualization of political debate and decision making, replacing deliberation over collective goals with underdeveloped individual preferences. Noting this fact, Gandy echoes Cass Sunstein's concerns about the impact of target marketing on participants in a mass-customized public sphere: "They are less likely to be concerned as members of a larger community that shares common and collective interests."[56]

To return to the formulation outlined above of the two forms of democratic publicity—of government activity on the one hand and public will on the other—we can now consider how the promise of database politics within the digital enclosure reformulates their mutual relationship. In the ideal model of democratic politics government publicity means the submission to public scrutiny of the decisions and reasoning of political leaders. Citizen publicity on the other hand might be described as the public expression of the deliberatively formed political will of the citizenry to its elected representatives. The citizenry has to "go public" at some point with its opinions and responses in order for their political leadership to respond and be held accountable. Thus all democracies have some mechanism for the collective expression of public opinion, even if they don't necessarily have well-developed conditions for the deliberative formation of such opinion. Database politics transforms government publicity into target marketing and citizen publicity into increasingly precise market research. It equates submission to detailed forms of monitoring with democratic participation—and feedback with shared control. In so doing, it reduces what Cass Sunstein calls "citizen sovereignty"—the collective expression of shared political concerns arrived at through public deliberation—to what he calls "consumer sovereignty"—the "individualized" preferences of the shopper. In so doing, it further enables the importation of marketing and public relations strategies into the political process. The goal of these strategies is not to become increasingly responsible to the public will, but to find ways of managing it more effectively before it expresses itself in action. As media theorist Jodi Dean observes, "Perhaps paradoxically, the very means of democratic publicity end up leading to its opposite: private control by the market."[57]

Surveillance

Public habituation to the political uses of surveillance is perhaps exemplified by the U.S. public's response to news that the Bush administration's National Security Administration had decided to engage in blanket monitoring of the calling patterns of U.S. citizens. After the newspaper *USA Today* revealed the existence of the program—a revelation that followed shortly on the heels of a similar exposé by the *New York Times* of government wiretapping—a public poll on surveillance and privacy revealed that more than 60 percent of those surveyed found the NSA phone monitoring program to be "acceptable" and 44 percent indicated that they "strongly endorsed the effort."[58] The newspaper coverage attributed the public response to "the belief that the need to investigate terrorism outweighs privacy concerns," suggesting once again the inefficacy of appeals to privacy within the contemporary context. But this explanation needs to be scrutinized within its broader historical context. The laws that the Bush administration circumvented in its covert surveillance programs were laws passed in response to a similar controversy in the 1970s: revelations about domestic surveillance during the Nixon administration. The Nixon-era surveillance had taken place when the nation was at war—and yet the revelations led to both public and political concern that manifested itself in an extended congressional investigation and the passage of new laws restricting the ability of intelligence agencies to spy on the U.S. population. These laws were passed not solely over concern for an abstract conception of privacy, but in response to documented abuses of unsupervised surveillance powers for political purposes.

The United States, in other words, has had previous experience with a similar situation to that presented by George W. Bush, his declared war on terror, and his vexed invasion of Iraq. In the mid-1970s, an administration that had been revealed to be both corrupt and duplicitous in the pursuit of a drawn-out and apparently unsuccessful war was discovered to have been engaging in covert surveillance of the U.S. populace in the name of national security and defense. Thirty years later, an administration wracked by charges and revelations of political scandal and duplicity, caught up in the pursuit of a drawn-out combination of wars, was discovered to have neglected the laws that had been passed in response to the covert monitoring practices of a previous administration. Instead of a public outcry and a call for impeachment and congressional investigation, the populace has expressed its willingness to submit to increasingly comprehensive forms of government monitoring— assuming, apparently, that if they have nothing to hide, they have nothing to be worried about. Or rather, that they have less to worry about than in a scenario in which the government is deprived of unlimited surveillance powers.

Perhaps this is more about a growing habituation to pervasive monitoring in the information society than it is about fears of national security or terrorist threat. Yes, the war on terror is a historically unique formation— but perhaps no more destabilizing and threatening than the combination of the cold war, the Vietnam war, and the forms of international terrorism that characterized the early 1970s. What distinguishes the war on terror from the Vietnam era, rather, is the subsequent monitoring embrace of the digital enclosure—a place in which submission to monitoring becomes an increasingly pervasive part of everyday life in all its facets. In a world in which we've become used to having details of our daily lives collected and sorted by Web browsers and credit card companies, in which we know that we are surrounded by surveillance cameras in public and private spaces alike, in which our employers can monitor our e-mail correspondence and our online activities, and in which surveillance has become such a popular form of entertainment that the expression "Big Brother" is just as likely to refer to a game show as to a fading cold war memory of authoritarianism, the government decision to track our phone calls might seem just one more natural extension of the everyday monitoring practices associated with the information age. Viewed against the background of a world in which our laptops and cell phones will track our locations in order to market to us directly and our cars will keep track of our speed and itineraries, government surveillance of our call records seems almost quaint and rudimentary by comparison. It can be portrayed to a surveillance-habituated public as just one more form of participation enabled by the digital enclosure.

iMonitoring
Keeping Track of One Another

With the Handy Truster, you can find out if your lover has been faithful, what your co-workers and boss really think, and how honest your friends and family truly are! . . . *Never Be Lied To Again!*

—Handy Truster ad copy

One of the attributes of what I've been calling the "digital enclosure" is that it facilitates not only commercial and state monitoring, but also what might be described as lateral or peer-to-peer surveillance. In a culture of constant connectivity and online self-disclosure, we can not only keep tabs on our friends and family members via cell phones, e-mail, and instant messaging, but we can check up on new acquaintances or old friends by going online. *To google* has become not only a verb, but a transitive one whose objects are often friends, acquaintances, significant others, colleagues, and whoever happens to cross the mind of curious Web surfers. Within the digital enclosure, the movements and activities of individuals equipped with interactive devices become increasingly transparent—and this makes monitoring technologies easier to obtain and use. The result is increasing public access to the means of surveillance—not just by corporations and the state, but by individuals. Cell phones, for example, are already equipped with GPS devices that allow users to relay information about their location to selected friends and relatives. This information will soon be available without having to make a call: parents calling their children, for example, will no longer have to ask the standard cell phone question: "Where are you?" They will already know.

The unifying theme of the preceding chapters has been an attempt to trace some of the ways in which interactivity is becoming synonymous with asymmetrical forms of monitoring, information gathering, and surveillance. My goal has not been to dismiss the potential of interactivity outright, but to point out how the promises of inclusiveness, participation, and power sharing associated with interactive technologies are deployed as alibis for information gathering in the service of top-down forms of political and economic control.

The lurking question—which I revisit in the conclusion to this chapter—regards how we might start to distinguish between those forms of interactivity that live up to the promise of democratization and those that fall short. Before engaging with this question, however, this chapter addresses another aspect of public habituation to interactivity as surveillance by considering how the commercial deployment of interactivity as an information-gathering strategy is being imported into the realm of personal relationships. This development shouldn't be surprising, considering the ways in which interactivity as a form of one-way information gathering has been modeled for the public by commercial entities and the state. To the extent that the model of interactivity as asymmetric monitoring has permeated daily life, it is perhaps not surprising that a similar deployment of interactivity comes to characterize a range of individual uses of the technology. Moreover, as I will argue in more depth later in this chapter, when networked communication technologies increasingly mediate interpersonal interactions, the perceived need for verification increases: are the people we meet online really who they say they are? Are the children or the significant others calling in on the cell phone really where they say they are? What is my child, employee, or significant other actually doing during the hours he or she spends online? These are the types of questions that the deployment of the technology mobilizes and promises to answer. Forms of mediation and simulation facilitated by new information and communication technologies raise potential risks that they address with proliferating technologies for verification.

The way in which interactivity enables an emergent culture of peer-to-peer monitoring that mimics and amplifies top-down forms of commercial and political surveillance is the subject of this chapter. As in other chapters, of central interest is the way in which the mobilization of techniques and technologies for lateral monitoring incorporate the imperatives of state and commercial entities into the fabric of social life within the digital enclosure, and the way in which it habituates the public to pervasive forms of one-way, nontransparent monitoring. Wearable computing guru Steve Mann uses the term "co-veillance"—as opposed to surveillance—to refer to what I describe as lateral or peer monitoring: not the state watching individuals or vice versa, but individuals monitoring one another.[1] Such monitoring has always been a part of social interaction, but interactive technologies create shifting strategies for self-representation, simulation, and anonymity. Moreover—and this is perhaps the central point of the chapter—they foster increasingly asymmetric forms of information gathering that replicate the model of commercial and state oversight for self-management in the name of efficiency and security.

Savvy Skepticism and Risk

One illustration of the emerging culture of detection in a savvy, skeptical era, was the announcement in the spring of 2004 by Court TV of its decision to renew a show called *Fake Out,* designed to train contestants and viewers in the art of lie detection. Perhaps building on a growing sense of skepticism as to whether contestants on shows in the booming reality TV genre were being "real" or just acting, Court TV billed the show as "the most compelling reality show in the investigative genre."[2] *Fake Out* offered lessons from "renowned polygraph expert and former FBI agent Jack Trimarco" and a test of the ability of the "average person"—in the form of selected contestants—"to lie and catch others in the act of lying."[3] The show featured an elimination competition designed to select the quickest learners and those with the best instincts for ferreting out deception. Viewers were invited to learn how to *really* watch and listen—and to do so for eminently practical purposes with a direct bearing on their own lives: "Is your teenager being untruthful? Is your spouse not telling you the whole story? Is your employee late to work again the fifth time because of a car accident on the road? Can you spot a lie?" In other words, can you, in good conscience and in today's world, afford *not* to learn how to cut through the tangle of potential falsehoods in which we are all caught up in the contemporary climate of dissimulation? The show promised that the players would benefit from Trimarco's expertise and that it would arm "viewers with the fundamental lie detection techniques that can be applied in everyday life."[4]

Those with the will but not the requisite instincts (a repeatedly invoked component of the investigator's arsenal) could compensate by going on-line (instead of relying on Trimarco's teachings) to equip themselves with a $99 portable "voice-stress analyzer" called the Handy Truster. The world of the Handy Truster has much in common with that of *Fake Out*. It is one in which those closest to us remain a potential source of risk and uncertainty. The Truster ad leads with three disturbing, loudly capitalized questions: "Is She Cheating on You? Is He Really Working Late? What Are Your Kids Really Doing?"[5] It is a world in which no one, barring verification, is necessarily who they seem—one that concedes the manipulative character of every individual's self-presentation, and therefore the generalized need for techniques of verification not just in commercial transactions and state policing, but in every aspect of public and private life.

Before dismissing gadgets like the Handy Truster as latter-day versions of the x-ray glasses advertised in the back of comic books—gimmickry targeting a fringe, slightly paranoid, adolescent secret-agent sensibility—it is worth considering their relationship to a climate of generalized postmodern skepticism that reduces anything that seeks to pass for truth as a ruse of power or manipulation. When an ingrained savviness about the staging of public facades and spectacles is fostered by an ongoing fascination with the behind-the-scenes access provided by an increasingly pervasive and invasive mass media, reliance on gut instinct and well-honed detection skills comes to be portrayed as a necessary supplement to public discourse. No less a public figure than George W. Bush framed his image as a leader in terms of his finely honed instincts and his ability to "read" character. Recall, for example, his highly publicized first meeting with Russian leader Vladimir Putin, when Bush, famous both for his creative awkwardness with words and his evident mistrust of them, noted that he had been able to bypass the niceties of speech and cut straight through to the essence of his interlocutor: "I looked the man in the eye; I found him to be very straightforward and trustworthy. . . . I was able to get a sense of his soul."[6] Bush would be an ideal contestant on *Fake Out*. Gut instinct, heart reading, and soul seeing are staples of the public packaging of Bush.

To complete the picture, a related hallmark of Bush's visceral leadership style—his predilection for instinct over facts—is his own well-publicized savvy skepticism toward political deliberation and the media institutions of public record, not to mention politicians themselves.[7] The exemplary indication of his putative honesty during the 2000 campaign was his willingness, in a flight of self-fulfilling prescience, to foreground the untrustworthiness of politicians themselves: "We don't trust bureaucrats in Washington, D.C. We don't believe in planners and deciders making decision on behalf of America."[8] Trust me, he seemed to proclaim cannily, because at least I concede the untrustworthiness of political discourse itself.

This appeal to postmodern savviness is a recurring theme that may help explain both GOP political strategy and the mainstream media's coverage of the two main political parties. As pundit Eric Boehlert has observed, one persistent media meme in the coverage of Democratic politicians is that even, or especially, when they're campaigning on the strength of substantive, even wonkish, policy, they're dismissed for being too wooden and appearing phony or boring (think of the coverage of Al Gore, Hillary Clinton, and Jimmy Carter, for example). By contrast, Republican candidates, even, or especially, when they are accused of being duplicitous or misleading, are portrayed, Bush style, as seeming "genuine, comfortable in their own skin" (Ronald Reagan and George W. Bush, for example).[9] If this may be in part a projection of reporters' personal experiences with congenial figures like Bush and Reagan onto the public at large—an attempt to explain the popular appeal of mediocre and duplicitous leaders—it is also, implicitly, a capitulation to the savvy skepticism described in the previous chapter—a cynicism about so-called truths and those who would claim access to them. Politicians who appear to trust themselves and their policy solutions *too* sincerely—and who invite the public to trust them in turn—paradoxically come across as phony because they haven't capitulated to the preemptive savviness that unmasks all campaign strategies as ruses of power or strategies of manipulation. Again, the tendency is to conflate the undeniable fact that all campaign appeals are strategic (insofar as they are aimed at gaining or consolidating political power) with the savvy assertion that they are entirely reducible to strategy—that they are nothing more than one more ruse. In the face of this savvy reductionism, for a politician not to concede the reality of manipulation is, paradoxically, to run the risk of coming across as an inept manipulator who takes the audience for dupes. Conceding the reality of manipulation by contrast perversely comes across as a form of honesty and respect for the audience. An acknowledgment of the manipulative character of politicians, concedes in advance what the public already knows rather than treating them as dupes—the ultimate insult to an aggressively in-the-know audience.

But this formulation doesn't go quite far enough. Even in the face of generalized savviness, authenticity is recuperated at one remove: in the form of honesty about the reality of manipulation. This move requires a further warrant, an appeal that paradoxically cuts through the climate of skepticism. Such was the carefully managed message of what came to be known as Ashley's Story, a 2004 campaign ad built around the widely circulated image of President Bush comforting the daughter of a 9/11 victim with a cradling embrace. The response of the young lady's father to this gesture of presidential consolation is featured in the ad, alongside a photograph of the hug: "What I saw is what I want to see in the heart and in the soul in the man who sits in the highest elected office in our country."[10]

Soul seeing, in other words, is not just the province of the savvy political leader, but also of those who recognize his talents. In an era of generalized risk and skepticism—in which politicians, like peers, are not necessarily who they seem—it is not enough to have a leader who has naturally internalized the lessons of *Fake Out*. The rest of us need a crash course in visceral literacy. We need to learn to find a way behind the facade—to develop strategies of investigation and verification not just for the claims of politicians, but for those of friends, family, lovers, and coworkers.

Surely there is nothing particularly new and earth-shattering about the fact that peers develop strategies for keeping track of one another, and those who write about new media might even go so far as to suggest that contemporary strategies for mutual monitoring merely rehabilitate, in technological form, the everyone-knows-everyone-else's-business world of more traditional forms of community, undoing the anonymity of urbanized modernity. However, there are two aspects of the contemporary version of lateral surveillance that are worth recognizing and emphasizing: the use of covert investigation as an alternative or substitute for debunked discourse (the attempt, as the philosopher Slavoj Žižek puts it, to appeal to the evidence of one's eyes rather than the words of others), and the democratization of access to technologies and strategies for cultivating investigatory expertise.[11] The use of the latter is characterized not just by the promise of participation, but by the threat of ubiquitous risk: the need to enlist monitoring strategies as a means of taking responsibility for one's own security in a networked communication environment characterized by the triumph of electronic mediation. Thus, part of the promise of the interactive information revolution is to provide the general public with access to the means of surveillance for do-it-yourself use in the privacy of one's home. This promise aligns itself with a series of strategies for offloading what might be described as the duties of monitoring in the name of efficiency and security onto the populace at large.

The Wariness of the Nonduped

As communication networks expand social networks into the virtual realm, the contrived character of self-presentation becomes increasingly apparent. Virtualization allows for the acceleration of online socializing and networking by disembedding interaction from social contexts that facilitate more traditional forms of verification and accountability. A world in which interpersonal interaction increasingly relies on deterritorialized and mobile forms of electronic mediation—cell phones, instant messaging, e-mailing—ushers in a related set of techniques and technologies of verification to address the risks associated with disembedding. As the pace and scope of interpersonal interaction accelerates, one result is the development of new strategies for the rationalization and management of risk.

Online dating, for example, is a form of online shopping that makes it possible to meet scores of potential dates and mates in a single sitting—without leaving the privacy of home. At the same time, it increases the potential risks associated with the fact that people aren't necessarily who they say they are. In her study of online identity, psychologist Sherry Turkle highlights ways in which the virtual world allows for forms of performative play with one's self-image—techniques for potential dissimulation about which those who have come of age with the Internet (or adapted to it) have grown reflexively savvy.[12]

One result is the development of strategies for countering the risks associated with online anonymity: the proliferation, for example, of background-check Web sites wallpapered with testimonials about the risks of online dating. A featured testimonial on Check-mate.com is typical:

I met him through a personal ad on the web . . . love on-line, what a concept. He seemed pretty honest and straightforward and we had a lot in common. We exchanged photos, talked on the phone and wrote letters. We became close very quickly. He lived far away so we met, and it was great. He told me he loved me and wanted to marry me. I thought I loved him too. And then I got a call from his wife.[13]

A new breed of dating sites, such as True.com, offer "criminal background screening" and threaten to prosecute "to the full extent of the law" married people who pass themselves off as single.[14]

Those who take advantage of the benefits of the technology—the fact that, for example, it's easy to meet scores of people online—can also find themselves increasingly reliant on the monitoring tools and strategies that it facilitates. Thus, the background check Web site Abika.com urges online daters to "screen them before you invest your time, emotions and resources. . . . Checking out that special someone's background and profile can help you avoid being taken advantage of and unnecessary grief."[15] Potential consumers are invited to reflect not just on the disturbing level of deceit that plagues romantic life (as the Infidelity Web Site puts it, "Every day, I get flooded with stories of the worst things imaginable going on in peoples' lives. The lies, the deceit, the betrayal, the broken hearts"[16]), but also on the unreliable character of verbal intercourse: because people lie, techniques, strategies, and technological devices must be used to cut through their verbal machinations.

One result is a culture of mutual detection characterized by generalized suspicion in which everyone can be treated similarly as a potential suspect. It turns out that the government's post-9/11 surveillance model is not all that different from what we're starting to do to ourselves by using the technology to cast as broad a net as possible, drawing on algorithms to sort through the clutter and conducting background checks on particular individuals. As in policing, electioneering, and marketing, so too in dating. Watching one another, it turns out, is one of our post-9/11 duties, not just for our government but for ourselves.

In a telling twist on the term *relationship marketing,* consider, for example, the importation of the language of data mining into the mate-shopping process as envisioned by the background check Web site Abika.com:

Checking out that special someone's background and profile can help you . . . estimate who that person really is. Do you want a second Date?—Studies show that

94% of people are nervous on their first date because they did not know much about what their dates really want. 82% also said they would have been able to make a much better impression on their date if they knew what their dates really wanted. Make a better impression on your date. Abikas' profiling system can help you estimate what your date really wants.[17]

If the market model for relationships has been around for a long time in various forms, its adoption of new media technologies allows for the further rationalization of the dating process. In one account of online dating, a reporter described, for example, the use of data-gathering and -sorting techniques used by those with digitally enhanced social lives to manage the scores of contacts available to them online. One kept "his dates and prospective dates arranged on an Excel spreadsheet"; another, who worked in human resources, "kept track of the multitude in a dating binder, printing out the profiles of every man who contacted her and filing them under different headings."[18] Frederick Taylor would have found the whole process a familiar one. Combine this database management with background checks and data mining, and the result is computerized scientific management of the dating and mating markets.

Romantic Risk Control

Bypassing reliance on traditional social networking institutions creates a context of generalized risk that foregrounds the importance of detection strategies not just in romantic relationships, but in personal and professional ones. Thus, on some background-check Web sites, employee surveillance rubs shoulders with advertisements for information about friends, family members, and significant others. In each case, taking responsibility for one's own security entails gathering information—often in nontransparent and asymmetrical ways—about one another. The embrace of surveillance techniques becomes a way of adopting and internalizing market and state imperatives, including the prioritization of efficiency and the privileging of adherence to behavioral norms that minimize perceived risk. The result is the cultivation of a population that in both private and public life is trained in the "norms and values of the market including those of 'responsibility, initiative, competitiveness, risk-taking, and industrious effort.'"[19]

Perpetual risk calculation, as we saw in Chapter 6, defers a critical examination of the way risk is defined, how it is mobilized, and the priorities incorporated into its management. The focus remains on developing the skills for negotiating a widening array of risks that require perpetual vigilance, investigation and assessment ("Is your partner/child/coworker lying to you—again?"). Perpetual risk management reduces experience to an experimental calculus—one that incorporates the sorting algorithms of commercial data-mining strategies along with policing techniques of detection and forensic examination. The following section explores some examples of technologies currently in place for managing personal interactions and ostensibly bypassing the deceptive character of self-presentation. The goal of lining up these devices and strategies alongside one another is to trace some of the ways in which the model of interactivity as surveillance is imported into the realm of personal relations.

Watching Each Other (Watch Ourselves)

> Whatever your reason, you may need video surveillance to monitor your home, you may want to detect suspected phone bugs, or test for a spouse's infidelity.
>
> —NetDetective Web site

In 2003, private investigators in the state of Georgia attempted to fight a move by the "verification services" company ChoicePoint (one of the nation's largest database companies) to mass market background-check software through a major retail chain. The move, they argued, transferred control over the data-gathering process from certified experts to anyone who wandered into Sam's Club with $60 and the wherewithal to purchase a $138 business license. As one disappointed private investigator put it, "It's almost like they're wanting to be the Wal-Mart of the information business."[20] According to ChoicePoint, a company that claims to have amassed more than 14 billion records about individuals and companies, retail background checking is apparently one of the new frontiers of the information economy.[21] The new "channel" for private investigation tools, in other words, is not institutional but personal: members of the general public are invited to become do-it-yourself private investigators. Perhaps professional private investigators need not despair, given that the generalization of surveillance as a strategy for negotiating the uncertainties of contemporary life has triggered a boom in the demand for their services, at least according to the U.S. Department of Labor, which has predicted a 33 percent increase in demand by 2010.[22] In this case, as in other spheres of social practice, the do-it-yourself industry doesn't dispense with experts but relies on their multiplication, not least in the form of trainers and consultants, including Jack Trimarco of *Fake Out* fame.

Additional competition in the mass marketing of surveillance technologies for personal use is coming from the World Wide Web, which has spawned a burgeoning industry in background check sites. The flip side of what Bill Gates described as the ability of the network to make "geography" less important is the loss of what had hitherto been provided by geography: local information networks that provided references, guarantees, and controls on social and economic interactions.[23] Similarly, the flip side of the freedom afforded by virtual space to experiment with identity and to play with subject positions and self-presentation is a growing savviness about the constructed character of online identity.[24] The unique addressability of e-mail accounts and cell phones as well as their spatial mobility, as compared with geographically fixed forms of communication, provide not just for constant contact, but the increased possibility of deceit. It is possible, for example, to download prerecorded background sounds for one's cell phone that provide an acoustically verifiable geographic alibi, providing, for example, the background noises of engines revving and cars honking to allow the cell phone user to claim to be stuck in traffic—wherever he or she may be.

In keeping with the so-called interactive revolution, individuals are invited not just to participate in the forms of entertainment they consume (interactive television) and in the production of the goods and services they consume (mass customization), but to also participate in formerly centralized forms of surveillance and verification. As the sociologist David Lyon has suggested, the obverse of postmodern paranoia about the prospect of being watched all the time is the paranoia that serves as an alibi for being always on the lookout, always watching.[25] One gateway Web site for background verification says solicitously, "We know how important it is to you to feel secure about the people you enter into relationships with—whether the relationships are business or personal. That's why we've compiled these background check resources. Now, using this website as your gateway to our nation's vast reservoir of public records, you can check out virtually anyone's background from your home or office."[26]

If we are at risk in the privacy of our homes from those who enter via the network—including identity thieves, online pedophiles, lying Internet dates, and pornographers—the network can also provide us with resources for monitoring the behaviors of others, and if need be, ourselves. As the database corporation ChoicePoint puts it on its consumer solutions Web site, "We buy products every day to protect our valuables. What are you doing to protect your family from people who enter your home?"—or, one might add, your life.[27]

Lateral surveillance, or peer-to-peer monitoring, covers (but is not limited to) three main categories: romantic interests, family, and friends or acquaintances. It also comprises several levels of monitoring, ranging from casually googling a new acquaintance to purchasing keystroke-monitoring software, surveillance cameras, or even portable lie detectors. Rather than providing an exhaustive taxonomy of surveillance technologies and practices, this section explores some representative examples of monitoring strategies in an effort to elaborate the logic of peer-to-peer surveillance that unites a constellation of practices ranging from the use of lie detectors on reality TV to the growing market for home surveillance products, and the everyday practices of peer monitoring via cell phone, instant messaging, or the Internet.

Although some of the practices described below might seem absurd, such as submitting children to portable lie detector tests, others have become so commonplace that they have passed into unreflective use, such as the reliance on caller ID, once a technology paid for by those with security concerns but now a service as ubiquitous as cell phones. The following sections explore three interrelated forms of lateral surveillance: the use of the Internet, the development of do-it-yourself information-gathering technologies and offline investigative tools. In each case, the goal is to use representative examples of the technologies to illustrate developments in lateral monitoring that don't receive the kind of attention—academic or otherwise—that more top-down forms of surveillance have generated. They are, I would argue, worthy of consideration in their own right—not as a unique phenomenon, but as part of the monitoring assemblage associated with the deployment of new information and communication technologies.

Background Screening Online

Perhaps one of the most highly marketed forms of peer surveillance is, as described above, that associated with online dating. Scores of services with names like DateSmart.com, Check-mate.com, and DateDetectives.com, urge customers to put the claims of would-be spouses and lovers to the test, to "find out who they really are and what part you play in their life," as one site puts it.[28] Typically such sites admonish potential clients not to be the "dupe" who actually believes the words of their prospective dates, offering cautionary tales that range from the disconcerting to the truly violent.

Background-check services offer a range of information, typically starting with facts that would be available to those who have even a passing acquaintance with the "suspect"—name, address, marital status. More detailed reports include public record checks that include financial information, criminal history, and child support records. A dating service called CertifiedDates.com, which advertises that it was "created by a licensed private investigator," provides different levels of screening, from a basic membership that verifies name, address, and date of birth, to a platinum membership for those who have been subjected to a "complete background investigation," which includes criminal background checks, sex offender status, and verification of educational background.[29]

Dating sites incorporate other forms of monitoring, as in the case of sites that allow users to keep track of one another's activity, so that, for example, a woman who thinks she has entered into an exclusive relationship with someone she met online can determine whether that person has been visiting the site to shop for other prospects. Still other dating and social networking sites, like Friendster, include the testimonials of fellow users in an attempt to create an online version of more traditional offline reputation systems. As one of the testimonials on Friendster's home site puts it, "We all know that meeting people out in the wild is a risky proposition. With Friendster, you meet people through people that you already know and trust. So it's like having an infinite social network."[30] Rather than inviting users to rely on professional investigatory expertise, as in the case of CertifiedDates.com, Friendster offers the security of a community of peers. In both cases, users are urged not to rely solely on the self-presentation of their prospective dates in an appeal that caters to both their savvy understanding of the ways in which appearances can deceive, and to their sense of the risks of social relations facilitated by the anonymity of the network.

The deceptive character of appearances is highlighted by the admonition of one background check site that couches its appeal to skepticism in the guise of social science: "If you or someone you know is romantically involved, knowing more than what is divulged in conversation could be important. In fact, anyone putting a measure of trust in another might want to verify their trust. According to Dr. Michael Lewis of the Robert Wood Johnson Medical School in New Jersey, 'In a single day, most people lie a minimum of 25 times.'"[31]

Do-It-Yourself Surveillance Technologies

Despite the relentlessly skeptical tone of the background-check Web site warnings, reliance on the expertise of peer networks conserves a certain faith in discourse—if not in the words of the individual being investigated, presumably in those of investigators, friends, and acquaintances. However, an awareness of the ways in which words themselves can be manipulated and in which appearances can deceive others and ourselves underwrites the appeal of alternative investigation strategies. In the case of online dating, for example, the technology that makes possible what one Friendster testimonial describes hyperbolically as "an infinite social network" also offers plenty of resources for those who don't want to place their trust in either the certification process or peer testimonials. The goal of do-it-yourself investigators is to gather information about their subject without that subject's knowledge.

One of the most common practices of online monitoring is search-engine surveillance. A 2002 study by the Pew Center's Internet and American Life project found that one in three Internet users had looked someone else's name up online, and that the searches were overwhelmingly for "personal reasons."[32] It's a safe bet that that number has only gone up in the interim—a period that saw the verb *to google* enter the vernacular. The efficacy of search-engine monitoring has been further promoted by popular press accounts. The *Boston Globe*, for example, ran a two-piece story on the googling phenomenon that led off with the story of a thirty-four-year-old man who discovered, to his dismay, that an article he'd written about his prison experience as a teenager had migrated online, making his criminal history a matter of the Google public record, freely available to dates, prospective employers, and landlords.[33] This is not to discount the fact that googling, according to numerous news accounts, has helped users ferret out corrosive forms of deception in the online dating scene by unmasking individuals who lie about their age, profession, or marital status. As one press account puts it, "Deborah Knuckey met a seemingly nice guy online and Googled him. Turns out he has his own personal Web site that contains his own personal musings about his own personal wife."[34] Such accounts highlight the ways in which monitoring and verification strategies help rationalize the search for a mate, a process that starts to bear an increasing similarity to that of online shopping.

For those willing to pay, the Internet provides access not only to more detailed forms of background checking, but also to tools that enlist the capabilities of the network itself as a monitoring system. DidTheyReadIt.com, for example, provides an e-mail utility that allows users to surreptitiously track when and where their e-mail messages are read (and how long the reader spent reading them). Such services offer to reterritorialize mobile communications, pinning down e-mailers to their geographic location and eliminating the slack in an asynchronous form of communication. Similarly, Abika.com allows users to trace the geographic origin of e-mail messages, IP addresses, and instant messages. It also offers a reverse-search service that promises to find the full names associated with instant messaging nicknames and e-mail addresses. The site also provides access to a variety of background search services that blur from the investigatory into the mystical, evoking the promise that information technology, suitably perfected, might provide direct access to the desires and fantasies of real or potential love objects. The appeal to the "scientific" power of the research reads like an updated version of old comic book advertisements for how-to hypnotist kits: "Studies have shown that people who rarely get rejected are the ones who know what the opposite sex wants. For some it is instinctive and for others it is an acquired skill. If you know enough about someone, you can persuade them to do almost anything. Click here to find out what that someone you like wants and avoid rejection."[35] The seemingly extreme example of the computer database as key to the truth of one's personality—if only the right algorithm can be found—merely amplifies a theme common to a range of investigatory techniques that ostensibly bypass the uncertainties of mediation, from phrenology to lie detector tests.

In the workplace, keystroke monitoring programs serve as a means of both monitoring and disciplining employees—a form of surveillance that has since migrated into the do-it-yourself market. Richard Eaton, the president of software manufacturer WinWhatWhere (later renamed TrueActive), said in one interview that he was taken by surprise by consumer demand for his company's keystroke monitoring software when it was first developed and marketed: "We started getting calls from spouses that are spying on their other spouse. . . . I had no idea it would ever be used for that. That never even crossed our mind. . . . It's something like 20 percent of our business now, and growing."[36] As of this writing, the company's Web site included a page devoted to the home market—one that grappled with the ethics of monitoring one's spouse: "A natural reaction is to dismiss monitoring a spouse's computer use. However, there ARE times where such use may be appropriate, even prudent. In cases of online affairs, cheating, gambling, and addiction, TrueActive is a powerful tool for getting at the truth."[37]

If Web sites and online detective services invite individuals to subcontract their searches, utilities like TrueActive and DidTheyReadIt.com allow consumers to become investigators from the privacy of their home computers. In both cases, the technology blamed for the risks of anonymous or distant relationships is retooled to provide an antidote in the form of additional, behind-the-scenes information, all of which sets up a self-proliferating spiral of monitoring technologies and cloaking ones. For every e-mail tracking software package, there is also likely to be an anonymizer; for every spyware utility, there is a spyware detection program. The result is the escalation of risk and suspicion as an engine for increasingly sophisticated forms of information gathering.

Researching the Watchers

This chapter has so far considered some of the technologies available to individuals for the practice of peer-to-peer monitoring. Against the background of such practices, this section explores the results of an online survey of the use of the Internet by college and graduate students for gathering information about one another. The survey was administered primarily to students in undergraduate classes at a large Midwestern university and circulated to colleagues in other states as well as in Europe and Asia. Over the course of a three-month period, results from more than five hundred responses—including comments to open-ended questions—were gathered and form the basis of the following discussion. Links to the online survey were circulated to classes and distributed over a campus social networking Web site. The sampling method was one of convenience rather than systematic random sampling, which suggests that the findings ought to be considered preliminary, suggestive, and illustrative. The goal of the survey was to provide more fine-grained detail about the peer monitoring activities of a technologically literate population. Its construction was based in part on the observation that forms of monitoring that might once have been considered borderline stalking have become commonplace and routine—a fact with implications not just for the ways in which we represent ourselves to one another, but also for shifting expectations regarding privacy and surveillance.

Now that, as the new media truism puts it, the Internet "allows everyone to become a producer of media content,"[38] we find ourselves generating information about ourselves that is increasingly available to our friends, acquaintances, and omnivorously curious Web surfers. Personal Web sites, journal sites, social networking sites, and Weblogs are just a few examples of places where people knowingly post information about themselves, their thoughts, preferences, and activities. Thanks to the migration of public records sites onto the Internet, as well as to the digital presence of such things as high school and campus newspapers, sports statistics, and telephone directories, a range of additional information about private individuals is working its way into the public realm.

In many cases, unless we start monitoring our publicly available data shadows, we're often unaware of the information available about ourselves online. We may suspect that there is information about us, but as in the case of information gathered by state and commercial agencies, we're not necessarily clear on the details of its availability and potential uses. Nor do we know who is surfing through it and why. Increasingly, however, those with access to the Internet are finding uses for this information.

Avoiding the perils of being duped is perhaps one of the imperatives of information age interactivity. When we aren't keeping in touch with one another, we can still keep track of each other. More than three-quarters of the respondents to my online monitoring survey said that they had used the Internet to search for information about someone they knew, and almost half

indicated that they did so several times a year or more. They described an array of monitoring practices incorporating cell phone call records, e-mail accounts, social networking Web sites, instant messaging, search engines, and
public-record Web sites.[39] Reflecting the social priorities of the age group, by
far the most common targets of the information-gathering activities were
friends and significant others. More than two-thirds of those who said they'd
searched for information online indicated they were looking up their friends,
and almost two-thirds had looked up information about a current or former
significant other.

The searches seemed to break down into two types: open-ended information fishing expeditions, and more directed searches for specific types
of information, including contact information, sports achievements, educational background, and criminal histories. Several respondents indicated
that googling friends online was a form of entertainment born of curiosity:
it was just something to do when whiling away the time online. Surveillance
as a form of entertainment is perhaps not unfamiliar to a generation raised
on reality shows like MTV's *The Real Word*. The open-ended responses to the
survey indicated that online searches led to a general awareness of the type of
information available, which, in turn, lead to more searching.

Unsurprisingly, given its popularity and high profile, Google was the
search engine of choice, but respondents listed a variety of other Web sites
they visited for background information, including other search engines
(Yahoo was the next most frequently listed), Facebook, state criminal records
Web sites, online white pages, online journals, social networking sites (like
MySpace), and online dating sites. The pattern of searching described in several of the responses is well described by one respondent: "Just looking to
see what I'd find. I search for addresses and phone numbers a lot. A few
trips to the . . . [state] criminal records to look up friends and fellow employees. Mostly, just to see if anything comes up—if I don't have a specific
goal in mind." Or, as another respondent put it, with reference to her online
searches, "I was just looking for random things my friends show up in, like
hearings before the state senate or the local newspapers."

Several respondents described more targeted forms of information gathering aligned with strategies described in previous sections. Facebook, for
example, was a popular site for people to learn more about prospective dates
and new acquaintances. One respondent noted that the site allowed her to

answer the question, "What kind of person am I dating or plan to date?" Another wrote, "I'm not a stalker. Mainly I just use thefacebook to remember stuff about people I meet at bars." This kind of information gathering, formerly conducted interpersonally through social networks that radiate information more or less symmetrically (the searcher knows that inquiries will likely be noted and duly reported to their target), can now take place in the register of marketing research: in relative anonymity and on a vastly expanded scale.

The asymmetric character of this kind of information gathering is highlighted by the fact that although more than three-quarters of the survey respondents said they had used the Internet for monitoring purposes, less than a third indicated knowing that they had been the target of searches. As one respondent noted, "Facebook . . . allows you to find out a lot of information about a person without even having them know you were inquiring about them." Instant messenger names are often listed on Facebook sites, and these profiles were popular sources for information gathering, used by more than 40 percent of respondents (although instant messaging users can, in some cases, find out who has looked at their profiles).

For those already in relationships, information gathering can take on the aspect of verification and surveillance. The search for high school and college sports statistics, for example, was a recurring theme in the U.S. responses, and one student said she went online because "I was wondering what my boyfriend's baseball stats were from his college. I wanted to know if he was really as good as I was told that he is." Another noted that she had done a background check for criminal records about her boyfriend: "I never found anything on him, but I found his brother's criminal records instead." Slightly more than 12 percent of the respondents indicated that they had used the Internet to do background checks for criminal activity.

In addition to the Internet, cell phones and e-mail were frequently cited as ways of checking up on partners: "I have checked a date's call log in his cell phone to see who he is staying in contact with the most. I know several people in my age group (male and female) who do/have done this sort of thing." Several respondents noted that ex–significant others with access to online passwords had used e-mail and online cell phone accounts as a means of checking up on them: "My ex used cell phone records online to view who I was speaking with after we separated since he had access to our online in-depth account and I did not."

The responses provide examples of users' exploration of the investigatory potential of new communication technologies and paint an emerging portrait of the repurposing—or the dual purposing—of interactive technologies for monitoring and verification. For the most part, respondents characterized their reasons for information gathering as either personal (48 percent) or entertainment (38 percent). Which brings us back to the topic of popular culture—in particular to a cultural moment in which the mobilization of interactivity as a form of peer-to-peer monitoring coincides with the popularity in (more or less) nonfictional TV programming of reality formats that portray of surveillance as a means of flushing out the phonies and, in fictional programming, of the *CSI* forensic detection franchise.

In is perhaps symptomatic of a generalized and reflexive skepticism that surveillance and detection (the evidence of "my eyes" over "your words") have emerged side by side as hegemonic forms of popular entertainment. The new crop of detection shows focuses attention on the techniques and technologies of empirical evidence gathering: not on piecing together the intricate interaction of character and motive, but on black-light body-fluid illumination.[40] One of the supervising producers of *CSI: Miami* noted, "In the old shows, no one could figure out how to make the analysis of evidence interesting. . . . What we did was slow things down to say, 'This is cool stuff'. . . . We wanted them to look through the microscope."[41]

The Return to the Body

If words can be contrived, if data can be manipulated, one remaining frontier of authenticity is the testimony of the flesh. The success of devices like the Handy Truster, and its online version, a software utility that, according to its manufacturers, turns "your computer or laptop into a truth verification device," should come as no surprise. The technology, purportedly originally developed for the military, has been priced for home use at less than $200, providing inexpensive access to the tools of professional investigators.[42] If words lie, perhaps voices don't; if discourse and even data can be manipulated, a final appeal is made to the direct and ostensibly unmanipulable evidence of the body.

As interactive technology comes to be more fully integrated with the body in the form of wearable devices and perhaps, down the road, various forms of implants, biometric information may come to be increasingly folded into the data gathered by interactive devices. The advent of the cyborg promises to coincide with that of the fully monitored body. Consider, for example, the prototype of an unobtrusive, low-attention video camera designed to be worn and left on so as to allow the user to participate in the events being filmed without having to worry about turning the camera on or off. To solve the problem of determining what part of the tape might be interesting to watch, the inventors designed a "marking" technology based on biometric monitoring: "A heart rate or skin monitor (as part of a watch, for instance) could register changes in pulse when camera wearers were stimulated by what they were seeing. Software running on a desktop computer could later find the markers."[43] The monitoring technology would be designed to determine the truth of the viewer's response, responding to those moments when "the body thought something interesting was happening."[44]

Such a device gives new meaning to the claim that the camera never lies—not about what's in the viewfinder, but about its user—a possibility with obvious applications for both surveillance and marketing. If the recourse to the body sounds a bit far-fetched, it may perhaps become less so as we find ourselves living in increasing proximity to our technology, and as the search for verification unearths strategies for bypassing the slippery medium of discourse, turning instead to the evidence of the flesh. As a recent edited volume on the future of surveillance technologies notes, one of the goals of contemporary security research in the post-9/11 era "is to measure the heartbeats of passengers as they pass through security screening and to compare the data with that of 'normal' individuals."[45] In an age of ongoing responsibilization of the populace, devices like the Truster anticipate a time when such technology becomes cheap and portable enough for a retail market in risk management.

Room Raiding

The MTV reality series *Room Raiders* provides a pop-culture portrayal of do-it-yourself detection in practice: viewers get to watch the spies in action as they "investigate" the bedrooms of potential dates before meeting them. The show might be considered a symptomatic example of the emerging surveillance culture because it provides a distillation for mass consumption of the themes described above: the promise that if appearances can be deceiving, one way of accessing the behind-the-facade reality of potential dates is to bypass face-to-face interaction and conversation by going straight into a surprise forensic examination.

The surprise, on the TV show, is a limited one: the participants have answered a casting call for seventeen- to twenty-three-year-olds available on the MTV Web site to participate in the show—so they're aware that the knock on the door could be coming. And when it does, it comes in the form of mock secret-police manhandling. As if highlighting the privatization and internalization of police-state protocols, each episode begins with a ritual kidnapping: anonymous figures knock on the front door, forcefully grab the targets, and unceremoniously frog-march them into the back of an "undercover" panel van. The targets, abducted while sleeping, showering, or dressing, are routinely dumped into the van in various states of undress—without shoes or, in the case of the men, shirts. One contestant endured an entire show wrapped only in a towel: she had been "abducted" while showering. To underline this element of surprise, the voice-over during the kidnapping segment at the start of every show announces, "They have no idea the crew is on the way. By catching them off guard, they'll have no time to clean up or hide anything."

The opening sequence is a prime-time pastiche of procedures that appear in more somber guise on the wartime evening news: people bursting into homes, forcibly removing their occupants before they have time to hide or dispose of anything, and then conducting room-to-room searches. In this case, however, the search and seizure is in the name of entertainment and dating—a way of capitalizing on the element of surprise to find out who someone really is before asking them out. The *Room Raiders* voice-over notes that the cast members are "in for the surprise of their lives when they find out they're being picked for a date not by their looks or charm, but by what's inside their bedrooms." The MTV Web site gets a little bit more graphic, gleefully noting the intrusiveness of the investigation: "No drawer will be left unopened and no bed stain unexamined as each victim—or potential date—is mercilessly scrutinized without advance warning."

The "raider" is equipped with a metal suitcase described in each episode as a "trusty spy kit," complete with rubber gloves, metal tongs, and a portable UV light—familiar to *CSI* fans as a tool for revealing traces of body fluids on sheets, carpeting, and clothing. The remainder of the show is devoted to following the "investigator" as he or she (the show mixes up the genders) conducts a search of three bedrooms and along the way provides a running monologue of observations and often obscure deductions, as if he or she were Sherlock Holmes for the MTV generation ("I like that he had a surfboard; it shows he has hobbies and some goals for himself").

Despite the fact that the camera crew following the "searcher" remains invisible, the show foregrounds the fact that the investigation is a performance for the camera: the investigators directly address the camera, describing their thought processes and revealing their personal preferences to the camera, and thus to the imagined gaze of the audience. This gaze is redoubled by that of the abductees, who, in the back of their panel van, watch the progress of the investigation on a video monitor. In this respect, the show highlights the exhibitionistic side of the voyeur: the way in which the role of the savvy investigator bypassing the manipulative facade of self-presentation is, in turn, a performance for the imagined gaze of the omniscient other of the audience—a point that will be taken up in more detail in the conclusion to this chapter.

For the purposes of a generalized consideration of distributed or lateral monitoring, three themes of *Room Raiders* are worth highlighting: the way in which interactive communication technologies double as surveillance tools, the norm-enforcing character of peer monitoring as a means of screening for deviance, and the confirmation of forensic investigation as a matchmaking tool. My goal in discussing the show is not to make the case that it is uniquely responsible for training audiences in strategies of peer-to-peer monitoring, but to explore it as a pop culture example of some of the themes I have been addressing in the book. A show like *Room Raiders* is little more than a blip on the cultural radar screen, but as such, it might nevertheless provide some insight into the larger cultural context in which it is embedded. Philosopher Theodor Adorno wrote, "the mind is indeed not capable of producing or grasping the totality of the real, but it may be possible to penetrate the detail."[46] Reality TV is a telling "detail" for any consideration of the emerging surveillance culture, not just because it exemplifies themes of the emerging surveillance culture, but also because it has become a successful entertainment genre by exploiting the equation of interactivity and surveillance. Its offer of audience participation doubles as an invitation to submit to detailed forms of monitoring, both on the part of the cast members and, in the case of interactive "voting" shows like *American Idol,* on the part of audiences who "participate" by serving as a nationwide focus group.

On *Room Raiders,* as in the case of many consumer-oriented shows targeting a youth demographic, computers and cell phones have a recurring role to play as forms of conspicuous consumption—signifiers of the high-tech connectedness of the Internet generation. In the investigative context of the show, they do double duty by facilitating strategies for asymmetrical, nontransparent monitoring. The multifunctionality of cell phones as portable telephone books and answering machines provides searchable data about prospective dates: how many people call them, whom they've spoken to recently, the number of people in their phone books, and so on. Room raiders frequently pick one or more people to call on their target's cell phones to interview for background information. They learn details about the looks, personality, and social lives of prospective dates by calling up friends and family members culled from the phone's built-in listings. Underlining the status significance of communication accessories, raiders will often comment on the quality and style of the cell phones they find as they conduct their searches. As one raider in an episode of *Room Raiders: Florida* observed on finding a fancy new cell phone in his prospective date's room: "I need a girl with style like that. I really liked her messaging phone, she's up on technology, and I like a girl I can keep in touch with." In the room of another target, he found a digital answering machine instead of a cell phone and checked it unsuccessfully for messages, noting, "It looks like you don't have any friends." In an example of fortuitous unpaid advertising, another raider expressed her approval for a prospective date's late-model cell phone: "You have a high-tech phone. I guess you're up to date on your stuff. . . . I like a guy who's up to date."

On *Room Raiders,* as in law enforcement and market research, computers double as communication devices and data-gathering technologies, providing detailed information about their users. If there is a computer in the room, the raiders will sooner or later search the virtual desktop for photos, music files, bookmarked Web sites, and whatever else they can find. The search is part social sorting—an attempt to rule out an incompatible person—and in part market research that recalls Abika.com's ostensibly research-based claim that most people "said they would have been able to make a much better impression on their date if they knew their date's personality and preferences in advance."

When it comes to sorting, one of the recurring red flags is pornography, which is such a frequently unearthed find in the targets' rooms that the show has a special logo for it: a flashing red skull and crossbones with the subtitle "X-rated" superimposed over the offending material. Computers are also storehouses of information about the user's career or scholarly achievements, tastes in music, and Web browsing habits. In this respect, the role played by computers on *Room Raiders* recalls the recurring news coverage of the emerging field of computer forensics—and its role in both police investigations and the state's declared war on terror, in which cell phones and computers double as communication tools and surveillance targets.

Because the stated goal of each episode is the choice of an appropriate person for the raider to date, the narrative arc relies on the raiders' distinctions between desirable characteristics and those that serve as grounds for disqualification. The finale of each episode features—in the form of "the reveal"—the judgment of the raider, along with an elaboration of his or her reasons for selecting one prospective date and disqualifying the others. The professed desiderata of the MTV demographic might come as a surprise to those who decry the debilitating moral influence of pop culture on its most avid fans. In keeping with the norms of self-governance, the themes that repeatedly emerge in the investigations include professional prospects, physical fitness, cleanliness, and hygiene. The spy kit includes a pair of tongs that are usually used to sort through laundry baskets and trash, and a pair of white gloves that are used, Felix Unger style, to test for dust. Reasons for dismissal include everything from smoking to untidiness, and there is often a scolding tone to the dismissals ("I didn't like that he didn't put his ironing board away—it was a simple task and it just shows that he's lazy and disorganized," or "I really didn't like the shower curtain: it was grimy and nasty. She needs to replace that").

To hear MTV tell it, today's youth are big on enforcing norms of (relatively) clean living, mainstream style, and responsible behavior. Reasons for dismissal in the twenty episodes I viewed for this chapter included the following: novelty handcuffs hidden in the closet ("I didn't like the love cuffs, he's a little too kinky for me and I'm not into that"), Goth artwork ("I really didn't like her gothic style, it's a little scary"), dirty flip-flops ("They were

just nasty"), a whip and a porn tape ("I'm really not into that stuff"), cigarettes (twice—"I'm not down with kissing someone with smoke breath"),
too many video games ("I don't want to sit home and play video games"),
too much pornography (in four episodes—all in the rooms of men), and a
dirty hairbrush ("if you can't take care of your hairbrush, I don't know if you
can take care of yourself"). The mantle of the spy seems to carry with it a
sense of duty to enforce socially sanctioned norms of private behavior. Not
surprisingly, in the postfeminist MTV world, grounds for disqualification
of women included the appearance of being too overtly sexual. One raider,
after finding a vibrator under the bed of a prospective date, decided, "I did
not like one of the rooms because it was very kinky, and even though I can
be kinky it's a little too kinky for me." Another raider dismissed a prospective
date after finding that her purse doubled as an overnight bag, complete with
toothbrush and deodorant: "Is this like your one-night-stand bag?" he asked
disapprovingly.

In the dating world of *Room Raiders,* anonymity can be an amplifier of
both risk and opportunity. When raiders are allowed the opportunity to exclude those whose rooms exhibit traces of deviance or dishonesty—or just
improper conduct—both raider and target are ensured in the closing wrap-
up that the correct choice has been made. The woman who was rejected for
being too kinky said, "I think my drawer and what he found in it probably
freaked him out, but that's OK—not everyone can handle it and I don't want
to be with anyone who can't."

In other words, if the common refrain of other challenge-oriented reality
shows is that of how great the experience was—how much it taught the cast
members about themselves and their relations with others—the recurring
concluding message of *Room Raiders* is that the investigations yielded the
correct choice. Only two of the twenty episodes I viewed for this essay ended
with the room raider expressing any misgivings about his or her final choice.
For the most part, the show repeatedly confirmed the viability of investigation and detection as effective tools for prescreening dates.

In this respect the show provides a pop culture echo of the findings of psychologist Samuel Gosling described by Malcolm Gladwell in his book *Blink*
about the power of first impressions and gut instincts.[47] Gosling had students fill out a standard personality test and then compared how well friends
evaluated the students' personalities with evaluations made by strangers who

had only briefly inspected the students' rooms. He found, as Gladwell put it, that "on balance . . . the strangers ended up doing a much better job. What this suggests is that it is quite possible for people who have never met us and who have spent only 20 minutes thinking about us to come to a better understanding of who we are than people who have known us for years."[48]

The timing of Gladwell's book and its finding that the "second brain"—the gut—can cut through the various distractions, miscues, and manipulations that taint more deliberative assessments fits neatly with the x-ray-vision style of the Bush administration and its attendant version of generalized post-modern skepticism. *New York Times* columnist Matt Miller has described one consequence of this generalized skepticism as the "death of persuasion"[49]: the debunking of rational, critical deliberation as little more than a ruse of power, and thus the foreclosure of persuasion's potential purchase. We are left with a default to the promise of the ostensibly direct evidence of our eyes and the stain in the black light as more reliable than the other's words.

Monitoring the Watchers

This brief discussion of some of the themes of *Room Raiders* is not meant to suggest that the show's viewers are conditioned by the show to put into practice investigative tactics that might not otherwise have occurred to them (nor is it to rule out this possibility). Rather, it is to suggest that, to the extent that popular culture serves as an admittedly selective form of societal self-representation, a show like *Room Raiders* might provide a useful distillation of themes that we can discern in other realms of social practice. Once we have traced the trajectory of the use of mutual monitoring as an investigative technique associated with a climate of savvy skepticism and generalized risk, we can use it to explore interconnections between forms of popular entertainment, political discourse, and social practice.

It is the staging of the spectacle of surveillance on reality shows like *Fake Out* and *Room Raiders* that highlights the reflexive character of the monitoring process itself. When the surveillance process is presented as a spectacle for popular consumption, the figure of the savvy spy—of the unduped skeptic—is portrayed as a performance for the imagined gaze of the watchers. Savviness is revealed as a self-conscious performance that expresses the desire not to be seen as a dupe—a desire that underwrites not only a generalized skepticism, but the deployment of detection schemes for getting behind potentially manipulating and misleading facades.

Conclusion: Exposing the Voyeurs

One familiar assessment of the lateral monitoring practices described above characterizes them as a displacement of the figure of "Big Brother" by proliferating "little brothers" who engage in distributed, decentralized forms of monitoring and information gathering. Surveillance scholar Reg Whitaker, for example, invokes the model of a "participatory Panopticon" in a double sense: it represents a form of consensual submission to surveillance in part because the watched are also doing the watching.[50] Mark Crispin Miller succinctly reformulated the Big Brother slogan for a reflexive era: "Big Brother is you, watching."[51] In an era of distributed surveillance, the amplification of panoptic monitoring relies on the internalized discipline not just of the watched, but also of the watchers. We are not just being habituated to an emerging surveillance regime in which we all know that we could be monitored at any time—a realization driven home by the repetitive drumbeat of investigative reports about commercial and state monitoring. At the same time, we are becoming habituated to a culture in which we are all expected to monitor one another—to deploy surveillance tactics facilitated at least in part by interactive media technologies—in order to protect ourselves and our loved ones and to maximize our chances for social and economic success.

The exposure of the watchers themselves as objects of the gaze is the participatory twist highlighted by the portrayal of surveillance as spectacle on a show like *Room Raiders*. The TV show offers a reflexive distillation of the role of the savvy subject, who, always on guard against the risks of deception, internalizes the norms and imperatives of surveillance, screening, and sorting. The contrived scene of surveillance on the show exposes practices of investigatory voyeurism as, simultaneously, forms of self-display. The drive to make oneself seen as someone not fooled by facades aligns itself with the performance of the savvy subject, who takes pride in the ability to discern the "real" agendas and personalities behind the phony facades presented by public discourses and symbolic mandates.

Such an interpretation prompts a reconsideration of the exhibitionistic character of what surveillance scholar Clay Calvert calls "voyeur nation":

a nation of watchers performing their verification practices with an eye to the gaze of an imagined other, in order to avoid being seen as a dupe.[52] The room raid is thus both examination and exhibition: by going through the rooms with investigative tools, searching dresser drawers and hard drives, the raider guards against potentially unpleasant surprises and performs for an imagined audience the skills of detection and risk monitoring necessary for negotiating a world in which people are not always who they say they are. Raiders are, of course, conscious that their actions will be broadcast for all to see—indeed, they have sought out the opportunity to display their investigatory expertise in the form of the detection and risk-management skills that protect them from the ruse of appearances. Practices of mutual monitoring, seen in this light, rely not just on a climate of generalized skepticism and wariness, but on conceptions of risk that instantiate social imperatives of productivity, hygiene, and security associated with the maximization of productive forces—imperatives that, as media scholar Laurie Ouellette argues, quoting Nikolas Rose, "transform . . . 'the goals of authorities' into the 'choices and commitments' of individuals."[53]

The image of the dupe is the phantasmic figure that haunts the imagination of postmodern skepticism. We feel the implied threat of being caught and exposed in our moments of credulity, potentially taken in by our partners, coworkers, perhaps our children and friends. If the advent of new media technologies promised more democratic access to the mode of information, the result has been not so much a democratization of politics and the economy, but the injunction to embrace the strategies of law enforcement and marketing at a micro level. Citizens are invited to conduct their own versions of market research and personal verification, thanks to their newfound access to information and communication technologies. The result has not been a diminution of either government or corporate surveillance, as evidenced by their converging role in the war on terror, but rather their amplification and replication through peer monitoring networks. The participatory injunction of the interactive revolution extends monitoring techniques from the cloistered offices of the Pentagon to the everyday spaces of our homes and offices, from law enforcement and espionage to dating, parenting, and social life. In an era in which everyone is to be considered potentially suspect, we are invited to become spies—for our own good.

9

Beyond Monitoring

The masses have the right to a change in property relations; Fascism seeks to give them a form of expression in the preservation of these relations.
—Walter Benjamin

The media coverage of the stunningly successful fifth season of the game show *American Idol* made much of host Ryan Seacrest's public boast about the 63.4 million votes that has been cast during the finale, "That's more than any president in the history of our country has ever received."[1] Although misleading on a number of counts, the comparison made its way into the headlines because of what it presumably said about American voters: that they were more likely to take the initiative to participate in their "bread and circuses" than their politics. It also highlighted what I have been describing as the misleading equation of interactive marketing with democratic politics and political empowerment. The nation's political newspaper of record, the *Washington Post,* cited survey results indicating that more than a third of those who voted for an *American Idol* contestant felt that the vote counted "'more than or as much as' voting in a presidential election."[2] One commentator took these results as an indication that the country might want to turn to the Fox network for a twenty-first-century model of democratic participation: "If we look at how 'American Idol' works, we might pick up a few cues for a better way to run our real election and inspire some passion for politics."[3]

What gets lost in this comparison is the distinction between what I have been calling cybernetic interactivity and democratic interactivity—the difference between assisting marketers and participating collectively in the setting of shared goals. Whatever else it might be, *American Idol* is not democratic: it is an interactive marketing campaign that treats the viewing audience as a nationwide focus group. The goals of the network and production company are not subject to collective deliberation. Audience feedback is used for the sole purpose of marketing a product—in this case, a recording artist—to as large a market as possible. Participation contributes to this marketing effort by providing data about tastes and preferences—information that marketers used to have to work hard for, going door to door, engaging in phone surveys, and even, as in the example of Crossley's pioneering market research work, sorting through trash.

The Tom Sawyer trick of *American Idol* is to offload this work onto the populace by portraying it as fun and empowering—a version of reality TV democracy that's more entertaining and rewarding than the real thing. Seacrest's boast that the *Idol* competition received more popular support than the political system amounts to a declaration of victory for consumer sovereignty over political sovereignty. The timing of his statement was suggestive, taking place, as it did, during a period of national disillusion over the reelection of President Bush, whose poll numbers had dropped precipitously in response to his apparently failed policies in Iraq, the eruption of scandal investigations reaching into his inner circle, and his administration's negligent response to the devastation caused by Hurricane Katrina. Reality TV democracy might have looked a lot less fraught with disturbing consequences than real politics at the time.

But even Cass Sunstein's notion of consumer sovereignty, understood as the unreflective exercise of individual consumer preferences, doesn't quite do justice to the ostensibly democratic character of *American Idol*. The show isn't just about selecting a pop star; it's about participating in the process whereby that star is marketed to oneself. This is the model of interactivity on offer, the one whose critique has been a recurring theme of this book: the invitation to participate in one's own manipulation by providing increasingly detailed information about personal preferences, activities, and background to those who would use the knowledge to manage consumption. In this regard, the spectacle of *American Idol* recalls critical theorist Susan Buck-

Morss's description of propaganda, which gives "to the masses a double role, to be observer as well as the inert mass being formed and shaped. And yet, due to a displacement of the place of pain, due to a consequent misrecognition, the mass-as-audience remains somehow undisturbed by the spectacle of its own manipulation."[4]

To update this formulation for the interactive era, we might add that not only does the public remain undisturbed, not only does it watch, but it participates in the spectacle of its own manipulation. And in one more reflexive twist, this participation becomes itself a form of manipulation insofar as it is passed off as a form of democratic empowerment—not just what Reg Whitaker calls a participatory panopticon, but a participatory spectacle—in the sense invoked by Guy Debord. The effort to gloss over the process of manipulation is, in the interactive era, displaced by its spectacular celebration. The somewhat dystopian theme running through this book is that people will not only pay to participate in the spectacle of their own manipulation, but that, thanks in part to the promise of participation, they will ratify policies that benefit powerful elites and vested interests at their own expense, as if their (inter)active support might somehow make these vested interests their own.

The culmination of this dystopian moment was identified in apocalyptic terms by the theorist and critic Walter Benjamin, who, in response to the rise of fascism, observed in 1936 that humanity's "self-alienation has reached such a degree that it can experience its own destruction as an aesthetic pleasure of the first order."[5] Although Benjamin was referring to the Futurist "cult of warfare as a form of aesthetics" and its attendant fascination with military technology, it is possible to discern the afterglow of this form of "aesthetic pleasure" in the post-9/11 United States. Shortly before the United States embarked on its invasion of Iraq, ostensibly to rid the world of a dangerous dictator and his cache of weapons of mass destruction, but also, tacitly, to "stabilize" a region vital to the U.S. economy, America's Motor City unveiled a spectacular celebration of the aesthetics of destructive consumption. The 2003 Detroit Auto Show, which featured the resurgence of overpowered muscle and luxury cars, amounted to a perverse display of defiance toward the legacy of antipathy toward the U.S. spawned in no small part by its oil-driven foreign policy in the Middle East. The array of pricey, overpowered gas gluttons, in part a reflection of increasing economic stratification in the United States, was also a stubborn assertion that neither the industry nor its upscale consumers would be cowed by the threat of instability into rethinking their commitment to environmentally and politically disastrous consumption patterns. As one press account noted, "The trend also speaks to the American mood as the country hunkers down in the shadow of war, terror, and oil-price fears. Some drivers see the gas-guzzling vehicles as an assertion of American self-confidence."[6] One of the top designers for the Ford Motor Company observed of the post-9/11 proliferation of overpowered vehicles, "Partly it may be a patriotic thing."[7] The star of the show was a 500-horsepower motorcycle with a ten-cylinder sports-car engine, a growling, gleaming hunk of chrome-plated mechanical muscle, something straight out of the Futurist fantasy of "the metallization of the human body."[8]

In light of this perverse reaction to the legacy of U.S. foreign policy, the threat of instability in the Middle East, and the increasingly clear signals about the environmental threat of global warming, it's hard not to see the recurring ads for powerful trucks and sport utility vehicles (interspersed between reruns of car-chase movies) as minispectacles of self-destruction presented as a form of entertainment. Audiences, in the interactive era, are no longer relegated to the role of merely watching such commercials. Thanks to the popularity of user-generated content, they have been offered the opportunity to participate in producing these commercials for themselves. In 2006, Chevrolet featured an interactive make-your-own ad campaign for its Tahoe sports utility vehicle. The promotion, which ran parallel to a product-placement segment on Donald Trump's reality show, *The Apprentice,* invited contestants to compose their own commercial by stringing together video clips (for example, the Tahoe sitting on a mountain peak, or driving through the desert or the wilderness) over which their original ad copy would be superimposed. There were plenty of spoof and critical ads, which were promptly circulated on the popular viral video site YouTube, but in the end, even the critics ended up spending more time on the Chevy Tahoe Web site than they would have otherwise—and ended up sending e-mail links for the site to their friends.

The Chevy campaign was just one of several user-generated content advertising campaigns that offloaded the work of creating and promoting advertising appeals onto audiences. Companies including Converse, Sony, JetBlue, MasterCard, and the USA Cable TV Network all jumped on the interactivity

bandwagon. In an era in which viewers have increased access to digital production tools, the goal of such campaigns is to put the audience to work. TV
networks including Bravo and VH1 have composed entire shows out of user-
generated content created from homemade viral videos. The biggest draw is
economic: "It's . . . cheaper by far than anything else VH1 produces, which is
to say, cheaper than almost anything else on television."[9] Moreover, thanks
to their success on the Internet, many of the clips come pretested: they've
already been subjected to the online focus group that much of the Internet
seems to be turning into.

These examples are of a piece with many of the other examples of interactivity highlighted in this book: they further illustrate some of the ways in
which the creative potential unleashed by the rapid spread of relatively inexpensive media technology and communication devices is being exploited for
the purposes of strengthening and feeding what media critic Ben Bagdikian
has called the "media monopoly"—the handful of major media corporations that control the lion's share of the commercial media that saturate
the cultural life of the United States. Under conditions in which those who
retain ownership of the means of media production continue to shape the
spectacle of manipulation, the offer of interactivity can only propose "as a
revolutionary solution, that everyone become a [self-]manipulator."[10]

If one of the age-old conundrums of democracy is that posed by the prospect of the democratic election of an authoritarian leader (a prospect that
hits close to home in the contemporary United States), the interactive era
updates this conundrum with its obverse: the prospect of an ongoing democratic practice that approaches what the philosopher Jean Baudrillard describes as "decentralized totalitarianism."[11] The threat posed by this version
of totalitarianism is not the eradication of the vote, but its ongoing deployment as an extension of the version of interactivity on offer by the commercial sector: a version of interactivity that amounts to "actively sustaining
the scene of one's own passive submission."[12] Perhaps even more frightening
than the authoritarian dismantling of mechanisms for democratic participation would be their repurposing for an ongoing process of ratified submission to exploitation and domination. The former society still holds forth the
prospect of rebellion; the latter has seemingly dispensed with it. A society
characterized by the deployment of interactivity for the purposes of decentralized totalitarianism might take the form of one in which consumers identify

strongly enough with the imperatives of those who manipulate and manage them to willingly submit to comprehensive monitoring; it is a society in which they actively provide politicians with the resources for targeted campaigning; and finally, it is a society in which the deployment of interactive information and communication technologies perfects the forms of social and economic control envisioned at the turn of the twentieth century.

Splitting the Audience

The crucial question raised by Susan Buck-Morss in her discussion of propaganda regards what she describes as the displacement of the "place of pain": how is it that the segmented and stratified mass audience fails to regard its own manipulation as such? Whence the blind spot that allows the anxiety born of a sense of political, economic, and environmental insecurity to seek relief through a double dose of the cause? Why reelect die-hard oilmen to address instability in the Middle East; or buy an overpowered truck to defy the threat posed by a wounded and sick environment, or the hatred spawned by oil-driven foreign policy? Why participate deliberately in the spectacle of one's own manipulation in the name of empowerment? Such questions get to the larger social context within which the promise of interactivity as participation is deployed and lead us into some speculative terrain. It is, I think, terrain that is well worth exploring, and I will spend a little time doing so before outlining a more practical critique of the promise of interactivity and some suggestions for distinguishing between democratic and cybernetic forms of interactivity—between collective deliberation and social Taylorism.

Propaganda, according to Susan Buck-Morss's formulation, relies on an internal split in its target audience that allows its members to adopt the role of observers at the scene of their own manipulation. To describe this split, she uses the metaphor of the operating theater—a site where the spectacle of an expert operating on a selected member of the public was made possible by the discovery of anesthesia, whose narcotic effect numbed the pain that might disturb the audience or trigger a sense of empathy or identification with the patient. Similarly, she argues, the rise of social theory and, I would add, social science, cultivates the ability to abstract away from the human scale at which suffering occurs and to adopt a removed Olympian stance of dispassionate observation. Communication philosopher John Peters offers a similar diagnosis of what he describes as the stoicism of statistical social science: "Statistics . . . offer the ultimate in Stoic distance. From their height no tragedy looks tragic any more, as in Stalin's chilly dictum, 'one death is a tragedy, a million deaths is a statistic.'"[13]

Negotiating what I have been describing, following Haskell, as the recession of causality imposes a complementary stance of abstraction on the part of the social scientist. Viewed from a distance, the social body spreads out across the landscape like a patient etherized upon a table. As Susan Buck-Morss puts it, the nineteenth century, captivated by the technologies of specialized manufacturing and long-distance communication associated with industrialization, ushered in social theories that "perceived society as an organism, literally a 'body' politic, in which the social practices of institutions . . . performed the various organ functions. Labor specialization, rationalization and integration of social functions created a techno-body of society, and it was imagined to be as insensate to pain as the individual body under general anesthetics."[14]

The recession of causality corresponds to a complementary recession of affect: members of the social body were presented with their own image as it were "from a distance," and thereby invited to view the operation performed on it from the perspective of spectators. To characterize the form of anesthetization that resulted from this response to the recession of causality, Buck-Morss invokes the comparison to medicine: "What happened to perception under these circumstances was a tripartite splitting of experience into agency (the operating surgeon), the object . . . (the docile body of the patient), and the observer (who perceives and acknowledges the accomplished result)."[15]

The formulation of a split audience, one that observes its own manipulation as that exerted on a "docile" body politic (or economic), relies on what Buck-Morss describes as a form of numbness: the inability of the observers to determine that they inhabit "the place of pain"—that the forms of manipulation to which they are privy are being exercised on them. A sense of reflexive savviness follows on and compensates for the "numbness" that Buck-Morss describes as a reaction formation to the "shocks" of the modern world. As she puts it, "Being 'cheated out of experience' has become the general state," insofar as the sensory system is "marshaled to parry technological stimuli in order to protect both the body from the trauma of accident and the psyche from the trauma of perceptual shock. As a result, the system reverses its role. Its goal is to numb the organism, to deaden the senses, to repress memory."[16]

This account of the impact of industrialization can be read alongside the recurring theme of the recession of causality. One of the messages of social science and contemporaneous and paternalistic forms of progressivism was that the everyday experience of the layperson—the nonexpert—was not sufficient to make sense of an increasingly interdependent social system, whose movements could only register as incomprehensible shocks. Perhaps local experience might be enough to make it through the day—to react to the demands and activities of daily life—but it stopped short of being able to make sense of the larger system within which these took shape. In the face of this larger system, acceptance of expert analysis relied on numbing down the faculties—a willingness to delegate particular forms of experience and sensibility to those "in the know," and thereby, perhaps, to accept the displacement of one's own sensibilities with regard to topics supposedly beyond the scope of the layperson.

This message is reinforced by the division of labor imposed by scientific management: the separation of planning and managing from execution. Schmidt, the steelworker whom Frederick Taylor guides to greater efficiency, doesn't need to understand the reasons behind the timing of his work. He is asked only to follow the commands of the managers whose opaque system is based on their ongoing observation of workers—data inaccessible to the workers themselves. On the one hand, managers and social scientists are required to adopt an "inhuman" perspective—to treat workers as objects to be managed. On the other hand, workers are required to relinquish the forms of understanding and experience that precede the separation of planning and conception from execution. There is an affinity here between the need for numbness in the face of the "shocks" of industrial life and the need to numb oneself down enough to simply, unthinkingly, automatically follow the motions and directives dictated by the managers: "Exploitation is here to be understood as a cognitive category. . . . The factory system injuring every one of the human senses, paralyzes the imagination of the worker. His or her work is 'sealed off from experience'; memory is replaced by conditioned response, learning by 'drill,' skill by repetition."[17]

As in the workplace, so too in society—at least according to the managers and the social scientists. Their Stoic sacrifice—the adoption of a removed, scientific perspective—also implicitly sets a limit to the power of everyday experience and the knowledge of the uninitiated. In an era of rapid transformation, in which proximate events are the results of remote, invisible, and interdependent causes, "immediate" experience remains reactive, unable to keep pace with the recession of causality. The resulting split between the perspective of the managerial and the working classes is reflected, as historian Michael Schudson points out, in the media culture of the late nineteenth century. The model of journalism that targeted working-class readers, Schudson argues, reflected their own experience of the world as one of dependence on forces beyond their control: "In tone and display it created the sense that everything was new, unusual, and unpredictable. There is reason to believe that this accurately reflected the life experience of many people in the cities, the newly literate and the newly urban."[18] That the sense of dependence and lack of control might be structural rather than merely the result of a temporary historical conjuncture is suggested by the enduring popularity of this journalistic model, which focuses both on providing lifestyle tips from "experts" and on stories that highlight the unpredictability and inexplicability of life even (or especially) for celebrity figures whose tabloid lives might be described as a tangled web of infidelities, addictions, and traumas. At worst, such journalism provides entertainment and information that mimics the predictable shocks of the workplace, reinforcing the anaesthetization of experience.

This is a grim picture—one which surely doesn't do justice either to the media or to workplace experience (at least in every case), but it captures the broad claims that underlie Susan Buck-Morss's argument: that the transition from traditional rural life to urban industrialization had what the sociologist Anthony Giddens describes as the "disembedding" effect of "'lifting out' . . . social relations from local contexts of interaction."[19] Uprooted from the established norms and practices of rural life, the workers who followed the jobs to the city and the factory were forced to seek out new social structures appropriate to their new way of life. As in the case of the factory, argues media historian William Leiss, the prescriptions for a reconfigured lifestyle—one in keeping with the new urban milieu—came from the new, self-styled lifestyle experts, the managers, in this case, of consumption: "The functions of older cultural traditions in shaping consumption patterns and the sense of satisfaction for individuals have been taken over by media-based messages through which are circulated a great assortment of cues and images about the relationship between persons and goods."[20] Historian Jib Fowles similarly argues that the emerging cult of media celebrity in the early twentieth century provided images of contemporary lifestyles for popular consumption—images that were particularly appealing to those uprooted from traditional lifestyles and in search of patterns from above for their lives and loves.[21]

The organized manufacture of images and information for popular consumption, insofar as it came to saturate everyday experience, became an integral part of social Taylorism and the management of consumption. The numbing down of experience is a crucial component of forms of social control that displaced workplace expertise by managerial guidance inside the factory and social expertise by mass-produced culture outside it. The point with respect to the culture industries is not that experience becomes increasingly mediated, because all experience is, arguably, mediated. Rather, it is that these industries provide a form of prefabricated mediation, in which the sense-making work has been done in advance. As in the workplace, what is foreclosed or suppressed by these constructed and rationalized forms of prefabricated experience are alternate experiences that might counter the lessons received from the managers of production or consumption. The management of consumption becomes reliant on the ways in which "sensory addiction to a compensatory reality becomes a means of social control."[22] Complementing this compensatory reality—the phantasmagoria of the pop culture imaginary—is the symbolic discourse of the experts. On the one hand, repetitive images of the ideals of consumer society circulate instructions for living; on the other, scientific research and analysis compensates for the recession of causality and helps to craft these images. One of the recurring messages of the former is to cede the analysis of important political and economic questions to the latter.

Debunking Expertise: The Postmodern Turn

And now, after a bit of a detour, we can revisit the initial question: how is it that the split public distances itself from the spectacle of its own manipulation—a spectacle from which it imagines itself to be removed? Just as the deskilling of the worker is compensated for by the emergence of a profes-

sional class of trained managers, the numbing down of the citizen is compensated for by the ostensible expertise of the trained social scientists (and,
to complete the trinity, that of the consumer by the expertise of the market
researcher, who comes to know the tastes of consumers "better than they
do themselves"). Without the scientific managers, a factory full of workers
trained only to follow instructions and provided with only a fragmented
view of the production process faces the prospect of disarray. Similarly, a
society comprised of deskilled, numbed-down citizens becomes reliant on
an implicit faith in the work of the symbolic analysts and their power to de-
cipher the complexities of an increasingly interdependent society.

The complexity of the postmodern moment, by contrast, results from the
fact that it is characterized by a savvy, reflexive critique of this faith—not just
in the talents of a particular group of experts, but in the efficacy of expert
discourse itself as a means of countering the recession of causality, of grasping the totality of interdependent social relations. The usual suspects behind
this demise, which Žižek describes as the "decline of symbolic efficiency," include the legacy of brutality and tragedy that characterized the efforts of the
twentieth-century technocrats, the co-optation of social science by marketing and public relations (both corporate and government), and the reflexively demystifying influence of the mass media.[23] The century that ushered
in the fantasy of an efficiently managed consumer paradise was characterized
in reality by a brutal litany of totalitarianism, fascism, genocide, exploitation,
world war, and the specter of global destruction. The "best and brightest"
brought us napalm warfare and secret bombings, the "smartest boys in the
room" corporate fraud and bankruptcy. TV amplified the fantasy of celebrity while it demystified authority figures, bringing us images of presidents
tripping and puking—images of their fallibility as well as their humanity. It
also brought us metacoverage—the behind-the-scenes spectacle of the revelation of the spectacle, which is perhaps the defining postmodern form of
entertainment and news. If the willing submission of the public to the ministrations of experts relied on a (suppressed) faith in symbolic efficacy, the
demise of this faith has important consequences.

To summarize the thrust of the argument so far, the recession of causality
served as the rationale for the rise of social scientific expertise and invited
members of the public to discount their own experience in the face of expert
analysis. The conundrum of the contemporary era of interactivity, then, is

that posed by the double movement of the replacement of traditional forms of knowledge and expertise by those of the symbolic analysts and the subsequent savvy critique of expertise itself. The demise of symbolic efficacy associated with this critique aligns itself with the exaltation of the compensatory world of popular culture. If a commitment to Enlightenment egalitarianism that is based on shared access to rational thought and deliberation has too often manifested itself in the form of tragedy, in the postmodern era, it appears in the form of farce: the ostensibly democratic assertion that, thanks to generalized debunkery (universalized skepticism), any worldview is as defensible as any other. The savvy citizen, equipped with preemptive knowledge of the ways in which all knowledge is a political ruse, can dismiss in canny scare quotes the scientific consensus about global warming alongside the promises of policy makers, political scientists, and pundits, who have all too often gotten it wrong.

The demise of symbolic efficiency refers not just to a well-warranted loss of faith in particular experts, but a questioning of the possibility of expertise itself. This is what renders it ostensibly democratic: the leveling of the hierarchical distinction between the realm of symbolic expertise and the prefabricated experiences of the industrially produced culture that it helped administer. This generalized skepticism also underwrites the narrowly construed version of interactivity critiqued in previous chapters. If modernism presented the audience with the spectacle of the expert management of a benumbed body politic, postmodernism promises the uncanny reanimation of this body in the guise of the manager's assistant. When expertise is debunked by the revelation of knowledge not merely as power's ruse but as entirely reducible to it, the distinction between spectator and expert dissolves. The audience is invited to elevate its imaginings (apparently forgetting their heteronomous origins in the culture industry) to the level of what heretofore counted as expertise, not by thinking them through, testing them out, and engaging in collective deliberation, but by discounting these processes—throwing out the bathwater of the Enlightenment with its misbegotten babies. The philosopher Alain Badiou has described the combination of an ersatz, market-based version of democracy with an ostensibly egalitarian relativism as "the abstract universality of our epoch": combining "the violent dogmatism of mercantile 'democracy' with a thoroughgoing skepticism."[24]

Žižek's invocation of Groucho Marx's question, "Who do you believe, your eyes or my words?" is meant to illustrate the role that symbolic efficacy plays in opening up a space of possibility beyond the seemingly irrevocably given character of directly experienced reality. It is not, of course, an uncommon experience to trust the evidence of the symbolic realm over our more "direct" experience, as when, for example, we concede that the earth orbits the sun. Most of us don't have access to the direct evidence that proves such an assertion; we rely on the system of meanings and institutions that guarantee it. Symbolic efficacy has, he suggests, an important role to play at the level of social and political institutions in which "the symbolic mask-mandate matters more than the direct reality of the individual who wears this mask and/or assumes this mandate."[25]

On Žižek's account, the efficacy of the symbolic—of the shared system of representations according to which we organize our world—relies on an acceptance of the nonidentical and contradictory character of discourse itself: the fact that, for example, it can be inadequate to the reality it designates—or vice versa. Thus, the notion of freedom might designate more than its real-world referent represented by the version of freedom that we find on offer in the "free" market or that invoked by Donald Rumsfeld's description of a "liberated" Iraq. A generalized savviness collapses such distinctions: there can no longer be a discrepancy between a portrayal and that which it ostensibly portrays, because the latter is fully absorbed into the former. The deadlock of the symbolic (always also its condition of possibility)—the contradictory character of redoubling reality by representing it (in order to access it)—is conveniently elided. In more concrete terms, this logic appears in contemporary political discourse as a kind of postmodern nominalism: if the United States, for example, pursues its imperialistic ambitions in the name of fostering democracy, then democracy itself is dismissed as nothing more than (or, in other words, entirely reducible to) a ruse for imperialism. There is a frustrating flatness to what passes for symbolic representations in a savvy, post-deferential context: they can't pull themselves away from the brute facticity of the given.

The impossibility of dispensing with the symbolic order altogether (universal skepticism relies, inevitably, on disavowed truth claims, and generalized debunkery is possible only as an abstract, self-contradictory exercise) results in what Žižek describes as the return of the symbolic in the register of the real: "two features which characterize today's ideological stance—cynical distance and full reliance on paranoiac fantasy—are strictly codependent: the typical subject today is the one who, while displaying cynical distrust of any public ideology, indulges without restraint in paranoiac fantasies about conspiracies."[26] Once the possibility of expertise is debunked, such fantasies are absorbed into the encompassing embrace of a pluralism of worldviews: each to one's own cultural imaginary—there's no accounting for fantasies (except at the box office). These imaginary possibilities remain products not of collective life and shared experience but of the serialized, isolating society of the spectacle. They serve not as the basis for collective action but as private matters—the kind of politics to be discussed only with people who already agree; or, more cynically, only with those who also recognize them as merely one more ruse of power—public relations for strategic gain. Hence the disconcerting hermeticism of contemporary political discourse and the talking heads of cable TV and talk radio.

The wonder of symbolic efficacy is that, in its contradictory relationship to a contradictory world, it opened up the possibility that things might be otherwise—that, for example, the actions we take in the name of democracy might not live up to its concept. Or, to put it more generally, that the very possibility of constructing a shared understanding of the world (as it could be) that differs from how it immediately appears is a function of potentialities in the (contradictions of the) world itself. As Žižek puts it, "in 'normal' symbolic communication, we are dealing with the distance (between 'things' and 'words') which opens up the space for the domain of Sense and, within it, for symbolic engagement."[27] What type of engagement or meaningful participation is possible without it? In the face of generalized wholesale skepticism, participation runs the risk of merely reproducing the limits imposed by the scientific management of culture on the imagination of an animated yet benumbed populace. Yes, they can participate, but the cultural imaginary that underwrites this participation comes prepackaged. Freedom will continue to mean the deregulation of the market; choice will continue to refer to a forced choice from a fixed range of goods and goals.

One of the most telling pop culture images of this version of technologically facilitated interactivity was the image of a mass-customized virtual world portrayed in the movie *Vanilla Sky*. The protagonist, a wealthy playboy who suffered a deforming accident and subsequent rejection by his new love, signed up with a high-tech firm to have his consciousness replaced by a virtual reality construct. Instead of having to endure the agony of life with his new deformation, he chose to live in a fantasy world in which his deformity is cured and he is reunited with his lost love. Here, perhaps, is an example of the perfection of numbness—and of the subterranean link hinted at by the shared etymology of the words *narcotic* and *narcissism*. The virtual world inhabited by the protagonist is a purely solipsistic one, crafted not out of new, shared experiences with other humans, but from a collection of memories supplied by the culture industry, including album covers, movies, and celebrity photos. As the movie's protagonist is told by a representative of the virtual reality company, "You sculpted your Lucid Dream out of the iconography of your youth. An album cover that once moved you. . . . A movie you saw once that showed you what a father could be like . . . or what love could be like." When provided with perfect freedom—the ability to, as it were, choose any life he liked, the lead character's choices were delimited by the prefabricated images of the culture industry. Moreover, as the movie notes, this solipsistic vision of technology-facilitated freedom was, in the end, made possible only, paradoxically, by complete dependence on next-generation forms of mediated entertainment. Virtual reality, in this example, represents the limit-case of the empowerment facilitated by interactive technology: "On the one hand, reduction of reality to a virtual domain regulated by arbitrary rules that can be suspended, [and] on the other, the concealed truth of this freedom, the reduction of the subject to an utter instrumentalized passivity."[28]

Alternative Interactivities

How might interactivity amount to something other than cybernetic feedback (or what I have been describing as active participation in self-manipulation)? Envisioning an alternative to the deployment of interactivity on offer by the culture industry requires more than describing alternative forms of practice. It presupposes a shift in the social conditions within which interactivity is deployed. It is perhaps overly simple to propose, as I do below, a list of criteria for what might count as more democratic versions of interactivity. Nevertheless, in an effort to parry the challenge of postmodern nominalism—the reduction of interactivity to what the culture industry says it is—the concluding section of this chapter is devoted to offering some outlines for the shape interactivity might take if it were to facilitate the promise of shared control that all too often serves only as its alibi.

Although it is common to invoke questions of privacy when critiquing the emerging surveillance society, I will not spend much time addressing privacy issues. A number of scholars, including, most recently, Jeffrey Rosen, have made eloquent cases for the importance of privacy protection to a regime of liberal democracy, and they raise interesting and important issues. Rosen, for example, claims that "privacy is necessary . . . to protect important social relationships—to make it possible for people to interact as citizens in the public square, as professionals in the workplace, and as friends, lovers, and family members in intimate group settings."[29] We don't want to know everything there is to know about friends, colleagues, students, and relatives, any more than they want to know everything about us. Privacy allows us to selectively shape our public persona in ways that may be at times incomplete, but which also facilitate social, political, and professional interactions. With privacy, in other words, comes a bit of control over our self-presentation—control that underwrites a sense of personal autonomy as well as helping to foster the conditions for collective action and public deliberation.

At the same time, privacy is used by private companies to claim control over transactional information generated by and about consumers and, paradoxically, by the government to refuse to disclose information about whom it has been monitoring. Most outrageously, the Bush administration claimed it was protecting the privacy rights of detainees held without trial as part of its post-9/11 secret detention program, refusing requests for information by family members. Privacy is not only a two-edged sword, it is also a culturally and historically variable one that has proven to be of only limited use in contesting the recent proliferation of government and commercial monitoring.

Part of the problem has been the tendency to think of privacy as a possession, something that can be acquired, surrendered, or exchanged, as implied by the question, "Are you willing to give up some of your privacy in exchange for greater security or convenience?" This book's discussion of interactivity, by contrast, has focused on monitoring as a power relation—one that can be used to extract and acquire benefits from the use of personal information within structured relationships. The question is not "how much privacy has been surrendered," but "who benefits from and who is disempowered by the deployment of interactivity as a monitoring strategy, and in what ways? Who is subjected to more sophisticated forms of management and control, and to what end? How does knowledge about individuals facilitate forms of control over them?"

The previous chapters have suggested, for the most part, that certain forms of commercial and state monitoring that take place within what I have been calling a "digital enclosure" foster asymmetrical and undemocratic power relations. Political and economic elites collect information that facilitates social Taylorism rather than fostering more democratic forms of shared control and participation. This is not to discount some very interesting and potentially powerful forms of collective action enabled by networked and interactive media, including open-source movements, collaborative media productions, and forms of online and offline activism. Rather, it is to focus on the practices for which these much-hyped forms of activism too often serve as an alibi.

Symmetry

One of the clearest distinctions between commercial and democratic forms of interactivity is the level of symmetry they allow in the information gathering process. As I argued in Chapter 6, democracy is predicated on the interplay of state and citizen publicity, which might also be understood as a specific form of symmetry. Rulers provide the public with access to their deliberations and the public expresses its will, to which the rulers are supposedly accountable. Democracy is, in this regard, a public enterprise on the part of both public and politicians. Symptoms of the default of publicity to public relations include, on the one hand, the gathering of market data about voters (the privatization and individualization of public opinion) and, on the other, the so-called politics of character (the publication of details of politicians' private lives). Commercial interactivity is, by contrast, asymmetrical: the decisions and actions of corporate entities remain opaque—private—even as consumers are rendered increasingly transparent to marketers and advertisers. Rather than accountability and transparency, commercial entities offer the promise of convenience and customization as an alibi for a shift in power relations: for the ability to discriminate invisibly and to gather information that facilitates market management and public manipulation. Perhaps not surprisingly, given its private sector provenance, this is the model of compensatory exchange offered by the Bush administration in its deployment of covert surveillance: the public is subjected to increasingly comprehensive forms of surveillance, for which the government seeks to exempt itself from accountability.

Invoking the notion of symmetry shifts the basis of the discussion from debates over privacy to an engagement with issues of centralized power and control. Engaging with these questions might help clarify ongoing debates over both government and commercial forms of monitoring facilitated by interactive technologies.

Consider, for example the defining fallacy of the post-9/11 surveillance debate: that the key question with regard to increasingly intrusive forms of government monitoring (including the collection of phone records and Internet search data) was that of the trade-off between privacy and security. Americans should be willing to sacrifice some of our privacy, we were told, in exchange for greater protection against future terrorist attacks. The public eventually learned that, after the attacks, the government had initiated a policy of eavesdropping without search warrants, apparently in violation of the law, that it had sought information from Internet search engines about user requests, and that it had reportedly acquired the calling records of millions of American citizens.

In the wake of a series of revelations during George W. Bush's second term about the government's various surveillance projects, the administration's defenders worked hard to portray the issue as one that pitted individual liberties against security and to tar critics with the charge of being soft on terrorism. Bush's second in command, Vice President Dick Cheney, who reportedly argued for unlimited wiretapping of domestic calls and e-mail in the wake of the 9/11 attacks, equated the claim that civil liberties were under attack with the "outrageous proposition that we ought to protect our enemy's ability to communicate its plots against America."[30] As the poll results cited in Chapter 6 suggest, the public for the most part bought Cheney's bluster—and in the process, perhaps inadvertently, accepted the right of the executive branch to exempt itself from the law of the land.

However, an invocation of the criterion of democratic symmetry and accountability reveals that the administration's push wasn't just in the direction of expanded monitoring power, but also, crucially, in the direction of diminished public scrutiny. At issue was the ability of the government to engage in blanket monitoring without judicial review or oversight. The move was much more than an invasion of privacy; it was a fundamentally undemocratic power grab. It was the adoption of a commercial model of information gathering: "We learn more about you, the consumer, but we are under no obligation to let you know what information we're gathering and how we're using it." Perhaps one of the reasons this fact didn't seem to register with the public was that the model of information gathering proposed by the administration reflected the forms of information gathering to which consumers are regularly subjected in the digital enclosure. Within this enclosure, we are becoming habituated not just to the notion that information is being gathered about our shopping practices, our online behavior, and even our movements throughout the course of the day, but also to the fact that we have no way of finding out what information has been collected, by whom, and for what purposes.

This asymmetric form of interactivity is inimical to democracy insofar as it inhibits collective action, meaningful participation, and shared control. Any form of interactivity that amounts to an unaccountable form of information gathering fails to live up to the promise of democratization. Calling interactive marketing campaigns like NIKE iD or *American Idol* democratic because they incorporate audience feedback does a disservice to the term and further underwrites the default of politics to marketing. If companies want to live up to the promise of the democratization that they mobilize as a marketing motif, then let them submit to forms of information gathering by, for example, independent public-interest organizations that gather detailed records about what type of information they gather and how they use it. This is not to say that symmetry is on its own sufficient to democratize interactivity. But it would be a step in the right direction. Knowing what companies are doing with transactionally generated information provides only a very limited form of accountability—certainly not shared participation in goal-setting decisions or in control over the databases and the means of interaction.

I harbor no illusions about the willingness of commercial entities to submit to symmetrical forms of information gathering—although some level of commercial transparency might encourage not only industry self-regulation, but the promulgation of legislation giving the public more control over information collected about them. It might also highlight the undemocratic character of asymmetrical forms of state monitoring, submission to which is presented not just as the public's duty, but as a form of participation in the war on terrorism—a way of doing one's part by sacrificing not just personal privacy but also, crucially, government publicity and accountability. This latter sacrifice, systematically exacted by the Bush administration, was largely overlooked in the debates over privacy, but it was perhaps the most telling. The logic of killing democracy in order to save it invokes the specter of refeudalization. It is a move away from public control and toward the portrayal of government as a protection racket. There is an exchange involved, but no longer in terms of reciprocal publicity or power. To avoid corroding the meaning of democracy, we need to resist the description of this model of interactivity (which is really partially coerced submission to comprehensive monitoring) as democratic.

Ends, Not Means

To continue the argument of the previous section, one way of restating this book's critique of the tendency to reduce politics to the market—to confuse consumer sovereignty with citizen sovereignty—is to assert that commercial forms of interactivity cannot be democratic, despite their repeated mobilization of democracy's promise. *American Idol* is not democratic, and neither is the NIKE iD marketing campaign. If it seems absurd even to have to point this out, the absurdity is a function of the contemporary confusion of political freedom with that of the "free" market—a confusion that is not limited to the marketing industry but extends to include those pundits and academics who described mass customization as democracy by another name. The *New York Times,* for example, went so far as to argue that because it relied on audience voting, the African version of the *Big Brother* reality TV show helped model democracy for a "strife-torn" continent.[31] In England, the chairman of the company that brought the popular reality show *Big Brother* to the United Kingdom, Peter Bazalgette, received widespread news coverage for his claim that reality TV might serve as model for boosting public interest in the political process, suggesting that the House of Commons might benefit from secret voting and regular online votes "to make Parliament more interactive"[32] Following the ratings—and voter turnout—success of *Big Brother,* Bazalgette was appointed in 2003 to the Conservative Party's Commission for Democracy, to help turn out the vote.[33] Finally, one British researcher issued a report called "A Tale of Two Houses," explaining what the House of Commons could learn from the public popularity of the *Big Brother* house.[34]

Presumably the pundits and academics understand that TV shows and advertising campaigns aren't literally political, insofar as they're about selling products, not making policy. Nevertheless, the thrust of their observations is that what works in one sphere might be readily translatable into the other—because, after all, getting out the vote is like attracting viewers and promoting a candidate is like selling a car. In the face of such apparent similarities, this book has argued that it is the crucial differences to which we need to pay careful attention. Relationship marketing and mass customization are nondemocratic not just because they're not about politics proper but also because they don't allow for shared participation in the goal-setting process. Market forms of feedback are cybernetic, not democratic.

As an example of the limits of cybernetic interactivity, consider the case of the *American Candidate* TV show, an attempt by producer and documentary filmmaker R. J. Cutler to realize, literally, the ostensibly democratic character of interactive TV. As Cutler envisioned it, the show would transpose the participatory model of *American Idol* (a show that allows viewers to vote for their preferred contestants) into the realm of politics, allowing "nonprofessional politicians of conviction"—real people with political passion and talent—to bypass normal political channels and run for president on TV. Viewers would select their favorite candidate, who would then, thanks to a cash prize and a TV season's worth of national publicity, be poised to run for office as a third-party candidate.

For Cutler, who devoted several years to developing it, the show represented the possibility that TV might heal the wounds it had inflicted on the political process in the form of prohibitive campaign costs and bland infotainment coughed up by media conglomerates unwilling to hold power accountable. For our purposes, *American Candidate* might be considered an attempt to jump the gap between feedback and shared control by channeling audience participation into the realm of the political—that of goal setting, not just strategy adjusting. Predictably, the project was thwarted. The F/X Network, owned by Rupert Murdoch's NewsCorp, picked up the show—and then, after a year in development, dropped it, citing costs—despite the fact that, according to Cutler, cost estimates had not significantly changed during development. The show was eventually produced as a mock presidential campaign, poorly promoted and relegated to the ratings hinterlands of Showtime, too late in the season to allow the winner to run for office.

As someone who continues to work with NewsCorp outlets, Cutler confines his frustration over the fate of the show to speculating that it was too political and participatory for the political elites on whose goodwill Murdoch's media empire depends: "The reported reason could not possibly be the full story," he insists.[35] From the perspective of cybernetic TV, the show represented an attempt to deliver on the promise of participation as power sharing—a promise that, regardless of the show's potential to deliver, stretched the limits of cybernetic TV beyond the comfort zone of the media oligopoly.

The market is a powerful economic machine—certainly among the most powerful and productive mechanisms harnessed by human society—but it is not a political substitute for democratic policies that facilitate deliberation over shared goals. Any version of interactivity that lays claim to democratic empowerment must allow feedback to shape collective goals as well as the means for achieving them. Moreover, a democratic version of interactivity cannot define feedback merely as a survey of consumer preferences, but must promote collective deliberation over shared goals. That is to say, it must foster what Cass Sunstein terms *political sovereignty* rather than consumer sovereignty. Democratic interactivity relegates the market to the status of a tool and facilitates shared control over the ends to which this tool is to be directed. Surveillance is not a substitute for deliberation, and the market is not a substitute for democratic participation.

A Public Enclosure

The digital enclosure that I have been describing throughout the course of this book is, for the most part, a privately controlled one. If the Internet was originally developed and funded by the state (and there are pockets of it within educational and political institutions that remain state subsidized), the recent history of the Internet has been one of privatization and commercialization.[36] Additional layers of what I have been calling the digital enclosure—mobile telephony, mobile e-mail and texting, Wi-Fi, GPS services—are, for the most part, privately owned and operated (although there are some exceptions in the case of Wi-Fi). The movement of digital enclosure, in other words, has largely corresponded to the privatization and commercialization of spaces and times that fall outside of those traditionally associated with production and consumption. The expansion of the enclosure represents the widening reach of monitoring practices that coordinate the simultaneous rationalization of production and consumption by blurring the barriers that helped keep marketing, advertising, and shopping distinct.

In the twentieth-century heyday of one-way electronic mass media, advertising remained, for the most part, distinct from shopping. The Home Shopping Network and "call now!" ads were anticipatory forms of convergence: a way to combine the mass advertising potential of broadcasting with the interactive capabilities of telephony. Interactive technologies extend this logic, making ads customizable and "actionable." Users can click on a pop-up ad for a book and buy it right away, generating not only one more sale, but also one more bit of demographic data for the marketing industry. At the same time, the commercial digital enclosure represents the expansion and overlap of the workspace and shopping mall. Thanks to the reach of interactive technology, these formerly delimited regions of social life promise to fill the available space. Or, to put it slightly differently, they promise to redouble (or "retreble") the available space to increase its commercial (and law enforcement) value. Sites of leisure and domesticity can become, simultaneously, sites of production and consumption.

As suggested in the previous section, the private, market-driven character of the digital enclosure imposes some significant limits on the promise of the Internet to, as the conservative blogger Andrew Sullivan put it (in a free-market parody of Marx), allow those with Internet access to "seize the means of production."[37] Consider, for example, the case of the Chinese political blogger Zhao Jing, who, when the government used its control over Internet routers to block his Web site, switched to the Microsoft Corporation's blogging tool, MSN Spaces. After he criticized the firing of an editor from one of China's more independent newspapers and called for a boycott of the paper, his blog was shut down by Microsoft at the Chinese government's behest. One press account noted, "What was most remarkable about this was that Microsoft's blogging service has no servers located in China; the company effectively allowed China's censors to reach across the ocean and erase data stored on American territory."[38]

Interestingly, Zhao Jing identified in published news accounts the nature of the line that he'd crossed: "If you talk every day online and criticise the government, they don't care. . . . Because it's just talk. But if you organise— even if it's just three or four people—that's what they crack down on. It's not speech; it's organising."[39] Microsoft, with an eye to the lucrative potential of the Chinese market, helped take the activism out of interactivity, with the explanation that in order to do business in China, it had to follow the laws that "require companies to make the internet safe for local users."[40] Sugges- tively, the company has also reportedly taken the democracy out of its blog service: "In China, Microsoft does not allow the word 'democracy' to be used in a subject heading for its MSN Spaces blog service." The company is not alone in making concessions with an eye to the bottom line: "Google . . . restricted search results for the Tiananmen Square massacre; and Yahoo handed over private e-mail information that reportedly led to the conviction of two internet dissidents."[41] U.S. politicians have been critical of the actions of these companies abroad, even while some of them defended the Bush ad- ministration's Justice Department's request for information about millions of searches made on popular search engines including Google, AOL, MSN, and Yahoo. It's not hard to imagine why large Internet companies with an eye to government regulators might be all too willing to comply (although Google did put up some resistance).

The tendency to celebrate the revolutionary, empowering potential of in- teractivity all too often fails to consider the actual conditions under which this potential is being developed: namely, the dependence of new forms of interactivity on the economic priorities of large corporations dependent on the goodwill of government bureaucracies for access to lucrative markets. The result is that the digital enclosure of information—detailed data about millions of users, including their online purchasing habits, their Web brows- ing habits, their blogging, and even their e-mail—concentrates an unprec- edented amount of control over digital information in the hands of a few. As information companies like Google continue to push a business model based on online content storage, users' information—their e-mail, their pho- tos, lists of favorites, perhaps eventually their music, their videos, their word processing documents, and even their spreadsheet data—will increasingly migrate into the control of those who own and operate privatized, commer- cialized digital enclosures. This transfer of control would be decidedly disempowering insofar as it would amount to a surrender of control over the decision of whether to reveal, for example, the contents of one's personal correspondence to a collection of media giants and their marketing adjuncts. Free marketers will argue that media companies are held accountable via the logic of the market—but this assumes a level of disclosure that is not forthcoming, and it reduces the process of control to a form of market signaling—as opposed to collective deliberation.

A privatized enclosure is not a democratic one, and the political potential of the interactions that take place within it are shaped by that fact. As described in Chapter 4, the U.S. Congress is pushing in the direction of changing the "common carrier" character of the Internet by allowing the companies that own the pipes that carry online information to charge differential rates to content providers. The likely effect will be to further consolidate centralized control over information by making it easier for major media companies to drive alternative sources of information and content off the Internet by jacking up the price of "shipping" information. In other words, a move is afoot to make the Internet look like all the other major media industries in the United States: another media oligopoly controlled by the usual suspects. In this brave new information world, it's more than likely that the swarm of influential political blogs providing commentary, insight, and useful links about the day's news on a shoestring budget will be picked off and silenced, not because no one wants to read them, but because they don't have a large enough budget to compete for bandwidth with the Time-Warners and News Corporations of the world.

If the prospects for a privatized digital enclosure look like a retrenchment of the media oligopolies—"the revolution of the fixed wheel"—what might an alternative, noncommercial enclosure look like?[42] New media guru Douglas Rushkoff describes one possible model, devised by a graduate student who built a portable computer system called WiFiBedouin that doubles as its own wireless network node: "The advantage afforded by Wi-Fi technology is not to provide access to the same old Web, but to create an independent web of activity where location, proximity and occupancy are primary factors informing the connected experience."[43] Several computers running this software could create what Rushkoff calls ad hoc, Internet-independent networks. If one of them is able to connect to the Internet via a municipal Wi-Fi connection, then all the computers in the "mesh" would be connected. Given enough computers, enough collaboration, and sufficient wireless broadcasting and receiving power, such mesh networks could create an alternative to commercially controlled networks. They could also facilitate noncommercial forms of information sharing. Rushkoff describes, for example, an ad hoc network technology that allows users to stream music to one another from their computers—to act, in short, as point-to-point network radios.

Similar forms of ad hoc networking are envisioned by MIT Media Labs founder Nicholas Negroponte, who is working on the prototype of a $100 laptop computer for circulation in the developing world as an educational and information networking tool. To keep the cost down and the technology as flexible as possible, the machines would be equipped with open-source software and wireless data connections to allow the computers to communicate with one another.[44] Powered by hand crank, such computers could allow ad hoc networks to spread over completely unwired territories and could amplify the reach of just one or two municipal Internet connections to hundreds of users.

These ad hoc or mesh networks come with a built-in sense of collaboration. Perhaps this might temper mutual monitoring practices (which mimic commercial forms of monitoring) with a sense of interdependence. In competition with Negroponte, Bill Gates is proposing, predictably, a cell phone–based system of inexpensive networked computing—one that would presumably rely on an external, privately operated digital enclosure to mediate the connections between individual users. In Negroponte's model, by contrast, the users are the network. The latter model seems to fit more neatly the model of an open, public digital enclosure, one less subject to unaccountable forms of centralized command and control. Negroponte's choice of open-source software is also telling. Open-source applications don't rely on advertiser or commercial support. Perhaps free marketeers will argue that the use of such systems will inhibit the development of software, but open-source development was one of the earliest models of software development and, as Negroponte puts it, if the code is available to everyone equipped with his computers, he'll have "100 million programmers I can rely on."[45]

Open-source code development is democratic in the sense outlined in the previous section: it allows users not just to work within a set of given parameters, but to collectively change the parameters themselves. The digital enclosures envisioned by Rushkoff and Negroponte are not extensions of commercially managed virtual spaces into other realms of life, but the outward expansion of collectively managed virtual space in which it is possible for databases to be distributed and subjected to collectively developed controls, rather than being left to the profit-driven whims of corporate media owners and managers.

If such public-enclosure models of technology development were to prevail (a prospect that seems unlikely at best), they could conceivably provide the developing world with a huge advantage when it comes to collaborative uses of the Internet and to computer literacy. They may also provide a sense of participation and interactivity significantly different from that which is emerging in the commercial digital enclosures of the developing world. Finally, if they do prevail, they would represent a real, perhaps even a truly revolutionary, break from the history of the development of electronic mass media. Betting on an open-source, open-network future may not be a particularly sure thing, but at the very least such models provide an ideal—one that reminds us that the democratic promise of interactivity, even as a ruse of the digital enclosure, promises the possibility of something beyond the communicative practices that have until now prevailed. This is a possibility to be preserved rather than rejected in a fit of postmodern nominalism that reduces the potential of new media technologies to the reality of their current deployment.

The political theorist Carole Pateman has argued that the cultivation of a sense of participation in nongovernmental spheres of life is crucial preparation for participation in democratic forms of self-governance.[46] That is to say, involvement in a participatory workforce better prepares its employees for participation in political self-governance. But this formulation doesn't quite go far enough. Those of us within the reach of the conveniences of the digital enclosure are become habituated to multiplying possibilities for participation—in designing our shoes, customizing our news, and voting on our TV shows. This book has argued that one of the unifying themes of this seeming multiplicity of practices is that they serve as participatory forms of labor. Such work is productive not least because it is a form of active participation in the marketing process: a form of "self-expression" that preserves and consolidates relations of power and property. Therefore, it is no longer enough to call for the cultivation of participation as an antidote to the undemocratic character of mass consumer culture. Rather, we have to imagine and cultivate heretofore untested forms of meaningful participation (and the conditions that might make them actual) against the background of the versions of participation on offer. We need to mine the contradictions embedded in a commercial information culture that exploits the promise of democracy as a means of furthering strategies of consumer and citizen management. Rather than dismissing the potential of interactivity out of hand, we need to turn this promise back against the forms of interactivity it has helped promote. Without undertaking a rethinking of the question of participation that I have attempted under the sign of "interactivity," we may well end up with more participatory forms of media production, but we run the danger of merely expanding and customizing what came before rather than transforming it. Distributed news gathering could provide us with endless celebrity voyeur shows and home-brewed reality TV formats, podcasts with a million yammering Rush Limbaughs. The interactively enhanced media-entertainment complex will provide us with the possibility of retreat: each into our customized, virtual, vanilla skies composed of mass-customized experiences.

The real challenge, in the end, is overcoming the numbness of eviscerated experience and its attendant ideology of quiescent postmodern savviness. It is to counter the assumption that concepts like interactivity, freedom, and democracy do not overflow the experiences to which they refer with an insistence on making reality live up to the promise of democracy mobilized by the promoters of interactivity. Faced with the specter of a benumbed populace, Susan Buck-Morss has argued that "in this situation of 'crisis in perception,' it is no longer a question of educating the crude ear to hear music, but of giving it back hearing. It is no longer a question of training the eye to see beauty, but of restoring 'perceptibility.'"[47] In the interactive era, it is also no longer a question of submitting to prefabricated forms of participation, but of restoring the democratic possibilities of participation.

NOTES

CHAPTER 1. INTRODUCTION

1. "Peek-a-boo Google Sees You," CNNmoney.com, 7 April 2006, at http://money.cnn.com/2006/04/06/technology/googsf_reut/index.htm?section=money_top-stories (accessed 28 October 2006).

2. My use of this term is influenced by James Boyle's article on the fate of intellectual property in the digital era. However, the analysis in this book combines the metaphorical and physical aspects of the enclosure movement. Whereas Boyle emphasizes the ways in which information that was actually or potentially in the public domain becomes private property, I am interested in both the privatization of personal and public information and the apparatuses used to capture this information—apparatuses that comprise a digital enclosure wherein behaviors are monitored and recorded. For more on Boyle's discussion of the digital enclosure, see James Boyle, "The Second Enclosure Movement and the Construction of the Public Domain," *Law and Contemporary Problems* 66 (winter–spring 2003): 33–74.

3. Vincent Mosco develops the notion of the "cybernetic commodity" in *The Pay-Per Society: Computers and Communication in the Information Age* (Toronto: Ablex, 1989).

4. Edward J. Dowan and Sally J. McMillan, "Defining Interactivity: A Qualitative Identification of Key Dimensions," *New Media and Society* 2, no. 2 (2000): 165.

5. Spiro Kiousis, "Interactivity: A Concept Explication," *New Media and Society* 4, no. 3 (2002): 371.

6. Scott McNeally, "On the Record: Scott McNeally," *San Francisco Chronicle,* 14 September 2003, sec. I1.

7. Paul Magnusson, "They're Watching You," *Business Week,* 24 January 2005, 22.

8. Frederic Jameson, "Reification and Utopia in Mass Culture," in *Signatures of the Visible* (New York: Routledge, 1992), 9–34.

9. Kathy Prentice, "TiVo's World," Media Life Magazine, at http://archives.medialifemagazine.com/news2000/jul00/jul3/news70705.html (accessed 1 March 2005).

10. Michael Lewis, "Boombox," *New York Times Magazine,* 13 August 2000, 36.

11. Ibid.

12. Harry Flood, "Linux, TiVo, Napster . . . Information Wants to be Free, You Got a Problem with That?" *Adbusters* 34 (March–April 2002): 17.

13. See, for example, Sut Jhally and Bill Livan, "Watching as Working: The Valorization of Audience Consciousness," *Journal of Communication* 36, no. 3 (1986): 124–43.

14. Mosco, *Pay-Per Society.*

15. The story about marketing to pregnant mothers comes from Erik Larson's *The Naked Consumer: How Our Private Lives Become Public Commodities* (New York: Henry Holt, 1992).
16. Slavoj Žižek, *The Ticklish Subject* (London: Verso, 1999).
17. Celia Pearce, *The Interactive Book* (New York: Penguin, 1997), 180.
18. Ibid., 183.
19. Howard Rheingold, *Virtual Community: Homesteading the Electronic Frontier* (Reading, Mass.: Addison-Wesley, 1993), 14.
20. Darin Barney, *Prometheus Wired: The Hope for Democracy in the Age of Network Technology* (Chicago: University of Chicago Press, 2000), 104.
21. Pearce, *Interactive Book,* 185.
22. Ibid., 244.
23. James Carey, "Historical Pragmatism and the Internet," *New Media and Society,* 17, no. 4 (2005): 444.
24. As quoted in Vincent Mosco, *The Digital Sublime: Myth, Power, and Cyberspace* (Cambridge, Mass.: MIT Press, 2004), 117.
25. Nicholas Negroponte, *Being Digital* (New York: Knopf, 1995), 229.
26. Norbert Wiener, *Cybernetics; or, Control and Communication in the Animal and the Machine* (New York: MIT Press, 1961), 19.
27. Ibid., 39.
28. Kiousis, "Interactivity," 59.
29. Wiener, *Cybernetics,* 19.
30. Ibid., 185.
31. Norbert Wiener, *The Human Use of Human Beings: Cybernetics and Society* (Boston, Mass.: Houghton Mifflin, 1954), 185.

CHAPTER 2. THREE DIMENSIONS OF iCULTURE
1. "Nike Retailing Innovation," Retail Systems, at http://www.retailsystems.com/ index.cfm?PageName=PublicationsTONHomeNew&CartoonArticleID=4394 (accessed 11 July 2005).
2. "Nike iD," NikeID.com, at http://nikeid.nike.com/nikeid/index.jhtml?_requestid =2357796#home(accessed 14 July 2005).
3. Ibid.
4. Josh Marshall, "Talking Points Memo," Talking Points Memo, at http://www .talkingpointsmemo.com/archives/week_2005_07_10.php (accessed 14 July 2005).
5. Ann M. Mack, "Power to the People," *Critical Mass,* 11 November 2000, at http:// www.criticalmass.com /about/news/view.do?article=cm_110100&year=2000 (accessed 18 July 2005).
6. "My Logo: Are We the New Brand Bullies? Hijacking the Brand," *Toronto Star,* 10 July 2005, sec. D4.
7. Reuters, "Nike Designs Get Personal," *Los Angeles Times,* 30 May 2005, sec. C5.
8. "My Logo."

9. Mack, "Power to the People."

10. Ibid.

11. Jonah Peretti, "The Life of an Internet Meme," at http://www.shey.net/niked.html (accessed 20 July 2005).

12. C. K. Prahald and Venkat Ramaswamy, *The Future of Competition: Co-Creating Unique Value with Customers* (Cambridge: Harvard Business School Press, 2004).

13. Suzanne D'Amato, "Custom Sties Let Users Cobble Their Own Shoes," *Washington Post*, 17 July 2005, sec. F1.

14. Walid Mougayar, *Opening Digital Markets: Battle Plans and Business Strategies for Internet Commerce* (New York: McGraw-Hill, 1998).

15. D'Amato, "Custom Sties."

16. Steve Inskeep, "Second Life: Real Money in a Virtual World," National Public Radio, Morning Edition, 6 November 2006, at http://www.npr.org/templates/story/story.php?storyId=6431819.

17. As quoted in ibid.

18. Richard A. Lanham, *The Electronic Word: Democracy, Technology, and the Arts* (Chicago: University of Chicago Press, 1993), 38.

19. Ibid., 51.

20. "The World's First Collaborative Sentence," Whitney Museum of Art, at http://www.whitney.org/artport/collection/index.shtml (accessed 30 July 2005).

21. PostSecret, at http://postsecret.blogspot.com (accessed 4 August 2005).

22. Danny Bradbury, "Remixing the Blogosphere," *The Guardian*, 9 June 2005, http://technology.guardian.co.uk/online/story/0,,1501809,00.html (accessed 15 August 2006).

23. "David Bowie Mash-up Contest," Davidbowie.com, at http://www.davidbowie.com/neverFollow (accessed 4 April 2004).

24. "Forget-Me-Not Panties: Contagious Media," Forgetmenotpanties, at http://forgetmenotpanties.contagiousmedia.org/testimonial.html (accessed 20 September 2004).

25. Jeffrey Rosen, *The Unwanted Gaze: The Destruction of Privacy in America* (New York: Random House, 2000), 200.

26. Zizi Papacharissi, "The Presentation of Self in Virtual Life: Characteristics of Personal Home Pages," *Journalism and Mass Communication Quarterly* 79, no. 3 (2002): 658.

27. Katha Pollitt, "Personal History: Webstalker," *New Yorker*, 19 January 2004, 39.

28. Sherry Turkle, *Life on the Screen: Identity in the Age of the Internet* (New York: Simon & Schuster, 1997), 18.

29. Ibid., 14.

30. "Check My Mate," Checkmymate.com, at http://www.checkmymate.com (accessed 28 September 2005).

31. Ibid.

32. "Customer Comments," NetDetective.com, at http://www.affiliatesuccess.net/cgi-bin/clickthru.cgi?pidb=ND (accessed 3 June 2006).

33. Thomas Streeter, "'That Deep Romantic Chasm': Libertarianism, Neoliberalism and the Computer Culture," in *Communication, Citizenship and Social Policy: Rethinking the Limits of the Welfare State,* ed. Andrew Calabrese and Jean-Claude Burgelman (Boulder, Colo.: Rowman and Littlefield, 1999); Paulina Barsook, *Cyberselfish: A Critical Romp through the Terribly Libertarian Culture of High Tech* (New York: Public Affairs, 2000). For an insightful and sophisticated historical account of the tensions that come to characterize the notion of online community, see Fred Turner, *From Cyberculture to Counterculture: Stewart Brand, the Whole Earth Network, and the Rise of Digital Utopianism* (Chicago: University of Chicago Press, 2006).

34. "Big Mother (or Father) Is Watching," *The Age,* 9 September 2005, at http://www.theage.com.au/news/technology/big-mother-or-father-is-watching/2005/09/08/1125772632570.html (accessed 20 September 2006).

35. Neil Swidey, "A Nation of Voyeurs," *Boston Globe,* 2 February 2003, sec. B1.

36. Jennifer Egan, "Love in the Time of No Time," *New York Times Magazine,* 23 November 2003, 66–70.

37. "Welcome to the U.S. HomeGuard: Learn More," USHomeGuard, at http://www.ushomeguard.org (accessed 12 July 2005).

38. Tom Feran, "Here's Your Chance to Target Terror," *Plain Dealer* (Cleveland), 8 July 2003, sec. E1.

39. Matthew Brzezinski, "Homeland-Security Neighborhood Watch," *New York Times,* 14 December 2003, sec. 7, 5.

40. "Former ASIO Officer Claims Islamic Extremists Are Living in Australia," Australian Broadcasting Corporation, ABC News Radio: Lateline, at http://www.abc.net.au/lateline/content/2005/s1428699.htm (accessed 3 August 2005).

41. Louis Althusser, "Ideology and Ideological State Apparatuses," in *Lenin and Philosophy and Other Essays* (New York: Monthly Review Press, 1971).

42. Cass Sunstein, *Republic.com* (Princeton, N.J.: Princeton University Press, 2002), 62.

43. "My Logo."

44. Carole Pateman, *Participation and Democratic Theory* (Cambridge: Cambridge University Press, 1970), 105.

45. Henry Jenkins, "Democracy, Big Brother Style," *Confessions of an Aca/Fan: The Official Weblog of Henry Jenkins,* 4 July 2006, at http://www.henryjenkins.org/.

46. Joe Trippi, *The Revolution Will Not be Televised* (New York: Regan Books, 2004).

47. Douglas Kellner, "Globalization from Below? Toward a Radical Democratic Technopolitics." *Angelaki: Journal of the Theoretical Humanities* 4, no. 2 (1999): 101–14.

48. Blog book.

49. Paul Krugman, "The New Gilded Age," *New York Times,* 20 October 2002, 34.

CHAPTER 3. iMANAGEMENT, THE EARLY YEARS

1. Percival White, *Scientific Marketing Management: Its Principles and Methods* (New York: Harper and Brothers, 1927), 39.

2. Ibid.

3. Frank Webster and Kevin Robins, *Information Technology: A Luddite Analysis* (Norwood, N.J.: Ablex, 1986), 312.

4. Leon Bramson, *The Political Context of Sociology* (Princeton, N.J.: Princeton University Press, 1961), 51.

5. Saul Hansell, "Marketers Trace Paths Users Leave on the Internet," *New York Times,* 15 August 2006.

6. Samuel Haber, *Efficiency and Uplift: Scientific Management in the Progressive Era, 1890–1920* (Chicago: University of Chicago Press, 1964), 164.

7. Ibid, x.

8. See, for example, Douglas Kellner, "Globalization from Below? Toward a Radical Democratic Technopolitics," *Angelaki: Journal of the Theoretical Humanities* 4, no. 2 (1999): 101–14; John Armitage, "Special Issue on Machinic Modulations: New Cultural Theory and Technopolitics," *Angelaki: Journal of the Theoretical Humanities,* 4, no. 2 (1999); and Richard Kahn and Douglas Kellner, "New Media and Internet Activism: From the 'Battle of Seattle' to Blogging," *New Media and Society* 6, no. 1 (2004): 87–95.

9. Bill Gates, *The Road Ahead,* 2nd ed. (New York: Penguin, 1996).

10. Robert Goldman, "'We Make Weekends': Leisure and the Commodity Form," *Social Text* 8 (winter 1984): 84.

11. Thomas L. Haskell, *The Emergence of Professional Social Science: The American Social Science Association and the Nineteenth-Century Crisis of Authority* (Baltimore, Md.: Johns Hopkins University Press, 2000), 33.

12. Ibid., 40.

13. James Carey, "Time Space and the Telegraph," in *Communication in History: Technology, Culture, Society,* ed. David Crowley and Paul Heyer (New York: Longman, 1999), 135–40.

14. Haskell, *Emergence,* 40.

15. Ibid., 43.

16. John Durham Peters, *Courting the Abyss: Free Speech and the Liberal Tradition* (Chicago: University of Chicago Press, 2005), 210.

17. Haskell, *Emergence,* 43.

18. Ian Hacking, *The Taming of Chance* (New York: Cambridge University Press, 1992), 5.

19. Haskell, *Emergence,* 5.

20. Peters, *Courting the Abyss,* 210.

21. Ibid.

22. James Beniger, *The Control Revolution: Technological and Economic Origins of the Information Society* (Cambridge, Mass.: Harvard University Press, 1986), 38.

23. Ibid., 427.
24. Ibid.
25. James Beniger, "The Control Revolution," in *Communication in History: Technology, Culture, Society,* ed. David Crowley and Paul Heyer (New York: Longman, 1999), 305.
26. Ibid., 308.
27. Kevin Robins and Frank Webster, *Times of the Technoculture: From the Information Society to the Virtual Life* (London: Routledge, 1999), 131 ff.
28. Frederick Taylor, *The Principles of Scientific Management* (New York: Harper & Row, 1967), 43.
29. Ibid., 62.
30. Ibid., 44.
31. Clifford Pratten, "The Manufacture of Pins," *Journal of Economic Literature* 18 (March 1980): 93–96.
32. Anthony Giddens, *A Contemporary Critique of Historical Materialism* (Berkeley: University of California Press, 1981).
33. Christian Parenti, *Soft Cage: Surveillance in America* (New York: Basic Books, 2003), 14.
34. Ibid.
35. Steve Mann, Jason Nolan, and Barry Wellman, "Sousveillance: Inventing and Using Wearable Computing Devices for Data Collection in Surveillance Environments," *Surveillance and Society* 1, no. 3 (2003): 331–55, at http://citeseer.ist.psu.edu/mann03sousveillance.html.
36. Robert Kanigel, *The One Best Way: Frederick Winslow Taylor and the Enigma of Efficiency* (New York: Viking, 1997), 233.
37. On the early uses of social science for state charities, see Haskell, *Emergence.*
38. Beniger, *Control Revolution,* 15.
39. Max Weber, *From Max Weber: Essays in Sociology* (New York: Oxford University Press, 1946), 216.
40. Erik Larson, *The Naked Consumer: How Our Private Lives Become Public Commodities* (New York: Henry Holt, 1992), 18.
41. Ibid., 18.
42. As quoted in Kanigel, *One Best Way,* 511.
43. Ibid., 510.
44. Ida Tarbell, "Taylor and His System," *Saturday Review of Literature,* 25 October 1924, 225.
45. Frank Copley, *Frederick W. Taylor: Father of Scientific Management,* vol. 2 (New York: Harper and Brothers, 1923), 53.
46. Congressional testimony.
47. Congressional testimony, 180.
48. Darin Barney, *Prometheus Wired: The Hope for Democracy in the Age of Network Technology* (Chicago: University of Chicago Press, 2000), 12.

49. Rupert Cuff, "Edwin F. Gay, Arch W. Shaw, and the Uses of History in Early Graduate Business Education," *Journal of Management History* 2, no. 3 (1996): 15.

50. As quoted in ibid., 15.

51. As quoted in ibid., 19.

52. Ibid.; Melvin Copeland, "Arch W. Shaw," *Journal of Marketing* 22, no. 3 (1958): 313–15.

53. Alfred Chandler, *The Visible Hand: The Managerial Revolution in American Business* (Cambridge, Mass.: Harvard University Press, 1977), 467.

54. Roland Marchand, *Advertising the American Dream: Making Way for Modernity, 1920–1940* (Berkeley: University of California Press, 1985), 2.

55. Walter Dill Scott, as quoted in Stuart Ewen, *Captains of Consciousness: Advertising and the Social Roots of the Consumer Culture* (New York: McGraw-Hill, 1976), 31.

56. Ibid., 33.

57. William Akin, as quoted in Frank Webster and Kevin Robins, "'I'll be Watching You: Comment on Sewell and Wilkinson," *Sociology* 27, no. 2 (1993): 247.

58. Ibid.

59. Karl Marx, *Grundrisse* (London: Penguin, 1993), 91.

60. Stuart Ewen, *PR! A Social History of Spin* (New York: Basic Books, 1996), 68.

61. Robert Bartels, *Marketing Theory and Metatheory* (Homewood, Ill.: Richard D. Irwin, 1970), 34.

62. Ewen, *PR!*, 132.

63. Ibid., 181.

64. Ibid., 71.

65. Historian David Potter, as quoted in Kevin Robins and Frank Webster, *Times of the Technoculture: From the Information Society to the Virtual Life* (London: Routledge, 1999), 100.

66. Robert Goldman, "'We Make Weekends': Leisure and the Commodity Form," *Social Text* 8 (winter 1984): 95.

67. Michael Schudson, *Advertising, the Uneasy Persuasion: Its Dubious Impact on American Society* (New York: Basic Books, 1984), 238.

68. Ewen, *Captains of Consciousness*, 33.

69. Ibid., 33.

70. Goldman, "We Make Weekends," 90.

71. Ewen, *PR!*, p. 64.

72. Robert McChesney, *The Problem of the Media: U.S. Communication Politics in the 21st Century* (New York: Monthly Review Press, 2004), 32.

73. James Carey, "The Press, Public Opinion, and Public Discourse," in *Public Opinion and the Communication of Consent*, ed. Theodore L. Glasser and Charles T. Salmon (New York: Guilford, 1995), 373–402.

74. Beniger, *Control Revolution*, 378.

75. Ibid., 383.
76. Ibid., 383.
77. Oscar Gandy, "Tracking the Audience: Personal Information and Privacy in Downing," in *Questioning the Media: A Critical Introduction,* ed. John D. H. Downing, Ali Mohammadi, and Annabelle Sreberny (London: Sage, 1990), 207–20. See also Sut Jhally and Bill Livan, "Watching as Working: The Valorization of Audience Consciousness," *Journal of Communication* 36, no. 3 (1986): 124–43.
78. Beniger, *Control Revolution,* 383.
79. Ibid., 383.
80. Malcolm Beville Jr., *Audience Ratings: Radio, Television, Cable,* 3rd ed. (Hillsdale, N.J.: Lawrence Erlbaum Associates, 1988), 3.
81. Ibid., 5.
82. Ibid., 3.
83. Ibid., 5.
84. Dorothy Crossley, *The Advertiser Looks at Radio* (manuscript held in author's personal archive).
85. Eileen Meehan, "Why We Don't Count: The Commodity Audience," in *Logics of Television: Essays in Cultural Criticism,* ed. Patricia Mellencamp (Bloomington: Indiana University Press, 1990), 123.
86. Ibid.
87. Larson, *Naked Consumer,* 109.
88. Ibid., 108.
89. Ibid., 109.
90. Ibid., 109–10.
91. Ibid.
92. Stan Seagren, Vice President for Strategic Research, A. C. Nielsen, personal interview with author, 5 March 2005.
93. Jon Gertner, "The Very, Very Personal Is Political," *New York Times Magazine,* 15 February 2004.
94. Seagren interview.

CHAPTER 4. iCOMMERCE: INTERACTIVITY GOES MOBILE

1. "Greatest Engineering Achievements of the 20th Century: 2. Automobile," Great Achievements, at http://www.greatachievements.org/greatachievements/ga_2_1.html (accessed 15 July 2005).
2. Henri Lefebvre, *The Production of Space* (Oxford: Blackwell, 1991).
3. Fiona Allon, "An Ontology of Everyday Control: Living and Working in the 'Smart House,'" *Southern Review* 34, no. 3 (2001): 21.
4. Anthony Giddens, *A Contemporary Critique of Historical Materialism* (Berkeley: University of California Press, 1981), 137.
5. Matthew Hart, "Calling for a Drink Fattens Telstra's Waistline," *Courier Mail* (Queensland, Australia), 23 December 2002, 21.

6. Jennifer Dudley, "In Future, Don't Leave Home without Your Mobile Phone," *Courier Mail* (Queensland, Australia), 6 November 2004, 17.

7. Jennifer Dudley, "Dial Your Own Future," *Courier Mail* (Queensland, Australia), 18 June 2005, 27.

8. Alison MacGregor, "Montreal Firm Hopes to Cash in on Mobile Phone Transactions," *The Gazette* (Montreal), 6 June 2005, sec. B1.

9. Dudley, "Dial Your Own Future," 27.

10. "About," Vindigo, at http://www.vindigo.com (accessed 2 August 2003).

11. Nikolai Dobberstein, John Livingston, and Prapavadee Sophonpanich, "On the Wireless Web Frontier, Asia is the Pioneer," *Business Times* (Singapore), 8 May 2000, 13.

12. Joan Yap, "Towards a User-Centric Model," *Business Times* (Singapore), 25 April 2001, 28.

13. Jorge Borges, "Funes the Memorious," in *Labyrinths: Selected Stories and Other Writings* (New York: New Directions, 1964).

14. Bill Gates, *The Road Ahead,* 2nd ed. (New York: Penguin, 1996).

15. David S. Bennahum, "Forget the World Wide Web on Your Cell Phone. The Key to the Always-On, Everywhere Wireless Internet Comes Down to Three Things: Location, Location, Location," *Wired* 9, no. 11 (November 2001): 159–60.

16. Michael Dresser, "Cell Phone Data Tracing Traffic in Md.; System 'Watches' Vehicles, Raises Fears about Privacy," *Baltimore Sun,* 18 November 2005, sec. 1A.

17. Ibid.

18. Matt Richtel, "Enlisting Cellphone Signals to Fight Road Gridlock," *New York Times,* 11 November 2005, sec. C1.

19. Karen Dearne, "Mobiles to Keep Tabs on Health," *The Australian,* 1 November 2005, 42.

20. Fiona Harvey, "M-Commerce: Paying for Goods with a Mobile Phone Was to be the Next Big Thing. But Disagreement on Standards Mean a Mass Market is Years Away in Europe and the U.S.," *Financial Times* (London), 23 October 2002, 13.

21. Gwen Ackerman, "On the Edge of a Cellular Shopping Revolution," *Jerusalem Post,* 19 November 2000, 9.

22. Hannah Arendt, *The Human Condition* (Chicago: University of Chicago Press, 1958).

23. Michel De Certeau, "Walking in the City," in *The Cultural Studies Reader,* ed. Simon During (London: Routledge, 1993), 128.

24. Ibid.

25. Ibid., 127.

26. Paula Bond, "ID Tags Make Products Talk," *Atlanta Journal Constitution,* 29 July 2003, sec. 1A.

27. "Research Proactive Computing," Intel, at http://www.intel.com/research/exploratory/ (accessed 2 August 2005).

28. Robert O'Harrow Jr., *No Place to Hide* (New York: Free Press, 2005), 105.

29. Harry Bruinius, "Here Come the Ads, Over Your Cellphone," *Christian Science Monitor,* 14 May 2002, sec. USA3.

30. Toby Lester, "The Reinvention of Privacy," *Atlantic Monthly* 287, no. 3 (March 2001): 28.

31. Ibid.

32. Joan O'C. Hamilton, "The New Workplace: Walls Are Falling as the 'Office of the Future' Finally Takes Shape," *Business Week* (29 April 1996), 106, at http://www. businessweek. com/1996/18/b34731.htm (accessed 18 July 2002).

33. Dearne, "Mobiles to Keep Tabs on Health," 42.

34. Kevin Robins and Frank Webster, *Times of the Technoculture: From the Information Society to the Virtual Life* (London: Routledge, 1999), 117.

35. Kevin Robins and Frank Webster, "Cybernetic Capitalism: Information, Technology, and Everyday Life," in *The Political Economy of Information,* ed. Vincent Mosco and Janet Wasko (Madison: University of Wisconsin Press, 1998), 52.

36. Mark Poster, *The Mode of Information* (Chicago: University of Chicago Press, 1990).

37. Lori Valigra, "Fabricating the Future," *Christian Science Monitor,* 29 August 2002, 11.

38. Mark Weiser, "Open House: *In Review,* the Web Magazine of the Interactive Telecommunications Program of New York University," *ITP Review 2.0,* March 1996, at http://www.itp.tsoa.nyu.edu/~review, 3.

39. Alex Pentland, "Perceptual Intelligence," *Communications of the ACM* 43, no. 3 (March 2000): 35.

40. "The MIThril Vision," at http://www.media.mit.edu/wearables/mithril/vision. html (accessed 20 May 2004).

41. Genevieve Bell, Tim Brooke, and Elizabeth Churchill, "Intimate (Ubiquitous) Computing," Ubicomp 2003 Adjunct Conference Proceedings, at http://ubicomp.org/ubicomp2004/ (accessed 12 March 2004).

42. Keith Bresnahan, "Housing Complexes: Neurasthenic Subjects and the Bourgeois Interior," *Space and Culture* 6, no. 2 (2003): 173.

43. Scott Lafee, "Geek Chic," *New Scientist,* 24 February 2001, 30.

44. Clive Thompson, "There Is a Sucker Born in Every Medial Prefrontal Cortex," *New York Times,* 26 October 2003, 54.

45. Lafee, "Geek Chic."

46. Ibid.

47. Ibid.

48. Nichoals Negroponte, *Being Digital* (New York: Knopf, 1995).

49. Nathan Cochrane, "Ulterior Motives Behind ID Tags Exposed," *The Age* (Melbourne), 15 July 2002, 1.

50. Pentland, "Perceptual Intelligence."

51. Gates, *Road Ahead.*

52. Libby Copeland "For DotComGuy, the End of the Online Line," *Washington Post,* 3 January 2001, sec. C2, telephone interview with DotComGuy, aka Mitch Maddox, 12 June 2000.

53. Theodor W. Adorno, *Kierkegaard: Construction of the Aesthetic,* trans. Robert Hullot-Kentor (Minneapolis: University of Minnesota Press, 1989), 42.

54. Ibid., 41.

55. Jamie Owen Daniel, "Achieving Subjectlessness: Reassessing the Politics of Adorno's Subject of Modernity," *Cultural Logic* 3, no. 1 (2001), at http://eserver.org/clogic/3-1&2/daniel.html (accessed 4 March 2004).

56. Walter Benjamin, *The Arcades Project,* trans. Howard Eiland and Kevin McLaughlin (Cambridge, Mass.: Belknap Press, 1999), 220.

57. Ibid., 20.

58. Ibid., 174.

59. Ibid., 20.

60. Graeme Gilloch, *Myth and Metropolis* (Cambridge: Polity Press, 1997), 124.

61. Susan Buck-Morss, *The Dialectics of Seeing: Walter Benjamin and "The Arcades Project"* (Cambridge, Mass.: MIT Press, 1995), 83.

62. Gilloch, *Myth and Metropolis,* 126.

63. Gates, *Road Ahead.*

64. Benjamin, *Arcades Project,* 56.

65. Lester, "Reinvention of Privacy," 29.

66. Associated Press, "Glasses that Focus on the Mind's Eye," *Newsday* (New York), 30 November 2003, sec. A40.

67. Bond, "ID Tags."

68. Mary Starrett, "I'd Rather Go Naked," NewsWithViews.com, 13 March 2003, at http://www. newswithviews.com/Mary/starrett4.htm (accessed 20 October 2003).

69. Crayton Harrison, "Gaining Frequency: Commitment from Wal-Mart May Boost Tracking Technology," *Dallas Morning News,* 15 July 2002, sec. D1.

70. Gregg Easterbrook, "All This Progress Is Killing Us Bite by Bite," *New York Times,* 11 March 2004, sec. 4, 5.

71. David Morley, *Home Territories: Media, Mobility, and Identity* (London: Routledge, 2000), 200.

72. Gary Marx, *Undercover: Police Surveillance in America* (Berkeley: University of California Press, 1988); Gary Marx, "Murky Conceptual Waters: The Public and the Private," *Ethics and Information Technology* 3, no. 3 (2001): 157–69.

73. Teresa Patents Riordan, "A Computer System with an Eye (and Ear) for Crime, or at least Re-enactments Thereof," *New York Times,* 13 October 1997, sec. D2.

74. Jeff Chester, "The End of the Internet?," *The Nation,* at http://www.thenation.com/doc/20060213/chester (accessed 3 February 2006).

75. Ibid.

76. Oscar Gandy, "Dividing Practices: Segmentation and Targeting in the Emerging Public Sphere," in *Mediated Politics: Communication in the Future of Democracy*, ed. W. Lance Bennett and Robert M. Entman (New York: Cambridge University Press, 2001), 141–59.

77. Oscar Gandy, "Data Mining, Discrimination, and the Decline of The Public Sphere," Dixons Public Lecture, London School of Economics and Political Science, 7 November 2002, 8.

78. "Terms of Service," Gmail, at http://www.google.com/mail/help/terms_of_use .htm (accessed 12 February 2006).

79. Daniel Wood, "Radio ID Tags Proliferate, Stirring Privacy Debate," *Christian Science Monitor*, 15 December 2004, 3.

80. "Research Proactive Computing."

81. Pamela Licalzi O'Connell, "Korea's High Tech Utopia, Where Everything Is Observed," *New York Times*, 5 October 2005, sec. A1.

CHAPTER 5. iMEDIA: THE CASE OF INTERACTIVE TV

1. Andrew Sullivan, "The Blogging Revolution: Weblogs Are to Words What Napster Was to Music," *Wired* 10, no. 5 (May 2002), at http://www.wired.com/wired/ archive/10.05/mustread.html?pg=2 (accessed 12 January 2006). Rebecca Blood quotes the observation by one media activist that "Media is a corporate possession. . . . You cannot participate in the media. Bringing that into the foreground is the first step. The second step is to define the difference between public and audience. An audience is passive; a public is participatory. We need a definition of media that is public in its orientation." For her, blogs create that redefined medium: "By writing a few lines each day, weblog editors begin to redefine media as a public, participatory endeavor." The quotes are from Rebecca Blood, "Weblogs: A History and Perspective. Rebecca's Pocket (Blog)," at http://www.rebeccablood.net/essays/weblog_history.html (accessed 12 January 2006).

2. Michael Bugeja, "Facing the Facebook," *Chronicle of Higher Education*, 23 January 2006, at http://chronicle.com/jobs/2006/01/2006012301c.htm (accessed 30 January 2006).

3. Ibid. The article provides the following examples of Facebook clubs: "'Baseball Addicts' and 'Kick Ass Conservatives' are Facebook groups while 'Baseball Fanatics' and 'Iowa Conservatives' are the names of commercial mailing lists. You can find 'PC Gamers,' 'Outdoor Enthusiasts,' and advocates for and against gun control on both Facebook and in marketing directories. Several Facebook groups resemble advertisements for products or lifestyles such as 'Apple Macintosh Users,' 'Avid Sweatpants Users,' or 'Brunettes Having More Fun.'"

4. Ibid.

5. Walter Benjamin, *Charles Baudelaire: A Lyric Poet in the Era of High Capitalism*, trans. Harry Zohn (London: NLB, 1973) 55.

6. Henry Jenkins, *Textual Poachers: Television Fans and Participatory Culture* (New York: Routledge, 1992), 23.

7. Carly Mayberry, "USA Network Casts Viewers for New Site," *VNU Entertainment News Wire*, 14 March 2006.

8. Marshall Sella, "The Remote Controllers," *New York Times Magazine*, 20 October 2002, 62.

9. Ibid.

10. Nick Couldry, *The Place of Media Power: Pilgrims and Witnesses of Media Age* (New York: Routledge, 2000).

11. Celebrants of the promise of interactivity include: George Gilder, *Life after Television: The Coming Transformation of Media and American Life* (New York: Norton, 1994); Derrick De Kerchhove as interviewed in Kevin Kelly, "What Would McLuhan Say?" *Wired* 4, no. 10 (October 1996), at http://www.wired.com/wired/archive/4.10/dekerckhove.html (accessed 18 July 2002).

12. Sella, "Remote Controllers," 66.

13. Tiziana Terranova, "Free Labor: Producing Culture for the Digital Economy," *Social Text* 63, no. 18 (2000): 33–57.

14. Ibid.

15. Nikolas Rose, *Powers of Freedom: Reframing Political Thought* (Cambridge: Cambridge University Press, 2001), 164.

16. Emily Nussbaum, "Confessions of a Spoiler Whore: The Pleasures of Participatory TV," *Slate*, 4 April 2002, at http://slate.msn.com/id/2063235/ (accessed 2 October 2003).

17. Grace Bradberry, "Review: Get a Shave, Carter: Forget TV Criticism," *The Observer*, 5 January 2003, 11.

18. Rebecca Gardyn, "The Tribe Has Spoken," *American Demographics* (September 2001): 34–40.

19. Mark Lacey, "Reality TV Rivets Africa, to the Church's Dismay," *New York Times*, 4 September 2003, sec. A8.

20. Sella, "Remote Controllers."

21. Paul F. Lazarsfeld and Robert K. Merton, "Mass Communication, Popular Taste, and Organized Social Action," in *The Communication of Ideas*, ed. Lyman Bryson (New York: Harper and Row, 1948), 95–118.

22. Jodi Dean, *Publicity's Secret: How Technoculture Capitalizes on Democracy* (Ithaca: Cornell University Press, 2002).

23. Ibid., 173.

24. Slavoj Žižek, *The Ticklish Subject* (London: Verso, 1999).

25. Todd Gitlin, "Blips, Bites and Savvy Talk: Television's Impact on American Politics," *Dissen* (winter 1990): 20.

26. Ibid., 21.

27. Žižek, *Ticklish*, 284.

28. Jürgen Habermas, *The Structural Transformation of the Public Sphere: An Inquiry into a Category of Bourgeois Society* (Cambridge, Mass.: MIT Press, 1991).

29. Sadie Plant, *Zeros + Ones: Digital Women and the New Technoculture* (London: 4th Estate, 1997).

30. Ibid., 144.

31. Darin Barney, *Prometheus Wired: The Hope for Democracy in the Age of Network Technology* (Chicago: University of Chicago Press, 2000), 147.

32. Henry Jenkins, "*Star Trek* Rerun, Reread, Rewritten: Fan Writing as Textual Poaching," *Critical Studies in Mass Communication* 5 (1988): 85–107.

33. As quoted in ibid., 86.

34. Jan Fernback, "Using Community to Sell: The Commodification of Community in Retail Web Sites," presented at the Annual Conference of the Association of Internet Researchers, 13–16 October 2002, Maastricht, The Netherlands.

35. Ibid., 11.

36. Kevin Robins and Frank Webster, *Times of the Technoculture: From the Information Society to the Virtual Life* (London: Routledge, 1999), 166.

37. Dean, *Publicity's Secret*.

38. Adam Clymer, "Government Openness at Issue as Bush Holds on to Records," *New York Times*, 3 January 2003, sec. A1.

39. Pew Research Center for the People and the Press, "Strong Opposition to Media Cross-Ownership Emerges: Public Wants Neutrality *and* Pro-American Point of View," 13 July 2003, at http://people-press.org/dataarchive/#2003 (accessed 21 August 2005).

CHAPTER 6. iWAR

1. Richard Stengel, "The First Internet War," *Time Magazine,* 25 October 2001, at http://www.time.com/time/columnist/stengel/article/0,9565,181350,00.html (accessed 5 October 2002).

2. Ibid.

3. "Ridge/Every Family," Homeland Public Service Announcement, Ad Council, 2003, at http://www.adcouncil.org/campaigns/homeland_security/ (accessed 20 August 2004).

4. Maureen Dowd, "Ready or Not . . . ," *New York Times,* 23 February, 2003, sec. 4, 11.

5. Leon Harris, "Ridge on Preparations for Possible Terror Attack," CNN, domestic news transcript 021901CN.V54, 19 February 2003.

6. George Will, "Acts of Character Building," *Washington Post,* 30 January 2005, sec. B7.

7. Rick Santorum, "The Great Test of This Generation: Naming and Defeating Enemy, Islamic Fascism," at article.nationalreview.com/?q=ODk3NWI3ZmFiM W

U3ZjMzNDI2MWE1NzkoOGFhMjZiNTI= (accessed 21 July 2006). Santorum also sought to make clear the war is more intensely personal than previous ones. One part of the problem is that defining the enemy correctly has a direct impact on our personal lives. It forces us to recognize that we, the infidels, are being hunted. This is not just happening someplace thousands of miles away. The enemy is doing his utmost to kill us because of who we are, wherever we are, at home or overseas.

8. Richard Schmidt, "Making America Safe," Richard Schmidt's Homerun Stock Alert, promotional mailing, May 2005.

9. "Are You Prepared," AreYouPrepared.com, at http://www.areyouprepared.com (accessed 12 September 2005).

10. Associated Press, "Bets Off on Terror Futures Index," 29 July 2003, http://www .wired.com/news/politics/0,1283,59813,00.html (accessed 28 December 2005).

11. Dowd, "Ready or Not. . . . "

12. Mitchell Dean, *Governmentality: Power and Rule in Modern Society* (London: Sage, 1999), 162.

13. "Ridge/Families in Florida," Homeland Public Service Announcement, Ad Council, at http://www.adcouncil.org/campaigns/homeland_security/ (accessed 20 August 2004).

14. I repeatedly qualify the phrase "war on terror" because it is not in any respect what is typically referred to by the term *war*. Rather, the term *war* is one mobilized by the Bush administration to legitimize seizure of power by the executive branch and bolster an array of policy initiatives.

15. Ulrich Beck, *Risk Society: Towards a New Modernity* (London: Sage, 1992).

16. Martin Amis, "Fear and Loathing," *Guardian Unlimited,* 18 September 2001, at http://www.guardian.co.uk/wtccrash/story/0,,553638,00.html (accessed 10 November 2006).

17. Tom Narin, "Black Pluto's Door," *Arena Magazine,* 1 October 2001, 12.

18. William J. Bennett, "Faced with Evil on a Grand Scale, Nothing is Relative," *Los Angeles Times,* 1 October 2001, sec. 2, 11.

19. William J. Bennett, "Maddening Deeds at U.S. Universities," *Boston Globe,* 4 November 2001, at http://empoweramerica.org/stories/storyReader$182 (accessed 20 October 2005).

20. Ulrich Beck, "The Silence of Words and Political Dynamics in the World Risk Society," *Logos* 1, no. 4 (fall 2002), at http://www.logosjournal.com/beck.pdf (accessed 2 October 2003).

21. Beck, *Risk Society.*

22. Beck, "Silence of Words."

23. Ibid., 9.

24. Ibid., 8.

25. Bill Frist, *When Every Moment Counts: What You Need to Know about Bioterrorism from the Senate's Only Doctor* (Boulder, Colo.: Rowman and Littlefield, 2002), 24–25.

26. Paul Virilio and Sylvere Lotringer, *Pure War* (New York: Semiotext(e), 1997).

27. Harris, "Ridge on Preparations."

28. David Brummer, "U.S. Homeland Security Chief Touts Ready Kids Terrorist Attack Program," *Associated Press Worldstream*, 2 February 2006.

29. John Markoff and John Schwartz, "Many Tools of Big Brother are Now Up and Running," *New York Times*, 23 December 2002, sec. C1.

30. Beck, "Silence of Words," 13.

31. Robert Rivas and Robert Windrem, "News Findings Run Counter to Recent Bush Administration Claims," NBC News, at http://www.msnbc.msn.com/id/5889435 (accessed 5 September 2004).

32. Virilio and Lotringer, *Pure War*, 176.

33. Robert O'Harrow Jr., *No Place to Hide* (New York: Free Press, 2005), 137.

34. Ibid.

35. Paul Marks, "Pentagon Sets its Sights on Social Networking Websites," NewScientist.com, at http://www.newscientist.com/article/mg19025556.200?DCMP=NLC-nletter&nsref=mg%0A19025556.200 (accessed 10 July 2006).

36. Frist, *When Every Moment Counts*, 26.

37. Dave Lindorff, "When Neighbors Attack," Salon.com, 6 August 2002, at http://www.salon.com/news/feature/2002/08/06/tips/index_np.html (accessed 22 September 2003).

38. Lloyd Grove, "The Reliable Source," *Washington Post*, 11 March 2003, sec. C3.

39. Kevin Dilworth, "Orange Seeks Volunteers to Tell of Crime via Web," *Star-Ledger*, 14 March 2006.

40. Ibid.

41. Mitchell Dean, *Governmentality: Power and Rule in Modern Society* (London: Sage, 1999).

42. New Jersey Office of Homeland and Security and Preparedness, at http://njhomelandsecurity.gov.

43. Ibid.

44. "Ready. Prepare. Plan. Stay Informed," Department of Homeland Security, at http://www.ready.gov.

45. Dean, *Governmentality*, 183.

46. Frist, *When Every Moment Counts*, 40–41, 38.

47. Dean, *Governmentality*, 172.

48. Giles Whittell, "The Rise of Condoleezza," *The Times* (London), 24 September 2001: 1.

49. Virilio and Lotringer, *Pure War*, 192.

50. Dean, *Governmentality*, 167.

51. Beck, "Silence of Words," 13.

52. "Ridge/Families in Florida."

53. "Crazy Like a Duct," *Hartford Courant*, 22 February 2003, sec. A2.

54. Nikolas Rose, *Powers of Freedom: Reframing Political Thought* (Cambridge: Cambridge University Press, 2001), 145.
55. "About Us," Safer America, at http://www.saferamerica.com (accessed 20 August 2004).
56. Seymour Hersch, "Lunch with the Chairman," *New Yorker,* 17 March 2003.
57. Dean, *Governmentality,* 12.
58. Ibid., 191.

CHAPTER 7. iPOLITICS
1. Thomas Edsall, "Democrats' Data Mining Stirs an Intraparty Battle," *Washington Post,* 8 March 2006, sec. A1.
2. Philip Howard, John N. Carr, and Tema J. Milstein, "Digital Technology and the Market for Political Surveillance," *Surveillance and Society* 3, no. 1 (2005): 60.
3. Celia Pearce, *The Interactive Book* (New York: Penguin, 1997), 180.
4. Ibid., 185.
5. Joe Trippi, *The Revolution Will Not be Televised* (New York: Regan Books, 2004), xix.
6. Ibid., xx.
7. Howard et al., "Digital Technology," 60.
8. Charles Briggs, *The Story of the Telegraph and a History of the Great Atlantic Cable* (New York: Rudd & Carleton, 1858).
9. Susan Douglas, *Inventing American Broadcasting, 1899–1922* (Baltimore, Md.: John Hopkins University Press, 1987), 306.
10. Ibid., 306.
11. I'm indebted for some of these quotes to similar assemblages of utopian predictions available online. It's unclear who got what from whom, but several sites with similar sets of quotes are: Annenberg Publications On-Line, Annenberg Washington Program, at http://www.annenberg.northwestern.edu/pubs/downside/downside02.1.htm; "Tom Munnecke's Journal," Tom Munnecke Blog, at http://www.munnecke.com/blog/archives/2004_11. html#000201; and "Imagining the Internet: A History and Forecast," Elon University/PEW project, at http://www.elon.edu/e-web/predictions/150/1930.xhtml.
12. Vincent Mosco, *The Digital Sublime: Myth, Power, and Cyberspace* (Cambridge, Mass.: MIT Press, 2004), 121.
13. As quoted in Darin Barney, *Prometheus Wired: The Hope for Democracy in the Age of Network Technology* (Chicago: University of Chicago Press, 2000), 19.
14. Spencer Reiss, "His Space," *Wired* 14, no. 7 (July 2006), at http://wired.com/wired/archive/14.07/murdoch_pr.html (accessed 18 July 2006).
15. Cathy Bryan et al., "Electronic Democracy and the Civic Networking Movement in Context," in *Cyberdemocracy: Technology, Cities, and Civic Networks,* ed. Rosa Tsagarousianou, Damian Tambini, and Cathy Bryan (London: Routledge, 1998), 5.

16. Howard Rheingold, *Virtual Community: Homesteading the Electronic Frontier* (Reading, Mass.: Addison-Wesley, 1993), 14.

17. Dan Schiller, *Digital Capitalism: Networking the Global Market System* (Cambridge, Mass.: MIT Press, 1999).

18. Trippi, *Revolution*, 235.

19. Howard et al., "Digital Technology," 62.

20. Jon Gertner, "The Very, Very Personal Is Political," *New York Times Magazine*, 15 February 2004.

21. Ibid.

22. Ibid.

23. Thomas Edsall, "Democrats' Data Mining Stirs an Intraparty Battle," *Washington Post*, 8 March 2006, sec. A1.

24. Ibid.

25. Michael Lewis, "The Two-Bucks-a-Minute Democracy," *New York Times Magazine*, 5 November 2000, 65 ff.

26. Slavoj Žižek, *The Plague of Fantasies* (London: Verso, 1997).

27. Howard et al., "Digital Technology," 63.

28. Drew Chalfant, "Facebook Postings, Photos Incriminate Dorm Party-goers," *The Northener*, 2 November 2005, 1.

29. Tom Brignall III, "The New Panopticon: The Internet Viewed as a Structure of Social Control." *Theory and Science* 3, no. 1 (2002), at http://theoryandscience. icaap.org /content/vol003.001/brignall.html (accessed 4 June 2007).

30. Howard et al., "Digital Technology," 63–64.

31. Jürgen Habermas, *The Structural Transformation of the Public Sphere: An Inquiry into a Category of Bourgeois Society* (Cambridge, Mass.: MIT Press, 1991), 232.

32. Ibid., 206.

33. Trippi, *Revolution*, 235.

34. Gertner, "Very, Very Personal."

35. Ibid.

36. Ibid.

37. Cass Sunstein, *Republic.com* (Princeton, N.J.: Princeton University Press, 2002).

38. Ibid., 37.

39. Guy Debord, *The Society of the Spectacle* (New York: Zone Books, 1995), 22.

40. Ibid., 22.

41. I'm indebted to Slavko Andrejevic for this description.

42. John Brenkman, "Mass Media: From Collective Experience to the Culture of Privatization," *Social Text* 1 (1979): 101.

43. Howard Rheingold, *Smart Mobs: The Next Social Revolution* (Cambridge, Mass.: Perseus, 2000), 169.

44. Jeff Howe, "The Rise of Crowdsourcing," *Wired* 14, no. 6 (June 2006), at http:// www.wired. com/wired/archive/14.06/crowds.html (accessed 5 June 2006).

45. Sunstein, *Republic.com*.

46. Joshua Micah Marshall, "The Post-Modern President," *Washington Monthly*, September 2003, at http://www.washingtonmonthly.com/features/2003/0309 .marshall.html (accessed 28 May 2006).

47. Bruno Latour, "Why Has Critique Run Out of Steam? From Matters of Fact to Matters of Concern," *Critical Inquiry* 30 (2004): 225–45.

48. Ibid., 228.

49. Marshall, "Post-Modern President."

50. Ibid.

51. Brenkman, "Mass Media," 105.

52. Oscar Gandy, "Data Mining, Discrimination, and the Decline of The Public Sphere," Dixons Public Lecture, London School of Economics and Political Science, 7 November 2002, 8.

53. Howard et al., "Digital Technology," 70.

54. Oscar Gandy, "Dividing Practices: Segmentation and Targeting in the Emerging Public Sphere," in *Mediated Politics: Communication in the Future of Democracy*, ed. W. Lance Bennett and Robert M. Entman (New York: Cambridge University Press, 2001), 157.

55. Wayne Steger, "A Quarter Century of News Coverage of Candidates in Presidential Nomination Campaigns," *Journal of Political Marketing* 1, no. 1 (2002): 91–115.

56. Gandy, "Data Mining," 10.

57. Jodi Dean, *Publicity's Secret: How Technoculture Capitalizes on Democracy* (Ithaca: Cornell University Press, 2002), 150.

58. Richard Morin, "Poll: Most Americans Support NSA's Efforts," *Washington Post*, 12 May 2006.

CHAPTER 8. iMONITORING: KEEPING TRACK OF ONE ANOTHER

1. Steve Mann, Jason Nolan, and Barry Wellman, "Sousveillance: Inventing and Using Wearable Computing Devices for Data Collection in Surveillance Environments," *Surveillance and Society* 1, no. 3 (2003): 331–55, at http://citeseer.ist.psu .edu/mann03sousveillance.html.

2. "It's True! Popular Court TV Lie Detection Series Fake Out Returns for Second Season," CourtTV, 18 May 2004, at http://www.courttv.com/press/fakeout_second _season_51804. html (accessed 22 September 2005).

3. Ibid.

4. Ibid.

5. "Truster," National Association of Investigative Specialists, at http://www.pimall. com/nais/truster.html (accessed 10 July 2004).

6. G. Robert Hillman, "Bush, Putin Swap Praise after Meeting," *Seattle Times*, 17 June 2001, sec. A2.

7. Ron Suskind's 2004 profile of President Bush focused attention on this aspect of his self-image—and public image—with an anecdote recounted by Democratic

Senator Joseph Biden: "'I was in the Oval Office a few months after we swept into Baghdad,' he began, 'and I was telling the president of my many concerns'— concerns about growing problems winning the peace, the explosive mix of Shiite and Sunni, the disbanding of the Iraqi Army and problems securing the oil fields. Bush, Biden recalled, just looked at him, unflappably sure that the United States was on the right course and that all was well. "Mr. President," I finally said, "How can you be so sure when you know you don't know the facts?" Biden said that Bush stood up and put his hand on the senator's shoulder. "My instincts," he said. "My instincts."'"

8. Alison Mitchell, "The 2000 Campaign," *New York Times,* 7 September 2000, sec. A27. This was, of course, long before George Bush dubbed himself the "decider" in the face of mounting criticism of Secretary of Defense Donald Rumsfeld.

9. Eric Boehlert, "The Media: Dems Are Phony, GOP Authentic. Here We Go Again," *Huffington Post,* 25 May 2006, at http://www.huffingtonpost.com/eric-boehlert/the-media-dems-are-hony_b_21591.html (accessed 2 June 2006).

10. Eric Boehlert, "The TV Ad that Put Bush over the Top," Salon.com, 5 November 2004, at dir.salon.com/story/news/feature/2004/11/05/bush_ads/index.html (accessed 2 June 2006).

11. Slavoj Žižek, *The Ticklish Subject* (London: Verso, 1999).

12. Sherry Turkle, *Life on the Screen: Identity in the Age of the Internet* (New York: Simon & Schuster, 1997).

13. "Welcome to Check-Mate.com," Check-mate.com, 2004, at http://check-mate.com/ (accessed 10 February 2005).

14. "True Prosecutes Felons and Marrieds," True.com, at http://www.true.com/magazine/saferdating_prosecute.htm (accessed 12 June 2005).

15. "Background Check of Date," Abika.com, at http://www.abika.com/Reports/PersonalityandRomance.htm (accessed 10 February 2005).

16. "Infidelity—How to Catch Your Cheating Lover," Catchacheat.com, at http://www.downloadfreetrial.com/society/how-to-catch-your-cheating-lover.html (accessed 4 June 2005).

17. "Background Check of Date."

18. Jennifer Egan, "Love in the Time of No Time," *New York Times Magazine,* 23 November 2003, 69.

19. Mitchell Dean, *Governmentality: Power and Rule in Modern Society* (London: Sage, 1999), 162.

20. Mary Lou Pickel, "Private Eyes Fight Database Company," *Atlanta Journal Constitution,* 18 December 2003, sec. 1C.

21. Ibid.

22. Nancy Bartley, "Private-Detective Trainees Get a Clue in UW Course: Old Hands Teach Ways of a Job in Hot Demand," *Seattle Times,* 3 December 2002, sec. A1.

23. Bill Gates, *The Road Ahead,* 2nd ed. (New York: Penguin, 1996), 204.

24. Turkle, *Life on the Screen.*

25. David Lyon, *The Electronic Eye: The Rise of Surveillance Society* (Minneapolis: University of Minnesota Press, 1994).

26. Background Check Gateway, at http://www.backgroundcheckgateway.com/ (accessed 1 June 2004).

27. "Family Security Background Check," ChoiceTrust.com, 2004, at http://www .choicetrust.com/servlet/com.kx.cs.servlets.CsServlet?channel=home&product =bgcheck&subproduct=default&anchor (accessed 10 February 2005).

28. "Welcome to Check-Mate.com."

29. "Learn More," Certifieddates.com, at http://www.certifieddates.com/learnmore .htm (accessed 10 July 2004).

30. "Testimonials," Friendster, 2004, at http://friendster.com/info/testimonials.php (accessed 10 February 2005).

31. "Background Check of Date."

32. Susannah Fox, "Pew Internet Project Data Memo: Search Engines," *Pew Internet and American Life Project*, 2002, at http://www.pewinternet.org/PPF/r/64/ report_display.asp (accessed 10 February 2005).

33. Neil Swidey, "A Nation of Voyeurs," *Boston Globe*, 2 February 2003, sec. B1.

34. Lenore Skenazy, "Googling be Gone." *Daily News* (New York), 10 November 2002, 47.

35. "Background Check Gateway"; "Background Check of Date."

36. Farewell David Brancaccio, "New High-Tech Surveillance Software Being Used by Jealous Spouses to Make Sure Their Mates Aren't Cheating," *Marketplace*, 20 October 2000, Minnesota Public Radio, LexisNexis, Online Brancaccio, 2000.

37. "Monitoring at Home," TruceActive.com, at http://trueactive.com/why/home .asp (accessed 11 April 2004).

38. Zizi Papacharissi, "The Presentation of Self in Virtual Life: Characteristics of Personal Home Pages." *Journalism and Mass Communication Quarterly* 79, no. 3 (2002): 658.

39. It's worth noting that the percentage of respondents indicating they'd sought information online would have been higher—more than 80 percent—if one set of European results, from Northern Ireland, were removed from the data. The sample from Northern Ireland was too small to make a significant comparison, but it was suggestive: whereas U.S. respondents treated googling and other forms of information gathering almost as a routine practice, almost all of the Irish respondents indicated that they did not use the Internet to find information about people they knew.

40. Stefan Lovgren, "'CSI Effect' is Mixed Blessing for Real Crime Labs," *National Geographic News* (23 September 2004), at http://news.nationalgeographic.com/ news/2004/09/0923_040923_csi.html (accessed 20 October 2005).

41. Ibid. Popular press accounts have linked the popularity of the *CSI* franchise with the popularization of forensic detection as a career: "Universities have seen a dramatic increase in applications to forensic science programs. Prosecutors,

meanwhile, are facing greater pressure from science-savvy juries to present so-phisticated forensic evidence in court" (ibid.). Rather than beg the question of whether TV shows "cause" such shifts, the argument presented here proposes ways of thinking about the place that both cultural representations and emerging social practices fit with a culture of savvy skepticism whose obverse is a default to an ostensibly unmediated empiricism.

42. "Truster."

43. Sabra Chartrand, "A Low-Attention Video Camera Lets the Photographer Focus Instead on the Action," *New York Times,* 25 August 2003, sec. C8.

44. Ibid.

45. David Wood, Eli Konvitz, and Kirstie Ball, "The Constant State of Emergency," in *The Intensification of Surveillance: Crime, Terrorism and Warfare in the Information Age,* ed. Kristie Ball and Frank Webster (London: Pluto Press, 2003), 137–50. Quotation on page 143.

46. Theodor W. Adorno, "The Actuality of Philosophy," in *The Adorno Reader,* ed. Brian O'Connor (Oxford: Blackwell, 2000), 38.

47. Malcolm Galdwell, *Blink: The Power of Thinking without Thinking* (New York: Little, Brown, 2005).

48. Ibid.

49. Matt Miller, "Is Persuasion Dead?," *New York Times,* 4 June 2005, sec. A6.

50. Reginald Whitaker, *The End of Privacy: How Total Surveillance Is Becoming a Reality* (New York: New Press, 1999).

51. Mark Crispin Miller, *Boxed In: The Culture of TV* (Chicago: Northwestern University Press, 1988).

52. Clay Calvert, *Voyeur Nation: Media, Privacy, and Peering into Modern Culture* (Boulder, Colo.: Westview, 2004).

53. Laurie Ouellette, "'Take Responsibility for Yourself': Judge Judy and the Neoliberal Citizen," in *Reality TV: Remaking Television Culture,* ed. Susan Murray and Laurie Ouellette (New York: NYU Press, 2004), 246.

CHAPTER 9. BEYOND MONITORING

1. Alessandra Stanley, "The TV Watch; Surprise (Well, Not Exactly)! 'American Idol' Finale Unfolds and Unfolds," *New York Times,* 25 May 2006, sec. B1.

2. Ethan Leib, "Why Not Dial-in Democracy, Too?" *Washington Post,* 28 May 2006, sec. B2.

3. Ibid.

4. Susan Buck-Morss, "Aesthetics and Anaesthetics: Walter Benjamin's Artwork Essay Reconsidered," *October* 62 (1992): 38.

5. Walter Benjamin, *Illuminations* (New York: Harcourt, Brace & World, 1968), 242.

6. Phil Patton, "Cultural Studies: A Proud and Primal Roar," *New York Times,* 12 January 2003, sec. 9, 1.

7. Ibid.

8. As cited in Benjamin, *Illuminations,* 241.

9. Jeff Howe, "The Rise of Crowdsourcing," *Wired* 14, no. 6 (June 2006), at http://www.wired. com/wired/archive/14.06/crowds.html (accessed 5 June 2006).

10. Jean Baudrillard, *For a Critique of the Political Economy of the Sign* (St. Louis, Mo.: Telos, 1981), 182.

11. Ibid., 181.

12. Slavoj Žižek, "In His Bold Gaze My Ruin is Writ Large," in *Everything You Always Wanted to Know about Lacan but Were Afraid to Ask Hitchcock,* ed. Slavoj Žižek (London: Verso, 1992), 284.

13. John Durham Peters, *Courting the Abyss* (Chicago: University of Chicago Press, 2005), 211–12.

14. Buck-Morss, "Aesthetics and Anaesthetics," 29–30.

15. Ibid., 30.

16. Ibid., 18.

17. Ibid., 17.

18. Michael Schudson, *Discovering the News: A Social History of American Newspapers* (New York: Basic Books, 1978), 119.

19. Anthony Giddens, *The Consequences of Modernity* (Stanford, Calif.: Stanford University Press, 1990).

20. William Leiss, Stephen Kline, and Sut Jhally, *Social Communication in Advertising: Persons, Products, and Images of Well-being* (Toronto: Metheun, 1990), 82.

21. Jib Fowles, "Mass Media and the Star System," in *Communication in History: Technology, Culture, Society,* ed. David Crowley and Paul Heyer (White Plains, N.Y.: Longman, 1995), 195–202.

22. Buck-Morss, "Aesthetics and Anaesthetics," 23.

23. Slavoj Žižek, *The Ticklish Subject* (London: Verso, 1999).

24. Alain Badiou, *Being and Event* (New York: Continuum, 2005), xii.

25. Žižek, *Ticklish,* 323.

26. Ibid., 362.

27. Slavoj Žižek, *The Indivisible Remainder: An Essay on Schelling and Related Matters* (London: Verso, 1996), 196.

28. Slavoj Žižek, "The Matrix, or, the Two Sides of Perversion," paper presented at Inside the Matrix—International Symposium at the Center for Art and Media, Karlsruhe, Germany, 28 October 1999, at http://container.zkm.de/netcondition/matrix/zizek.html (accessed 2 May 2005).

29. Jeffrey Rosen, *The Unwanted Gaze: The Destruction of Privacy in America* (New York: Random House, 2000), 216.

30. David Sarashohn, "Softness on Terror?," *The Oregonian* (Portland), 17 March 2006, sec. D06.

31. Mark Lacey, "Reality TV Rivets Africa, to the Church's Dismay," *New York Times,* 4 September 2003, sec. A8.

32. Gabt Hinsliff, "Is Big Brother Key to Winning Next Election?" *The Observer*, 1 June 2003, 15.

33. Robert Hanks, "Last Night: Reality TV Has Yet Another Winner but Who Loses?" *The Independent*, 14 December 2002, 9.

34. Stephen Coleman, "A Tale of Two Houses: The House of Commons, The Big Brother House," Hansard Society, at http://www.clubepublic.org/eve/030708/Hansardb_b.pdf (accessed 24 July 2005).

35. Personal interview with the author, 12 November 2005.

36. Bettina Fabos provides some good background on the privatization of the Internet in *Wrong Turn on the Information Superhighway: Education and Commercialization of the Internet* (New York: Teachers College Press, 2004).

37. Andrew Sullivan, "The Blogging Revolution: Weblogs Are to Words What Napster Was to Music," *Wired* 10, no. 5 (May 2002), at http://www.wired.com/wired/archive/10.05/mustread.html?pg=2 (accessed 12 January 2006).

38. Clive Thompson, "The Great Firewall of China," *The Advertiser* (Australia), 29 April 2006, sec. W9.

39. Ibid.

40. Richard Spencer, "Microsoft Pulls Plug on China Protest Blog," 6 January 2006, at http://www.telegraph.co.uk/news/main.jhtml?xml=/news/2006/01/06/wmicro06.hml&sSheet=/news/2006/01/06/ixworld.html (accessed 2 June 2006).

41. "War of the Words," *The Guardian*, 20 February 2006.

42. Kevin Robins and Frank Webster, *Times of the Technoculture: From the Information Society to the Virtual Life* (London: Routledge, 1999).

43. Julian Bleecker quoted in Douglas Rushkoff, "Networks without the Net," TheFeature.com, 22 September 2004, at http://www.thefeaturearchives.com/topic/Networks/Networks_Without_the_Net.html (accessed 3 October 2005).

44. John Markoff, "Microsoft Would Put Poor Online by Cellphone," *New York Times*, 30 January 2006, sec. C1.

45. Ibid.

46. Carole Pateman, *Participation and Democratic Theory* (Cambridge: Cambridge University Press, 1970).

47. Buck-Morss, "Aesthetics and Anaesthetics," 18.

"About." Vindigo, at http://www.vindigo.com (accessed 2 August 2003).

"About Us." Safer America, at http://www.saferamerica.com (accessed 20 August 2004).

Ackerman, Gwen. "On the Edge of a Cellular Shopping Revolution." *Jerusalem Post,* 19 November 2000, 9.

Adorno, Theodor W. "The Actuality of Philosophy." In *The Adorno Reader,* edited by Brian O'Connor, 23–39. Oxford: Blackwell, 2000.

———. *Kierkegaard: Construction of the Aesthetic.* Translated by Robert Hullot-Kentor. Minneapolis: University of Minnesota Press, 1989.

Allon, Fiona. "An Ontology of Everyday Control: Living and Working in the 'Smart House.'" *Southern Review* 34, no. 3 (2001): 21.

Althusser, Louis. "Ideology and Ideological State Apparatuses." In *Lenin and Philosophy and Other Essays.* New York: Monthly Review Press, 1971.

Amis, Martin. "Fear and Loathing." *Guardian Unlimited,* 18 September 2001, at http://www.guardian.co.uk/wtccrash/story/0,,553638,00.html (accessed 10 November 2006).

Annenberg Publications On-Line. Annenberg Washington Program, at http://www.annenberg.northwestern.edu/pubs/downside/downside02.1.htm.

"Are You Prepared." AreYouPrepared.com, at http://www.areyouprepared.com (accessed 12 September 2005).

Arendt, Hannah. *The Human Condition.* Chicago: University of Chicago Press, 1958.

Armitage, John. "Special Issue on Machinic Modulations: New Cultural Theory and Technopolitics." *Angelaki: Journal of the Theoretical Humanities* 4, no. 2 (1999).

Associated Press. "Bets Off on Terror Futures Index," 29 July 2003, at http://www.wired.com/news/politics/0,1283,59813,00.html (accessed 28 December 2005).

———. "Glasses that Focus on the Mind's Eye." *Newsday* (New York), 30 November 2003, sec. A40.

Fabos, Bettina. *Wrong Turn on the Information Superhighway: Education and Commercialization of the Internet.* New York: Teachers College Press, 2004.

"Background Check of Date." Abika.com, at http://www.abika.com/Reports/PersonalityandRomance.htm (accessed 10 February 2005).

Background Check Gateway, at http://www.backgroundcheckgateway.com/ (accessed 1 June 2004).

Badiou, Alain. *Being and Event.* New York: Continuum, 2005.

Barney, Darin. *Prometheus Wired: The Hope for Democracy in the Age of Network Technology.* Chicago: University of Chicago Press, 2000.

Barsook, Paulina. *Cyberselfish: A Critical Romp through the Terribly Libertarian Culture of High Tech.* New York: Public Affairs, 2000.

Bartels, Robert. *Marketing Theory and Metatheory.* Homewood, Ill.: Richard D. Ir-win, 1970.

Bartley, Nancy. "Private-Detective Trainees Get a Clue in UW Course: Old Hands Teach Ways of a Job in Hot Demand." *Seattle Times,* 3 December 2002, sec. A1.

Baudrillard, Jean. *For a Critique of the Political Economy of the Sign.* St. Louis, Mo.: Telos, 1981.

Beck, Ulrich. *Risk Society: Towards a New Modernity.* London: Sage, 1992.

———. "The Silence of Words and Political Dynamics in the World Risk Society." *Logos* 1, no. 4 (fall 2002), at http://www.logosjournal.com/beck.pdf (accessed 2 October 2003).

Bell, Genevieve, Tim Brooke, and Elizabeth Churchill. "Intimate (Ubiquitous) Com-puting." Ubicomp 2003 Adjunct Conference Proceedings, at http://ubicomp.org/ubicomp2004/ (accessed 12 March 2004).

Beniger, James. "The Control Revolution." In *Communication in History: Technol-ogy, Culture, Society,* edited by David Crowley and Paul Heyer, 305–14. New York: Longman, 1999.

———. *The Control Revolution: Technological and Economic Origins of the Informa-tion Society.* Cambridge, Mass.: Harvard University Press, 1986.

Benjamin, Walter. *The Arcades Project.* Translated by Howard Eiland and Kevin McLaughlin. Cambridge, Mass.: Belknap Press, 1999.

———. *Charles Baudelaire: A Lyric Poet in the Era of High Capitalism.* Translated by Harry Zohn. London: NLB, 1973.

———. *Illuminations.* New York: Harcourt, Brace & World, 1968.

Bennahum, David S. "Forget the World Wide Web on Your Cell Phone. The Key to the Always-On, Everywhere Wireless Internet Comes Down to Three Things: Lo-cation, Location, Location." *Wired* 9, no. 11 (November 2001): 159–60.

Bennett, William J. "Faced with Evil on a Grand Scale, Nothing is Relative." *Los Ange-les Times,* 1 October 2001, sec. 2, 11.

———. "Maddening Deeds at U.S. Universities." *Boston Globe,* 4 November 2001, at http://empoweramerica.org/stories/storyReader$182 (accessed 20 October 2005).

Beville, Malcolm, Jr. *Audience Ratings: Radio, Television, Cable.* 3rd ed. Hillsdale, N.J.: Lawrence Erlbaum Associates, 1988.

"Big Mother (or Father) Is Watching." *The Age,* 9 September 2005, at http://www.theage.com.au/news/technology/big-mother-or-father-is-watching/2005/09/08/1125772632570.html (accessed 20 September 2006).

Blood, Rebecca. "Weblogs: A History and Perspective. Rebecca's Pocket (Blog)," at http://www.rebeccablood.net/essays/weblog_history.html (accessed 12 January 2006).

Boehlert, Eric. "The Media: Dems Are Phony, GOP Authentic. Here We Go Again." *Huffington Post,* 25 May 2006, at http://www.huffingtonpost.com/eric-boehlert/the-media-dems-are-hony_b_21591.html (accessed 2 June 2006).

———. "The TV Ad that Put Bush over the Top." Salon.com, 5 November 2004, at dir.salon.com/story/news/feature/2004/11/05/bush_ads/index.html (accessed 2 June 2006).

Bond, Paula. "ID Tags Make Products Talk." *Atlanta Journal Constitution,* 29 July 2003, sec. 1A.

Borges, Jorge. "Funes the Memorious." In *Labyrinths: Selected Stories and Other Writings,* 23–28. New York: New Directions, 1964.

Boyle, James. "The Second Enclosure Movement and the Construction of the Public Domain." *Law and Contemporary Problems* 66 (winter–spring 2003): 33–74.

Bradberry, Grace. "Review: Get a Shave, Carter: Forget TV Criticism." *The Observer,* 5 January 2003, 11.

Bradbury, Danny. "Remixing the Blogosphere." *The Guardian,* June 9 2005, http://technology.guardian.co.uk/online/story/0,,1501809,00.html (accessed 15 August 2006).

Bramson, Leon. *The Political Context of Sociology.* Princeton, N.J.: Princeton University Press, 1961.

Brancaccio, Farewell David. "New High-Tech Surveillance Software Being Used by Jealous Spouses to Make Sure Their Mates Aren't Cheating." *Marketplace,* 20 October 2000, Minnesota Public Radio, LexisNexis, Online Brancaccio, 2000.

Brenkman, John. "Mass Media: From Collective Experience to the Culture of Privatization." *Social Text* 1 (1979): 94–109.

Bresnahan, Keith. "Housing Complexes: Neurasthenic Subjects and the Bourgeois Interior." *Space and Culture* 6, no. 2 (2003): 169–77.

Brzezinski, Matthew. "Homeland-Security Neighborhood Watch." *New York Times,* 14 December 2003, sec. 7, 5.

Briggs, Charles. *The Story of the Telegraph and a History of the Great Atlantic Cable.* New York: Rudd & Carleton, 1858.

Brignall, Tom, III. "The New Panopticon: The Internet Viewed as a Structure of Social Control." *Theory and Science* 3, no. 1 (2002), at http://theoryandscience.icaap .org/content/vol003.001/brignall.html.

Bruinius, Harry. "Here Come the Ads, Over Your Cellphone." *Christian Science Monitor,* 14 May 2002, sec. USA3.

Brummer, David. "U.S. Homeland Security Chief Touts Ready Kids Terrorist Attack Program." *Associated Press Worldstream,* 2 February 2006.

Bryan, Cathy, et al. "Electronic Democracy and the Civic Networking Movement in Context." In *Cyberdemocracy: Technology, Cities, and Civic Networks,* edited by Rosa Tsagarousianou, Damian Tambini, and Cathy Bryan. London: Routledge, 1998.

Buck-Morss, Susan. "Aesthetics and Anaesthetics: Walter Benjamin's Artwork Essay Reconsidered." *October* 62 (1992): 3–41.

———. *The Dialectics of Seeing: Walter Benjamin and "The Arcades Project."* Cambridge, Mass.: MIT Press, 1995.

Bugeja, Michael. "Facing the Facebook." *Chronicle of Higher Education,* 23 January 2006, at http://chronicle.com/jobs/2006/01/2006012301c.htm (accessed 30 January 2006).

Calvert, Clay. *Voyeur Nation: Media, Privacy, and Peering into Modern Culture.* Boulder, Colo.: Westview, 2004.

Carey, James. "The Press, Public Opinion, and Public Discourse." In *Public Opinion and the Communication of Consent,* edited by Theodore L. Glasser and Charles T. Salmon, 373–402. New York: Guilford, 1995.

———. "Time Space and the Telegraph." In *Communication in History: Technology, Culture, Society,* edited by David Crowley and Paul Heyer, 135–40. New York: Longman, 1999.

———. "Historical Pragmatism and the Internet." *New Media and Society,* 17, no. 4 (2005): 443–55.

Chandler, Alfred. *The Visible Hand: The Managerial Revolution in American Business.* Cambridge, Mass.: Harvard University Press, 1977.

Chartrand, Sabra. "A Low-Attention Video Camera Lets the Photographer Focus Instead on the Action." *New York Times,* 25 August 2003, sec. C8.

"Check My Mate." Checkmymate.com, at http://www.checkmymate.com (accessed 28 September 2005).

Chester, Jeff. "The End of the Internet?" *The Nation,* at http://www.thenation.com/doc/20060213/chester (accessed 3 February 2006).

Clymer, Adam. "Government Openness at Issue as Bush Holds on to Records." *New York Times,* 3 January 2003, sec. A1.

Cochrane, Nathan. "Ulterior Motives Behind ID Tags Exposed." *The Age* (Melbourne), 15 July 2002, 1.

Coleman, Stephen. "A Tale of Two Houses: The House of Commons, The Big Brother House." Hansard Society, at http://www.clubepublic.org/eve/030708/Hansardb_b.pdf (accessed 24 July 2005).

Copeland, Libby. "For DotComGuy, the End of the Online Line." *Washington Post,* 3 January 2001, sec. C2, telephone interview with DotComGuy, aka Mitch Maddox, 12 June 2000.

Copeland, Melvin. "Arch W. Shaw." *Journal of Marketing* 22, no. 3 (1958): 313–15.

Copley, Frank. *Frederick W. Taylor: Father of Scientific Management.* Vol. 2. New York: Harper and Brothers, 1923.

Couldry, Nick. *The Place of Media Power: Pilgrims and Witnesses of Media Age.* New York: Routledge, 2000.

"Crazy Like a Duct." *Hartford Courant,* 22 February 2003, sec. A2.

Crossley, Dorothy. *The Advertiser Looks at Radio.* Manuscript held in author's personal archive.

Cuff, Rupert. "Edwin F. Gay, Arch W. Shaw, and the Uses of History in Early Graduate Business Education." *Journal of Management History* 2, no. 3 (1996): 15.

"Customer Comments." NetDetective.com, at http://www.affiliatesuccess.net/cgi-bin/clickthru.cgi?pidb=ND (accessed 3 June 2006).

D'Amato, Suzanne. "Custom Sties Let Users Cobble Their Own Shoes." *Washington Post,* 17 July 2005, sec. F1.

Daniel, Jamie Owen. "Achieving Subjectlessness: Reassessing the Politics of Adorno's Subject of Modernity." *Cultural Logic* 3, no. 1 (2001), at http://eserver.org/clogic/3-1&2/daniel.html (accessed 4 March 2004).

"David Bowie Mash-up Contest." Davidbowie.com, at http://www.davidbowie.com/neverFollow (accessed 4 April 2004).

Dean, Jodi. *Publicity's Secret: How Technoculture Capitalizes on Democracy.* Ithaca: Cornell University Press, 2002.

Dean, Mitchell. *Governmentality: Power and Rule in Modern Society.* London: Sage, 1999.

Dearne, Karen. "Mobiles to Keep Tabs on Health." *The Australian,* 1 November 2005, 42.

Debord, Guy. *The Society of the Spectacle.* New York: Zone Books, 1995.

Dobberstein, Nikolai, John Livingston, and Prapavadee Sophonpanich. "On the Wireless Web Frontier, Asia is the Pioneer." *Business Times* (Singapore), 8 May 2000, 13.

De Certeau, Michel. "Walking in the City." In *The Cultural Studies Reader,* edited by Simon During, 126–33. London: Routledge, 1993.

Dilworth, Kevin. "Orange Seeks Volunteers to Tell of Crime via Web." *Star-Ledger,* 14 March 2006.

Douglas, Susan. *Inventing American Broadcasting, 1899–1922.* Baltimore, Md.: Johns Hopkins University Press, 1987.

Dowan, Edward J., and Sally J. McMillan. "Defining Interactivity: A Qualitative Identification of Key Dimensions." *New Media and Society* 2, no. 2 (2000): 157–79.

Dowd, Maureen. "Ready or Not . . . " *New York Times,* 23 February 2003, sec. 4, 11.

Dresser, Michael. "Cell Phone Data Tracing Traffic in Md.; System 'Watches' Vehicles, Raises Fears about Privacy." *Baltimore Sun,* 18 November 2005, sec. 1A.

Dudley, Jennifer. "Dial Your Own Future." *Courier Mail* (Queensland, Australia), 18 June 2005, 27.

———. "In Future, Don't Leave Home without Your Mobile Phone." *Courier Mail* (Queensland, Australia), 6 November 2004, 17.

Easterbrook, Gregg. "All This Progress Is Killing Us Bite by Bite." *New York Times,* 11 March 2004, sec. 4, 5.

Edsall, Thomas. "Democrats' Data Mining Stirs an Intraparty Battle." *Washington Post,* 8 March 2006, sec. A1.

Egan, Jennifer. "Love in the Time of No Time." *New York Times Magazine,* 23 November 2003, 66–70.

Ewen, Stuart. *Captains of Consciousness: Advertising and the Social Roots of the Consumer Culture.* New York: McGraw-Hill, 1976.

———. *PR! A Social History of Spin.* New York: Basic Books, 1996.

"Family Security Background Check." ChoiceTrust.com, 2004, at http://www.choice trust.com/servlet/com.kx.cs.servlets.CsServlet?channel=home&product=bgchec k&subproduct=default&anchor (accessed 10 February 2005).

Feran, Tom. "Here's Your Chance to Target Terror." *Plain Dealer* (Cleveland), 8 July 2003, sec. E1.

Fernback, Jan. "Using Community to Sell: The Commodification of Community in Retail Web Sites." Presented at the Annual Conference of the Association of Internet Researchers, 13–16 October 2002, Maastricht, The Netherlands.

"Forget-Me-Not Panties: Contagious Media." Forgetmenotpanties, at http://forget menotpanties.contagiousmedia.org/testimonial.html (accessed 20 September 2004).

"Former ASIO Officer Claims Islamic Extremists Are Living in Australia." Australian Broadcasting Corporation, ABC News Radio: Lateline, at http://www.abc.net.au/ lateline/content/2005/s1428699.htm (accessed 3 August 2005).

Flood, Harry. "Linux, TiVo, Napster . . . Information Wants to be Free, You Got a Problem with That?" *Adbusters* 34 (March–April 2002): 17.

Fowles, Jib. "Mass Media and the Star System." In *Communication in History: Technology, Culture, Society,* edited by David Crowley and Paul Heyer, 195–202. White Plains, N.Y.: Longman, 1995.

Fox, Susannah. "Pew Internet Project Data Memo: Search Engines." *Pew Internet and American Life Project,* 2002, at http://www.pewinternet.org/PPF/r/64/report _display.asp (accessed 10 February 2005).

Frist, Bill. *When Every Moment Counts: What You Need to Know about Bioterrorism from the Senate's Only Doctor.* Boulder, Colo.: Rowman and Littlefield, 2002.

Galdwell, Malcolm. *Blink: The Power of Thinking without Thinking* (New York: Little, Brown, 2005).

Gandy, Oscar. "Data Mining, Discrimination, and the Decline of The Public Sphere." Dixons Public Lecture, London School of Economics and Political Science, 7 November 2002, 8.

———. "Dividing Practices: Segmentation and Targeting in the Emerging Public Sphere." In *Mediated Politics: Communication in the Future of Democracy,* edited by W. Lance Bennett and Robert M. Entman, 141–59. New York: Cambridge University Press, 2001.

———. "Tracking the Audience: Personal Information and Privacy in Downing." In *Questioning the Media: A Critical Introduction,* edited by John D. H. Downing, Ali Mohammadi, and Annabelle Sreberny, 207–20. London: Sage, 1990.

Gardyn, Rebecca. "The Tribe Has Spoken." *American Demographics* (September 2001): 34–40.

Gates, Bill. *The Road Ahead.* 2nd ed. New York: Penguin, 1996.

Gertner, Jon. "The Very, Very Personal Is Political." *New York Times Magazine,* 15 February 2004.

Giddens, Anthony. *The Consequences of Modernity.* Stanford, Calif.: Stanford University Press, 1990.

————. *A Contemporary Critique of Historical Materialism.* Berkeley: University of California Press, 1981.

Gilder, George. *Life after Television: The Coming Transformation of Media and American Life.* New York: Norton, 1994.

Gilloch, Graeme. *Myth and Metropolis.* Cambridge: Polity Press, 1997.

Gitlin, Todd. "Blips, Bites and Savvy Talk: Television's Impact on American Politics." *Dissen* (winter 1990): 18–26.

Goldman, Robert. "'We Make Weekends': Leisure and the Commodity Form." *Social Text* 8 (winter 1984): 84–103.

Grove, Lloyd. "The Reliable Source." *Washington Post,* 11 March 2003, sec. C3.

Haber, Samuel. *Efficiency and Uplift: Scientific Management in the Progressive Era, 1890–1920.* Chicago: University of Chicago Press, 1964.

Habermas, Jürgen. *The Structural Transformation of the Public Sphere: An Inquiry into a Category of Bourgeois Society.* Cambridge, Mass.: MIT Press, 1991.

Hacking, Ian. *The Taming of Chance.* New York: Cambridge University Press, 1992.

Hamilton, Joan O'C. "The New Workplace: Walls Are Falling as the 'Office of the Future' Finally Takes Shape." *Business Week* (29 April 1996), 106, at http://www. businessweek. com/1996/18/b34731.htm (accessed 18 July 2002).

Hanks, Robert. "Last Night: Reality TV Has Yet Another Winner but Who Loses?" *The Independent,* 14 December 2002, 9.

Hansell, Saul. "Marketers Trace Paths Users Leave on the Internet." *New York Times,* 15 August 2006.

Harris, Leon. "Ridge on Preparations for Possible Terror Attack." CNN, domestic news transcript 021901CN.V54, 19 February 2003.

Harrison, Crayton. "Gaining Frequency: Commitment from Wal-Mart May Boost Tracking Technology." *Dallas Morning News,* 15 July 2002, sec. D1.

Hart, Matthew. "Calling for a Drink Fattens Telstra's Waistline." *Courier Mail* (Queensland, Australia), 23 December 2002, 21.

Haskell, Thomas L. *The Emergence of Professional Social Science: The American Social Science Association and the Nineteenth-Century Crisis of Authority.* Baltimore, Md.: Johns Hopkins University Press, 2000.

Harvey, Fiona. "M-Commerce: Paying for Goods with a Mobile Phone Was to be the Next Big Thing. But Disagreement on Standards Means a Mass Market is Years Away in Europe and the U.S." *Financial Times* (London), 23 October 2002, 13.

Hersch, Seymour. "Lunch with the Chairman." *New Yorker,* 17 March 2003.

Hinsliff, Gabt. "Is Big Brother Key to Winning Next Election?" *The Observer,* 1 June 2003, 15.

Howard, Philip, John N. Carr, and Tema J. Milstein. "Digital Technology and the Market for Political Surveillance." *Surveillance and Society* 3, no. 1 (2005): 69–73.

Howe, Jeff. "The Rise of Crowdsourcing." *Wired* 14, no. 6 (June 2006), at http://www .wired. com/wired/archive/14.06/crowds.html (accessed 5 June 2006).

Hillman, G. Robert. "Bush, Putin Swap Praise after Meeting." *Seattle Times,* 17 June 2001, sec. A2.

"Imagining the Internet: A History and Forecast." Elon University/PEW project, at http://www.elon.edu/e-web/predictions/150/1930.xhtml.

"Infidelity—How to Catch Your Cheating Lover." Catchacheat.com, at http://www .downloadfreetrial.com/society/how-to-catch-your-cheating-lover.html (accessed 4 June 2005).

Inskeep, Steve. "Second Life: Real Money in a Virtual World." National Public Radio, Morning Edition, 6 November 2006, at http://www.npr.org/templates/story/ story.php?storyId=6431819.

"It's True! Popular Court TV Lie Detection Series Fake Out Returns for Second Season." CourtTV, 18 May 2004, at http://www.courttv.com/press/fakeout_second _season_51804. html (accessed 22 September 2005).

Jameson, Frederic. "Reification and Utopia in Mass Culture." In *Signatures of the Visible,* 9–34. New York: Routledge, 1992.

Jenkins, Henry. "Democracy, Big Brother Style." *Confessions of an Aca/Fan: The Official Weblog of Henry Jenkins,* 4 July 2006, at http://www.henryjenkins.org/.

———. "*Star Trek* Rerun, Reread, Rewritten: Fan Writing as Textual Poaching." *Critical Studies in Mass Communication* 5 (1988): 85–107.

———. *Textual Poachers: Television Fans and Participatory Culture.* New York: Routledge, 1992.

Jhally, Sut, and Bill Livant. "Watching as Working: The Valorization of Audience Consciousness." *Journal of Communication* 36, no. 3 (1986): 124–43.

Kahn, Richard, and Douglas Kellner. "New Media and Internet Activism: From the 'Battle of Seattle' to Blogging." *New Media and Society* 6, no. 1 (2004): 87–95.

Kanigel, Robert. *The One Best Way: Frederick Winslow Taylor and the Enigma of Efficiency.* New York: Viking, 1997.

Kellner, Douglas. "Globalization from Below? Toward a Radical Democratic Technopolitics." *Angelaki: Journal of the Theoretical Humanities* 4, no. 2 (1999): 101–14.

Kelly, Kevin. "What Would McLuhan Say?" *Wired* 4, no. 10 (October 1996), at http:// www.wired.com/wired/archive/4.10/dekerckhove.html (accessed 18 July 2002).

Kiousis, Spiro. "Interactivity: A Concept Explication." *New Media and Society* 4, no. 3 (2002): 355–83.

Krugman, Paul. "The New Gilded Age." *New York Times,* 20 October 2002, 34.

Lacey, Mark. "Reality TV Rivets Africa, to the Church's Dismay." *New York Times,* 4 September 2003, sec. A8.

Lafee, Scott. "Geek Chic." *New Scientist,* 24 February 2001, 30.

Lanham, Richard A. *The Electronic Word: Democracy, Technology, and the Arts.* Chicago: University of Chicago Press, 1993.

Larson, Erik. *The Naked Consumer: How Our Private Lives Become Public Commodities*. New York: Henry Holt, 1992.

Latour, Bruno. "Why Has Critique Run Out of Steam? From Matters of Fact to Matters of Concern." *Critical Inquiry* 30 (2004): 225–45.

Lazarsfeld, Paul F., and Robert K. Merton. "Mass Communication, Popular Taste, and Organized Social Action." In *The Communication of Ideas,* edited by Lyman Bryson, 95–118. New York: Harper and Row, 1948.

"Learn More." Certifieddates.com, at http://www.certifieddates.com/learnmore.htm (accessed 10 July 2004).

Lefebvre, Henri. *The Production of Space*. Oxford: Blackwell, 1991.

Leib, Ethan. "Why Not Dial-in Democracy, Too?" *Washington Post,* 28 May 2006, sec. B2.

Leiss, William, Stephen Kline, and Sut Jhally. *Social Communication in Advertising: Persons, Products, and Images of Well-being*. Toronto: Metheun, 1990.

Lester, Toby. "The Reinvention of Privacy." *Atlantic Monthly* 287, no. 3 (March 2001): 28.

Lewis, Michael. "Boombox." *New York Times Magazine,* 13 August 2000, 36.

———. "The Two-Bucks-a-Minute Democracy." *New York Times Magazine,* 5 November 2000, 65 ff.

Lindorff, Dave. "When Neighbors Attack." Salon.com, 6 August 2002, at http://www.salon.com/news/feature/2002/08/06/tips/index_np.html (accessed 22 September 2003).

Lovgren, Stefan. "'*CSI* Effect' is Mixed Blessing for Real Crime Labs." *National Geographic News* (23 September 2004), at http://news.nationalgeographic.com/news/2004/09/0923_040923_csi.html (accessed 20 October 2005).

Lyon, David. *The Electronic Eye: The Rise of Surveillance Society*. Minneapolis: University of Minnesota Press, 1994.

MacGregor, Alison. "Montreal Firm Hopes to Cash in on Mobile Phone Transactions." *The Gazette* (Montreal), 6 June 2005, sec. B1.

Mack, Ann M. "Power to the People." *Critical Mass,* 11 November 2000, at http://www.criticalmass.com /about/news/view.do?article=cm_110100&year=2000 (accessed 18 July 2005).

Magnusson, Paul. "They're Watching You." *Business Week,* 24 January 2005, 22.

Mann, Steve, Jason Nolan, and Barry Wellman. "Sousveillance: Inventing and Using Wearable Computing Devices for Data Collection in Surveillance Environments." *Surveillance and Society* 1, no. 3 (2003): 331–55, at http://citeseer.ist.psu.edu/mann03sousveillance.html.

Marchand, Roland. *Advertising the American Dream: Making Way for Modernity, 1920–1940*. Berkeley: University of California Press, 1985.

Markoff, John. "Microsoft Would Put Poor Online by Cellphone." *New York Times,* 30 January 2006, sec. C1.

Markoff, John, and John Schwartz. "Many Tools of Big Brother are Now Up and Running." *New York Times,* 23 December 2002, sec. C1.

Marks, Paul. "Pentagon Sets its Sights on Social Networking Websites." NewScientist.com, at http://www.newscientist.com/article/mg19025556.200?DCMP=NLC-nlet ter&nsref=mg%0A19025556.200 (accessed 10 July 2006).

Marshall, Joshua Micah. "The Post-Modern President." *Washington Monthly,* September 2003, at http://www.washingtonmonthly.com/features/2003/0309 .marshall.html (accessed 28 May 2006).

———. "Talking Points Memo." Talking Points Memo, at http://www.talkingpoints-memo.com/archives/week_2005_07_10.php (accessed 14 July 2005).

Marx, Gary. "Murky Conceptual Waters: The Public and the Private." *Ethics and Information Technology* 3, no. 3 (2001): 157–69.

———. *Undercover: Police Surveillance in America.* Berkeley: University of California Press, 1988.

Marx, Karl. *Grundrisse.* London: Penguin, 1993.

Mayberry, Carly. "USA Network Casts Viewers for New Site." *VNU Entertainment News Wire,* 14 March 2006.

McChesney, Robert. *The Problem of the Media: U.S. Communication Politics in the 21st Century.* New York: Monthly Review Press, 2004.

McNeally, Scott. "On the Record: Scott McNeally." *San Francisco Chronicle,* 14 September 2003, sec. I1.

Meehan, Eileen. "Why We Don't Count: The Commodity Audience." In *Logics of Television: Essays in Cultural Criticism,* edited by Patricia Mellencamp, 117–37. Bloomington: Indiana University Press, 1990.

Miller, Matt. "Is Persuasion Dead?" *New York Times,* 4 June 2005, sec. A6.

Miller, Mark Crispin. *Boxed In: The Culture of TV.* Chicago: Northwestern University Press, 1988.

Mitchell, Alison. "The 2000 Campaign." *New York Times,* 7 September 2000, sec. A27.

"The MIThril Vision," at http://www.media.mit.edu/wearables/mithril/vision.html (accessed 20 May 2004).

"Monitoring at Home." TruceActive.com, at http://trueactive.com/why/home.asp (accessed 11 April 2004).

Morin, Richard. "Poll: Most Americans Support NSA's Efforts." *Washington Post,* 12 May 2006.

Morley, David. *Home Territories: Media, Mobility, and Identity.* London: Routledge, 2000.

Mosco, Vincent. *The Digital Sublime: Myth, Power, and Cyberspace.* Cambridge, Mass.: MIT Press, 2004.

———. *The Pay-Per Society: Computers and Communication in the Information Age.* Toronto: Ablex, 1989.

———. *The Political Economy of Communication.* London: Sage, 1996.

Mougayar, Walid. *Opening Digital Markets: Battle Plans and Business Strategies for Internet Commerce.* New York: McGraw-Hill, 1998.

"My Logo: Are We the New Brand Bullies? Hijacking the Brand." *Toronto Star,* 10 July 2005, sec. D4.

Narin, Tom. "Black Pluto's Door." *Arena Magazine,* 1 October 2001, 12.

National Academy of Engineering. "Greatest Engineering Achievements of the 20th Century: 2. Automobile." Great Achievements, at http://www.greatachievements .org/greatachievements/ga_2_1.html (accessed 15 July 2005).

Negroponte, Nichoals. *Being Digital.* New York: Knopf, 1995.

New Jersey Office of Homeland and Security and Preparedness. NJHomelandSecu rity.gov, at njhomelandsecurity.gov.

"Nike iD." NikeID.com, at http://nikeid.nike.com/nikeid/index.jhtml?_requestid=23 57796#home(accessed 14 July 2005).

"Nike Retailing Innovation." Retail Systems, at http://www.retailsystems.com/index .cfm?PageName=PublicationsTONHomeNew&CartoonArticleID=4394 (accessed 11 July 2005).

Nussbaum, Emily. "Confessions of a Spoiler Whore: The Pleasures of Participatory TV." *Slate,* 4 April 2002, at http://slate.msn.com/id/2063235/ (accessed 2 October 2003).

O'Connell, Pamela Licalzi. "Korea's High Tech Utopia, Where Everything Is Observed." *New York Times,* 5 October 2005, sec. A1.

O'Harrow, Robert, Jr. *No Place to Hide.* New York: Free Press, 2005.

Ouellette, Laurie. "'Take Responsibility for Yourself': Judge Judy and the Neoliberal Citizen." In *Reality TV: Remaking Television Culture,* edited by Susan Murray and Laurie Ouellette. New York: NYU Press, 2004.

Papacharissi, Zizi. "The Presentation of Self in Virtual Life: Characteristics of Personal Home Pages." *Journalism and Mass Communication Quarterly* 79, no. 3 (2002): 643–60.

Parenti, Christian. *Soft Cage: Surveillance in America.* New York: Basic Books, 2003.

Pateman, Carole. *Participation and Democratic Theory.* Cambridge: Cambridge University Press, 1970.

Patton, Phil Patton. "Cultural Studies: A Proud and Primal Roar." *New York Times,* 12 January 2003, sec. 9, 1.

Pearce, Celia. *The Interactive Book.* New York: Penguin, 1997.

"Peek-a-boo Google Sees You." CNNmoney.com, 7 April 2006, at http://money.cnn. com/2006/04/06/googsf_reut/index.htm?section=money_topstories (accessed 28 October 2006).

Pentland, Alex. "Perceptual Intelligence." *Communications of the ACM* 43, no. 3 (March 2000): 35.

Peretti, Jonah. "The Life of an Internet Meme," at http://www.shey.net/niked.html (accessed 20 July 2005).

Peters, John Durham. *Courting the Abyss: Free Speech and the Liberal Tradition.* Chicago: University of Chicago Press, 2005.

Pew Research Center for the People and the Press. "Strong Opposition to Media Cross-Ownership Emerges: Public Wants Neutrality *and* Pro-American Point of View," 13 July 2003, at http://people-press.org/dataarchive/#2003 (accessed 21 August 2005).

Plant, Sadie. *Zeros + Ones: Digital Women and the New Technoculture.* London: 4th Estate, 1997.

Poster, Mark. *The Mode of Information.* Chicago: University of Chicago Press, 1990.

PostSecret, at http://postsecret.blogspot.com (accessed 4 August 2005).

Pollitt, Katha. "Personal History: Webstalker." *New Yorker,* 19 January 2004, 38–42.

Prahald, C. K., and Venkat Ramaswamy. *The Future of Competition: Co-Creating Unique Value with Customers.* Cambridge: Harvard Business School Press, 2004.

Pratten, Clifford. "The Manufacture of Pins." *Journal of Economic Literature* 18 (March 1980): 93–96.

Prentice, Kathy. "TiVo's World." Media Life Magazine, at http://archives.medialife magazine.com/news2000/jul00/jul3/news70705.html (accessed 1 March 2005).

"Ready. Prepare. Plan. Stay Informed." Department of Homeland Security, at http://www.ready.gov.

Reiss, Spencer. "His Space." *Wired* 14, no. 7 (July 2006), at http://wired.com/wired/archive/14.07/murdoch_pr.html (accessed 18 July 2006).

"Research Proactive Computing." Intel, at http://www.intel.com/research/explor atory/ (accessed 2 August 2005).

Reuters. "Nike Designs Get Personal." *Los Angeles Times,* 30 May 2005, C5.

Rheingold, Howard. *Smart Mobs: The Next Social Revolution.* Cambridge, Mass.: Perseus, 2000.

———. *Virtual Community: Homesteading the Electronic Frontier.* Reading, Mass.: Addison-Wesley, 1993.

Richtel, Matt. "Enlisting Cellphone Signals to Fight Road Gridlock." *New York Times,* 11 November 2005, sec. C1.

"Ridge/Every Family." Homeland Public Service Announcement, Ad Council, 2003, at http://www.adcouncil.org/campaigns/homeland_security/ (accessed 20 August 2004).

"Ridge/Families in Florida." Homeland Public Service Announcement, Ad Council, at http://www.adcouncil.org/campaigns/homeland_security/ (accessed 20 August 2004).

Riordan, Teresa Patents. "A Computer System with an Eye (and Ear) for Crime, or at least Re-enactments Thereof." *New York Times,* 13 October 1997, sec. D2.

Rivas, Robert, and Robert Windrem. "News Findings Run Counter to Recent Bush Administration Claims." NBC News, at http://www.msnbc.msn.com/id/5889435 (accessed 5 September 2004).

Robins, Kevin, and Frank Webster. "Cybernetic Capitalism: Information, Technology, and Everyday Life." In *The Political Economy of Information,* edited by Vincent Mosco and Janet Wasko, 45–75. Madison: University of Wisconsin Press, 1998.

————. *Times of the Technoculture: From the Information Society to the Virtual Life.* London: Routledge, 1999.

Rose, Nikolas. *Powers of Freedom: Reframing Political Thought.* Cambridge: Cambridge University Press, 2001.

Rosen, Jeffrey. *The Unwanted Gaze: The Destruction of Privacy in America.* New York: Random House, 2000.

Rushkoff, Douglas. "Networks without the Net." TheFeature.com, 22 September 2004, at http://www.thefeaturearchives.com/topic/Networks/Networks_Without_the_Net.html (accessed 3 October 2005).

Santorum, Rick. "The Great Test of This Generation: Naming and Defeating Enemy, Islamic Fascism," at article.nationalreview.com/?q=ODk3NWI3 ZmFiMWU3Zj MzNDI2MWE1Nzk0OGFhMjZiNTI= (accessed 21 July 2006).

Sarashohn, David. "Softness on Terror?" *The Oregonian* (Portland), 17 March 2006, sec. D06.

Schiller, Dan. *Digital Capitalism: Networking the Global Market System.* Cambridge, Mass.: MIT Press, 1999.

Schmidt, Richard. "Making America Safe." Richard Schmidt's Homerun Stock Alert. Promotional mailing, May 2005.

Schudson, Michael. *Advertising, the Uneasy Persuasion: Its Dubious Impact on American Society.* New York: Basic Books, 1984.

————. *Discovering the News: A Social History of American Newspapers.* New York: Basic Books, 1978.

Seagren, Stan. Vice President for Strategic Research, A. C. Nielsen, personal interview with author, 5 March 2005.

Sella, Marshall. "The Remote Controllers." *New York Times Magazine,* 20 October 2002, 62.

Skenazy, Lenore. "Googling be Gone." *Daily News* (New York), 10 November 2002, 47.

Spencer, Richard. "Microsoft Pulls Plug on China Protest Blog," 6 January 2006, at http://www.telegraph.co.uk/news/main.jhtml?xml=/news/2006/01/06/wmicro06.hml&sSheet=/news/2006/01/06/ixworld.html (accessed 2 June 2006).

Stanley, Alessandra. "The TV Watch; Surprise (Well, Not Exactly)! 'American Idol' Finale Unfolds and Unfolds." *New York Times,* 25 May 2006, sec. B1.

Starrett, Mary. "I'd Rather Go Naked." NewsWithViews.com, 13 March 2003, at http://www. newswithviews.com/Mary/starrett4.htm (accessed 20 October 2003).

Steger, Wayne. "A Quarter Century of News Coverage of Candidates in Presidential Nomination Campaigns." *Journal of Political Marketing* 1, no. 1 (2002): 91–115.

Stengel, Richard. "The First Internet War." *Time Magazine,* 25 October 2001, at http://www.time.com/time/columnist/stengel/article/0,9565,181350,00.html (accessed 5 October 2002).

Streeter, Thomas. "'That Deep Romantic Chasm': Libertarianism, Neoliberalism and the Computer Culture." In *Communication, Citizenship and Social Policy: Rethinking the Limits of the Welfare State,* edited by Andrew Calabrese and Jean-Claude Burgelman, 49–64. Boulder, Colo.: Rowman and Littlefield, 1999.

Sullivan, Andrew. "The Blogging Revolution: Weblogs Are to Words What Napster Was to Music." *Wired* 10, no. 5 (May 2002), at http://www.wired.com/wired/archive/10.05/mustread.html?pg=2 (accessed 12 January 2006).

Sunstein, Cass. *Republic.com*. Princeton, N.J.: Princeton University Press, 2002.

Swidey, Neil. "A Nation of Voyeurs." *Boston Globe*, 2 February 2003, sec. B1.

Taylor, Frederick. *The Principles of Scientific Management*. New York: Harper & Row, 1967.

Tarbell, Ida. "Taylor and His System." *Saturday Review of Literature*, 25 October 1924, 225.

"Terms of Service." Gmail, at http://www.google.com/mail/help/terms_of_use.htm (accessed 12 February 2006).

Terranova, Tiziana. "Free Labor: Producing Culture for the Digital Economy." *Social Text* 63, no. 18 (2000): 33–57.

"Testimonials." Friendster, 2004, at http://friendster.com/info/testimonials.php (accessed 10 February 2005).

Thompson, Clive. "The Great Firewall of China." *The Advertiser* (Australia), 29 April 2006, sec. W9.

———. "There Is a Sucker Born in Every Medial Prefrontal Cortex." *New York Times*, 26 October 2003, 54.

"Tom Munnecke's Journal." Tom Munnecke Blog, at http://www.munnecke.com/blog/archives/2004_11.html#000201.

Trippi, Joe. *The Revolution Will Not be Televised*. New York: Regan Books, 2004.

"True Prosecutes Felons and Marrieds." True.com, at http://www.true.com/magazine/saferdating_prosecute.htm (accessed 12 June 2005).

Pickel, Mary Lou. "Private Eyes Fight Database Company." *Atlanta Journal Constitution*, 18 December 2003, sec. 1C.

"Truster." National Association of Investigative Specialists, at http://www.pimall.com/nais/truster.html (accessed 10 July 2004).

Turkle, Sherry. *Life on the Screen: Identity in the Age of the Internet*. New York: Simon & Schuster, 1997.

Turner, Fred. *From Cyberculture to Counterculture: Stewart Brand, the Whole Earth Network, and the Rise of Digital Utopianism*. Chicago: University of Chicago Press, 2006.

Valigra, Lori. "Fabricating the Future." *Christian Science Monitor*, 29 August 2002, 11.

Virilio, Paul, and Sylvere Lotringer. *Pure War*. New York: Semiotext(e), 1997.

"War of the Words." *The Guardian*, 20 February 2006.

Weber, Max. *From Max Weber: Essays in Sociology*. New York: Oxford University Press, 1946.

Webster, Frank, and Kevin Robins. "'I'll be Watching You: Comment on Sewell and Wilkinson." *Sociology* 27, no. 2 (1993): 243–52.

———. *Information Technology: A Luddite Analysis*. Norwood, N.J.: Ablex, 1986.

Weiser, Mark. "Open House: *In Review,* the Web Magazine of the Interactive Tele-communications Program of New York University." *ITP Review 2.0,* March 1996, at http://www.itp.tsoa.nyu.edu/~review.

"Welcome to Check-Mate.com." Check-mate.com, 2004, at http://check-mate.com/ (accessed 10 February 2005).

"Welcome to the U.S. HomeGuard: Learn More." USHomeGuard, at http://www.ushomeguard.org (accessed 12 July 2005).

Whitaker, Reginald. *The End of Privacy: How Total Surveillance Is Becoming a Reality.* New York: New Press, 1999.

White, Percival. *Scientific Marketing Management: Its Principles and Methods.* New York: Harper and Brothers, 1927.

Whittell, Giles. "The Rise of Condoleezza." *The Times* (London), 24 September 2001.

Wiener, Norbert. *Cybernetics; or, Control and Communication in the Animal and the Machine.* New York: MIT Press, 1961.

———. *The Human Use of Human Beings: Cybernetics and Society.* Boston, Mass.: Houghton Mifflin, 1954.

Will, George. "Acts of Character Building." *Washington Post,* 30 January 2005, sec. B7.

Wood, Daniel. "Radio ID Tags Proliferate, Stirring Privacy Debate." *Christian Science Monitor,* 15 December 2004, 3.

Wood, David, Eli Konvitz, and Kirstie Ball. "The Constant State of Emergency." In *The Intensification of Surveillance: Crime, Terrorism and Warfare in the Information Age,* edited by Kristie Ball and Frank Webster, 137–50. London: Pluto Press, 2003.

"The World's First Collaborative Sentence." Whitney Museum of Art, at http://www.whitney.org/artport/collection/index.shtml (accessed 30 July 2005).

Yap, Joan. "Towards a User-Centric Model." *Business Times* (Singapore), 25 April 2001, 28.

Žižek, Slavoj. "In His Bold Gaze My Ruin is Writ Large." In *Everything You Always Wanted to Know about Lacan but Were Afraid to Ask Hitchcock,* edited by Slavoj Žižek. London: Verso, 1992, 211–92.

———. *The Indivisible Remainder: An Essay on Schelling and Related Matters.* London: Verso, 1996.

———. "The Matrix, or, the Two Sides of Perversion." Paper presented at Inside the Matrix—International Symposium at the Center for Art and Media, Karlsruhe, Germany, 28 October 1999, at http://container.zkm.de/netcondition/matrix/zizek.html (accessed 2 May 2005).

———. *The Plague of Fantasies.* London: Verso, 1997.

———. *The Ticklish Subject.* London: Verso, 1999.

INDEX

Abika.com, 219–220, 226, 235–236
Activism, use of interactive technology, 49–50, 51
Adbusters, 10
Adorno, Theodor W., 116–117, 234
Advertising
  automobile, 31–32, 244
  development of industry, 73, 75, 77, 79–80
  effectiveness, 78
  goals, 77, 78
  homeland security readiness campaign, 166–167, 181–182
  influence on consumer tastes, 47
  interactive billboards, 22
  magazine, 77
  market research and, 81, 82, 113
  mass, 128
  monitoring exposure to, 90
  physiological reactions, 39, 113
  political, 196, 217
  product placement, 12
  radiofrequency ID tags in, 90
  relationship to journalism, 80
  ubiquity, 90
  use of scientific management techniques, 79
  See also Marketing; Television commercials
Advertising, customized
  based on content of e-mail messages, 129–131
  based on data collected about individuals, 11, 12, 13, 14–15, 114–115, 128, 131
  based on feedback, 21
  blocking, 97–98
  contextual, 1–2
  delivered on cell phones, 97–98
  location-specific, 1–2, 97–98, 104

  mistargeted, 104
  online, 11, 54, 129–131, 263
  political, 196
  targeted to vulnerable consumers, 131
  television, 12, 13
Africa, *Big Brother* show, 148
Agre, Philip, 108
Alias, 138–139
Al Qaeda, 169–170
Althusser, Louis, 45
Amazon.com, 11, 14, 131
American Candidate, 261–262
American Idol, 241–243, 260
American Society of Mechanical Engineers, 67
Amis, Martin, 167
Apple Computer, 10, 197
The Apprentice, 12, 244
Arbitron, 90, 91
Arcades, shopping, 118–120
AreYouPrepared.com, 166
Art, computer, 29
Asymmetrical monitoring
  in daily life, 213
  data gathering, 40–42
  by government, 7–8, 44–46, 258–259
  by individuals, 230
  in marketing, 65–66, 131–132, 257, 259–260
  in scientific management, 65
  See also Monitoring
Audi, 31–32
Audimeters, 87, 88, 195
Audit Bureau of Circulation, 82
Australia, citizen participation in security surveillance, 43
Automobiles
  advertising, 31–32, 244
  large, 243–244
  tracking teenage drivers, 39
  traffic management, 100–101

[309]

Internet searches
  anonymity, 41
  for data on family members, friends,
    and acquaintances, 35, 37, 212, 225–
    226, 227–231
  information available, 35, 40, 228
  recorded by Google, 41
  state surveillance using, 258, 264
  student survey on, 227–231
Interpassive participation, 175–177, 195
"i" prefix, 4–5
Iraq war, 174, 184, 242, 243
Islamic terrorists, 168–170, 174
iTunes, 109, 197

Jackson, Janet, 11
Jameson, Fredric, 9
Jenkins, Henry, 50, 137–138, 158
Journalism, 80, 82, 204, 249
  See also Mass media
J. Walter Thompson, 82

Kahl, John, 183
Kanigel, Robert, 67, 70
Keystroke monitoring software, 36, 71,
    227
Kierkegaard, Soren, 117
Kiousis, Spiro, 18
Knight, Phil, 24
Knowledge Networks, 194–195, 196, 197
Krugman, Paul, 51

Labor
  of audiences, 13, 142–144, 152–153, 158
  de-differentiation from leisure, 107, 108
  of fans on Web sites, 138–139, 143, 148,
    158
  in online economy, 143–144
  participatory, 267–268
  unpaid, 157, 158
  See also Citizen labor; Consumer
    labor; Workers
Lanham, Richard A., 29

Laptop computers, for developing
    countries, 266
  See also Personal computers
Larson, Erik, 68
Lateral surveillance. See Surveillance,
    do-it-yourself
Latour, Bruno, 206
Law enforcement
  citizen participation, 40, 43, 178
  use of private databases, 130–131,
    175–176
  use of surveillance technology, 125–126
Lee, Ivy, 76, 199
Lefebvre, Henri, 93
Lehman Brothers, 101
Leiss, William, 249–250
Lester, Toby, 106
Lewis, Michael, 225
LexisNexis, 175
LG CNS, 133
Lovejoy, Margot, "Turns," 29
Lyon, David, 222

Magazines, 77, 82, 84
Mann, Steve, 67, 214
Manufacturing, role of consumer
    feedback, 25
  See also Industrialization; Scientific
    management
Maps, interactive, 99–100
Marchand, Roland, 73
Marketing
  business school classes, 73
  connection to scientific management,
    54–56, 65–66
  creation of demand, 52–53
  customized pricing, 126
  data collected in, 25–26
  development of industry, 73, 75, 78–79
  differences from industrial
    management, 74–75
  identification with process, 136–137
  interactive, 22–26